Ending Empire

A volume in the series

Cornell Studies in Political Economy

EDITED BY PETER J. KATZENSTEIN

A full list of titles in the series appears at the end of the book.

Ending Empire

CONTESTED SOVEREIGNTY
AND TERRITORIAL PARTITION

HENDRIK SPRUYT

CORNELL UNIVERSITY PRESS

Ithaca and London

First published 2005 by Cornell University Press
First printing, Cornell Paperbacks, 2005

Printed in the United States of America

Library of Congress Cataloging-in-Publication Data

Spruyt, Hendrik, 1956–
    Ending empire : contested sovereignty and territorial partition / Hendrik
Spruyt.
        p. cm. — (Cornell studies in political economy)
    Includes bibliographical references and index.
    ISBN 0-8014-4314-8 (alk. paper) — ISBN 0-8014-8972-5 (pbk. : alk.
paper)
    1. World politics—1945–1989. 2. World politics—1989–
3. Decolonization. 4. Postcolonialism. I. Title. II. Series.
    D840.S63 2005
    909.82′5—dc22

                                                              2004023499

Cornell University Press strives to use environmentally responsible
suppliers and materials to the fullest extent possible in the publishing
of its books. Such materials include vegetable-based, low-VOC inks
and acid-free papers that are recycled, totally chlorine-free, or partly
composed of nonwood fibers. For further information, visit our
website at www.cornellpress.cornell.edu.

Cloth printing   10 9 8 7 6 5 4 3 2 1
Paperback printing   10 9 8 7 6 5 4 3 2 1

For Lucy Lyons
—mijn levensgezel

Contents

Maps and Tables

Preface

The second half of the American century has been described by some of the most prescient scholars of our time as "the long peace." Despite brushes with nuclear holocaust, the conflict between the two great powers did not result in war. The United States created a relatively stable order and ultimately even triumphed in its cold war against the Soviet Union. But the notion of a "long peace" obscures how the post–World War II era saw many bloody conflicts in which contending polities laid claim to the same territory. What subject populations saw as legitimate national aspiration, the governments in the center saw as illegal secessionism.

In the aftermath of the Second World War, territorial challenges emerged with particular salience in the European colonial empires. Was Algeria part of France, or should it become an independent state? Were Portugal's "overseas territories" in Africa indeed part of Portugal?

However, nationalist challenges to existing territorial configurations continue to emerge even now. Indeed, the number of independent states has multiplied fourfold in the last fifty years. Who would have thought in the 1980s that the breakup of the USSR was imminent? Borders and claims to sovereignty remain contested in many parts of the world. Is the West Bank part of Israel, or should it be an independent Palestinian state?

Ending Empire attempts to explain why compromise and accommodation resolved some nationalist conflicts and why hard-line policies led to conflict and bloodshed in other instances. I argue that fragmented political governments provided more opportunities for hard-liners to forestall concessions to nationalist demands, thus making violent conflict more likely. While the international environment provided catalysts for change, domestic politics explains the variation in policies.

Any explanation of macrolevel, complex historical events must be partial. Where historians layer and provide nuance, investigate hidden meanings, and weave a tapestry of details, political scientists reduce and simplify, even as they try to be true to the historical record and the intricacies of human agency. Such is the fate of theory building. Indeed, in offering a model that places considerable emphasis on domestic politics in contrast to realist explanations that emphasize strategic unitary-state calculations, I only tangentially test other rival explanations. I lay no claim to a covering-law explanation that uniformly accounts for all features of territorial partition in all instances. Contrary to the common dictum, history never repeats itself.

Nevertheless, we can gain much from systematically studying decision making in the central governments that faced nationalist demands. By parsing the many causes at work we can analyze how much might be gained from an institutionalist analysis of territorial questions—a heretofore underdeveloped line of investigation.

Although this book has been inspired by scholarly concerns, theory and personal experience have at times intersected unexpectedly. Having been born in Hong Kong, I witnessed the last vestiges of British rule in Asia. As a Dutch national, I viewed the changing ethnic composition of the Dutch population as a constant reminder of colonial legacies. My mother's Portuguese-speaking family, when evicted from Shanghai in 1949 by the Communist regime, dispersed to virtually every corner of the Portuguese Empire. My father, who had been a prisoner of war in the Japanese camps for most of World War II, was pressed back into the Dutch military after 1945 to aid in the suppression of Indonesian nationalism. Incidents such as these serve as a reminder that the costs of holding territory rather than letting go are not just tallied on the accountant's balance sheet.

At times this book seemed to take more time to write than the life span of a few empires. This inevitably comes with the attempt to marry historical narrative with theory. Throughout this intellectual journey I have incurred many debts, which regretfully I can acknowledge only in passing. David Lake and Peter Katzenstein were intellectual beacons providing insight, critique, and suggestions for the final manuscript. Many others read portions of the book or provided other inspiration. I cannot possibly list all who have aided and abetted; thus, with apologies to those accidentally omitted, I thank Karen Alter, Stefan Andreasson, David Auerswald, Deborah Avant, Mark Blyth, Alex Cooley, Peter Cowhey, Colin Elman, Miriam Elman, Robert Jervis, Miles Kahler, Michael Loriaux, Arvid Lukauskas, Jack Matlock, Peter McDonough, Patrick McGowan, Rajan Menon, Chris Nevitt, Phil Roeder, James Ron, Jack Snyder, Kathy Thelen, Michael Wallerstein, Carolyn Warner, and Alexander Wendt. Many others provided comments at institutions where parts of the argument were presented: I single out Beth

Kier and John Mercer's seminar at the University of Washington and the PIPES seminar at Chicago run by Duncan Snidal and Charles Lipson. An earlier version of parts of the book was presented to the challenging and inspiring audience at the University of California at San Diego. Bruce Parrott gave me a venue to present an early sketch of the Soviet chapter at the Paul H. Nitze School of Advanced International Studies at Johns Hopkins University, and Bruce Parrott and Karen Dawisha provided the opportunity to float very preliminary ideas at their "After Empire" conference in San Diego in 1997. My thanks to both.

Part of this work was generously supported by the Junior Fellowship program from the Smith Richardson Foundation. Jack Matlock was a generous host at the Institute of Advanced Study in Princeton and offered an insider's view of the last years of the USSR. I thank him and the institute for providing an intellectual home.

Throughout, I have been lucky enough to be at three wonderful institutions. The Institute of War and Peace Studies at Columbia University was a stimulating venue for starting this research. The intellectual stamp of my former colleagues will undoubtedly be apparent to the careful reader. Arizona State University subsequently supplied me with exciting colleagues and assistants who helped greatly, gathering information and suggesting insights of their own. My thanks to Michael Kidonakis and Akan Malici for their exceptional work. Finally, Northwestern University has given me the opportunity to (finally) wrap up this project in an environment where the intersection of domestic and international politics, and the connections between history and politics, are pursued to the fullest. One could not want more from one's academic institutions.

Roger Haydon at Cornell University Press proved, once again, why so many of us deem him a superlative editor. Not only did he shepherd the book through the pragmatic hurdles of production but he furnished key substantive insights as well. I would also like to thank Karen Hwa for supervising the final production process and John Raymond for his exceptional editing.

The book is dedicated to Lucy Lyons—who else?—proving that behind every scholar, or at least this one, stands a better and wiser half.

HENDRIK SPRUYT

Evanston, Illinois

Ending Empire

Introduction:
Contested Territories and Empire

> I have not become the King's First Minister in order to preside over the liquidation of the British Empire.
>
> —WINSTON CHURCHILL, November 10, 1942

Winston Churchill's uncharacteristic lack of prescience might be forgiven.[1] He was by no means alone. At the dawn of the twentieth century imperial powers controlled most of the globe and dominated hundreds of millions of people. A belief in racial and cultural superiority reinforced utilitarian reasons for territorial aggrandizement. Even if the interwar years saw demands for greater independence, partially inspired by Wilsonian ideas, only the defeated empires of World War I had their territories severed. In 1938 the Dutch governor-general anticipated that the rule of the Netherlands in Indonesia could still last decades, perhaps even centuries. The Free French government submitted in 1944 that autonomy for the colonies remained unthinkable, even though their support was deemed critical to retaking France itself.

Yet within a few decades, most of the great empires had dissolved. The vast British territories dwindled to a handful of islands and strategic posts. Belgium, the Netherlands, France, Spain, and Portugal similarly surrendered virtually all of their possessions abroad. More recently, continental empires and large multinational polities have similarly fragmented. The Soviet Union not only lost its external empire in Eastern Europe, but its internal empire (the Soviet Union itself) fragmented with remarkable speed into fifteen new independent states. Such cases of territorial dissolution re-

---

1. According to one high-ranking colonial officer, the British had "unlimited time in which to work." Betts 1985, 61.

allocated sovereignty, severed hierarchical ties, and created new independent international actors.

The process of reallocating patterns of authority, from internal hierarchy to interstate relations, proved far more contentious in some cases than in others. The British government reconfigured its territorial framework without getting embroiled in colonial quagmires, save for incidental clashes such as in Kenya and Malaya. The swift and relatively bloodless breakup of the Soviet Union presents an even greater puzzle. Given the brutality of the Soviet system in the past, the prevalence of a large standing army and internal security forces, its expansionist policies of many decades, the Soviet economy's high degree of integration, and twenty-five million ethnic Russians in the "near abroad" (Russia's label for the other former union republics), this would be the last case where one would have expected the quick territorial dissolution that occurred.

Other governments, by contrast, fought wars that drained their economies, compelled huge sacrifices of life and limb, and caused domestic upheaval and revolution. Portugal, for example, committed hundreds of thousands of men overseas, and incurred, proportionally speaking, more casualties than the United States suffered in Vietnam, at a time when far more powerful states had withdrawn years earlier from their colonies. The Dutch deployed 150,000 troops to retake Indonesia, suffered thousands of casualties, and inflicted many more on the Indonesians. French policies in Indochina and Algeria stand out as exemplars of brutality and futility, which even threatened the fabric of French society and democracy itself.

What explains these variations in territorial policy? More specifically, why do some governments seemingly have greater latitude to alter existing territorial arrangements while others have little room for maneuvering?

The answer lies in large part in the domestic institutional structures of the central governments. In *Ending Empire* I start by examining the decolonization process of the Western maritime powers. I then generalize my argument by focusing on cases that fit the imperial label less well. The insights gleaned from studying imperial decolonization and breakup can also shed light on multiethnic polities and contested territories—although some readers will undoubtedly object to the very idea that the Soviet Union or Israel's policies on the West Bank can be discussed using the vocabulary of decolonization and end of empire.

Colonialism and empire have become pejorative terms today. But to many politicians and publics in the Western empires colonialism and empire did not possess the negative attributes we now associate with those concepts. To speak of "overseas territories" was sometimes a rhetorical ploy, but it also conveyed a claim to legitimate authority and rule. Concepts such as empire, the multinational state, and legitimate sovereignty appear only in hindsight as clearly distinct and easily recognizable. In practice one person's empire is another's multinational state. Russians tended to view the former USSR through lenses different from those of non-Russian ethnic groups that formed part of the Soviet population. The political struggles about empire and independence of decades past are not logically distinct from the conflicts over territorial sovereignty today. The point is not whether a given policy is imperial. Rather, the question is whether domestic institutional structures affect the range of policy choices for political leaders when they are confronted by challenges to the existing territorial order.

THE STUDY OF EMPIRE, MULTIETHNIC POLITIES, AND DECOLONIZATION

Given that the pursuit of empire has been one of the main causes of the twentieth century's great wars, and given that imperialism has meant the subjugation of hundreds of millions of people, social scientists and historians have rightly devoted great analytic efforts to comprehend the pursuit of empire and the construction of multinational, composite polities. The best among these scholars have looked beyond the isolated case study and have tried to understand the pursuit of empire from a comparative vantage point.[2]

Broad theoretical explanations of how states undergo territorial dissolution are a good deal scarcer. Although there is a vast literature with ideographic, single-case analyses, there is far less that systematically compares and contrasts the causes of fragmentation. Edited volumes by Karen Barkey and Mark von Hagen and by Karen Dawisha and Bruce Parrott pioneered some of the work on the comparative decline of empires. These volumes excel in generating hypotheses by some of the most knowledgeable area specialists, but they have not generated a more systematic examination of the relative explanatory power of the various accounts. Combining theory building and knowledge of individual cases is always a difficult exercise.[3] A few exemplary works suggest how the particular constellations of politics and ideology in metropolitan centers have influenced territorial policy.[4]

In *Ending Empire* I seek to add to that literature by systematically examining, through deductive propositions and historically informed analyses, how institutional configurations in the center have complicated decisions about contested territories. The focus of this book is on formal empire rather than informal empire or hegemony. To use Michael Doyle's definition, "An empire is a system of interaction between two political entities,

2. Doyle 1986; Snyder 1991; Kupchan 1994.
3. Barkey and von Hagen 1997; Dawisha and Parrott 1997.
4. Kahler 1984; Lustick 1993; Levine 1994. For a useful compilation of case-specific arguments, see T. Smith 1975.

one of which, the dominant metropole, exerts political control over the internal and external policy—the effective sovereignty—of the other, the subordinate periphery." In most cases the term "metropole" refers to a distinctive dominant territory. However, in the Soviet case (due to its particular nature) I will refer to the "center" or the "all-Union government," because the dominant geographical unit (Russia) arguably viewed itself as subject to the imperial government, the central government as formalized in the Communist Party hierarchy.[5]

The Argument in Brief

Changes in the International Environment

Systemic changes in the military and economic environment following the Second World War affected the will of metropoles and central governments to control contested territories and their ability to do so.[6] Militarily, the control of large territories decreased in value as a security asset. As the world moved to bipolarity and the Cold War, and as nuclear weapons and advanced weaponry changed the modes of warfare, imperial reserves of troops and resources became less important for the great powers. As Charles de Gaulle and Nikita Khrushchev explicitly acknowledged, great power status hinged on nuclear capability and advanced technological weapons, not on empire.

The value of territory as an economic asset also declined because of the rise of a global liberal economic system and the decline of imperial preference schemes, which discriminated against trade with areas outside the empire. To paraphrase Richard Rosecrance's insight, gains through commerce have displaced gains through territorial acquisition.[7] Traditionally, empires had been pursued in order to acquire protected markets and to guarantee access to scarce resources. But economic liberalism, bolstered by increasing global transactions, prohibited such imperial preference schemes. With American hegemony dictating the terms of the postwar economic settlement, mercantilist imperialism had to give way. As liberalism spread globally, even the closed economies came under pressure, though authoritarian domestic elites succeeded in obfuscating the costs.[8] Even if authoritarian governments could initially contain such external pressures from the international environment, the costs for such isolation gradually became prohibitive.

5. Doyle 1986, 12.
6. I use Robert Jervis's notion of how one should understand the notion of a "system," rather than the sparse neorealist conceptualization (Jervis 1997, 6).
7. Rosecrance 1986.
8. See Frieden and Rogowski (1996), and Evangelista's response in Keohane and Milner 1996.

4

In addition, nationalist sentiments that emerged in Europe in the nineteenth century ultimately made their way to the colonies as well. In the interwar years, the metropolitan powers succeeded in stifling most of these demands for independence. After 1945 this no longer proved possible. Indigenous nationalist elites and their external supporters raised the costs for maintaining imperial and multinational hierarchies.[9]

These factors did not affect all countries to the same degree. Changes in the military benefits of empire particularly concerned great powers such as Britain and France. The Soviet Union, as an emerging superpower, evaluated territory in terms of its value in the bipolar competition.

States such as the Netherlands and Portugal were more concerned with the economic aspects of empire. As small powers they had traditionally relied on the support of great powers to guarantee their own security. But while empires might provide economic benefits, the smaller powers were in no position to dictate imperial preferences to larger economic powers such as the United States. The desire for imperial preference thus had to be weighed against the benefits of access to and support from the larger developed economies.

Nationalism also differed in intensity and type. Some nationalists embraced socialist principles and catered to the Soviets and Chinese for support. Others, such as the Indonesian nationalists, explicitly distanced themselves from left-wing beliefs in the hope of retaining the support of the United States. Some nationalist cadres showed close intellectual affinities with the elites of the metropolitan governments. Others felt alienated and resentful.

I discuss the variant impact of military and economic concerns in chapter 2. Nationalism, although arguably part of a systemwide phenomenon, manifested itself partially in reaction to the particular policies that the metropolitan governments pursued. The Dutch and French, for example, pursued a hard line in dealing with nationalists during the interwar period, leaving them with few moderate intermediaries after the war. By contrast, their more flexible response made the British credible negotiation partners. Consequently, I discuss the interaction of the metropolitan government and nationalist elites in the empirical case chapters.

Domestic Preferences and Institutions as Conduits of International Effects

Various theories of realism would predict that the behavior of the central governments that are the focus of this book might be explained by changes in the international milieu alone. In Kenneth Waltz's parsimonious struc-

---

9. Jackson (1993) puts particular emphasis on normative issues within the metropoles. I argue that international norms particularly served to mobilize the periphery (Spruyt 2000).

tural realist conception, "State behavior varies more with differences in power than with difference in ideology . . . or in governmental form."[10] Fareed Zakaria suggests that classical realism "supposes that a nation's interests are determined by its power . . . relative to other nations: nations thus expand when they can."[11] Conversely, then, we would expect them to contract when their relative positions decline or when the international milieu no longer favors the existing territorial configuration.

Changes in the international environment no doubt play an important role. Without changes in the security environment or in the economic benefits of empire, we would expect the status quo to prevail. After all, territorial change and readjustment of boundaries comes at significant cost: military bases might have to be surrendered, industrial plants handed over, settlers relocated. The changes in the post–World War II environment thus provided the antecedent conditions for changes in existing territorial configurations.

Neither the variation in position of these states, nor the variation in their economic interest in empire, adequately explains territorial policy, however. As defensive realists or neoclassical realists argue, a structural realist account that stresses unitary, strategic state calculations has weak explanatory power. Domestic analysis must form part of any comprehensive explanation.[12] In this book, therefore, I aim to provide a systematic analysis of exactly how domestic politics interacts with international constraints and opportunities.

I argue that the institutional structures in the core affect the processes through which these dynamics play out. To put it succinctly: the more fragmented the decision-making process in the core, the greater the resistance to change in territorial policy and decolonization. The number of veto players can be used to measure the degree of centralization or fragmentation in the core. The number of veto players in the core territory or central government thus constitutes the independent or explanatory variable. In this theory, the likelihood of change in the existing territorial policy constitutes the dependent variable.

A veto player is an "individual or collective actor whose agreement is necessary for a change of the status quo."[13] Consequently, the number of veto players influences the latitude that governments will have to change policy. If a proposed policy confronts many veto players with variant preferences,

---

10. Waltz 1986, 329.
11. Zakaria 1998, 8–9.
12. For discussions of these alternative conceptualizations of realism, see Walt 2002, 204, 210–211; G. Rose 1998. Even Fareed Zakaria's own work (1998), although he calls it state-centric realism, stresses the domestic relative balance of power between the American executive and Congress.
13. Tsebelis 1999, 591.

the veto of any player can forestall compromise. In strategic choice parlance, political systems that present many veto points in the decision-making process will demonstrate policy stability, leading to the "impossibility of significant change of the status quo."[14]

Extrapolating from the general premise regarding the likelihood of policy change to the question of territorial policy leads to the following conclusion: the more veto opportunities that are present in a political system, the more likely it is that opponents to territorial partition can stifle attempts to negotiate with nationalists and draft new borders that are acceptable to all. A hard-line policy response will be more likely. Hard-liners need not constitute a majority of the populace. Indeed, as I will show in greater detail in the following chapters, if institutional arrangements create multiple veto opportunities, those who hold veto power and who have an interest in maintaining the territorial status quo (that is, they prefer not to compromise with secessionists or nationalists) may win the day even if they constitute a minority.

I assume that politicians act rationally in at least some minimal sense. They evaluate the options at their disposal, try to be consistent in their preferences, and trade off different values against each other.[15] But we should not presume that the institutional environment fully explains the choices of individual leaders. Agent volition and preferences matter. The institutional context constrains and channels how certain preferences are translated into policy; but institutions themselves cannot explain outcomes.

Thus, while this work borrows from strategic choice theory, it proceeds in the tradition of configurative macroanalysis and deploys "institutions as middle-level mediations between large-scale processes and the microdynamics of agency and action."[16] Both the strategic choice and historical institutionalist literatures generate deductive propositions regarding territorial policy. Deductive accounts allow us to generate and test propositions in a more exacting way than we could using inductive methods alone. But whether these propositions indeed explain what happened in practice requires us to examine the process through which preferences are articulated and pursued. Process tracing of how actors perceive their interests, and how they pursue such interests given a particular institutional configuration and within a specific historical context, thus becomes an important part of the analysis.[17]

This has an important bearing on our analysis of territorial policy for several reasons. First, an institutional account provides educated first guesses

14. Tsebelis 1999; Immergut 1992, 63. I interchangeably use the terms "veto players," "veto points," and "veto gates." See also Tsebelis 1995.
15. See Elster 1989, 23 and n. 4.
16. Katznelson 1997, 84; Katznelson 1998.
17. See Thelen and Steinmo 1992, 7–10.

regarding the potential number of vetoes that might be exercised to fore-stall changes in territorial policy. But it does not tell us whether some actors indeed wish to exercise such a veto. If preferences overlap, then the mere presence of constitutional and partisan veto points does not explain out-comes. In other words, our analysis calls for the tracing of "disposition" and "opportunity."[18]

Two social groups in particular have historically often had a stake in af-fecting territorial policy: business interests with direct investments in the contested territories and settler populations. Both may have incentives to oppose changes to the territorial status quo with little regard to the costs for the populace as a whole.[19] Economic actors that benefit from trade and in-vestments throughout the empire or multinational state will oppose frag-mentation out of fear that their business will be hurt. If such interests have large investments in the peripheries, and if these investments are of a site-specific nature, these groups will be strong proponents of empire.[20]

Settler populations will likewise favor continuation of metropolitan con-trol. Indeed, they have perhaps the most to lose from imperial retrench-ment. They have acquired properties, plantations, and other unmovable assets. Their metropolitan heritage, furthermore, gives them a privileged status in these colonies and overseas territories, while, conversely, their colonial background might diminish their status should they return home.

In subsequent chapters I argue that the institutional environment greatly affects whether politicians have any incentive to cater to these actors. Where politicians have incentives to cater to the median voter, or the na-tional electorate as a whole, special interests who oppose a change in terri-torial policy will have less opportunity to influence policy. In multiparty systems, by contrast, politicians have fewer incentives to cater to the elec-torate as a whole or the median voter; rather, they defend a particular position across the political spectrum.[21] In the latter situation, veto oppor-tunities will likely increase. Parties will stake out different preferences based on their constituencies.

Conversely, voters, realizing that their votes will not go to waste, will have little incentive to alter their views. Institutions do not merely influence politicians' behavior in pursuit of votes; the very nature of institutions al-lows individuals to hold (or even develop) preferences that receive a voice in such institutions.

Ultimately, it remains moot whether politicians cater to special interests out of strategic calculation or because of shared perspectives and ideologi-

18. Bermeo 1992a.
19. One could expand this list of potential hard-line actors without invalidating the veto points logic of analysis.
20. Frieden (1994) articulates this argument following Williamson 1975, 1986.
21. Laver 1997, 117–21.

cal affinity. The question is whether the institutional configuration provides politicians the institutional avenues to block a change in the territorial order.

Extending the Veto Points Approach

Ending Empire extends the existing literature by including an analysis of civil-military relations and by extending the approach to authoritarian regimes. Both the strategic choice and historical institutionalist literatures focus primarily on constitutional and electoral rules to determine the number of veto actors. But other actors besides those holding formal office or providing political representation may exercise vetoes as well.

In territorial disputes, a key veto point resides with the military. If civilians exercise weak oversight, the preferences of the military may in fact determine policy. The military can act extra-institutionally, disregarding institutional rules of procedure, electoral laws, and constitutional constraints, because it has coercive means at its disposal.

The military's disposition toward territorial unity will largely depend on its role definition and organizational interest in maintaining the existing territorial structure. Thus, if the metropolitan military has traditionally played the role of a colonial army, and if imperial functions are important justifications for revenue, career advancement, and esprit de corps, then it will be predisposed to favor military action to prevent secession. Alternatively, the armed forces might have little interest in maintaining the territorial status quo if corporate interests dictate that they divest themselves from the territories.

Most analyses of the effects of domestic institutions have focused on democratic systems.[22] Nevertheless, the line of reasoning developed in this book can be extended to authoritarian regimes as well.

Authoritarian systems with concentrated decision making and a dominant executive will show a greater likelihood of policy change. Leaders can implement their preferences with few impediments. Conversely, the lack of public oversight, due to the authoritarian nature of the regime, and the lack of input by a ruling coalition make the direction of policy change difficult to predict.[23]

Authoritarian systems with multiple veto points, by contrast, will not move from the status quo. If authoritarian rulers depend on the support of a broad ruling coalition to maintain office, the likelihood will increase that one of these supporting groups will successfully oppose territorial with-

22. An exception is MacIntyre 2003.
23. These types of authoritarian systems would look similar to Snyder's unitary authoritarian polities; see Snyder 1991.

drawal. Each member of the ruling oligarchy can thus veto compromise solutions if its parochial interests are at stake.

Given that parochial interests may exercise undue influence in democratic and authoritarian systems alike, the differences in regime type—democratic or authoritarian—in and of themselves do not explain why some territorial dissolutions occur peacefully while others do not. The variation in outcomes cuts across regime type and depends on the ability of veto groups to block territorial retrenchment.

OVERVIEW

Let me be clear from the outset. Political elites rarely engage in careful, overt calibration of costs and benefits. Few leaders devise grand strategies for territorial withdrawal, although Britain has probably come the closest. Like captains caught in turbulent seas, they often jury-rig solutions with little eye for the ultimate sequence of events. Mikhail Gorbachev, although pushing for openness and reform, did not set out to dissolve the USSR. However, as governments have had to react to changes in the international environment and to indigenous nationalist demands, existing institutional arrangements have influenced the modes of decision making—allowing for flexible responses in some cases and leading to paralysis in others.

Chapter 1 clarifies the causal logic and the method of analysis that I briefly advanced in this introduction. It also clarifies case selection and the logic of comparative analysis. I then discuss the broad environmental changes that transpired in the wake of World War II but which cannot explain the divergent territorial policies. Each empirical chapter will discuss in greater detail how these changes operated in that specific instance. The clear-cut "imperial" cases come first, starting with three Western democracies: France, Britain, and the Netherlands. I then expand the logic of analysis to authoritarian governments by examining Portuguese decolonization and the dissolution of the Soviet empire, primarily focusing on its internal empire. The Soviet Union demonstrates the value of my argument for a category of cases in which the concept "empire" is contested (at least by some). Finally, I discuss the Arab-Israeli conflict and the problems created by the multiple veto points facing Israel's leaders. This presents a case even further removed from the original context of the maritime imperial examples and suggests the broader payoff of the theoretical framework.

CHAPTER ONE

Institutional Frameworks
and Territorial Policy

> In order to have a majority, one needs an electoral system that will pro-
> duce one. This was what my government decided upon when it passed
> the new electoral law by virtue of its special powers, rejecting propor-
> tional representation, dear to the rivalries and vetoes of the parties, but
> incompatible with the maintenance of a continuous policy.
>
> > CHARLES DE GAULLE, commenting on the
> > reforms that established the Fifth Republic

> Decolonisation . . . first required the growth of nationalist sentiments.
> But this growth alone was never the whole story. Whilst in reality inter-
> national aspects were rarely of great significance, what was then of pri-
> mary importance were the particularities of the imperial response,
> which to a major degree determined the nature of the confrontation
> which then ensued.
>
> > —ANTHONY LOW, Cambridge University

The late-nineteenth-century Scramble for Africa epitomized the might of
the European continental powers. In a manner reminiscent of the Treaty of
Tordesillas, by which Spain and Portugal had divided the yet to be explored
New World four centuries earlier, the Europeans divided vast tracts of land
by the mere exchange of signatures and without a hint of consultation with
their new subjects.

But by the middle of the twentieth century the international environment of empire had changed dramatically. Imperial possessions no longer
yielded the military benefits they once did. International economic flows
had become increasingly inter-empire rather than intra-empire. Moreover,
after the Second World War the United States opposed any renewed imperial preference schemes. Nationalist resistance also became a far more for-

midable force than it had been before the war. Exacerbating an already difficult situation, the two superpowers started to compete for the loyalties of the colonies by supporting the termination of empire, and international organizations gave voice to new nonaligned countries.

As the empirical narrative demonstrates, the governments of the various empires and multinational states reacted very differently to these changes in their environment. Internal politics explain the variation in metropolitan responses to a great extent. True, the changing international environment provided the antecedent conditions for change. But the changes in that environment do not adequately explain the diverse patterns of dissolution. Britain and France faced roughly similar environments—both were great (but not super) powers; both were liberal capitalist states; both operated within the Western alliance; and both faced recalcitrant subject territories that demanded secession from the empire. They nevertheless developed completely different territorial policies in response to such demands. As Michael Fry points out, for the British, decolonization "was meant to be a process of orderly, timely change based on negotiation, avoiding conflict, and contributing to British postwar recovery and influence." Even though violence erupted at a modest level in Kenya, Rhodesia, Cyprus, and Malaya, it "never approached the magnitude of the French experience in Vietnam and Algeria."[1]

How metropolitan governments react to challenges to the existing territorial order depends on whether institutional arrangements give pro-imperial actors a veto on territorial revisions. This requires an analysis of preference and opportunity. A military with a corporate interest in the empire, and groups that stand to lose from any change in the existing territorial order—particularly settlers and certain business interests—will demand that the status quo be maintained . . . if necessary through hard-line reactions. These groups pursue narrow private benefits and often have well-developed means of collective organization—for example, the Parti Colonial in France.

Political elites may take up the imperial cause for various reasons. Some leaders will be swayed by ideological arguments regarding the need to stand by "kith and kin." Others might believe that without the contested territories the country might be relegated to secondary status. Some Dutch politicians argued that the Netherlands without Indonesia would be relegated to being another Denmark. French elites claimed that France without empire would become no more than Montenegro. When coupled with domino theories that the defense of Europe starts in Africa, virtually no territory could be relinquished without dire consequences.

1. Fry 1997, 142, 145.

More strategic motives were also at work. In some instances settlers voted directly in metropolitan elections, as in Algeria. French settlers also financed favorite sons and daughters in a variety of political parties. Some leaders in the Dutch Catholic Party were closely affiliated with business interests in Indonesia. Particular institutional frameworks could also provide incentives for politicians to cater to groups with particular interests. Electoral systems that were highly proportional and that led to a multiparty system allowed parties to cater to groups across the political spectrum rather than having to pursue the median voter.

Ultimately, we need not account for why politicians held certain preferences. It suffices to demonstrate that preferences diverged. The question then becomes whether the institutions in the center provided the holders of hard-line positions the opportunity to block concessions.

The number of veto opportunities in a particular polity provides the key variable that predicts the likelihood of change in the existing territorial policy. The degree of civilian oversight of the military, as well as the constitutional and electoral rules, determine how many veto points exist in a given system.[2]

This leads to the following predictions:

First, if the military dominates civilian decision making, the preferences of the armed forces will be critical. If the armed forces have the ability to veto policy change and they wish to exercise that veto, this will often provide a necessary and sufficient explanation for the lack of policy change and negotiated adjustment.

Second, if a civilian government does control the military, and there is a two-party parliamentary system or a government that constitutionally provides the executive with autonomous powers, policy change will be more likely. Unified executive authority, whether in a democracy or an authoritarian regime, will provide hard-liners less opportunity to stall territorial retrenchment.

Third, even if a civilian government controls the armed forces, if there is also a multiparty parliamentary system, or a weak presidential system that confronts many checks and balances, or an oligarchical authoritarian regime, there still might be policy stasis. Such systems create multiple veto opportunities. Settlers and business groups with site-specific investments are likely to find political allies to oppose retreat. Given the availability of multiple veto points, these groups need not convince a majority of politicians or the electorate, but only those political actors needed to implement the desired veto.

---

2. This approach has much in common with Arvid Lukauskas's (1997) research on whether an institutional structure induces politicians to provide private, narrowly defined benefits or public goods. See also Bates 1981.

THE DOWNSTREAM EFFECT OF INSTITUTIONS

Regimes and Territorial Policy

One might conjecture that regime type explains whether a country will pursue peaceful adjustment or hard-line policies in contested territories. After all, a large body of literature suggests that democracies overall are less war-prone than authoritarian governments.[3] More specific to our question, some scholars submit that oligarchical political systems are more likely to be rife with logrolling and are, consequently, more likely to engage in imperialism.[4] Jack Snyder's masterful study shows how pro-imperial interests build coalitions by distributing specific benefits to political allies. Because the costs of empire are distributed over the larger, and weakly represented, broader population, difficulties with organizing collective action limit the degree of opposition to the pro-empire group.[5] Because oligarchical regimes manage to roll over the real costs of empire, the pursuit of empire might very well be irrational for the state as a whole, but it will come about nonetheless.

Democratic and unitary authoritarian regimes are less prone to catering to narrow private interests. That is, they will evaluate policies in terms of their overall costs and benefits to the state as a whole. Democratic regimes will do so given that information asymmetries are less pronounced than in oligarchical-cartelized regimes, and there are fewer barriers to entry for opponents of the parochial associations. Leaders also have to receive broad-based support to stay in power and will thus appeal to the median voter. Snyder suggests this is the case whether the system is a two-party, winner-take-all type or whether it is based on proportional representation and multiple parties.[6]

Unitary authoritarian systems show similar traits since power is "concentrated in the hands of a single dictator or unitary oligarchy" with a "relatively encompassing view of the state's interests."[7] Because rulers in essence appropriate all benefits and bear all costs they cannot roll over the costs from one group to another.

Extrapolating from these insights one can infer that well-entrenched interest groups, which benefit from empire, will likewise hold disproportionate influence when decisions are made regarding imperial retrenchment. Pro-empire groups will be better organized than those advocating retrenchment, and the benefits of maintaining the territorial status quo will be con-

---

3. For an overview, see M. Elman 1997.
4. Snyder 1991, 31.
5. The general proposition derives from Olson 1965.
6. Snyder 1991, 50 and n. 81.
7. Snyder 1991, 32.

centrated, whereas the benefits of retreat will flow to the population at large.

Others, however, are less convinced about democracy's virtues.[8] One study of colonial withdrawal maintains that "democratic states are particularly prone to using force against secessionist movements, even when those areas hold little strategic value" because parochial interests can set the political agenda. By contrast, "Authoritarian regimes in which settler interests have no seat at the table, may also be less likely to engage in violent confrontation with secessionist areas."[9]

Some scholars conclude that a focus on regime type is too broad and that electoral and constitutional rules mediate the effects of regime type. Miles Kahler, for example, notes how a lack of party discipline wreaked havoc in the multiparty French Fourth Republic.[10] Political elites will be reluctant to disengage from territories if it will hurt their chances for election or reelection. Politicians will seek to get the better of their rivals by engaging in an ever-increasing rhetorical spiral in support of empire. Two-party systems with party discipline will allow executives more room for retrenchment. In multiparty systems, where several parties cover the same political spectrum and voters shift allegiances, political elites will compete for the pro-empire vote.[11] However, in multiparty systems with stable constituencies, politicians will have fewer incentives to outbid one another and cater to pro-imperial, parochial interests.[12]

Even if they come to slightly different conclusions, jointly these studies suggest the need for domestic-level institutional analysis. How does regime type or institutional rules affect policy?

The Literature on the Downstream Effects of Institutions

Much of the debate has focused on whether presidentialism or parliamentarism favors the development of democracy and government stability, and on the effects of two-party versus multiparty systems.[13] Juan Linz and Arend Lijphart, for example, favor power sharing among multiple parties because it diminishes the winner-takes-all character of presidential and

8. Some political economists suggest that authoritarian East Asian countries have been able to implement export-oriented policies and to establish restrictive financial systems because they are less likely to be captured by special interests. Amsden 1989; Lukauskas 1997.

9. Levine 1994, 3, 57.

10. Kahler 1984.

11. Alicia Levine (1994) also argues that multiparty systems can generate policies that favor parochial interests, but she concentrates particularly on the consequences of logrolling in such systems.

12. For example, if they are divided according to religious and ethnic criteria, multiparty systems will resemble two-party configurations; Kahler 1984, 69.

13. Diamond and Plattner (1996) provide a good overview of some of these debates.

Westminster-type polities.[14] Cindy Skach and Alfred Stepan similarly suggest that parliamentarism creates a more supportive evolutionary framework for nascent democracies than does pure presidentialism.[15]

Others come to different conclusions. Scott Mainwaring and Matthew Shugart defend presidentialism by noting how parliamentary systems may show the vices mentioned by Lijphart and Linz to an even greater degree. Specifically, majoritarian parliamentary systems, such as the British, create even more pronounced winner-takes-all politics than do presidential polities. They suggest that a presidency with limited legislative powers and with few but disciplined parties can be conducive for promoting democracy.[16]

Others focus on how presidential systems tend to insulate political leaders from interest group pressures.[17] Because the president is elected on a nationwide rather than a district level, he or she will have less incentive to cater to localized interests. As David Lake suggests, "In the pursuit of national wealth and power, and in responding to its national rather than regional electorate, the foreign policy executive must . . . make judgments about what is good for the country as a whole."[18] Given the need to cater to the public at large and to maximize the likelihood of winning, and contrary to the dynamics in multiparty systems, presidential candidates will thus cater to the median voter. Furthermore, because presidents often sit for fixed terms, they tend to be less susceptible to the lobbying pressures brought to bear on the legislative body.

Two-party parliamentary systems can give the executive considerable authority as well. In a two-party system with disciplined parties, as in Britain, the prime minister wields considerable power because defection from party ranks is costly to the individual legislator. Moreover, significant policy shifts may occur if the party is not returned to office. Thus the prime minister maintains considerable leverage over the individual party member.[19]

Conversely, a prime minister in a multiparty system lacks such means of keeping the rank and file in control. Indeed, parties within the coalition might have incentives to bring the government down to reconstitute it in a form more to their liking. Even the loyalty of the members of the prime minister's own party cannot be taken for granted, and narrower interests may prevail over the will of the general electorate. The executive will have limited autonomy.

14. Linz 1996; Lijphart 1977, 1994. Sartori (1994) takes a middle road, arguing for a limited multiparty system (with four to five parties) or a "strong intermittent presidency."

15. Skach and Stepan 1993.

16. Mainwaring and Shugart 1997.

17. Lukauskas 1997; Moe and Caldwell 1994.

18. Lake 1988, 37.

19. Mainwaring and Shugart 1997, 453.

Clearly then, while the institutional literature provides valuable insights, it is also fraught with apparent contradictions.[20] Adam Przeworski's evaluation of the institutional literature and democratic transitions holds broad applicability: "We have intuitions about the impact of presidentialism versus parliamentarism, we know the effects of alternative electoral systems . . . but our current empirical knowledge leaves a broad margin for disagreements about institutional design."[21]

Jon Elster similarly notes the difficulties of trying to trace the downstream effects of institutional arrangements.[22] Terry Moe and Michael Caldwell concur: "Most everyone believes that institutions matter. But exactly how they matter, and thus how one might choose among them, remains something of a mystery."[23]

VETO OPPORTUNITIES AND THE LIKELIHOOD OF POLICY CHANGE

Although the research on the effects of institutions remains a subject of continuous analysis and controversy, there is considerable agreement on the impact of veto points and policy change. Indeed, strategic choice theorists and historical institutionalists, while working in different epistemological and methodological traditions, come to similar conclusions.

The degree of unity or fragmentation in the center affects the likelihood that executives can change policy when international circumstances warrant. More specifically, an analysis of the number of veto points provides deductive propositions about the downstream effects of institutional arrangements.

The comparative study of public policy pioneered this line of inquiry. Various scholars noted how the degree of centralization of a state's policy networks had consequences for the type of policies states adopted during the recession of the 1970s.[24] Peter Katzenstein's analysis of policy change in West Germany described how federalism, coalition governments, and parapublic institutions created a decentralized state: "The restraint that the interaction of these three nodes of the policy network imposes on the exercise of state power explains why policy change in the Federal Republic is incremental even when a new government is voted into office."[25] In other words, fragmented institutions lead to policy stasis.

20. Variation in subtypes further complicates generalization; see Duverger 1980.
21. Przeworski 1991, 35.
22. Elster 1997, 225.
23. Moe and Caldwell 1994, 171.
24. Katzenstein 1978.
25. Katzenstein 1987, 81.

Ellen Immergut's study of health care reform in western Europe introduced the notion of veto points even more explicitly. Rather than explaining policy outcomes by the relative power of interest groups, she emphasizes the key importance of institutional configurations: "Political decisions require agreement at several points along a chain of decisions. . . . The fate of legislative proposals depends upon the number and location of opportunities for veto along this chain."[26] Health care reform was less likely the greater the number of veto points there were in the policy process. She notes how, in general, "the ability of an executive government to introduce policy depends on its capacity for unilateral action."[27]

In comparing Westminster parliamentary systems with the separation of powers in the American presidential system, Moe and Caldwell argue that a crucial difference is that the former has few veto points, while the latter has many.[28] American presidents and British prime ministers, although both oriented toward the national electorate, face different structural settings.

Surveying the literature on institutions, R. Kent Weaver and Bert Rockman likewise submit that having fewer veto points create a greater likelihood of policy change. They note that scholars sometimes criticize the American separation of powers because in parliamentary institutions "the concentration of legislative power and party discipline is likely to enhance governmental capacity to impose losses and to innovate in policy by removing veto points."[29] Although they do not state it explicitly, they are comparing the American system to a two-party parliamentary system of the Westminster variety.

George Tsebelis has pursued this line of inquiry in the strategic-choice literature. He believes that debates about the effects of institutions are often misguided because they present false dichotomies between presidential and parliamentary or two-party and multiparty systems, and because they focus on government and regime stability.[30] Instead, he suggests focusing on the number of veto players, that is, any "individual or collective actor whose agreement is required for a policy decision."[31]

The likelihood of policy change will depend on the size of the winset, the range of acceptable policies for the majority. Larger winsets mean that more options for change are available, and thus increase the likelihood of

---

26. Immergut 1992, 63.
27. Immergut 1992, 65.
28. Moe and Caldwell 1994, 177.
29. Weaver and Rockman 1993, 17.
30. Most of the literature deals with the effects of institutions on government and regime stability, not policy stability (stasis), which is the focus of this work. For the discussion of various perspectives, see Lijphart 1977, 12–13, 63; 1989a.
31. Tsebelis 1995, 293; Tsebelis 1999. For Tsebelis, policy stability (the lack of policy change) constitutes the dependent variable, not government or regime stability.

a move away from the status quo. Tsebelis advances two propositions that are key to the analysis of *Ending Empire:*

1. As the number of players who are required to agree for a movement of the status quo increases, the winset of the status quo does not increase. [Policy change does not become more likely.]
2. As the distance of players who are required to agree for a movement of the status quo increases along the same line, the winset of the status quo does not increase. [The likelihood of policy change diminishes.][32]

Thus, the more players required to make a decision, the less likely it is that we will see a policy shift. In addition, if the parties required for a change in policy are ideologically far apart, the likelihood of a policy shift will decline as well. The more actors that have been involved in achieving the current winset (the existing policy), and the greater their policy differences, the less likely policy change will occur.

Tsebelis further distinguishes between institutional veto players and partisan veto players. The number of institutional veto players is determined by constitutional rules. Party and coalitional dynamics determine the number of partisan veto players. The consequences of varying institutional arrangements, and their bearing on veto points in the policy process, may thus be derived deductively.[33]

EXTENDING THE VETO POINTS APPROACH

Authoritarian Systems

Institutionalist arguments have for obvious reasons largely focused on democracies. Democratic governments, after all, operate according to formal constitutional and electoral rules. In authoritarian systems the political

---

32. Tsebelis 1995. He also introduces a third proposition: Less cohesive collective actors increase the size of the winset (policy change becomes more likely). That is, if the players—for example parties—exercise less party discipline the range of options that are acceptable will be larger, in that there is no single preference point. The third proposition is less clear-cut. A lack of cohesion and a lack of party discipline will indeed increase the range of the winset (because each collective actor will show a greater spread in policy positions). Thus, weak party discipline should make policy shifts more likely. However, one could conversely argue that lack of party discipline would make commitment to a certain range of policies less credible and thus make cycling more prevalent. If that were the case, policy change would be more difficult to achieve. In later articles Tsebelis also has focused on the number of parties and ideological distance; see Tsebelis 1999. MacIntyre (2003, 27) suggests, as do I, that weak party discipline increases veto opportunities.

33. For applications of veto points arguments in political economy, see Birchfield and Crepaz 1998; Crepaz 2002; Hallerberg and Basinger 1998; MacIntyre 2003. This approach has so far made few inroads in security studies. However, see Peterson and Wenk 2001.

game is rigged. Institutions are specifically designed to keep "the powers that be" in office. Electoral results may be annulled and opposition leaders jailed. Similarly, military regimes can act outside the formal rule of law. Guns trump rules of procedure.

There is nothing, however, that prevents us from extending the veto points argument to nondemocratic systems. Indeed, some studies of veto players and economic policy have already moved in that direction. Andrew MacIntyre suggests that veto points analysis can shed light on how East Asian countries responded to the financial crisis of 1997.

Authoritarian systems can be distinguished in two types: those in which there is a narrow coalition of private and public actors (what Snyder calls cartelized systems) and those in which private and public functions have been usurped by one actor and are highly centralized (Snyder's unitary system).[34] In the first type, oligarchical-authoritarian governments have multiple veto points. The partners in the ruling coalition (such as the armed forces, landed interests, and big business) will have the ability to veto policies they consider antithetical to their interests. Historically the "iron and rye" coalition of Wilhelmine Germany would fit this category, as would corporatist authoritarian systems of the Mediterranean and Latin American types.

In hierarchical authoritarian systems, by contrast, there are few veto opportunities. Similar to a strong executive in a democratic system, a unitary authoritarian government, which concentrates authority in a collective entity (such as a Communist party) or a single individual (in a dictatorship), can alter policies without many obstacles.

Although hierarchical authoritarian states may change policies without much opposition, like presidential systems with a strong executive or two-party parliamentary systems, one important caveat applies. The direction of policy change will be difficult to predict, because the government of a hierarchical authoritarian state need not cater to the electorate or median voter. Policies may change swiftly and take the state's external constraints and opportunities into account, that is, behave as a realist might predict, or they may disregard such structural imperatives. Nevertheless, an executive of such a state will still have the latitude to choose a policy that is not beholden to special interests.

34. Snyder (1991) argues that unitary authoritarian governments (such as the USSR) cannot roll over the costs of empire. Hence, the USSR adjusted. I would argue instead that such governments do roll over the costs of empire on the general population, but that there were few veto players who could block the adjustment when international circumstances dictated withdrawal. Our findings look similar, but the logic of our explanations differs.

The Armed Forces as a Veto Player

While the institutionalist literature largely looks at how civilian interest groups may influence decision making, the civil-military literature focuses more explicitly on the extra-institutional means through which the military can affect policy.[35] There are several distinct research programs dealing with civilian oversight.[36] One strand of literature focuses particularly on the propensity of the military to intervene in civilian politics.[37] A second body of research looks at the military within the new institutionalist framework of principal-agency theory and argues that a divided civilian government gives the military more autonomy.[38] Another strand of literature focuses on the question of whether and when civilians set grand strategy rather than the military.[39]

Our concerns are with the first and, to a lesser extent, the second approach. Under what conditions will the military contest civilian government and violate constitutional rules? The amount of influence that the military exercises over civilian decision making runs the gamut from political passivity on one end to forceful intervention, coups d'état, and rebellions on the other. Between these two extremes may lie political participation within the existing institutional and legal framework and aggressive institutional advocacy.[40]

Timothy Colton uses an analysis of relative predominance in three issue areas to distinguish civilian dominance from military supremacy.[41] He bases his work partially on Samuel Huntington's description of objectively controlled militaries, which have distinct noncivilian values and preferences. These militaries have specific professional traits and claim autonomy in their area of expertise but do not claim any expertise in other areas. In polities with objectively controlled militaries there is a mutual understanding and division of labor between civilian government and the military.[42]

Several factors will influence the likelihood of civilian control over the military. First, if external threats to the state are high and internal threats to

35. Nancy Bermeo, among others, has argued for more attention to the role of the military in democratic transitions; see Bermeo 1992a. I argue for greater attention to the role of the armed forces in territorial questions.

36. In Timothy Colton's words, "There is no such thing as an accepted global theory of civil military relations." Colton 1990, 6. See also Feaver 1996. Feaver 1999 provides a comprehensive overview of the state of this literature.

37. See the classic work by Huntington (1957).

38. Avant 1994.

39. Posen 1984; Snyder 1984.

40. Norden 1996, 10–12.

41. Colton 1990. For an application to Soviet civil-military relations, see Meyer 1991–92.

42. Huntington 1957, 83, 88–89; Feaver 1996; Desch 1993, 455.

the state are low, civilian control will be robust.[43] If external threats are low but internal threats are high, civilian control will be the least likely.

Second, divided civilian oversight will allow the military to play civilian leaders off against one another. Deborah Avant thus notes how the U.S. military has managed to evade stringent oversight due to the fragmented nature of decision making. The British military, however, has consistently faced unified oversight.[44]

In short, when civilians control the military, the armed forces will not have a veto over the policy process. If civilian control is weak, the military will be able to exercise a veto. Indeed, in that situation, the institutional ability of the military to intervene can override the preferences of civilian interest groups and political elites. In other words, in political systems where the military is poorly controlled and where it intervenes in many aspects of civilian government, the preferences of the military will provide a necessary and often sufficient explanation of territorial policy. Political leaders will have strategic incentives to follow the preferences of the military in order to secure and maintain their political office.

HYPOTHESES AND PROPOSITIONS

My objective is to explain change in territorial policy (the dependent variable of this study). A government may choose not to change the existing territorial order despite nationalist demands. It will try to maintain the territorial status quo by using force if necessary. At the other end, a government may concede that the colonial game is over, yield to nationalist demands, and withdraw. The number of veto points (the independent variable) provides the key explanation for the likelihood of such a policy change.

The dependent variable comes with an important corollary. If governments have greater latitude to deal with territorial demands, they will be more likely to evaluate the costs and benefits of maintaining the territorial status quo to the state as a whole. Thus, if the cost of holding contested territories has gone up while the benefits of the territories have gone down, a government that faces few veto actors will more likely entertain concessions to territorial demands. This will particularly be true in democratic systems with few veto opportunities, because governments will cater to the general public and the median voter. A unified authoritarian ruler likewise will have greater opportunity to change the existing territorial configuration, but

43. This argument follows Michael Desch 1999. Desch's argument does not make fully clear whether an internal threat means a challenge to the internal order of the state overall, or a more narrow threat to the corporate interests of the military.

44. Avant 1994.

Table 1.1. The likelihood of change in territorial policy

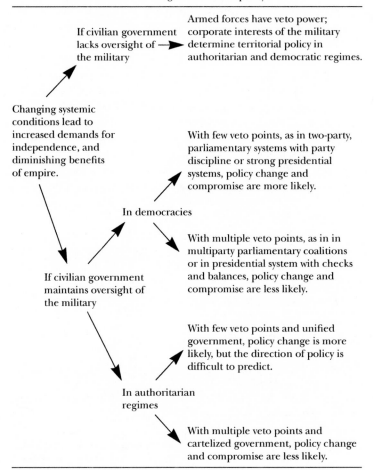

If civilian government lacks oversight of the military → Armed forces have veto power; corporate interests of the military determine territorial policy in authoritarian and democratic regimes.

Changing systemic conditions lead to increased demands for independence, and diminishing benefits of empire.

With few veto points, as in two-party, parliamentary systems with party discipline or strong presidential systems, policy change and compromise are more likely.

In democracies

With multiple veto points, as in in multiparty parliamentary coalitions or in presidential system with checks and balances, policy change and compromise are less likely.

If civilian government maintains oversight of the military

With few veto points and unified government, policy change is more likely, but the direction of policy is difficult to predict.

In authoritarian regimes

With multiple veto points and cartelized government, policy change and compromise are less likely.

since the leader is not subject to democratic oversight, the direction of policy change will hinge on the preferences of that individual, making prediction difficult.

For our analysis of how governments deal with secessionist demands this means that territorial policies of democratic governments with few veto points will more accurately reflect changes in the international environment than governments with many veto points. Changes in the existing territorial composition will be easier to make. Political rulers who decide that the existing territorial composition should not be maintained will be able to alter policies without special interest groups blocking compromise solutions with the secessionists.

My argument holds even if political elites do not make a deliberate choice for territorial dissolution. Whatever the causes of the incipient breakup, the actors who oppose territorial dissolution will be unable to veto such changes. My account does not require a government to engage in an elaborate cost-benefit analysis of the merits of the existing territorial arrangement. British prime minister Harold Macmillan did ask for such an explicit reckoning as soon as he assumed office in 1957, but this certainly was not the norm. This analysis focuses instead on the question of whether opponents to any change in the existing territorial configuration have the institutional ability to obstruct such potential changes. Thus while President Mikhail Gorbachev did not engage in the careful calibrations that Macmillan did, when he refused to call out the army to maintain the territorial integrity of the Soviet Union, pro-imperial groups could not forestall the dissolution of the USSR, because the political institutions did not provide them with any veto power.

Table 1.2. Hypotheses regarding the probability of policy change and territorial compromise

Situations in which policy change is more likely

H1. Governments that exercise civilian oversight of the military will have greater latitude to change territorial policy.

    H1a. Compromise solutions will be more likely if the costs of maintaining the territorial status quo have increased.

H2. Democratic governments with few constitutional or partisan veto points will have greater latitude to change territorial policy.

    H2a. Compromise solutions will be more likely if the costs of maintaining the territorial status quo have increased.

H3. Unified authoritarian governments will have greater latitude to change territorial policy.

    H3a. Given that authoritarian leaders are not beholden to a national electorate, the direction of policy change will be indeterminate, even if the costs of maintaining the territorial status quo have increased.

Situations in which policy change is less likely

H4. A change in territorial policy will be less likely if the government lacks civilian oversight.

    H4a. The preferences of the armed forces will determine policy outcomes.

    H4b. Hard-line policies will be more likely if this is in the military's corporate interest.

H5. A change in territorial policy will be less likely in multiparty coalition governments in parliamentary systems, or in presidential systems with checks and balances.

    H5a. The lack of policy change will make a hard-line response to demands for territorial adjustments more probable.

H6. Cartelized authoritarian regimes will have less latitude to change territorial policy.

    H6a. Less latitude to deal with nationalist demands will make a hard-line response more likely.

STAKEHOLDERS, POLITICIANS, AND PREFERENCES

Institutional analysis thus provides deductive propositions about the likelihood of a change in territorial configuration. Analysis of institutional configurations alone, however, is not sufficient. An examination of actors' preferences is also required.

The veto points model describes how institutional arrangements create potential obstacles to policy change. It does not tell us whether the opportunity for a veto will indeed be seized in practice.[45] Without an account of preferences we might misread our evidence and erroneously falsify or corroborate our theory. For example, if we have a system with multiple veto points and yet observe a change in policy, one might falsely conclude that institutions play no independent role. However, it is possible that none of the actors with a veto opportunity chose to exercise it because they all had similar preferences in favor of change.

Institutional configurations matter when preferences diverge. If all parties hold a similar position, the policy winset will be very large. Similarity of preferences reduces the number of vetoes. Tsebelis calls this the "absorption rule." Institutional architectures only provide an empty shell, the context in which actors pursue their preferences.[46] He further notes that the larger the divergence in ideological positions, the smaller the winset will be. The divergences in preferences between opponents and proponents of policy change make the institutional veto points salient. Strategic choice theory thus cautions us not to derive consequences from institutional analysis alone. Adherents of the "analytic narratives" approach, although their work is deductively driven, similarly caution that one should inductively seek "to understand the actors' preferences, their perceptions, their evaluations of alternatives."[47]

Historical institutionalists make this point even more forcefully. Institutions not only shape strategies but the very goals that actors pursue. As Ira Katznelson reminds us, relations between environmental conditions, institutions, and individual agents are matters of unique configuration and thus call for a careful reading of the empirical record. Institutions act as "mediations between large-scale processes and the microdynamics of agency and action."[48] Individual and group behavior cannot simply be inferred from a sparse accounting of exogenous costs and benefits. Consequently, *Ending Empire* examines how preferences may change over time, and how the

---

45. Bermeo (1992a) argues that explanations of democratic transitions need to account for "opportunities" as well as "dispositions." Milner similarly submits that institutional analysis requires an account of interests and preferences; Milner 1997, 10–18.

46. Tsebelis 2002, 12, 18.

47. Bates et al. 1998, 11.

48. Katznelson 1997, 84, 93. See also Thelen and Steinmo 1992; Katznelson 1998.

choices made at a particular juncture may constrain subsequent choices. Comparative statics across cases need to be augmented by a dynamic accounting of the actual decision process in each individual case.[49]

These observations, however, do not relegate us to a pure inductive analysis of preferences. We can reasonably have a priori expectations when the armed forces and key interest groups will try to forestall territorial changes. Similarly, we can have deductive expectations regarding the preferences of politicians from the institutional configuration in which they operate.

Business, Military, and Settler Preferences for the Territorial Status Quo

Observers have long noted that the pursuit of empire must often be attributed to the particular motives of key actors in a polity who have an undue influence on government.[50] In the 1950s Joseph Schumpeter suggested that societies with landholding aristocracies were particularly predisposed to aggressive foreign policies.[51] Even if modern militaries appear to have little resemblance to older privileged, aristocratic warrior elites, the militaries' prominence in imperial policies should not be underestimated. The armed forces might argue for empire to justify larger budgets, to enlarge their autonomy vis-à-vis other actors, to placate political superiors who favor aggressive foreign policies (such as Kaiser Wilhelm II, for example), or to defend a particular esprit de corps.[52]

Civilian interest groups have traditionally tried to exercise undue influence as well. In the early twentieth century John Hobson observed astutely that imperialism did not necessarily result from careful cost-benefit calculations of the state. Private benefit often triumphed over public good: "Irrational from the standpoint of the whole nation, it is rational enough from the standpoint of certain classes in the nation."[53]

Many empires thus find their roots in the benefits that they yield to specific segments within polities. Beyond the purview of the state, individuals and groups pursuing their own narrow interests draw the metropoles further and further into imperial expansion.

Just as the pursuit of empire finds its roots in the pull and tug of domestic politics in the metropole, so too can internal politics explain the opposition to changes in the existing territorial order. Some of the key actors, who

49. For a comparison of rational choice and historical institutionalism on the issue of preference formation, see Thelen 1999, 9.
50. For a comprehensive overview of some theories that emphasize the importance of domestic elites, see Doyle 1986.
51. Schumpeter 1955.
52. Snyder (1984) and Posen (1984) ascribe similar motives to the military in its pursuit of offensive doctrine.
53. Hobson 1961 [1902], 12.

advocated empire in the first place, may stand to lose the most if the metropole decides to retreat from the periphery. Moreover, given that concentrated groups as business and landed interests can more readily overcome collective action problems than diffusely organized groups, they have a distinct advantage over the social actors who favor disengagement. Consequently, these groups will try to prevent territorial dissolution by any means—some within the constitutional rules of political competition, others outside those rules (through coups d'état, even assassination).

Several groups are likely to be vociferous opponents of change in the territorial order: settler communities, the armed forces, and business communities with substantial investments in the colonies. To discern the preferences of actors largely requires empirical specification. Nevertheless, there are reasons to expect that some of these groups will be proponents of maintaining the existing territorial order.

The preferences of settlers are the most straightforward to deduce. These are people who have left their motherland to settle on a distant shore, perhaps never to return. They might own property and dwellings in the colony and intermarry with locals. In all circumstances settlers occupy a privileged legal and political position in the subject areas, which they cannot hope to duplicate in the metropole. Consequently, of all actors this group stands to lose the most, and, hence, this set of individuals should be expected to have intense preferences against metropolitan dissociation. The Algerian "pieds noirs," the Portuguese farmers in Angola, and the Dutch settler communities in Indonesia were among the most vociferous opponents of dissolution. They created armed militias and opposed peaceful territorial disengagement.[54]

The business community, with considerable transaction-specific investments in the empire, is another group with likely preferences for continued metropolitan control over the contested areas. Jeffry Frieden suggests that such holdings may be a key reason why formal empire followed private direct investments.[55] Likewise, Charles Lipson has shown that portfolio investments (bond loans, equities) tend to lead to different metropolitan responses than direct investments, the latter requiring more overt metropolitan action for their protection.[56]

---

54. By contrast, settlers were less pro-imperial where they had largely exterminated or dominated local populations (United States, Canada, Australia, New Zealand, South Africa). Indeed, such white settler states might favor secession. This set of cases falls outside my purview. I am interested in situations where the central government faces demands from expatriates to maintain its territorial hold rather than to retreat.

55. Frieden 1994. Similarly, O. Williamson (1975) suggests that when firms engage in asset-specific transactions, they will seek vertical integration. See also Yarborough and Yarborough 1987.

56. Lipson 1985.

The implication for the analysis of territorial policy is that corporations and individuals that have considerable transaction-specific investments in territories that are seeking independence will favor continued metropolitan rule. Like the settlers, these economic interest groups argue that the contested territories are vital to the motherland. To justify a serious commitment of political and military resources to keep the peripheries under control, these interests have to portray that what is at stake is the broad public good rather than narrow private benefits.

Just as the military may act as a veto player it also may display preferences for maintaining the territorial status quo. Given its past history as a key instrument of empire, and given prevailing recruitment patterns, promotional incentives, budget allocation, as well as strategic doctrine, the military will often have a corporate interest in maintaining the existing territorial configuration. Particularly those armed forces whose budget and functional role have been specifically geared toward the pursuit and defense of the empire will have a vested interest in opposing territorial retrenchment.

The preferences of the armed forces are, however, not as easy to infer *ex ante* as the preferences of settlers and economic actors with large investments in the colonies. For settlers, imperial disengagement might mean having to return to the home country. Similarly, for corporations with site-specific investments in the periphery, the very nature of their holdings makes a swift retreat from empire a painful proposition. Their first preferences are not malleable.

Conversely, military organizations might decide to pursue their organizational interests through nonimperial policies. As Robert Jervis reminds us, although the armed forces have a corporate interest in securing large budgets, organizational autonomy, and prestige, ultimately they also need to win the next war.[57] Indeed, the continued pursuit of empire might run counter to the military's corporate interests—if it draws away personnel from the main strategic area of concern, or if military defeat seems imminent. Although the armed forces will wish to increase their share of government revenue, true to their organizational interests they must also keep in mind that an ill fated war might involve heavy casualties and will lead to loss of prestige. Alternative policies that create new career opportunities and warrant large budgets might be preferable.

Preferences and Politicians in Two-Party and Multiparty Systems

Diverse institutions not only provide diverse opportunities to exercise vetoes on policy, but, by structuring the framework and context of political

57. Jervis 1995.

contestation, they influence the very nature of politicians' preferences. We could, as does much of the strategic choice literature, postulate that politicians are primarily concerned with reelection.[58] Different institutional configurations will thus lead to divergent political strategies in order to achieve reelection. But, even if one does not assume that politicians are motivated by narrow self-interest, the institutional structure will tend to select politicians whose preferences match those of their key constituencies.

Electoral rules critically affect the likelihood that a two-party or multiparty system will emerge. Proportional representation (PR) electoral systems tend to lead to multiparty legislatures, whereas majoritarian systems tend to lead to two-party systems. The particular method of calculating votes can also affect the propensity of systems to become two-party or multiparty.[59] In addition, district magnitude influences the number of effective parties in the legislature. In general, the fewer members per district the greater the advantage for larger parties.[60] Finally, a high threshold for parties to gain representation can form a barrier to smaller parties (as with the 5 percent rule in Germany and Russia).

These institutional rules have direct (proximal) effects and indirect psychological (or distal) effects on voters' strategic calculations, and thus on the behavior of politicians. These rules can also influence the level of party discipline. Systems with a low electoral threshold will pose few entry barriers to new parties, which in turn might erode party discipline, since party members can break away from existing parties to form new ones. Disloyalty to party leadership need not be the end of one's career.

Formal theory suggests several reasons why multiparty rule, and more specifically multiparty coalitions, might lead to the selection of candidates with parochial interests. First, multiparty systems give political entrepreneurs no reason to cater to the median voter. Politicians and parties that move to the median might see other parties encroach on their left or right, thus diminishing their original support. Indeed, tacit collusion may occur to maintain distance from the center, even if most voters cluster around the median point on the political spectrum.[61]

Second, multiparty systems will also be particularly prone to logrolling, argue William Riker and Steven Brams, because they meet the conditions under which logrolling may occur.[62] Logrolling requires actors to have various intensities on different issues, and "traders must be on opposite sides on two motions. One trader must be in the initial majority on the first

---

58. See, for example, Milner 1997, 33.
59. The D'Hondt system, for example, favors larger parties over small. Lijphart 1994, 24; Cox 1997, 58.
60. Lijphart 1994, 12; Taagepera and Shugart 1989, 117.
61. Laver 1997, 118–19.
62. For a general discussion, see D. Mueller 1989, 82–95.

motion, and the initial minority on the second."[63] This cannot occur when there is a legislature with two parties and winner-takes-all characteristics.

Despite the lack of vote trading that Riker and Brams observe in the British Parliament, logrolling between individual members of a two-party system can occur, if the parties lack internal discipline.[64] Indeed, the American system has been the locus classicus for students of such behavior. Logrolling is thus not simply a function of the number of parties but also of party discipline. Moreover, as Weaver and Rockman suggest, "knowing that legislators are not bound by party discipline makes it easier for constituents to put pressure on their representatives."[65] Parochial interests thus stand a better chance in such an environment.

If multiparty systems are operating with disciplined parties, logrolling between parties occurs en bloc, without individuals crossing party lines. In coalition governments where no party holds a majority, the coalition members concede on issues on which they have less intense preferences in return for which they expect support on issues they greatly care about. Consequently, cabinet formations tend to be complicated, as cabinet positions will have to be divided according to the anticipated issues in which logrolling will occur (for example, left-wing parties will want labor and social welfare cabinet seats; right-wing parties will want finance and security).

Multiparty systems, with little discipline, might precipitate continuous logrolling between parties and between party members. This raises the possibility of continuous cycling without party leadership being able to establish procedural rules to minimize the range of the winset.[66] In this scenario parochial interest groups have considerable influence on territorial policy.

In addition to logrolling and politicians eschewing the median position, coalitional dynamics may provide a third reason why parochial interests may surface in multiparty systems. If the ruling coalition's majority in the legislature is substantial, a small breakaway need not have dire consequences. But if the majority is fragile (for example, if the coalition is a minimum winning one) then the hard-line party may hold a pivotal position and be able to hold the coalition hostage.[67]

These insights have particular relevance for territorial politics and for the question of whether policy change is likely. Any political group with strong preferences might be able to decisively influence policy outcomes if that party can hold the coalition hostage. Paradoxically, if a party represents sin-

---

63. Riker and Brams 1973, 1, 238.
64. See also Milner 1997, 41. "Unified government is most likely in two-party systems. But even in these cases unified control depends on another factor: party discipline."
65. Weaver and Rockman 1993, 16.
66. For a discussion of cycling and winset limitation, see Shepsle and Weingast 1984.
67. On the dynamics of coalition formation and size, see Laver and Schofield 1998; Laver 1997, chap. 7.

gle-peaked preferences, that party might be a desirable coalition partner because it is willing to logroll on any other issue.[68]

Consequently, multiparty democratic systems give politicians reasons to seek niche constituencies (in the strategic choice view), or they will reward those politicians whose preferences are similar to their various constituencies (a structural selection argument). Logrolling between the parties and coalitional dynamics might give niche constituencies even more influence.

In short, electoral rules that lead to multiparty coalitions create not only more actors whose consent is necessary for policy change; they also increase the likelihood that the preferences of the political actors will diverge. Policy change will thus be unlikely.

A historical institutionalist argument might take this even one step further. If the institutional framework allows politicians to give voice to the preferences of niche clienteles, that very articulation may fortify the position of narrowly defined interest groups. There is no reason to bring one's position in line with the mainstream in order to be heard. In a highly proportional system, a political entrepreneur might even seek to *create* a narrow specialized constituency as a way to gain office. In this manner the preference of the politician may create the preferences of an interest group, which heretofore had not been articulated.

RESEARCH DESIGN AND CASE SELECTION

Measuring the Number of Veto Points

Tsebelis distinguishes between institutional veto players defined by a constitution (such as the president, the House of Representatives, and the Senate in the United States) and partisan veto players created by the political system (such as coalition partners in European parliamentary democracies).[69] Thus the number of institutional veto players is derived from the constitutional rules that specify which actors consent is required to change the status quo. Is, for example, power allocated to both an independently elected executive and a legislature?

Tsebelis's differentiation between constitutional veto players and partisan veto players resembles Arend Lijphart's method for delineating systems

---

68. Another reason why parties with single-peaked preferences are attractive partners is their credibility of commitment. Their preferences are clear as is their willingness to logroll on issues that are of little interest to them. For the logic of prisoner's dilemma games and iteration in logrolling, see D. Mueller 1989, 92.

69. Tsebelis 2002, 2. I prefer the term "constitutional veto players," since in my view the number of partisan veto players also derives from institutional rules (electoral formula, district threshold, and so forth).

along two dimensions.[70] Lijphart's analysis focuses on the degree to which governments are unitary or federalist in character, and on the degree to which influence primarily resides in executives or parties. Extrapolating from that logic I will classify political systems as having few constitutional veto points if the government is unitary (rather than federal); if the executive depends on legislative support to hold office; if the legislature is unicameral (rather than a bicameral one with equally strong and differently constituted houses); and if it lacks judicial review.

The political institutions of a given country provide few partisan veto opportunities if executive power resides with a single party or a bare majority cabinet (rather than large multiparty coalitions); if the executive dominates the legislature; if the system is two-party; and if the electoral system is majoritarian rather than proportional.

The American system is thus an example of a political system with multiple constitutional vetoes. Institutionally, the constitutional rules deliberately create a system of checks and balances. The Constitution allocates power to the president, the Senate, and the House of Representatives. The legislature is bicameral; the Supreme Court exercises judicial review; and state powers are considerable.

Multiparty coalition governments in parliamentary systems also create multiple veto opportunities, even in unicameral legislatures. Parliamentary systems of the European variety are based on electoral proportionality yielding multiparty coalitions. They evince a balance between executive and legislative decision making.

The proportional electoral system will lead parties to take up various positions on the political spectrum rather than cater to a median voter. Thus, parties have incentives to retain ideological distance. This divergence of preferences between the parties will exacerbate the salience of veto points.

Two-party parliamentary governments of the Westminster variety show the opposite qualities.[71] These systems have few constitutional and partisan veto points. Constitutionally, legislature and executive powers are bundled, as the prime minister requires legislative support to retain office. These systems are also unitary not federalist, and they lack judicial review. Given the disproportionality of the electoral system and given two-party winner-takes-all electoral competition, the party that wins the election will be able to implement its policies without having to broker deals with coalition partners. Indeed, Tsebelis classifies Britain as having a single veto point.[72]

---

70. For a discussion of these similarities, see Crepaz 2002, 175–76.

71. Minority governments in multiparty parliamentary systems may show traits similar to two-party parliamentary governments.

72. Tsebelis 2002, 4.

Case Selection

I assess the explanatory power of my proposed theory by closer inspection of five primary cases: British withdrawal from East Africa; the French Fourth and Fifth Republics' handling of the Algerian question; Dutch policy in Indonesia; the Portuguese empire in Africa; and the fragmentation of the Soviet Union. I then discuss Israel and the occupied territories to demonstrate how this analysis has broad applicability, even for cases not traditionally described as "imperial."

These cases show maximum variation of the independent variable. The number of veto points in the political system varies from a single point in the British parliamentary system to multiple veto opportunities in the Dutch system and the French Fourth Republic. Similarly, in extending the logic of veto points analysis to authoritarian systems, I show that the fascist-corporatist rule of Portugal contained multiple veto actors, whereas the Soviet system contained relatively few.

The research proceeds thus by "small-N" case comparison. Given the relatively small number of empires involved in decolonization this is to some extent inevitable. However, I try to avoid the danger of choosing too few cases in a mistaken search for total control over some of the independent variables.[73]

The cases also show variation on the dependent variable.[74] Britain and the USSR willingly changed their territorial policy. They engaged in negotiations and reconfigured the existing territorial order without resort to force. By contrast, the Dutch, Portuguese, and French governments proved unwilling to move from the existing territorial status quo. They refused to enter into negotiations with the nationalists, and as a result nationalists and central governments ended up in violent conflict.

My design allows us to compare three democratic processes of decolonization, that of the British Empire, the French, and the Dutch.[75] The British two-party parliamentary system contrasts with the French and Dutch systems, which were multiparty parliamentary systems with coalition governments. Comparison of these three cases allows for control for the effect of civil-military relations and isolates the causal effect of institutions, since the French case is overdetermined. In France, civilians lacked oversight, and the political system presented multiple partisan veto points. In both Britain and the Netherlands civilians retained control over the military, but the Netherlands contained multiple veto points in contrast to British institutions.

73. See Lieberson 1992.
74. King, Keohane, and Verba 1994, 129–30.
75. See Stephen Walt's discussion of "significant events" as a justification for case selection. Walt 1996, 14.

The Dutch and Portuguese cases also serve as tough tests for the proposed internal politics argument.[76] Received wisdom in the international relations literature suggests that the international environment dictates the foreign policies of small states, while domestic politics play a larger role for great powers.[77] Leaders of small states should be particularly sensitive to input from the international strategic environment. If we find that internal politics, nevertheless, played a key role in determining Dutch and Portuguese decolonization policy, this will be added corroboration for the importance of the internal-institutionalist argument advanced here.[78]

One might argue that adding the United States would expand the range of cases by including a presidential system with divided powers. However, as I am focusing on the dissolution of formal empires after World War II, it falls out of the scope of this analysis. Moreover, the United States was always far more reluctant to engage in formal empire than its European counterparts, even if it arguably exercised hegemony over much of the Americas.[79] The United States thus did not face the demands of imperially oriented forces or of large numbers of settlers abroad. The objective of my analysis, by contrast, is to focus exactly on the question of how governments deal with such demands. However, counterfactually, if such actors had been present, the multiple veto points in the U.S. system would lead us to expect that withdrawal would have been less likely.

This comparative case study also excludes cases of territorial disengagement where outright defeat in an international war was the primary cause of the breakup, such as the cases of the German, Ottoman, and Austrian Empires following World War I. In those cases, external powers dictated the dismantling of the defeated empires, and there is no reason to analyze the strategic calculations of the imperial state or the various contending groups within that state. The systemic environment provides a sufficient explanation.

Comparative Case Strategy and Theory Assessment

My research proceeds both by diachronic comparison within a given case and synchronic comparison between distinct cases. Diachronic comparison

76. For the logic of "tough tests" for one's own theoretical model, see Eckstein 1975, 118–20. See also Stinchcombe 1978.

77. For the argument that small states respond to the international environment, see Katzenstein 1985; M. Elman 1995. Small states should be cautious and less belligerent; see Snyder 1991, 62, 317–18.

78. Other cases could be included but have been omitted from this analysis for reasons of length. Belgium might be an additional case of multiparty systems facing decolonization; at face value it would not seem to contradict the argument. Scholars have noted the ineptitude with which the Belgian government disengaged from the Congo; see Stengers 1982.

79. Formal empire was not pursued with ardor. From the very beginning American interest in the Philippines was minimal. Kimball 1991, 130.

allows for analysis of the causes of policy change through before-after comparison within the same case, thus allowing for control for many causal factors. Thus, I analyze the transition from the Fourth to the Fifth French Republic in a quasi-experimental fashion. The institutional changes at the end of the Fourth Republic that gave the presidency in the Fifth Republic substantively new powers allows us to examine the effects of institutional change, while France's international position, the preferences of the military, and French ideology remained relatively constant.

Synchronic comparison across cases allows us to examine how various factors influenced outcomes. While controlling for alternative explanatory variables, such as regime type, I analyze why states adopted widely divergent imperial policies.[80]

I further use a method of agreement, asking why France and the Netherlands, despite significant differences (civilian oversight in the Netherlands but not in France, different international positions) both chose to fight for their imperial holdings. Which independent variable led to a similar policy outcome, despite other variables being so different? This does not produce selection bias.[81]

In a perfect research environment, with a large number of cases, one might be able to derive probabilistic statements with considerable certainty. But in explaining macrohistory, the world looks more like clouds than clocks.[82] Individual choices, while driven by actions that are rational at the microlevel, affect outcomes at the macrolevel through a maze of contingency and constraint.

Consequently, although I pursue the greatest possible explanatory power from comparing by methods of difference and agreement, the narrative within each case provides the basis for structured, focused comparison. Applying "standardized, general questions" to each historical case, "the investigator . . . seeks to identify the variety of different causal patterns that can occur for the phenomenon in question."[83] Such a method is appropriate when the number of cases is limited and many explanations appear possible.[84]

---

80. For discussions of the method of difference and method of agreement, see Lijphart 1971; Little 1991, 31–37; Skocpol 1984, 374–91; Eckstein 1975.

81. Bunce 1999, 16; J. Mahoney 2003, 351.

82. Almond and Genco 1977.

83. George 1979, 60.

84. See Jentleson, Levite, and Berman 1993; George and Smoke 1974; King, Keohane, and Verba 1994, 45. I make no claim to provide nomothetic causal statements but rather try to explicate the mechanisms that can account for the observed events. "A mechanism is a specific causal pattern that can be recognized after the event but rarely foreseen." Elster 1989, 7–10. However, I do approach the data with a specific deductive model, rather than try to decipher any regularity in observations post hoc.

Thus, while *Ending Empire* takes its cue from deductive theorizing, the actual mechanisms through which actors operate, and the particular context and struggles of the political contest, must be traced by historical, inductive analysis.[85] Tsebelis similarly notes how many types of actors such as the army, the courts, and key interest groups can exercise a veto. As he further suggests, such veto players can vary per issue and over time. Careful process tracing of the policy decisions in a particular case must form an essential component to any deductive propositions.

THE INTERNAL POLITICS OF PARTITION

I argue, therefore, that the institutional framework of the metropolitan power, or the central government, affects the likelihood of change in the existing territorial policy. When key groups (such as business elites, settlers, or the military) take a hard-line stance, and when politicians share their preferences for strategic or ideological reasons, a change in territorial policy becomes less likely if political institutions provide many veto opportunities. Under such circumstances peaceful adjustment to nationalist and secessionist demands becomes less likely. As Lisa Martin and Beth Simmons suggest (in a different context) "domestic institutions can be captured by preference outliers who hold policy hostage to their demands."[86]

I stress that nothing in this argument precludes a government with few veto points from choosing a hard-line policy or refusing to relinquish territory. However, in a democratic system with few veto opportunities, the decision to maintain or change the existing territorial configuration will be driven by broad electoral concerns rather than by the demands of narrow constituencies. A British government might thus choose to hold a particular territory for its strategic or economic value to the state as a whole. A fragmented government such as the French Fourth Republic or the Israeli government in the 1990s, facing multiple veto points will not be able to engage in such a calculus, as each veto player will be more concerned with the private goods that the territorial status quo yields than with the public goods that emanate from the territory under control. In short, democratic governments with few veto players will choose policies that come closer to what unitary-state realist theories would predict than governments with multiple veto players. My conclusion here is similar to Helen Milner's: "The more control over policy choices one actor alone, say, the executive, possesses—that is, the less he or she has to share decision-making power with others—the more the situation resembles that of a unitary actor."[87]

85. See Bates et al. 1998.
86. Martin and Simmons 1998, 748.
87. Milner 1997, 12.

Table 1.3. Predicted territorial policy (if states face changed systemic conditions)

Cases	Civilian oversight of the military (military as veto player?)	Institutional structure (partisan and constitutional vetoes)	Predicted outcome	Observed outcome
Britain	Strong civilian oversight	Two-party system, disciplined parties, and strong executive. Few constitutional and partisan veto points.	Policy change and adjustment.	Calibrated withdrawal; incidental conflicts.
France (4th Republic, 1946–58)	Contested oversight; military try to exercise veto.	Multiparty parliamentary system, coalitions, and undisciplined parties. Multiple partisan veto points.	No policy change, hard line more likely.	Hard-line and colonial wars.
France (5th Republic, 1958–)	De Gaulle reasserts civilian control.	Constitutional revisions (Art. 16) give president special powers. Reduction of veto points.	Policy change and adjustment.	France starts negotiations and withdraws from Algeria.
Netherlands	Strong civilian oversight	Multiparty system, coalition governments with disciplined parties. Multiple partisan veto points.	No policy change, compromise less likely.	Hard line. Dutch launch two police actions, 1947–48.
Portugal (Salazar-Caetano)	Weak civilian oversight	Cartelized authoritarian system (church, big business, military, landed elites). Multiple veto points.	No policy change, compromise less likely.	Hard line. Colonial wars, 1961–74.
Portugal 1974	Military coup d'etat	Unified authoritarian system. Single veto player.	Policy change but direction unpredictable.	Corporate interests of the military dictate speedy withdrawal within a year from all territories.
USSR (1945–85)	Strong civilian oversight	Unified authoritarian system. Single veto player.	Policy change, direction unpredictable.	No policy change. Systemic conditions favorable for USSR; geo-strategic and economic benefits (but declining).
USSR (Gorbachev, 1985–91)	Strong civilian oversight	Unified authoritarian; emerging strong presidential system. Single veto point.	Policy change, direction unpredictable.	Gorbachev unwilling to use force to maintain external or internal empire.

The claim that special interests can exert undue influence on foreign policy, and more particularly imperial policy, is not new. Scholars have often explained this influence by noting how the benefits and costs of territorial expansion are distributed asymmetrically.[88] Imperial proponents will win the political contest because the benefits of expansion are concentrated, while the benefits for anti-imperialists are diffuse. Given diffuse benefits, individuals will become free riders and anti-imperial coalitions will yield less influence than pro-imperial groups. Similarly, one might argue that when it comes to territorial adjustment hard-liners will be better organized than those who favor compromise solutions, who face free-riding problems and information and transaction costs in starting an alternative lobby.[89]

This might very well be the case, but note that the veto player logic does not require this argument. The key question is whether institutions create many veto opportunities or few. Even if hard-liners and compromisers are equally well organized the very presence of veto opportunities for hard-liners will allow them to forestall a move away from the status quo.

Needless to say, while internal politics played a crucial role in the cases analyzed here, states do not operate in a vacuum. Indeed, changes in the international environment often precipitated the changes in territorial orders. Consequently, the next chapter examines the nature of the international environment for each state in our analysis. Simply put, did the various policies follow from realist calculations of costs and benefits and the relative position of the state? Although I recognize the importance of the international context, the ensuing empirical cases demonstrate that a domestic institutional analysis is needed in order to explain why some governments chose policies that would not be expected based on realist premises. Relative position in the international system and military and economic interests do not adequately explain why some states failed to reconfigure their territorial order.

---

88. Snyder 1991.

89. Richard Baldwin notes how interest groups fight harder to avoid losses than to achieve gains (Baldwin et al. 1995, 34).

CHAPTER TWO

The Changing Fortunes of Empire

For what means can England have, which is not even a military state, of resisting the rebellion of two hundred and fifty million subjects.

J. R. SEELEY, 1883

Sir John Seeley, staunch imperialist and author of *The Expansion of England,* foresaw with remarkable prescience the fate that would befall the British Empire. British power, wealth, and standing in the world hinged on its possessions overseas. Its rule conveyed not only benefits to the metropole but also led to the advancement of the less developed world.[1] But he also realized that British imperial rule might be the result of a temporary convergence of factors that allowed Britain to exercise power far beyond the means of a small island state.

His fears of rebellion in the colonies came true after World War II, not only in the British Empire but also in many other polities. Most empires and multinational states, after all, had acquired their territories as a result of the relative imbalance in military power and economic resources and the political disorganization in the peripheries. The moment such discrepancies diminished and unified resistance emerged, the demands to change the existing territorial order could not be stifled.

As realists point out, anarchy forces states to be concerned with their security.[2] Consequently, states seek to expand their own resources (balance internally), ally with others (balance externally), or rely on collective security arrangements for their survival. Empire forms a means of internal balancing. By subjugating and annexing other territories, states gain access to useful commodities and manpower. At the same time, this strategy denies the adversary access to those same resources. Although the costs of gover-

1. James 1994, 204–5.
2. Waltz 1979, 91–9 3.

nance tend to be higher in an empire than in an alliance (given the necessity of repressing the opposition and creating an imperial administration),[3] one conversely needs to rely less on unstable alliances and noncredible partners.[4]

States also seek economic gains, to enhance their relative standing vis-à-vis rivals (as part of a realist strategy) or to improve their welfare on absolute grounds (as economic liberals might expect). Empire provides preferential access to raw materials as well as dumping grounds for surplus goods.[5] Imperial preference schemes confer insurance against cyclical downturns. The economic benefits help enhance security and provide material benefits for political elites and collective goods for the population.

Historically, such motives for establishing empires have coincided with the opportunity to do so. From the late fifteenth century on, new military technologies, modes of transportation, and superior logistics gave the European polities a decisive advantage over the nonmodernized states in the rest of the world.[6] Moreover, changes in Europe led to the development of high-capacity states that could mobilize societies on a truly national scale. Metropolitan modernization went hand in hand with nationalism and nation building in the core.[7] Together, these features gave the European powers the decisive advantage to subjugate virtually every corner of the globe.

Arguably, this trend had started to reverse itself before World War II, but the war more than any other event turned the old order upside down. Before the war, Britain, France, Germany, and Japan could pretend that they could stand toe to toe with any of the great powers, including the United States and Soviet Union. After the war, only the latter two could claim superpower status. Before the war, only the United States had made serious commitments to grant independence to its colonies (the Philippines in particular). After the war, in less than two decades, virtually all the European empires had to grant their overseas areas sovereignty. Before the war—although the League of Nations became a venue for discussions on the status of colonies and mandates in the interwar period—the imperial powers continued to justify their holdings with paternalistic arguments and outright use of force. The areas taken from defeated Germany and Turkey after World War I were transferred to new categories of foreign domination. "Mandates" were often colonies by another name.[8] After 1945, by contrast, the United Nations became a vibrant arena for challenging the imperial hold.

3. Lake 1996, 1999.
4. For discussion of the various strands of realism see Rose 1998.
5. See, for example, Hirschman (1980) on Germany's ambitions.
6. Cipolla 1965.
7. Gellner 1983.
8. See Betts 1985.

Several causes precipitated these changes. First, the benefits of empire for metropolitan defense diminished. As the world moved to bipolarity and the Cold War, and as nuclear weapons changed the mode of warfare, imperial reserves of troops and resources became less relevant for the security of the great powers. Second, a liberal trading order emerged, guaranteed by a hegemonic United States, that favored a system of sovereign states and open borders rather than imperial preference. This changed the economic logic of empire. Originally confined to the capitalist states, over time even the nonmarket economies could not escape its pressure. Third, the economic and political development of the peripheries and the support of the two superpowers for nationalist movements—in vying for greater spheres of influence of their own—enhanced the ability of the subjugated peoples to resist their erstwhile metropolitan masters. Ideational changes and new international rules of conduct, such as adherence to the principle of territorial sovereignty, further aided the nationalist cause.[9]

Because nationalism emerged in various patterns and in specific responses to the types of policies pursued by the central governments, I discuss this in the following chapters. This chapter examines whether relative position in the international system, security concerns, or economic benefits could justify holding on to the contested territories in the empires in question. Simply put, can realist accounts that focus on relative power and the pursuit of economic and military benefits adequately explain the policies chosen?[10]

This chapter explores whether policies of the central governments might be perceived as strategically rational by examining the objective evidence that leaders had at their disposal. At a minimum, we should ask ourselves whether elites even tried to systematically ascertain the gains and losses of the territories under question. Some states, as I will show, did a much better job in assessing the costs and benefits of their territorial possessions, and responding accordingly.

Consequently, this chapter examines the broader international context in which central governments conducted their territorial policy. In all instances forces were at work that affected their ability to hold subject territories, as well as the benefits of doing so. However, they did not operate uniformly. As small states, the Netherlands and Portugal faced different conditions than the great powers such as France and the United Kingdom. The pressures that would befall a superpower such as the USSR differed again from the Western cases.

9. See Jackson 1993; Zacher 2001.

10. Testing (neo) realist theory is notoriously difficult. Indeed, some of its proponents reject any attempts to evaluate it as a theory of foreign policy. I take the view of Colin Elman (1996). Realism does generate specific expectations about policy.

Overall, changes in the military environment and the expansion of a global, relatively liberal economic order set the stage for subsequent reactions and policy changes in the five cases under scrutiny. The long-term trend in the post-1945 world swung against empires and large multinational states. This chapter discusses how these changes specifically affected each country.

Changes in relative power and economic circumstances, however, cannot adequately explain the choices made by the central governments. Treating states as unitary and strategic actors does not explain their territorial polices. Although some governments conducted their policies as realists might expect, others behaved quite differently.

EMPIRES OF ARMS

Empire and Territory as Diminishing Security Assets

During the First World War colonial possessions figured prominently in metropolitan orders of battle, particularly among the great powers. The subject areas of the British and French Empires contributed vast quantities of manpower. For example, almost a million and a half Indians fought in the European trenches and in the Middle East.[11] Such calculations continued to figure in the interwar era. The ability to fall back on the empire enticed Britain to devise a strategy whereby it could initially pass the buck in meeting the German threat to other continental powers.[12] Its imperial reserves allowed it to wait for the final outcome of the French-German engagement after which—if necessary—the Commonwealth and empire could come to Britain's aid. The French likewise anticipated bringing troops from North Africa to the front as the German threat drew nearer in time.[13]

Russia's calculations in World War I differed because its internal empire abutted Russia itself. The territories surrounding Russia could be a buffer zone against western threats. Some strategists advocated a defense in depth, in which Byelorussia and Ukraine would be sacrificed if necessary and the enemy would be engaged in a manner similar to Russia's response to Napoleon's invasions in 1812. For political reasons, however, these strategists succumbed to the temptation to support others who advocated decisive offensive operations in World War I (with disastrous consequences in the early stages of the war).[14] Even though defense in depth and the idea of

---

11. Betts 1985, 14. See also Albertini 1969.
12. See Posen 1984.
13. For the French calculations, see Kupchan 1994.
14. Kokoshin 1998, 147–57.

Table 2.1. Relative position and the costs and benefits of empire

Case	Military contribution to home defense	Military contribution to imperial defense	Support of greater powers	Economic benefits
Britain (great power)	Significant contributions from India and Commonwealth in World War I and II.	Significant. Empire largely self-policing, particularly India. Contributions from East Africa debated.	U.S. advocates decolonization and hand over to noncommunist nationalists.	Declining. Supports liberal trading order. Trade emphasis shifts to U.S. and Europe.
France (great power)	Significant contributions in World War I and II but contributions inflated.	Significant before World War II, thereafter increasing drain on metropole.	U.S. critical of French colonialism but some support in Indochina, not in Algeria.	Alleged but objectively declining.
Netherlands (small power)	None. Defense based on great power support.	Partially local troops, partially metropolitan contingents. Large drain on metropole after 1945.	Active British and U.S. opposition to Dutch policies.	Alleged but objectively declining (even before World War II).
Portugal (small power)	None. Defense based on great power support.	Partially local troops, partially metropolitan contingents. Large drain on metropole after 1961.	U.S. and Western great powers tolerate Portuguese actions but offer little active support.	Large benefits asserted but based on self-imposed autarky.
USSR (superpower) 1945–1970s	Significant contributions from external and internal empire (buffer zones, forward bases, and manpower).	Partially self-policing with communist regimes, partially Soviet forward deployments.	Active balancing by great power and superpower rivals.	Significant economic benefits.
USSR 1980s	Need for forward basing and buffer zones declines. Reduction of manpower requirements.	Nationalist and reformist pressures in external and internal empire. Increasing costs to metropole.	Active balancing by super- and great power rivals.	Diminishing benefits with rising costs of external and internal empires.

buffer zones lost out, the benefits of the vast territories of the Soviet Union were evident as World War I progressed. During World War II large reserves of manpower from the entire Soviet Union would eventually replenish the horrendous losses of 1941–42, and the hinterland managed to produce many of the industrial and military resources lost in the west.

In short, the subject territories of the greater imperial powers conveyed significant security benefits. At the same time, however, the preservation of the empire also demanded that the metropole expend resources for its defense. How much of the fleet should be positioned around home waters? How much allocated to distant colonies and sea-lanes?[15] Indeed, trying to defend and hold distant territories might jeopardize the very security of the home country. For all imperial metropoles, empire invited trade-offs.

A variety of changes in the postwar security realm dramatically affected such estimates. Foremost among such changes, nuclear weapons raised doubts about vast imperial holdings as a sine qua non for home country defense.[16] Nuclear weaponry presented a quantum leap in the mode of warfare, requiring new understandings of the very nature of warfare itself.[17] Even some proponents of structural realism, who emphasize the number of great powers in the system and their relative distribution of power as key variables, have suggested that the nuclear era has led to a different security milieu that cannot be accounted for by shifts in polarity or the particular balance of power.[18] Indeed, the very logic of American strategy emphasized how a large-scale conventional threat (the USSR's advantages in manpower, proximity to Europe, and some types of matériel) could be offset with nuclear weapons. Moreover, American hegemony mitigated security dilemmas among the erstwhile Western European enemies and extended its nuclear guarantee for their protection as well. Over time, even the USSR came to retreat from its older doctrine of massed manpower reserves.

More recent advances in military technology and operational logistics similarly call into question the need for large conscript armies and vast reserves of manpower. In this third revolution in military affairs (the first was during World War I and the second in the nuclear era), advanced communications and high-technology weapons systems call for simultaneous and swift engagement across vast areas. The weaker side is unlikely to have the opportunity to stall enemy troops and fall back in a protracted war.[19]

15. For example, the British had traditionally calculated how best to utilize the empire's resources for home defense and had examined early on how their resources should be spread across the empire. See Aaron Friedberg's study (1988) of the 1895–1905 period.

16. For John Herz nuclear weapons rendered borders obsolete, and thus even challenged the function of the nation-state as a sufficient provider of protection. Herz 1976.

17. For a comprehensive discussion of how nuclear weapons have affected traditional calculations of offense, defense, and war in general see Jervis 1989.

18. See particularly Waltz 1990. See also Mearsheimer 1990 and Gaddis 1986.

19. This particularly became salient for Soviet planners; see Odom 1998.

Structurally, bipolarity also created different choices than those previously presented by the multipolar environment. With only a few exceptions the European system of the past centuries had pitted multiple great powers against one another in a pattern of fluid alliances and treaties. After the Second World War the separate category of the "superpowers" emerged, with which all the other great powers would align in two stable camps. Germany, moreover, became increasingly entrenched in the Western security system (the rationale for NATO was "to keep the Americans in, the Russians out, and the Germans down"). Consequently, if Lord Curzon could still remark after World War I, with some plausibility, that France was likely to be Britain's next enemy (because of disagreements over the spoils of war in the German colonies in Africa and the Middle East),[20] such a remark would be nonsensical in the era after 1945.

Thus, if one of the primary reasons for the Scramble for Africa had been the multipolar competition among the European great powers, such calculations now became obsolete.[21] Michael Doyle argues that multipolar competition, because of its lack of clarity, tends to induce formal annexation, whereas bipolarity reduces the need for formal empire.[22] Similarly, Kenneth Waltz suggests that bipolarity largely renders the periphery irrelevant.[23]

As the benefits of controlling peripheries and subject areas receded, the costs of controlling those territories rose. An asymmetry of interests made nationalist revolts more difficult to squelch. Whereas nationalist movements were fighting for their independence, metropoles were fighting for opaque strategic interests. When metropolitan forces required large numbers of conscript troops, the motivation of these forces rarely matched the tenacity of their foes.

Moreover, as various scholars have noted, the spread of relatively simple military technologies and asymmetry of interest made it possible for nominally weak states to humble even the largest powers. As the United States later experienced in Vietnam, so France and the Soviet Union realized that relative power alone did not foreordain the outcome of struggles in the periphery.[24]

Admittedly, these changes in the security realm did not affect metropolitan calculations uniformly or immediately. The remainder of this chapter surveys these alterations in the international environment for each country. I make no foolhardy claim to provide a comprehensive account of the inter-

20. Betts 1985, 18.
21. See Doyle 1986, 136.
22. Doyle 1986, 251.
23. Waltz 1979, 190–91.
24. Mack 1975.

national relations of all these states. However, I do suggest that some governments did a far better job in assessing these changes than others.

The French "Empire Coloniale" as a Declining Military Asset

France had long regarded its overseas territories as critical military assets. The colonies constituted a pool of reserves of manpower and resources, which became ever more important given the declining relative position of France and its demographic stagnation in the nineteenth century.[25] Its opponents also outclassed it in other regards. Britain's industrial potential in 1880 was three times that of France. While French industrial potential slightly more than doubled between 1880 and 1913, that of Germany quadrupled.[26] Britain pressed home its advantage in imperial contests and the Scramble for Africa, while Germany did so in the Franco-Prussian War of 1870 and started to challenge France in Africa after 1890. The Franco-Russian alliance of 1892 constituted a partial remedy, but it still required France to raise considerable numbers of troops. The Left and Center, however, objected to expanding conscription and defense funding, partially because of the Dreyfus affair. Colonial units (La Coloniale and the Armée d'Afrique) thus became ever more important for metropolitan defense.

During the First World War hundreds of thousands of Africans, and to a lesser extent Asians, served in the French army. French West Africa (AOF, Afrique Occidentale Française) supplied more than 150,000 troops, primarily from Upper Senegal and Niger.[27] Algeria contributed as many as 160,000.[28]

The victory in 1918 brought temporary relief. The dismantling of the Austro-Hungarian Empire and the harsh terms at Versailles seemed to make France once again master of the Continent. But such hopes quickly faded. British reluctance to balance on the Continent, American isolationism, and the lack of an alliance with Stalinist Russia soon put France in the uncomfortable position of being the only major power to face down Nazi Germany on the Continent.[29]

In the face of such challenges the empire became the panacea for all problems. The lobbyists for empire (broadly encompassed by the Parti Colonial), who had faced a disinterested public before World War I, increasingly gained a foothold in the public imagination. The military

25. From the latter half of the nineteenth century until the Second World War, France suffered from depopulation. Blondel 1974b, 9.

26. Kennedy 1985, 14.

27. Estimates for the contributions from French West Africa range from 154,155 to 193,349. Michel 1973, 644–45.

28. Brubaker (1992, 139), citing Mennier.

29. For the British strategy of passing the buck, see Posen 1984.

obliged by publicizing inflated numbers of the imperial contribution in the First World War.[30]

The manpower issue became ever more important because conscription in the metropole had been reduced to one year, whereas conscripts from Africa still had to serve three years.[31] Fantastic schemes replaced sound strategic thought. General Charles Mangin claimed in 1920 that France could count on a "black force" of 300,000 during peacetime and "millions more combatants during war."[32] General Jules-Antoine Bührer spoke in January 1940 of six million troops and workers coming to metropolitan France's aid.[33]

Moreover, General Jean-Baptiste Estienne's ideas for a smaller mechanized army, centered on the use of tanks supported by airpower (already advocated in 1920), had lost out. Instead, France would pursue a defensive strategy based on a stalling action behind the Maginot Line—forcing Britain to commit itself on the Continent—and the mobilization of the empire.[34] Imperial manpower thus once again became a key to survival.

At the outbreak of the war North African riflemen (*tirailleurs*) accounted for 38.6 percent of French infantry, with Algeria providing 28 percent of the total. During the May–June campaigns in 1940, out of 101 French divisions, the Armée d'Afrique contributed twelve divisions of infantry and three brigades of cavalry, and La Coloniale added eight divisions and two demi-brigades.[35]

The imperial contributions notwithstanding, the German juggernaut crushed France within eight weeks.[36] Marshal Pétain took over the government on terms largely dictated by the German occupier. The Third Republic thus came to an unceremonious end. In exchange, unoccupied France remained nominally independent, and the North African possessions remained French. The Vichyists later argued that one reason for their cooperation with Germany had been fears of British, Italian, and Spanish encroachment on French colonial territories.[37]

---

30. The official figures mentioned 518,638 troops and 183,928 workers. The colonial lobby reported 612,000 troops and 200,000 workers. Ageron 1982, 20, n. 10. See also Kupchan 1994, 214–20.

31. Clayton 1988, 37.

32. Ageron 1982, 11–12.

33. See, for similar figures and a discussion of this imperial mythology, Kupchan 1994, 227–38.

34. Ironically, the French and British who pioneered the use of tanks and air support neglected to follow through. The Germans, on the other hand, did not forget those lessons. See Shirer 1969, 175–76; Clayton 1988, 37.

35. Clayton 1988, 38, 124, 126. See also Hargreaves 1996, 51ff.

36. See Shirer 1969; Posen 1984; Mearsheimer 1983, chaps. 3–4.

37. Clayton 1988, 132–35.

The colonies, in other words, had not been able to save France. Instead, France's surrender had been partially driven by the desire to "save" its colonies. But did this lead to a reevaluation of their role in French grand strategy after the Second World War, as it should have? Quite the contrary.

Instead, French elites propagated the myth that the empire had helped save France. Although the empire had not stopped the immediate on-slaught, the colonies played key roles during the liberation. The French Army in Africa at the time of liberation consisted of 175,000 French citizens and 230,000 North Africans. Moreover, French colonial units had played important roles in the campaigns in Italy and southern France in 1943–44.[38] And had not de Gaulle and the Free French launched their counterattack from the North African territories? As one observer noted, "Without her Empire, France would be nothing more than a liberated country. Thanks to her Empire France is a victorious country."[39]

Moreover, France would regain its former grandeur through its overseas possessions. Without them, it would only be a minor European state. With them, France would be a great power; indeed, it would provide an alternative to a world dominated by the United States and the USSR.

Consequently, the army continued to reflect an important colonial orientation. The percentage of colonials within the army as a whole continued to increase. In 1946, ethnic French soldiers still made up 89 percent of the army. By 1949 this had decreased to 63 percent and by 1954 to 59 percent, partly due to changing conscription demands in the postwar period.[40]

Might one, therefore, argue that French recalcitrance to reassess the military benefits of empire was based on solid realist calculation? Actually, the narrower corporate interests of the armed forces dictated the pro-empire position.

First, despite the significant contributions of overseas contingents in 1940, German victory had been swift. Although manpower was still important, the ability to wage mechanized warfare and technological superiority in the air and at sea proved to be the keys to success.

Second, even before the war it had become clear that France could not hold all its positions in the empire. Thus, although Indochina was to supply twenty thousand troops to the metropolitan war effort according to a 1938 plan, in reality the army had to admit that Indochina was indefensible.[41] Britain and the United States would have to check aggression in East Asia.[42] Rather than contribute to metropolitan defense, the metropole would have to expend troops to retain control of its colonies.

38. Clayton 1988, 38–39, 143, 407 n. 51.
39. Gaston Monnerville in 1945. Cited in Clayton 1988, 395 n. 19.
40. Clayton 1988, 42.
41. Chonchirdsin 1997, 274; Ageron 1982, 20 n. 8.
42. Kupchan 1994, 223.

Third, although the army trotted out inflated estimates of millions of colonial troops before the war, such numbers never materialized. General Bührer, who in 1940 had spoken of six million men, noted in 1947 that in September 1939 the colonial army had only 65,930 men, of which 43,000 were in Europe.[43] The idea of moving three hundred to five hundred thousand infantry to come to France's aid has been rightly described by French analysts as "évaluations fantastiques" and as a "mythe de compensation."[44] In a work poignantly published on May 3, 1940, just before the German attack, two French authors argued that for France "l'idée imperiale est le talisman le plus precieux" because it guaranteed salvation.[45]

Nor were de Gaulle, the colonies, the Allied powers, and the Free French forces as unified as alleged. The Middle East campaign in 1941, for example, led to serious disagreements between the British and the Free French. De Gaulle feared a British attempt to replace France in that area.[46] De Gaulle was also not informed of the North African invasion, since Britain and the United States feared (rightly) that the Vichy forces would fight and believed that de Gaulle had only limited support in the colonies.[47]

Fourth, and most important, French strategic calculations should have adapted to critical changes in the security environment. If colonial manpower reserves could not counter the swift mechanized attack in 1940, one could hardly expect they could do so against a similar Soviet incursion. Economic necessities and political opposition had led to a swift 20 percent reduction in military expenditure by the end of 1945, so that by 1946 only 110,000 troops were deployed in the metropole.[48] The General Staff admitted in 1948 that it could resist a Soviet attack for only six days.[49] Moreover, given French reluctance to rearm Germany, France would have to face such an onslaught alone.[50] And finally, unlike the smaller powers, France could

43. Ageron 1982, 12–13. (Allowing for a buildup between September 1939 and May 1940, this could square with the twenty divisions mentioned by Clayton for May and June, considering a division size of about seven thousand.)

44. Ageron 1982, 11, 20.

45. "The imperial idea is the most precious amulet." Ageron 1982, 22 n. 42.

46. Mickelsen 1996. De Gaulle's Free French only numbered about two thousand by the start of the campaign. Ultimately, of the 37,000 Vichy forces, less than 6,000 joined the Free French. See also Hourani 1991, 356, 357.

47. See, for example, the Gaulle-Lyttelton agreement and the Clark-Darlan agreement. Hurewitz 1979, doc. nos. 124, 135, 144, 156, 168. All these show the clear tensions between de Gaulle and his allies, and the relative weakness of his position. See also Dallek 1998, 57–58.

48. Kupchan 1994, 272.

49. Girault 1986, 60.

50. Paris favored a much harsher treatment of Germany not dissimilar to the 1918 Versailles Treaty. It wished to internationalize the Ruhr, establish French authority on the west bank of the Rhine and in the Saar, and obtain reparations from Germany. It also opposed partition of Germany out of fear this would lead to German rapprochement with the USSR. Hill 1994, 109; Girault 1986, 58–59; Rioux 1987, 83; Williams 1966, 47.

not expect to free ride and automatically count on American support.
Franco-American tensions during the war continued after 1945.

French calculations were thus rife with inconsistencies. The deployment
of troops to Indochina, when its own position on the Continent was precarious, reveals the utter inconsistency of French policy.[51] Rather than a manpower reserve, Indochina and North Africa had become a drain on French
manpower and expenditure.

Instead, chapter three will show how the narrow corporate interests of
the armed forces influenced grand strategy and metropolitan policy. Despite the advent of mechanized warfare and of nuclear weapons, the extrav-
agant ideas of prewar imperial France resurfaced after the war.[52] In 1945,
Raymond Aron was a lone voice when he suggested, on realist grounds, an
assessment of the contributions of empire in terms of its benefits to the
metropole.[53]

The British Imperial Sunset

Whatever effect American independence might have had on the disposition of George III, Albion had not yet acquired the full extent of its glory.
Its subsequent victories put it in command of French and Dutch colonies.
Britain completed the subjugation of India in the second half of the nineteenth century, while the Scramble for Africa in the 1870s and 1880s
enlarged its African holdings. Although some of the colonies moved to dominion status, they remained loyal subjects of the Crown that could be
called on in time of war and economic trouble. After World War I Britain
acquired Turkish holdings in the Middle East and German holdings in
Africa and the Pacific. By 1918, the British Empire controlled an uninterrupted corridor in East Africa from the Cape of Good Hope to Egypt, something once only imaginable in Cecil Rhodes's phantasmagoric schemes.

Despite this geographical expansion some chinks started to appear in the
British armor. In 1838 Charles Trevelyan had argued that "the existing connection between two such distinct countries as England and India cannot,
in the nature of things, be permanent."[54] Incipient nationalist movements
also started to emerge even before World War I, tentatively in Africa, more
forcefully in Asia. The demands of war provided an opportunity for some
nationalists to demand reforms and even incite rebellion, as in Ireland.

Overall, though, most of the dominions and colonies remained loyal during World War I and contributed vast quantities of manpower and re-

51. Kupchan 1994.
52. Rioux 1987, 85.
53. He resumed this role when he asked for a realist assessment of the value of Algeria for
France. Rioux 1987, 289.
54. Chamberlain 1999, 7.

sources. Britain had secured its Asian flank by its alliance with Japan, and thus its Asian manpower could be unambiguously committed to the war in Europe and the Middle East. The Indian contribution was particularly important.[55] The Canadians threw themselves into the war with vigor, and Australian and New Zealand troops played an important role in the Middle East.

The interwar years saw several changes in British strategy. Militarily, relative British decline and Japanese ascendance led London to seek protection in Asia by tightening its relations with the United States.[56] It did not renew its alliance with Japan and instead sought to limit its military prowess through the Washington Naval Treaty. The British forces would concentrate on the defense of Singapore, which would become the linchpin of Britain's entire eastern position, with Hong Kong operating as an early warning system.[57] Troops from the dominions, India, and Burma would then be brought to bear on any Japanese landings. This of course precluded those troops from being used in Europe and the Middle East.

But the colonies and the dominions no longer believed that self-defense automatically meant metropolitan defense at any cost. Australians and New Zealanders were hardly assured by London's assertion that, at the first sign of trouble, ships would be shifted from the Mediterranean to East Asia within seventy days.[58]

Consequently, British politicians increasingly had to take the preferences of the imperial forces into account. Chamberlain feared, rightly, that colonial and dominion support would not be forthcoming if Britain went to war over the Sudetenland, or even entire Czechoslovakia.[59] This exacerbated the paradox that already confronted the British government on the European mainland. It knew that France had deliberately left the Maginot Line incomplete, giving the Germans an incentive to attack through Belgium, forcing Britain's hand. But the lack of imperial support constrained London's ability to deter German aggression.[60]

The growth of nationalism further complicated British rule, particularly in India. During World War I, the metropolitan government had made significant promises in order to raise Indian support. British rulers aimed to establish "responsible government" and drafted the Montagu-Chelmsford

55. Albertini 1969, 19; Clayton 1999.
56. James 1994, 459–63.
57. Keay 1997, chaps. 8–9.
58. Clayton 1999, 283. The Australians favored either rapprochement with Japan or an explicit alliance with the United States. Britain opposed the latter, since this would amount to an admission that it could no longer defend the Asian dominions (James 1994, 471).
59. Clayton 1999, 286; James 1994, 473.
60. At the same time British reluctance to raise taxes (see Narizny 2003) made imperial contributions imperative.

reforms of 1918–19, which created eleven autonomous provinces with elected Indian ministers. Even imperialists such as Leo Amery advocated that the British Empire be reconstituted as a federation with a common executive and parliament.[61] Shortly after the war, however, Britain retreated from these reformist measures, sparking nationalist agitation. Forceful repression, such as the Amritsar massacre, in which 379 Indians were killed, only strengthened the position of the Indian National Congress.[62] Grudgingly, the Conservatives came to the conclusion that ultimately independence for India seemed unavoidable, but put it off into the distant future. Secretary of State for India Samuel Hoare devised a system in which the Indian princes and loyalists could block a possible Congress Party majority. Proponents argued this would keep Britain in India for "another thirty-five years at least."[63]

World War II dramatically changed the prospects of the British Empire. In some respects Britain had fared better than its continental European counterparts. The imperial metropole had not been occupied nor had it been riven by cleavages between collaborators and resisters (as had Vichy France). British troops had held in Egypt and the Middle East. India had remained safe (although Malaya and Burma had fallen). But in exchange for Indian support Britain had to concede that India would be granted independence shortly after the cessation of hostilities. Sub-Saharan Africa also had escaped unscathed. And, despite occasional tensions, most of the dominions had supported the British efforts with manpower and matériel and resources (South Africa reluctantly so, given the pro-German sentiments among many whites there). Britain could legitimately claim that it alone had stood against German military might in the period between France's fall and the attack on the Soviet Union.

Nevertheless, Britain's overall military status had diminished. If the metropole had remained unoccupied, it did so only through the combination of British resolve and American Lend-Lease (as well as less overt American support) until the United States entered the war in December 1941. Offensive operations through Allied landings on the Continent could only commence once American troops started to appear in numbers. And throughout the war, British political and military leaders had to acknowledge the American veto, most poignantly demonstrated by agreeing to overall American supreme command. Still, despite these constraints, Britain and the empire had demonstrated considerable strength in the European and North African theaters.

61. Betts 1985, 19. See also Albertini 1969, 22–23.
62. This is Betts's estimate (1985, 171).
63. Bridge 1976, 178.

The Changing Fortunes of Empire

In Asia, however, British forces had been unceremoniously dispatched. Japanese forces had landed in Malaya several hours before the strike on Pearl Harbor, even though the British General Staff had estimated Japan could not launch an attack until the spring of 1942. The battleship, and battle-cruiser *Prince of Wales* and *Repulse,* the anchors of the battle fleet at Singapore, were sunk within several days after the initial attack by air bombardment, also considered impossible. Churchill's dismissal of Japanese military competence—he described the Japanese as the "Wops of the East"—proved fatally flawed.[64] The smaller Japanese force captured Singapore by the end of January, aided by the fact that the land approach had never been fortified.[65] The lopsided victory of the Japanese fleet at Java Sea completed the takeover of Indonesia. From then on the Asian theater of war became primarily a Japanese and American contest.

Throughout the war, the United States made clear that it was not fighting to reconstitute the British Empire in Asia. Although Roosevelt saw Dutch and British imperial administration in a more favorable light than French colonialism, his dislike of empire remained a source of tension among the Allies.[66] Following 1945, with the Cold War imminent, the Americans continued to pressure the British to accept noncommunist nationalism as the best line of defense against communism.

The changing military context did not escape British politicians and military planners. The Colonial Office conceded that the fall of Singapore meant that East Asia could not be held by force.[67] Similarly, the military concluded that India could not be held without much larger numbers of British troops.[68]

Consequently, even though Britain had fared better than France or the Netherlands in the war, political elites debated the overall military value of the empire. Clement Attlee, the new Labour prime minister, who had dealt Churchill a stunning defeat at the polls in the summer of 1945,[69] believed that the eastern Mediterranean, the Middle East, and other areas beyond that were of questionable value.

64. James 1994, 491, 460, 483.
65. Gilbert 1991, 716; Keay 1997, chap. 9.
66. See, for example, Betts 1985, 190. Some British officials argued that the United States threatened to displace Britain not only in Asia but in Africa as well (Hargreaves 1996, 58). Americans hardly trusted the British either. Roosevelt purportedly observed about the British that "they are always foxy and you have to be the same with them." General Stillwell, Chiang Kai-Shek's chief of staff until 1944, saw the British as "bastardly hypocrites who do their best to cut our throats on all occasions. The pig fuckers" (James 1994, 454, 518).
67. Cell 1980, 238.
68. Cell 1980, 250.
69. In the 1945 election, 226 seats changed hands in this reversal of fortune for the Conservatives. Dragnich and Rasmussen 1974, 66; T. Lloyd 1993, 269.

Is it clear that the benefits which we should have to purchase at so great a cost are worthwhile? . . . We must not, for sentimental reasons based on the past, give hostage to fortune. It may be we shall have to consider the British Isles as an easterly extension of a strategic era [area?] . . . rather than as a power looking eastwards through the Mediterranean to India and the East.[70]

Moreover, the advent of nuclear weapons and an incipient Cold War had altered the nature of home defense. The key to Britain's security, for the adherents of Atlee's views, lay in a closer relationship with the United States, not in the vast extensions of empire.[71] Empire in this perspective had diminished as a military asset, while its costs had risen.

Others, military as well as civilian officials, believed that empire still had a significant role to play. Almost 3.6 million men and women from the colonies and dominions had served in the war effort, compared to 4.6 million from Great Britain. Britain had suffered 233,000 war dead, while the dominions and colonies counted more than 87,000 dead.[72] Moreover, although Indian independence had become an inevitability by the end of World War II, African manpower might serve as a substitute. By some calculations, perhaps four hundred thousand men could be raised in Africa. This possibility, combined with the importance of the Suez Canal and Middle East oil, propelled some to argue that Britain's role, although diminished, was far from insignificant. Fears of renewed American isolationism lent further weight to the imperial argument.[73]

In short, while the tide had started to turn on the British Empire, there were still significant differences of opinion on the merits of empire. Virtually all agreed, however, that India, the primary source of British manpower in the past, could no longer be denied independence.

In other words, Britain, which had fared reasonably well in the war and had gained much from dominion and colonial support, had a stronger case than France to try to maintain its holdings. Moreover, Britain, unlike France, had a much better relationship with the United States and could count both on its protection and on Washington's support for much of its foreign policy. Thus, conceivably Whitehall might have followed a hard-line response to incipient nationalist demands (except in India). However, in the 1950s the British government came to the conclusion that maintaining its holdings by force was not in its best strategic interest.

70. Hyam 1992, pt. 3, no. 276. Attlee to the Cabinet Defence Committee. March 2, 1946. See no. 277 for Bevin's retort as well as the cabinet discussions in no. 283, 284. Also see Clayton 1999, 294; Hargreaves 1996, 110.

71. Adamthwaite 1985; Hyam 1988, 158, 171.

72. James 1994, 504, 507, 520.

73. James 1994, 529–33.

The Dutch Hold on Indonesia

The Dutch Empire emerged from the republic's rise as a maritime power in the late sixteenth and seventeenth centuries.[74] During these centuries the United East-India Company, the "Verenigde Oost-Indische Compagnie" (VOC), controlled the archipelago as its own fiefdom.[75] After the company went bankrupt in 1795 the Dutch government took direct control over the Dutch East Indies.[76] Shortly thereafter, however, Napoleonic France annexed the Netherlands, while the British seized Indonesia. After the end of the Napoleonic era, Britain returned these lands to the Netherlands, as part of its grand strategy to prop up the Netherlands as an intermediate-range power. By the early nineteenth century the Dutch already needed foreign help to hold their possessions.

Unlike the British and French, however, the Dutch did not draw matériel and manpower from the colonies for the defense of the homeland. Indigenes in Indonesia were used solely for the defense of the colonies. Roughly half the colonial forces deployed in Indonesia were of Dutch origin; the other half were largely of non-Javanese (particularly Moluccan) descent.

The Hague recognized that it could not defend Indonesia from encroachment by greater powers such as Japan. In 1913 it rejected a plan for a Dreadnought fleet.[77] Its strategy from then on relied on free riding on the British and the Americans, who could ill afford to lose resource-rich Indonesia to Japan. The Four Power Treaty of December 13, 1921, and the Washington Naval Treaty of February 1922, reinforced this view.[78]

The Dutch thus did not assess the benefits of empire in terms of the self-defense of the homeland. As a minor power, the Netherlands had long relied on its ability to maintain neutral—as in World War I—and, more importantly, on the support of great powers such as Britain. Dutch grand strategy focused on the inverse question: How could the core country defend the periphery without too much expense?[79]

Consequently, with the American setbacks in late 1941 and the fall of Singapore, the Netherlands was in no position to stop the Japanese. A crushing

---

74. For an overview of the development of the Dutch empire, see Boxer 1965.

75. van den Doel 1996, 10.

76. Before 1945, the Dutch referred to Indonesia as Dutch East-India. To avoid confusion I use the contemporary "Indonesia," but will occasionally use the terms interchangeably if the translation warrants.

77. Teitler 1979; Bootsma 1978, 114.

78. In retrospect, the outcome of the conference was arguably disadvantageous to the Dutch. The price that the United States paid for having Japan agree to a 10:10:6 standard (rather than the 10:10:7 standard preferred by Japan) was abstaining from developing large naval bases on Guam and the Philippines. This left Singapore as the critical linchpin for Dutch defense. Bootsma 1978, 117.

79. Gouda 1994.

defeat in the Java Sea led to swift occupation of the islands. Nationalists would later remark how the feebleness of Dutch power had emboldened the nationalist movement.

In the immediate postwar era, the Dutch government assumed that great power support would once again be forthcoming in restoring Dutch control over the islands.[80] If the United States and Britain before the war could not let Japan take over the Indies, now they could not let communist-inspired (in the Dutch view) nationalists take over.[81] The Hague emphasized how Dutch control would forestall such developments and warned that the Soviet Union and China (should it fall to the communists) would take advantage of the power vacuum in the wake of Dutch withdrawal.

From the outset it became clear that defeating the nationalists, who had declared Indonesia independent when the Japanese surrendered, would require substantial resources from the mother country. Lieutenant Governor-General H. J. van Mook calculated early on that 24,000 troops would be needed to restore the peace in the chaotic period after the war, and that at least 75,000 men would be required to defeat the nationalist-proclaimed republic.[82] As it turns out, it required more than twice those numbers. The Netherlands allocated the vast majority of its military budget to defeating the nationalists. At the end of 1948, despite rising tensions in Czechoslovakia, Berlin, and the corresponding push to conclude western alliances, the Dutch had drained their home allocation to the point that "it could not defend itself or provide assistance in the case of aggression, as called for in the Treaty of Brussels."[83]

From a military perspective, Indonesia contributed little to home defense. Indeed, it drained resources from the mother country, and the Netherlands had to rely on other powers to defend its overseas territories. After the nationalists seized power, The Hague moved troops to Indonesia, even as military strategists were noting the danger of a Soviet advance on the European continent, which would be even more difficult to dislodge than the German occupation.

Nor could Dutch strategic calculations be justified by the support of greater powers. Indeed, The Hague dramatically misread the interests of its major allies. In the months after the Japanese defeat, the British troops, under whose sector the Indonesian islands fell, sought to restore order amid the chaos of yet-to-be-demobilized Japanese troops and nationalist fomentation. The British even bombed Surabaya in retaliation for an attack on some of its units. The Hague assumed Britain would then restore the territories to Dutch rule.

80. Low 1991, 131.
81. For an overview of Southeast Asian developments, see Stargadt 1989.
82. Duynstee en Bosmans 1977, 612.
83. Bogaarts 1989, vol. A, 731.

But London had different intentions and agendas. From its point of view Indonesia and India were both destined for independence. Lord Mountbatten, supreme commander in East Asia, was adamant in refusing to offer British support to the Dutch to retake Indonesia. Attlee's Labour government likewise wished to remain aloof from any turmoil in Indonesia.[84]

The British government also had a different reading of the implications of the Communist threat. It agreed that a Communist regime in Indonesia was to be avoided at all costs—not, however, by bringing the Dutch back, but by making common cause with the nationalists. Before the Dutch commencement of the Second Police Action (December 1948), British Ambassador Philip Nichols relayed the message in no uncertain terms to The Hague:

> Since the resources of the Western Powers in this region are limited, it follows that we must rely upon active co-operation with the peoples to resist the Communist advance. This, in our view, makes it imperative that the nationalist movements of South-East Asia should be on our side and we must at all costs avoid a situation in which the Nationalists and the Communists are impelled to form an alliance against us.[85]

Even more important, the Dutch could not count on the United States. In the 1920s American perceptions of Dutch colonial rule had been positive, even if such assessments were colored by paternalistic, racial overtones. Consul-General Chas Hoover spoke approvingly of Dutch colonial rule over the "apathetically conservative people of these islands." His successor argued that "the whites—particularly the 30,000 Dutch who are doing it—are experts in the art of government" who were willing to "discuss with friendly interest the aspirations of the brown people to learn how to govern themselves."[86] However, by the 1930s American views began to change, particularly when the relatively tolerant Dutch colonial government of the 1920s was replaced by a more conservative one under Governor B. C. de Jonghe (1931–36). The crackdown on nationalists in Indonesia led to a reevaluation by American diplomatic personnel in Indonesia and Washington.[87] World War II widened the rift. As Sumner Wells phrased it at the State Department in 1944, the United States would not rebuild a world "half free, and half slave," while "in Roosevelt's mind, the monster of colonialism threatened to bite if not devour the world by plunging it into another huge war."[88]

---

84. van den Doel 1996, 278–79.
85. *Officiële Bescheiden Betreffende de Nederlands-Indische Betrekkingen 1945–1950* (hereafter *NIB*) 1991, vol. 16, doc. 37, 69.
86. As quoted in Gouda 1994, 242–43.
87. Gouda 1994.
88. For this assessment of Roosevelt's views, see Kimball 1991, 128.

And, like the British government, Washington thought that communism was best stopped by supporting independence movements, rather than forcing them to seek help from Russia and China. The Indonesian nationalists were well aware of their potential attraction as a third alternative to colonial rule or Communist regimes. With the suppression of the Communist-inspired Madiun revolt on Java in September 1948, the nationalists gained substantial allies in Washington. The United States explicitly warned the Dutch against military action. In an aide-mémoire of December 1948, the American government stated that the United States was critical of the Netherlands' negotiating position. It also declared that it would not accept a Federation of Indonesia without inclusion of the Republic as the Dutch were attempting to construct. The aide mémoire further submitted that the Republic was too strong to overcome by force. It concluded with a warning that any other course of action than negotiation "could result in weakening the newly emerging Western European structure."[89] Nevertheless, the Dutch government paid little heed to the international environment. The high commissioner of the Crown, Louis Beel, essentially the viceroy, urged during the height of the military actions in 1948 that the Dutch government declare United Nations resolutions against its policies as "unacceptable" and urged The Hague to "ignore them as impossible to implement."[90]

In short, realist calculations should have generated territorial adjustment. Indonesia did not contribute to Dutch home defense. To the contrary, maintaining its hold required a sizeable deployment of Dutch professional military in the form of the Dutch Colonial Army. The empire was thus hardly self-policing. Moreover, one would expect a small power such as the Netherlands to pay heed to the international environment. The Netherlands also had been devastated and impoverished during World War II, and its forces in Asia had proved no match for the great powers in the Pacific. Its key allies, Britain and the United States, had emphatically criticized Dutch hard-line designs. And yet, the Netherlands deployed more than 150,000 troops overseas, when it could least afford it, and even endangered its own position in the Western European defense system.

Portugal's Colonial Quagmire

Like the Netherlands Portugal did not use its empire as a source of manpower for the home country's defense. As a small power in the European system it had traditionally relied on greater powers for its protection. Britain in particular underwrote its independence as early as the Treaty of Windsor in 1386. It renewed its close ties through the Treaty of Methuen in

---

89. *NIB* 1991, vol. 16, doc. 31, 55–58.
90. Giebels 1996, 300.

1703.[91] In exchange Portugal granted Britain the use of maritime bases throughout the empire, most critically, the use of the Azores.

Like the Dutch, the Portuguese used indigenous people to defend the colonial territories but not the metropole. Tens of thousands of Africans served in the Portuguese colonial army, but there was no assumption—as with the French or English—that the empire was a pool of manpower that could be used to defend the metropole in times of crisis, or even that these territories could be self-policing.

Rather than contribute to metropolitan defense, the colonies drained military manpower from the metropole. The empire was not self-supporting, as the British Empire to a large extent had been. Before the Second World War the costs of colonial policing had been manageable. Even as late as 1961 the colonial army in Africa totaled no more than forty thousand troops, composed mainly of Portuguese augmented with some indigenous elements. Portugal had not yet introduced conscription. But in response to the nationalist rebellions it greatly expanded the size of the armed forces to more than 150,000.[92] To fortify its colonial position, Portugal reduced its NATO contributions. It retained two divisions in Portugal, one devoted to NATO and the other deployed as part of the treaty with Spain to defend Iberia. Both, however, were below full strength.[93] The colonial deployment was a considerable burden on a population base of 8.5 million.

The African conflicts also imposed significant economic burdens. In 1967 the government allocated 40 percent of its budget to defense; by 1971, the figure had risen to 45.9 percent.[94] As a percentage of gross domestic product (GDP), Portugal spent 6.4 percent in 1961 and 7.6 percent by 1971 on defense—proportionately more than any other NATO country.[95]

Could Portugal's decision to pursue a hard-line policy in Africa be justified by support of its allies? Here the evidence is less clear-cut than in the Dutch case. Portugal's colonial wars overseas came at the expense of its NATO commitment, but NATO members were reluctant to press the issue, since they were concerned about Communist influence in Africa.[96] The

---

91. Maxwell 1995, 18.

92. The colonial army consisted of roughly 138,000 Portuguese and another 40,000 African troops. (Raby 1988, 220; Maxwell 1995, 33; Maxwell 1976, 252; Wheeler 1979, 195; Wheeler 1970, 779; Bender 1972a, 331–33, nn. 6 and 9; Newitt 1981, 230; Bandeira 1976, 20–21).

93. Keefe et al. 1977, 385.

94. Wheeler 1970, 777; Raby 1988, 244. Pimlott (1977, 336) mentions that 42.4 percent of the total budget went to defense. Bender (1972a, 331) suggests that outlays lay between 45 percent and 50 percent for defense. For slightly different figures, see Wheeler 1979, 204; Schmitter 1975a, 14–16.

95. SIPRI 1974, 208–9.

96. Minter (1972, chaps. 5, 7) argues that NATO did not merely tolerate but actually supported Portuguese efforts.

United States occasionally criticized Portuguese colonial policies, but, given Soviet, Cuban, and Chinese forays into Africa and the importance of the Azores as a refueling base, it muted its opposition. However, support meant American restraint rather than outright military assistance.

More important, Portugal faced quite different circumstances in Africa than had the British, the Belgians, or the French. By 1961, when hostilities started in Angola, the other colonial powers had withdrawn or were close to agreements regarding the transfer of power. Consequently, during the Portuguese colonial wars (1961–1974), Portugal not only could not count on much European support but the nationalist movements in Angola, Mozambique, and Guinea could draw on the support of newly independent African states and, in the case of leftist groups, the support of socialist countries such as the Soviet Union. Although the Portuguese armed forces did receive support from South Africa, the effort largely remained a Portuguese one.

Moreover, it became clear as early as 1963, barely two years into the wars of liberation, that the military situation, particularly in Guinea, would pose serious problems for the armed forces.[97] With long supply lines and vast territories to control, achieving ultimate victory soon proved unlikely.

In short, from a realist perspective one could hardly justify the empire as a key asset for the military security of the home country. It drained manpower and military assets from Portugal, while Lisbon received only modest support from stronger military powers.

Empire as an Element of Soviet Grand Strategy

The Soviet empire arose as a direct successor to the tsarist empire for which territorial conquest had been a strategic imperative.[98] The First World War and the collapse of the tsarist empire coincided with rebellion in several subject territories, but—with the exception of Poland, the Baltic countries, Moldavia, and parts of Galicia—the new Communist government succeeded in reestablishing a hold over much of the tsarist territorial space.

World War II and its aftermath saw more territorial gains. In the east the USSR added some of the Chinese and Japanese possessions to the internal empire, and in the west it gained Lithuania, Latvia, Estonia, and Moldavia. Although many of the Eastern European nations remained nominally independent, they could more accurately be described as part of the Soviet Union's external empire.

97. Africa Institute 1963, 286.
98. See Bendix 1978; Raeff 1984; D'Encausse 1992.

Both external and internal empires served a variety of military purposes. First, these territories provided buffer zones against potential aggressors. This followed a long historical practice: "Russia has always been interested in creating a buffer zone of acquired territories and allies along its borders to protect its heartland from intrusion."[99] Second, Russia and later the Soviet Union had always aimed at acquiring secure open-water ports. Third, the external empire provided substantial resources and manpower. By the mid-1950s Western sources estimated that the Russian military consisted of 175 line divisions (and a total of 2.5 million men) and that it could be rapidly increased to 300 divisions. Of these 175 line divisions, about one hundred were forward-deployed. The non-Soviet Warsaw Pact states added another eighty divisions, so that on the central Western front they made up roughly 45 percent of the total force structure.[100]

In the internal empire, with roughly one-third of the Soviet population being officially non-Russian, the republics were important components of the large Soviet Army. Even though the West overestimated Warsaw Pact conventional strength, the total number of personnel under arms remained substantial.[101]

Contrary to the Western view, Stalin saw nuclear weapons as potentially useful but maintained that they did not alter the character of war. Nuclear-armed missiles were seen as an extension of the artillery.[102] Soviet military doctrine thus continued to emphasize the importance of a great land war, fought mainly by large numbers of ground forces. In this scheme Eastern Europe served as an extension of the "fortress Soviet Union."[103]

Moreover, during the first decades of the cold war the USSR relied on forward basing of its conventional and nuclear arsenal. This provided a further rationale for Moscow to maintain tight control over its fixed military assets in Eastern Europe and within the USSR itself.[104]

Soon after Stalin's death, however, some politicians started to question existing military doctrine. Unlike Stalin, Khrushchev recognized that

99. Berman and Baker 1982, 23.

100. Duffield 1992, 209. Despite Warsaw Pact contributions, the chain of command remained decidedly Soviet, unlike the more integrated NATO command structure. Clarke, *Radio Free Europe/Radio Liberty* (hereafter cited as *RFE/RL*) 1, no. 8 (February 24, 1989), 13–14. See also Liberman 1996, chap. 7.

101. Holloway (1983, 35) suggests that the number of men under arms in 1955 might have been as high as 5,763,000.

102. Berman and Barker 1982, 41. Rice suggests that even after 1954 some argued that intercontinental ballistic missiles were not different than long-range artillery. Rice 1991, 156. Major-General Kozlow remarked that "Stalin's scornful statements about atomic weapons were the reason why our military thought was not directed in time to an objective and far-reaching evaluation of the new instruments of warfare." Cited in Holloway 1983, 28.

103. Rice 1991, 153–54; Berman and Baker 1982, 22, 29.

104. Lake (1999) argues that the nature of assets deployed explains the type of security policies that states choose.

nuclear weapons had fundamentally changed the character of war. He renounced the "inevitability of war" thesis but believed that, should war come, it would become a strategic nuclear war.[105] "In our time the defense capability of the country is defined not by how many soldiers we have under arms," Khruschev wrote, "[it] depends to a decisive degree on what firepower and what means of delivery that country has at its disposal."[106] Consequently, Khrushchev aimed to reduce the number of men under arms from 5.7 million in 1955 to 3.6 million by 1958, and he suggested even further cuts to 2.4 million.

But the military never implemented such reductions in full. Although the army welcomed a rethinking of the importance of nuclear weapons for doctrinal purposes it was not ready to relinquish older habits easily. Marshal V. D. Sokolovskii, the chief of the General Staff from 1952 to 1960, argued in an influential publication that nuclear war was winnable and that mass armies would continue to be essential for future military success. Minister of Defense Rodion Malinovsky sided with the military in opposing Khrushchev's "one variant war." Even when Khrushchev institutionalized a new segment in the Soviet force structure, the Strategic Rocket Forces (1959), the artillery branch of the ground forces managed to influence its organizational structure.[107] New strategic concepts were intermixed with old notions of large-scale conventional warfare. Nuclear war was an aggravated form of conventional conflict but would still have a victor.

Coit Blacker suggests that this view of the winnability of nuclear war lasted from the late 1950s until the late 1970s.[108] Soviet views remained largely untempered by the prospects of a potential Armageddon, and expansionist policies continued as a result. Some party members continued to expound that the USSR should be strong enough to oppose any coalition against it.[109] And in the external empire, General-Secretary Leonid Brezhnev, after the Soviet invasion of Czechoslovakia, propounded the right to interfere in any socialist country "threatened" by reform.[110] In the nuclear and conventional arenas, the Soviet Union engaged in an expansive program of building large ICBMs (the SS-18), a fourth generation of missiles, and new Delta-class nuclear submarines.[111]

By the mid-1970s the United States and the Soviet Union had reached parity in their nuclear rivalry. Soviet planners started to retreat from the

105. Berman and Baker 1982, 35; Rice 1991, 154.
106. As cited in Holloway 1983, 39–40. See also p. 35.
107. Berman and Baker 1982, 14; Holloway 1983, 40–41; Rice 1987, 60.
108. Blacker 1991, 432.
109. Gelman 1991, 6, 26.
110. Holloway 1983, 99. See also Schoepflin, *Report on the USSR* 1, no. 4 (January 27, 1989), 1–3.
111. Berman and Baker 1982, 65–68.

thesis that nuclear war could be won. In 1981 Brezhnev publicly proclaimed the unwinnability of nuclear war in favor of the principles of mutual assured destruction and mutual deterrence.[112]

But while parity induced caution in the overall superpower contest, it did not diminish Soviet ambitions elsewhere. The Soviet Union started to assert itself in Africa, the Caribbean, and the Middle East, culminating in the war in Afghanistan. Moreover, the Brezhnev administration continued to develop an array of sophisticated nuclear weapons: mobile missile launchers, highly advanced nuclear submarine capability, and greater blue water capability.

Its efforts were counterproductive.[113] The Western allies deployed new weapons systems of their own, such as Cruise missiles and the Pershing II. An American naval buildup offset the maritime ambitions of the USSR. The United States, France, and South Africa checked Soviet ambitions in Africa. In the Caribbean, Washington made clear that it would counter any extension of Soviet influence by intervening in El Salvador, Nicaragua, and Grenada. The Camp David accords diminished Moscow's leverage in the Egyptian-Israeli rivalry. And in Asia, the rapprochement of the United States and the People's Republic of China undermined the Soviet position even further. Finally, the war in Afghanistan threatened to become the Soviet Union's own version of a Vietnamese quagmire, occupying 130,000 ground troops by mid-1986.[114]

But an even more dramatic development was taking place that affected the USSR's own security: the third revolution in military affairs of the twentieth century. By the late 1970s Soviet analysts identified four trends: a qualitative modernization of nuclear weaponry; rapid development in military electronics; qualitative changes in conventional weaponry; and in general "new physical principles" of combat.[115] This ongoing development, argued William Odom in 1985, will "probably place nuclear weapons modernization into a secondary role as the competition with the West shifts into areas where the Soviet Union is less well prepared to compete."[116]

112. Holloway 1983, 48; Roeder 1993, 201–4; Rice 1987, 70. One analyst (John Collins), evaluating the situation in 1980–85, rated the United States superior in 67 categories, the USSR ahead in 28, and the two countries at parity in 31 other categories. See n. 46 in Desch 1993. William Odom questions the extent to which Brezhnev's Tula speech of 1977 really marked a strategic departure. Odom 1998, 443 n. 91.

113. Snyder (1991) notes this as a logical consequence of any expansionist strategy.

114. Mendelson 1993, 352. Overall, about half a million Soviet troops were deployed in Afghanistan. Official figures put the Soviet death toll, as of May 1988, at 13,310, with more than 35,000 wounded. Private sources suggest higher figures. Konovalov, *Report on the USSR* 1, no. 14 (April 7, 1989), 1. Odom (1998, 249) notes 16,000 dead (combat and accident-related) with 27,000 wounded (combat and noncombat).

115. Petersen and Trulock 1988, 12–13.

116. Odom 1985, 2.

Concurrent with an awareness of these Western technological break-throughs Soviet planners recognized the need for sophisticated combined operations—contracted in time but spread out over a vast area. In those scenarios, speed, logistics, and advanced communications would be essential. And in all those areas, the Soviet military concluded it was lacking.[117] The chief of staff, Marshal Nikolai Ogarkov, argued for a reevaluation of strategy and a reexamination of existing resource allocations.[118] Ogarkov was dismissed for his criticism of his civilian superiors, but his successor, Marshal Sergei Akhromeyev, warned similarly that "changes in the character of war are now proceeding more rapidly."[119] Akhromeyev's successor, Mikhail Moiseev, echoed his predecessor.[120]

Moreover, the need for forward deployment of nuclear weaponry receded. If Moscow still required such deployments in the 1950s to offset American bombers in Europe, by the 1980s its intercontinental capabilities and submarine development no longer made forward deployment necessary.

When Gorbachev came to power in 1985 he quickly integrated some of these military perspectives into his views. At the 27th Congress of February 1986, he argued that future military force levels should be based on "reasonable sufficiency."[121] He succinctly introduced his core beliefs: first, nuclear war could not be won, and, second, security depended ultimately on political, not military, means.[122] Furthermore, he linked military doctrinal and technological obsolescence to the overall state of the economy, and he questioned the paramount position that military expenditures had taken in the budget.[123] The Soviet Union itself was secure by its own estimation.[124] Consequently, Gorbachev eagerly embraced détente and concluded agreements on Intermediate Range Nuclear Forces (INF) and strategic nuclear weapons.

Finally, the subsiding of the Cold War had profound effects on the cohesion of the Warsaw Pact. Georgii Shakhnazarov, an aide to Gorbachev, stated the administration's position succinctly:

> The significance of small armies [Warsaw Pact allies] without nuclear rockets will be trivial. If somehow nuclear weapons are not used, then there are no

117. Odom 1985, 5–8.
118. Blacker 1991, 443; Gelman 1991, 8.
119. Petersen and Trulock 1988, 11–12.
120. Quoted in Foye, *RFE/RL* 1, no. 12 (March 24, 1989), 6.
121. Petersen and Trulock 1988, 18, 20.
122. Blacker 1991, 435. Mendelson suggests that Gorbachev empowered a coalition of new thinkers who could then go on to change foreign policy with respect to Afghanistan; Mendelson 1993. Her argument dovetails with learning arguments that account for changes in the Gorbachev administration by emphasizing the introduction of new personnel; see particularly Blacker 1991; Legvold 1991.
123. See Rice 1991.
124. See the discussion in Kokoshin 1998, 184–92.

guarantees that, say, the Hungarians will unquestionably follow the orders of our staff . . . [they might] even go over to the side of the West. I strongly doubt the GDR Germans will want to fight on Russia's side against their western kinsmen.[125]

The argument could be extended to the integrity of the USSR itself. As Karen Dawisha and Bruce Parrott suggest, "Whereas the siege atmosphere of the Cold War had justified the need to maintain a centralized state, the buoyant optimism of the 'new political thinking' provided no compelling geopolitical justification for the maintenance of the Union."[126]

In sum, in the decades after World War II both the external and internal empire served important military functions for the USSR. They yielded considerable numbers of troops (even if the USSR had to deploy troops of its own to police the external empire). They provided forward bases and buffer zones. Given its preponderant power and its ability to control these areas, this imperial strategy made sense from a realist perspective.

Gradually, however, these benefits receded. Countervailing alliances had checked the Soviet Union's continued expansionist attempts. Also, the Soviet Union achieved nuclear parity, and like the West, came to the conclusion that nuclear war was ultimately unwinnable. The need for forward deployment of nuclear weapons also diminished. The subsequent revolution in military affairs required a transformation from a large conscript-based army to highly trained professionals—as the Western armies were gradually becoming. It also required sustained technological development within the USSR itself. As Bill Wohlforth notes, the Soviet leaders came to the conclusion that they could not continue their military rivalry with the United States.[127]

Evaluating these declining benefits, the leaders of the Soviet Union and Russia behaved rather as realists might expect. Although the center still commanded considerable resources and despite the more than twenty-five million Russians in the other Soviet republics, the center readjusted to the new international conditions and its relative decline vis-à-vis the United States. In this case domestic politics did not trump the strategic calculations of the state.

EMPIRES OF WEALTH

It hardly needs restating that economic motives have often been key factors in the pursuit of empire and territorial expansion. Many an empire has

125. Quoted in Odom 1998, 105.
126. Dawisha and Parrott 1994, 20.
127. Wohlforth 1994–95.

been driven by the assumption that territorial conquest yields positive benefits, in the form of taxes, tributary payments, or preferential trading zones—which may benefit the state as a whole or narrow interest groups.[128]

More recent literature from the field of new institutional economics also stresses the economic logic of seeking formal hierarchy over other territories. For example, Jeffry Frieden suggests that empire tends to correlate with site-specific investments that are vulnerable to expropriation and seizure, such as mining and resource extraction.[129]

Territorial acquisitions yielded not only benefits in return on investments and markets for goods but also provided a fallback during trade crises. The imperial option played an important role in British retreat from hegemonic leadership.[130] In response to the Hawley-Smoot Tariff Act of 1930, Britain and France retreated to imperial preference schemes. This was partially instigated by the metropolitan powers but also by their dominions and colonies, which saw external markets for their goods closed. The British designed the Ottawa agreement of 1932, while France and the Netherlands pursued similar preferential trading schemes for their territories.

But it became readily apparent that imperial preferences were poor substitutes for a liberal trading regime. Imperial preferences tended to be trade diverting.[131] Moreover, the United States came to realize that nondiscriminatory tariffs led to its exclusion from foreign markets. Consequently, by 1934 it started to shift toward a discriminatory tariff scheme (through the Reciprocal Trade Agreements Act), under which the United States could bilaterally and selectively trade tariff concessions for reciprocal liberalization.[132]

Therefore, even while World War II was still in progress, the United States sought to more firmly establish itself as an economic leader. Whereas it had been reluctant to do so in the interwar period, the victory of internationalist coalitions now propelled Washington to seek far-ranging liberalization in trade and stabilization in financial markets. Fixed exchange rates, aid for reconstruction and development, and international lending authorities to guarantee liquidity would combine with the General Agreement on Tariffs and Trade (GATT) to open up and stabilize a liberal trading regime. As Miles Kahler notes, a global liberal trading system diminishes the attraction of imperial preference schemes.[133] Tariff reduction and the "most

128. For a useful set of essays on economic imperialism, see Boulding and Mukerjee 1972. See also Lenin 1939; Hobson 1961.

129. Frieden 1994. Lipson (1985) similarly notes that direct investments lead to greater intervention than portfolio investments.

130. Kindleberger 1979, 77–78.

131. The gravity model of trade provides one means of measuring such trade distortion. Baldwin et al. 1995.

132. See Lake 1988; Oye 1992.

133. Kahler 1997.

favored nation" principle were antithetical to the economic logic of mercantilist, imperial preference.

At the same time liberal trading environments make secession less costly. In a mercantilist international environment size confers great benefits. Scale correlates with substantial markets for production and consumption. Small states with insignificant domestic markets, by contrast, will face numerous barriers to trade. Consequently, a mercantilist environment discourages the quest for independence. In a liberal trading environment those efficiency-of-scale considerations no longer hold. Diminished barriers to trade give small states access to larger markets beyond their borders. "In the extreme case of total world economic integration there would in principle be no costs to separation in terms of trade, since political independence would no longer be related to trade barriers."[134]

In short, mercantilist international orders correlate with scale advantages. Liberal trading orders, by contrast, correlate inversely with size. There are fewer advantages for metropoles to seek territorial aggrandizement, while would-be secessionists face smaller costs in forming their own state.

Aside from the increasing liberalization of the economic order, other trends diminished the economic rationale for empire as well, particularly for the maritime empires. Trade between the advanced industrial states expanded faster than trade between the metropoles and peripheries. This occurred partially because of the liberalization of the postwar era, but also because of changes in the nature of goods traded. Increasingly trade became intrasectoral and more relation-specific, thus diminishing the value of such assets in alternative uses.[135] Simultaneously, the value of raw materials declined as a share of finished goods.

Finally, increasing globalization of trade and finance magnified the importance of becoming part of the trading scheme advanced by the hegemonic United States and its allies. In discussing the effects of internationalization of the economy, Jeffry Frieden and Ronald Rogowski succinctly capture the problem of mercantilist and imperial preference strategies in today's world: "The easier are international economic transactions in general, the greater the social cost of sustaining economic closure for any one country, and the greater the social impact of global economic trends on any one country—no matter how economically closed the country in question."[136]

Broad trends manifested themselves to different degrees in various countries, however. In many cases political elites tried to shield the metropole

134. Polèse 1985, 116. For a formal economic argument, see Alesina and Spolaore 1994. Meadwell and Martin (1994) develop that argument with specific reference to Quebec.
135. Yarborough and Yarborough 1987.
136. Frieden and Rogowski 1996, 34.

and the subject territories from the impact of this new international economic order. Thus, while the economic rationale for holding empire and territory had shifted, some states proved more adept than others at recognizing and responding to this new reality.

The Declining Economic Rationale for Empire in France

Before World War I, the Parti Colonial, the colonial lobby, argued strenuously that the empire yielded great riches. In reality, though, the economic gains in this period were modest. Only 10–12 percent of French trade went to its colonies, as did only 10 percent of its capital exports.[137] Jacques Marseille suggests that the colonies were not critical for France as a whole, although they had become important for specific sectors such as agriculture, transportation, banking, and mining.[138]

The economic importance of empire increased during the Great Depression. France, traditionally more protectionist and interventionist than Britain, intensified its efforts to curtail access by other states to its colonies during the global downturn.[139] France partly engaged in imperial preference because of the weaker development of its colonies compared to the British. The colonies provided largely unfinished, raw materials, and thus did not compete with metropolitan firms.[140] Ken Oye estimates that the turn to empire and discrimination increased the French Empire's share of total world exports from 7.6 percent in 1929 to 9 percent by 1933, even before devaluation of the franc.[141] While only 13 percent of French trade occurred with the empire, by 1933 the empire took in 33 percent of French exports and made up 23 percent of all French imports.[142] Jacques Marseille's calculations suggest an even greater economic role for the colonies. In 1927 France exported 1.4 billion francs (in 1914 constant prices) to the empire out of 7.8 billion in exports. By 1931 the empire made up 1.6 billion worth of exports out of 5.2 billion. And in 1936 the empire accounted for a full 1.3 billion out of only 2.6 billion.[143]

After the Second World War some politicians, therefore, saw not only military but also economic salvation in the empire. A modernized Union

---

137. Fieldhouse 1971.

138. See Marseille 1985, 127–30.

139. Due to bilateral agreements, French Equatorial Africa practiced an open door policy, while the other areas practiced protectionism even before the 1930s. Fieldhouse 1971, 595, 604; Marseille 1985, 132. See also Kupchan 1994, 249–52.

140. Kahler 1981, 403.

141. Oye 1992, 88.

142. Lustick 1993, 84. Even then, argues Lustick, economic considerations remained secondary to security concerns.

143. Marseille 1984, 44. While exports declined overall because of the Depression and tariff wars, the exports to the overseas territories remained the same.

Française with close ties between metropole and periphery would reinvigorate the French economy. Indeed, the share of French exports to the French Union as a percentage of total exports increased from 27 percent in 1938 to 36 percent in 1950.[144]

One should not, however, conclude that the pursuit of empire after the war was driven by careful economic considerations. France's precarious economic position should have precipitated a reevaluation of its strategy. If the government had systematically evaluated its holdings it would have noted that in the interwar period the economic advantages of the colonies had become less apparent. The most important colony, Algeria, benefited more than the mother country from its customs union with the metropole, accounting for 40 percent of colonial imports into France and 45 percent of all French exports to the empire.[145] Because of the customs union, trade between the metropole and Algeria was unaffected by the 1930s tariffs, which impinged on other bilateral trade relations. Algerian products, largely semifinished or unfinished goods, continued to gain access to the metropole. However, the finished goods that the mother country exported to Algeria declined more in relative price than the unfinished goods and raw materials that Algeria exported. France consequently had a negative trade balance with Algeria. These policies benefited the Algerian colons, whose purchasing power increased during this period.[146]

Moroccan and Tunisian goods, however, did not receive similar protection. France figured less prominently in their exports. Morocco received 39 percent of its imports from the metropole and exported 46 percent of its trade to France—still significant, but far less than Algeria, which got 74 percent of its imports from France, while France accounted for 85 percent of Algeria's exports.[147]

It was even less clear whether relations with the rest of the overseas territories, such as French Equatorial Africa (Afrique Equatoriale Française, or AEF) and French West Africa (AOF), yielded economic gains. On the one hand, these areas provided raw materials and unfinished goods, and private companies derived considerable profits from West and Equatorial Africa. In her study of two French conglomerates that together accounted for 30 percent of private investment in AOF and AEF, Catherine Coquery-Vidrovitch shows that these firms saw handsome profit margins until 1952, partially due to the demand for primary products and raw materials in the postwar period and the demand created by the Korean War.[148] On the other hand, their profits declined rapidly after that down to the lows of the 1930s.

144. Frank 1986, 273.
145. Marseille 1976, 530.
146. Marseille 1976, 533–35.
147. Marseille 1976, 531–32.
148. Coquery-Vidrovitch 1975, 595, 612.

Coquery-Vidrovitch suggests that their archaic colonial methods of production simply could not measure up to competition. Moreover, such private gains in West and Equatorial Africa had to be measured against considerable public expenditure. French public funds accounted for 50 percent of local budgets in AOF from 1946 to 1960.[149]

In general, the desire to foster closer economic integration between metropole and periphery and the attempt to raise the value of empire through developing the periphery—the "mise-en-valeur" policy started in the interwar period—did not follow market dictates. France used preferential purchasing arrangements and monopolies to maintain its privileged position in the colonies. "All these territories . . . continued to receive preferences for their exports to France,"[150] and the metropole purchased goods above world market prices.[151]

The postwar period also presented the metropole with a set of difficult quandaries. Rebuilding the French economy required considerable investment capital. At the same time, if the colonies were to become valuable economic partners, they would have to be developed and modernized. This required the French government to allocate considerable funds to the overseas territories. French public expenditure in its colonies in this period was roughly four to six times larger than British expenditure.[152] Nevertheless, this public expenditure had little effect.[153]

Most critical of all, Paris grudgingly had to acknowledge American economic hegemony. To rebuild its economy, France had to rely on aid from Washington on American terms, and those terms were decidedly anti-imperial and anti-protectionist.[154] The United States had come to the conclusion that economic autarky led to military conflict, and that liberal trade and international security were inseparable.[155] Under American hegemony a return to prewar levels of protectionism and government intervention was out of the question. France had to turn to the International Monetary Fund and the International Bank for Reconstruction and Development for loans. Moreover, while the Blum-Byrnes agreements of 1946 achieved desirable results—war debt became interest free and was added to the loans for reconstruction—they came at a price: France had to open its markets to

149. Berthélemy 1980, 304.
150. Fieldhouse 1971, 604–5.
151. Berthélemy 1980, 307. "La France achète les produits de l' Union française plus cher que sur la marché mondial." See also Fieldhouse 1971, 605, 625.
152. Fieldhouse 1971, 631–32.
153. Berthélemy 1980, 313–17.
154. Already in the interwar period France and Britain had come into conflict with American insistence on open door policies in the colonies and mandates. See particularly the clashes on Middle East oil agreements and the exchange between Ambassador Davis and Foreign Secretary Lord Curzon in May 1920. Hurewitz 1979, doc. 52.
155. Hill 1994, 106.

American products.[156] Marshall Plan aid provided further leverage. By 1948, 70 percent of French government investments came out of Marshall Plan funds.[157] Discrimination and empire preference rapidly became anachronistic.[158] Although liberals such as Jean Monnet did not immediately draw the conclusion that modernization and liberal trade diminished the rationale for empire, the Quai d'Orsay gradually won the argument against the traditionalists.[159]

Even before the war some economists had started to ask whether French economic modernization would accelerate if France let its colonies go. Paul Bernard and Albert Sarraut had suggested that the overseas territories retarded growth by protecting less competitive industries and raising prices.[160] Claude Gruson similarly suggested that "the idea of colonial riches is . . . no doubt true for Victorian England. But for France, I believe that idea has always been wrong."[161] France, he added, would do better to expend its resources at home. The later Jeanneney Report echoed Bernard's analysis: economic protectionism was irrational. It protected less-competitive industries and artificially raised prices.[162]

In the 1950s economists also started to compare the French colonial experience to that of the Netherlands. Had not the Netherlands undergone a dramatic spurt in growth in the five years since its retreat from Indonesia? Raymond Cartier, in three articles in *Paris Match,* traced the Dutch economic takeoff in the 1950s to its surrender of Indonesia.[163] Cost-benefit calculations, known as Cartiérisme, started to seep into at least some French minds.

If one calculated the economic benefits of the overseas territories against the costs of trying to maintain the French Union by force, positive benefits seemed even more illusory. Even with U.S. aid, the Indochinese war drained one-third of the French budget. The Algerian War likewise imposed heavy burdens on the economy. In 1957 the direct costs of the war came to $1.1 billion, out of a total budget of $11.3 billion. Social economic policies had to be sacrificed to pay for the armed forces. The total expenses for the war amounted to 50–55 billion French francs (10–11 billion dollars).[164]

156. Frank 1986, 277; Rioux 1987, 84.
157. Girault 1986, 63.
158. On this point, see Fry 1997, 131; Kahler 1981, 408.
159. See T. Smith (1981) on French tendencies toward protectionism, partially due to the large agricultural labor force (Blondel 1974a, 16).
160. Marseille 1984; Fieldhouse 1971, 597. Sarraut had not argued against colonialism per se but against monopoly colonialism, which worked to the detriment of the metropole.
161. Cited in Marseille 1984, 351.
162. Marseille 1976, 536.
163. Marseille 1984, 11; Hargreaves 1996.
164. Horne 1978, 538; Lustick 1993, 137; Rioux 1987, 281. Between 1949–57 the value of a dollar amounted to 350 francs, and in 1958 the dollar was equal to 431 francs. After the currency reform in 1959 a dollar equaled 4.90 francs (Loriaux 1991, 21).

In short, there were many reasons to question whether an imperial strategy made economic sense for the state as a whole. Anti-imperial voices, however, were drowned out. Although Cartier asked in his 1956 articles whether the empire still made sense economically, and Raymond Aron did the same in 1957,[165] they hardly typified the political debates of the 1950s. Politicians, except the Communists, favored the position of Pierre Moussa (the director of economic affairs at the Ministry of Overseas Territories): economic hardship would befall France without overseas territories.[166] It was not until April 1961 that a politician, Charles de Gaulle, fully applied the Cartierist argument: "Algeria costs us, to say the least, more than she is worth to us."[167] A rationalist, unitary state perspective focusing on economic gains does not help explain why France refused to change its territorial policies for so long.

The British Choice for a Liberal Order

Economic turmoil in the 1920s and the 1930s also sparked British reactions. With the Conservatives leading the way, Britain ratcheted up its tariffs on agricultural goods to deal with falling prices in the late 1920s. The American Hawley-Smoot tariffs, which dealt with agricultural and manufactured goods alike, led to reciprocal moves and a push for imperial preference. Initially that move came from some of the empire's subjects. Canadian Prime Minister R. B. Bennett championed "Canada and Empire First" policies, although Britain still preferred liberal trade and tried to push for international coordination together with the Dutch—to no avail.[168]

Changing economic circumstances and the replacement of the Labour Party government by a national coalition government in 1931 paved the way for British protectionism and empire preference. Empire preference was not simply a blind reaction to American protectionist sentiments but an attempt to revitalize the empire and the British Commonwealth. Preferential tariffs might aid British exports, but they would also tie the dominions closer to Britain through their exports to the motherland. Chamberlain thus described the Ottawa agreements of 1932 as "an attempt to bring the Empire together again and to supplement and support the common sentiment by bringing more material interests into line with it."[169] This marked "a decisive step away from Free Trade."[170] The primary proponent of free

---

165. Lustick 1993, 117; Marseille 1985.
166. Marseille 1984; 1985, 127.
167. Cited in Lustick 1993, 290.
168. Kindleberger 1973, 77–78, 135; Mansergh 1969, 242–44.
169. Quoted in Rooth 1992, 71. See also James 1994, 479–80.
170. T. Lloyd 1993, 177.

trade within the national coalition, the Liberals, suffered a catastrophic defeat in the 1935 election, gaining only 6.4 percent of the vote.[171]

Not all colonies and commonwealth members, however, supported the move. Some of the dominion countries, particularly Australia and New Zealand, feared losing access to American markets. They did not perceive the British market as a sufficiently large substitute.[172] From 1913 to 1929, the percentage share of Canadian exports to Great Britain had dropped from 49.9 percent to 24.7 percent; for Australia, from 45.5 percent to 38.1 percent; and for South Africa, from 80.4 percent to 49.5 percent.[173]

For Britain the dominions and empire still remained important even if the nature of British exports to the empire had changed. For example, Britain exported 430 million rupees worth of textiles to India in 1913–14. That figure had dropped to 90 million by 1935–36. Exports of manufactured goods, however, increased. Machine exports increased from 48 million in 1913–14 to 93 million by 1935; cars from 7 million to 19 million.[174]

Given the dominion opposition, the Ottawa agreements achieved less than London had hoped for. Nevertheless, overall the Ottawa agreements did substantially redirect British trade. By 1936–38 the agreement countries accounted for 40 percent of British exports, whereas in 1928–30 they had accounted for less than 30 percent.[175] In short, the empire and the commonwealth played an important economic role in British welfare in overall terms and in the types of British exports.

As with the other European states, the war severely affected Britain's economy. To finance the war effort and its purchases of American arms, London had gone into debt. Some had argued against accepting Lend-Lease aid on those grounds, but realistically Britain had no choice. During the war Britain sold off £1.2 billion to cover its imports of arms and other needed supplies.[176] Not only did it owe Washington, but it had also drawn from its colonies. Britain had insisted on self-financing in the colonies, with independent budgets, so the transfers from the colonies to London were considered intergovernmental loans. Because the government had agreed to finance the Indian troops deployed outside India, India's debt, amounting to £350 million in 1939, had been transformed into a British debt to India of £1,200 million.[177] Lord Keynes, speaking of a "financial Dunkirk," estimated that in 1945 alone Britain would be faced with overseas expendi-

171. T. Lloyd, 191.
172. Rooth 1992, 320. See also James 1994, 457.
173. Rooth 1992, 33.
174. Marseille 1984, 252. See also Rooth (1992, 32) for figures on overall exports to the empire.
175. Rooth 1992, 317.
176. T. Lloyd 1993, 271.
177. James 1994, 509; T. Lloyd 1993, 271.

tures of £2.9 billion with an overseas income of only £800 million. The overall deficit he estimated at about £5 billion.[178]

Basic commodities, such as fuel and food, remained in short supply for years after the war. Given Britain's debt, the metropolitan government could ill afford to buy its commodities from nonempire countries. Moreover, exports from some of the colonies in exchange for dollars could prove to be valuable additions to the Exchequer's income. Malayan rubber and tin, and various products from the Gold Coast and Nigeria, were deemed vital in this regard. The British government thus engaged in a variety of mechanisms to guarantee its ability to purchase needed commodities below world market prices, and to force such countries, through licensing agreements, to sell a certain percentage at that price to Britain, while charging a higher price to dollar-paying countries.[179]

Various voices in the Labour government started to push for a renewal of imperial preferences and for a tightening of the sterling area. This would diminish the pressure on London's dollar reserves, and a return of intra-imperial trade would replenish the critical supplies. Ernest Bevin, the foreign minister, even argued for the creation of a commonwealth customs union.[180]

Thus, London faced the quandary of other Western colonial powers. A return to sound economic footing might be possible with colonial access, imperial preference, and American financial support. But Washington saw these principles as incompatible. Britain would have to choose one or the other. To the Americans, the equal access clause of the Atlantic Charter meant that Britain had already pledged itself to greater openness.[181] British officials themselves were aware of the problem. Creech Jones at the Colonial Office noted that

> His Majesty's Government must consider not only the . . . effects of the price policy on the balance of payments position, but also international obligations . . . of freedom of access to Colonial raw materials and by their acceptance in principle of the American proposals for an international trade charter.[182]

Moreover, the Colonial Office relinquished the prewar notion that the colonies had to be self-financing. Like the French, the British government

---

178. Hyam 1992, pt. 2, no. 74. Cabinet memorandum Keynes: "Our overseas financial prospects"; 13 August 1945.

179. Hyam 1992, pt. 2, no. 78. Discussions of marketing of colonial produce in Colonial Office; January–November 1947.

180. Hargreaves 1996, 108, 111.

181. Hargreaves 1996, 59.

182. Hyam 1992, pt. 2, no. 79. Cabinet memorandum, "Prices of colonial export products"; March 1947. See also the Colonial Office memorandum by Sir S. Caine regarding the access of "American private investment in the colonies." Hyam 1992, pt. 2, no. 87.

recognized that development of the colonies had to be an integral element of metropolitan rule. Such development would diminish the appeal of radical nationalists while enhancing the economic value of the colonies as future economic partners.

However, because the empire was ultimately supposed to strengthen the British Exchequer, the treasury insisted that between 1946 and 1951 £250 million from colonial export trade be deposited in Britain to support the pound.[183] As David Fieldhouse argues, the British attempt at mise en valeur (the French strategy to improve and develop the colonies) never took on the proportions it did in France.[184]

Here too the empire posed a dilemma. Developing the colonies meant that they would drain much-needed financial resources from Britain. But this eroded the very rationale of having colonies in the first place. With debts to India, the potential costs of developing other parts of the empire, and the prospects of liberal international trade, the empire no longer constituted the economic asset that it once was believed to be.

The Dutch "Positive Balance Sheet" Gone Astray

Dutch colonial strategy traditionally embraced the "positive balance policy" (*batig slot politiek*). Only viable producing areas were to be colonized under the Cultivation System (the Cultuur Stelsel).[185] The policy proved highly efficient. By the early 1850s, almost one-third of governmental revenue came from Indonesia. In the course of the nineteenth century Dutch colonial policy changed. As the empire expanded into other peripheral areas in Indonesia—despite directives from the central government to the contrary—oil and mineral exploitation grew in significance.

The Dutch government saw little contradiction between their holding of Indonesia and the emerging international trade regime. While the Dutch had created monopoly positions in the nineteenth century, as a small country they had to open up the Indonesian economy by the twentieth century. They were in no position to bar entry to greater powers. Only in oil did they initially try to restrict American companies in order to give Royal Dutch Shell a privileged position. But after diplomatic pressure that noted these violations to "equal opportunity" to the resources of the Indies, Standard Oil of New Jersey was given access.[186]

In other words, the Dutch remained in their eyes economically intertwined with their holdings in Indonesia, but these economic connections

183. James 1994, 528.
184. Fieldhouse 1971.
185. For a discussion of the content of this policy, see Geertz 1963; Penders 1977, docs. 1–4, 7; van den Doel 1996, 63; Lindblad 1989.
186. Gouda 1994, 244–45.

were based on levels of investment and historically established patterns of trade, rather than exclusionist imperial preferences. Indeed, their hold on Indonesia arguably would have come to a much earlier end if they had tried to restrict the greater powers' access to Indonesian resources.

By Dutch calculations Indonesia still provided substantial benefits, though less so than the large amounts of revenue that the Dutch had extracted in the mid-nineteenth century.[187] Calculations in the early 1930s indicated that empire remained critical for Dutch revenue and job creation. Economists Jan Tinbergen and J. B. D. Derksen calculated that one out of ten jobs in the Netherlands depended on control over Indonesia.[188] They further calculated that in 1938 Indonesia provided 13.7 percent of Dutch national income.[189] Some business and government estimates went even higher (ranging up to 50 percent).[190] Selective use of data reinforced such estimates. Some suggested that in relinquishing Indonesia the Netherlands would be reduced to the status of Denmark—a fate apparently too horrific to entertain.

But elites did not calculate the costs and benefits of empire in a broader strategic sense. While the government calculated revenues spent and gained, it did not examine the opportunity costs involved. Indeed, later research suggested that the empire retarded Dutch industrialization.[191]

A more incisive analysis would have shown how Dutch economic preeminence had waned substantially before the Second World War. The Netherlands no longer constituted Indonesia's primary import or export partner. In 1913 the Netherlands still accounted for 34 percent of Indonesia's total exports. By 1939 this had dropped to 15 percent. The U.S. share, by contrast, had risen from 2 percent to 21 percent in that same period. Dutch goods accounted for 36 percent of Indonesia's imports in 1913 but for only 15 percent in 1935. Japanese goods, only 2 percent of imports in 1913, accounted for 30 percent by 1935. Moreover, the Indonesian economy was highly export-oriented, with exports exceeding imports by about 75 percent in the 1913–1938 period.[192] Other calculations show a similar trend, with the United States accounting for an average of 9.7 percent of Indonesian imports and 13.5 percent of its exports between 1925 and 1930. Twenty percent of rubber production was in the hands of American companies.[193] In short, Dutch-Indonesian trade had declined sharply.

187. Klein 1981.
188. van Doorn 1995a, 19.
189. van den Doel 1996, 248; Baudet 1975, 434. Angus Maddison argues that the total income from abroad added 8.6 percent to the Dutch domestic product between 1921 and 1938 (Maddison 1989, 647).
190. See Gouda 1994, 241, n. 15.
191. See Campo 1980.
192. Maddison 1990; van den Doel 1996, 234.
193. Gouda 1994; Homan 1983, 125; Homan 1984, 426–27.

Moreover, as H. Baudet argues convincingly, the statistics used to calculate the alleged benefits of empire were highly suspect. For example, C. G. S. Sandberg, the title of whose book, *Indonesia Lost, Disaster Born* (*Indie Verloren, Rampspoed Geboren*), had become a pro-imperial slogan in 1914, argued that half of Dutch national income was invested in Indonesia. More accurate calculations, however, would have shown a figure of about 18 percent of national income, or even 7.5 percent.[194] Not only was the relative share of investments in Indonesia as a share of national income overstated but the profitability of the Dutch colonies was similarly inflated. If the 1920s still yielded profit margins on investments of 7 percent, by 1935–1938 those margins amounted to no more than 2–3.9 percent, hardly indicative of a goose that lays golden eggs. There was little reflection on whether those investments needed Dutch sovereignty over the islands for their protection, or whether such investments elsewhere would be more profitable. Only the high estimates surfaced in political debates.[195]

Dutch calculations about the costs and benefits of retaking Indonesia after the nationalists had declared independence in 1945 were equally suspect. The Hague's forecasts contained two major errors. First, it deflated the military budget for the overseas interventions. The minister of war in the Beel cabinet (1946–48), H. H. Fievez, presented "a militarily impossible and financially dubious" picture of the operation in Indonesia.[196] Only after Indonesian independence, in 1951, did the full costs of the police actions become clearer.

Second, the Dutch based their calculations on the separate budgetary accounts in The Hague and in Indonesia. While the costs of transporting and equipping the troops would fall on the Dutch taxpayers, the costs of maintaining and supplying the troops in Indonesia would be posted to the Indonesian government's account. The Hague thus intended that the population in Indonesia would finance the military operations after Dutch authority had been reestablished.[197]

The Dutch government could not hope to shield Indonesia as a zone of imperial preference, as Britain and France had done with their colonies. Examination of the economic relations of the Netherlands with Indonesia would have shown how the Dutch position had changed. Its so-called eco-

---

194. Baudet 1975, 438.
195. Bogaarts 1989, vol. B, 1205.
196. The description is from Bogaarts 1989, vol. A, 725.
197. In one of the more bizarre moments of the decolonization process, the Dutch government insisted that the costs of its military efforts had become part of the federal Indonesian government's debt when it granted Indonesia independence in 1949. Bogaarts 1989, vol. A, 720ff.; vol. B, 1215. The Indonesian government defaulted on this debt in 1956. See also Maas and van Oerle 1987.

nomic rationale to retake Indonesia amounted to wishful thinking and poor analysis. The earlier economic benefits no longer existed.

The Portuguese Poor Man's Empire

The economic rationale for maintaining control of the overseas territories seemed, at face value, more convincing in the Portuguese case. In the interwar period, empire was justified as a solution to the economic depression of the 1930s.[198] In the postwar period, Angola and Mozambique conveyed economic benefits. The overseas territories provided raw materials below market prices, export earnings from the colonies to other countries, precious minerals (gold and diamonds), and protected markets for Portuguese wine and finished textiles.[199]

Angola in particular yielded natural resources and agricultural commodities, especially cotton. The Portuguese textile industry employed 120,000 people and relied on the African colonies as an outlet.[200] Oil production also became increasingly attractive with rising oil prices. By the early 1970s, the Cabinda region was producing 160 million barrels a day.[201]

The territories also provided other sources of revenue. Tax revenue came from the "imposta da palhota," or hut tax, of the indigenous population. Customs duties and railroad fees paid by South Africa for the use of the port of Lourenço Marques added other benefits. Laborers working abroad, particularly in South Africa, would remit money back to their Portuguese colonies of origin, which would show up as a positive gain on the colonial balance sheet.[202]

Overall, the earnings from the African territories contributed about 5 percent of GNP, or $540 million, to the Portuguese economy.[203] Prime Minister Marcelo Caetano could thus plausibly claim that the overseas areas yielded significant gains.[204]

The overseas territories seemed all the more important given Portugal's own precarious economic position and appalling social development. As much as 40 percent of the adult population could not read or write.[205] Moreover, the more enterprising elements of the workforce migrated to more developed European countries such as France and Germany to gain much higher wages in their booming economies. Despite 6–7 percent an-

198. Birmingham 1993, 156, 164.
199. Ferreira 1974, 47–48; Maxwell 1995, 19.
200. Maxwell 1995, 141.
201. Ebinger 1976, 877.
202. Friedland 1979, 118–23. Portuguese colonials working in South African mines were paid in gold (Patrick McGowan, personal communication).
203. Maxwell 1995, 97.
204. Bender 1974, 140.
205. Blackburn 1974, 7.

nual growth in the 1960s and early 1970s Portugal ranked among the poorest European countries. GDP per capita amounted to $760. Thirty-one percent of the workforce was still employed in agriculture.[206] Decades of isolationist policies and fascist corporatism had taken their toll.

Indeed, such economic weakness was a result partially of design. "I wish," said Prime Minister Antonio Salazar to Minister of Foreign Affairs Franco Nogueira in 1963, "this country poor but independent; and I do not wish it colonized by American capital."[207] He succeeded. By 1960 foreigners owned only 1.5 percent of Portuguese industry.[208] On the one hand, the self-chosen isolation and underdevelopment of the Portuguese economy could be turned into positive arguments for maintaining the empire. A weak domestic economy thus justified an intransigent colonial position. At the same time, the availability of overseas income could be used to justify a non-European focus. At face value, maintaining Portugal's presence in Africa seemed to be a rational policy to gain much-needed foreign earnings. Angola's positive trade balance could be siphoned off to compensate for Portugal's negative trade balance.[209]

But closer scrutiny reveals how the imperialist policies of Salazar and Caetano distorted the costs of empire to the country as a whole, and veiled the contradictions that had gradually started to emerge within their policy. To combat nationalist demands for independence the metropolitan government had to open up the Portuguese economy. Increasing military expenditures required economic growth in the Portuguese homeland, and this in turn required foreign capital. Moving from self-imposed autarky thus severed the logical connection between self-isolation (from Europe and the United States) and overseas commitment.

Stemming nationalism abroad also required greater investments in development and education overseas. Even then the per capita budget allocation in Angola was only 3 percent of that in Portugal.[210] To diminish the attraction of the nationalist demands to the local population, Portugal would have had to step up its efforts at development, but it lacked the resources to do so.[211] Moreover, allocating money overseas contradicted the imperial logic in which the overseas areas were supposed to aid the weak Portuguese economy.

Such paradoxes thus required a shift from Salazar's strategy. Suspending the Portuguese economy in limbo to forestall political change could no

---

206. Pimlott 1977, 340–41.
207. Maxwell 1995, 49.
208. Pimlott 1977, 336–37.
209. Maxwell 1976, 259.
210. Bender 1972a, 359 n. 72.
211. Raby (1988, 220) makes this connection between opening up the Portuguese economy as a strategy to facilitate development in the overseas territories.

longer be reconciled with other objectives. Attracting foreign capital required a shift in focus to Europe. Indeed, between 1961 and 1967 foreign investment was almost ten times that of the 1943–1960 period.[212] Business interests increasingly came to see the European Economic Community, not the overseas territories, as Portugal's economic future.

The argument for the economic benefits of empire also did not take into account the costs of keeping more than 150,000 troops in the field. Portuguese military expenditures drained almost 7 percent of its GNP and more than 40 percent of its annual budget. The view that empire constituted an economic asset focused only on the availability of resources and the benefits of colonial remittances, not on the military costs of empire, the indirect costs such as market and investment distortions, or the opportunity costs of European exclusion.

Andrew Green suggests that a withdrawal from empire as early as 1964 would not have had a significant detrimental effect on the Portuguese economy. Even though Portugal ran up a $1 billion trade deficit with all other countries between 1960 and 1964, it still showed a positive balance of payments. Its positive trade balance with the overseas territories of only $84 million, however, cannot account for this. The reason Portugal had a positive balance of payments despite the negative balance of trade had far more to do with remittances from workers in Western Europe and increasing tourism than with the unequal terms of trade with its colonies.[213]

Moreover, if one takes the negative effects on the labor supply into account, the case for the colonial wars becomes even weaker. The war directly siphoned off labor to serve in the military, while indirectly it provided incentives to the most capable elements in the workforce to seek employment elsewhere in Europe. As a consequence, Portugal could not parlay its low-wage advantage into attracting more foreign investors.

And, if an argument could be made for maintaining Angola and Mozambique on economic grounds, that argument could hardly be extended to places such as Portuguese Guinea. Nevertheless, Lisbon decided to deploy a considerable force in Guinea (between 26,000 and 30,000 troops) to control a small territory (roughly 14,000 square miles) and a small local population (about 800,000).[214] Economically, however, it conveyed few benefits.

But the ruling Portuguese coalition did not take its cue from cost-benefit calculations for the country as a whole. Already by the 1950s the Eisenhower administration had started to question the ability of the Portuguese to hold on to their territories. Ambassador Burke Elbrick suggested to the Salazar government that the British had exported more to India after inde-

212. Raby 1988, 221; Kohler 1981, 27.
213. Green 1969, 347–48.
214. For a description of the Portuguese in Guiné (later Guinea-Bissau) see Forrest 1992.

pendence than before, and that Portugal might wish to emulate Britain's commonwealth arrangement. Foreign Minister Marcello Mathias disdainfully replied that "for us, business was never the essential question."[215] Colonization, like the Estado Novo itself, found its basis in patrimonial and functionalist organization rather than in capitalist, market-driven desire. One might, like Howard Wiarda, link it to the almost feudal organization of Salazarist corporatism. In this sense, he argues, "capitalism was not the motor force driving Portuguese colonization."[216]

Economic calculations about the merits of empire for the country as a whole did not drive Lisbon to choose to fight rather than readjust. Instead, key actors in the ruling coalition sparked its imperial desires. Imperial income rather than European trade could be used to maintain fascist corporatism at home. Keeping Portugal out of Europe and in Africa diminished demands for democracy and weakened anti-Salazarist sentiments.

The Failure of the Soviet Union's Socialist Experiment in a Capitalist World

Although I am primarily interested in the dissolution of the Soviet internal empire, the separation of the USSR from Eastern Europe and the internal dissolution of the USSR are closely related. Although the retreat from the external empire need not have precipitated the breakup of the USSR, the trading arrangements between the Soviet Union and its Council for Mutual Economic Assistance (CMEA) partners showed dynamics similar to the economic relations between Russia and the Soviet republics. In both situations empire increasingly became a liability rather than an asset. To be sure, there was no master plan envisioning retreat from Eastern Europe and then the partition of the USSR, but high officials such as Foreign Minister Eduard Shevardnadze realized by 1989 that the retreat from Eastern Europe could have dire consequences for the integrity of the USSR itself. External and internal empire were linked.[217]

The External Empire. In the immediate postwar years the external empire yielded many benefits and few costs. Valerie Bunce suggests that in many ways it formed the ideal empire, with independent states and separate economies, although de facto under Soviet political control.[218] This imposed not only fewer costs on the Soviet Union but gave indigenous Communist elites control over their local economies.

215. Quoted in Maxwell 1995, 49.
216. Wiarda 1974, 16.
217. See Wohlforth 1994–95, 119.
218. Bunce 1985.

After the Stalinist period, however, their economic fortunes required increasing Soviet support. Given its security interests, Moscow provided cheap primary products, tolerated changing terms of trade, and supported the Communist regimes (the GDR and Czechoslovakia in 1953, and Hungary and Poland in 1956) with emergency aid.[219] Moreover, it tolerated a cost calculation that disadvantaged the USSR. Given the absence of a capitalist pricing system, the prices of traded goods in the CMEA were set by calculating moving averages of the prices of goods traded on the world market. The USSR largely exported primary goods to its CMEA partners that did not accurately reflect the rise in world market prices.[220] Conversely, because the USSR bought East European finished products according to world market prices, although these were inferior to Western goods, it overpaid for finished products.

Bunce claims that these subsidies made the external empire far less attractive, with subsidies to Eastern Europe rising from 6.2 billion current dollars in 1974 to $21.7 billion by 1980. Josef Brada, by contrast, argues that these subsidies were not inherently different from the cross subsidies of partners of the European Economic Community (EEC) and that they amounted to about $10 billion by the late 1970s and early 1980s.[221] Peter Liberman, although he argues that the burdens were not that severe, quotes research suggesting that subsidies between 1970 and 1984 amounted to between $30 billion and $97 billion.[222]

Be that as it may, the subsidization of the CMEA partners combined with a stagnating economy in the USSR led some decision makers to reexamine the economic benefits of the external empire. By November 1988, Moscow was demanding hard currency for its energy shipments to its Eastern European allies.[223]

Moreover, given its ability to generate external revenue by selling primary products on the world market, the USSR had an incentive to divert these goods from subsidized trade with the CMEA to Western trading partners. In view of the plans to reform its own economy, the trading schemes with the Eastern Europeans made little sense.[224]

The Internal Empire. The internal economy of the Soviet Union created more dilemmas. Throughout its history the Soviet regime tried a variety of

---

219. Bunce 1985, 12.

220. Assessing the economic system under Brezhnev, Alec Nove states that "prices play hardly any role in shaping the volume and pattern of foreign trade." Nove 1977, 280.

221. Brada 1988, 640ff.

222. Liberman 1996, 132.

223. Wohlforth 1994–95, 114.

224. See particularly Randall Stone's (1996) discussion of how the Eastern European states tried to maximize their subsidies from the USSR.

reforms to reconcile republic economic planning with that of the Soviet system as a whole. However, from 1965 on, all-Union ministries and institutions dominated decision making.[225] With the abolition of the *sovnarkhoz* system, which attempted to provide republican leaders with greater incentives to use local knowledge, central decision making reigned supreme. In the Soviet accounting system the ratio of all-Union industrial output to union republic and local industrial output in 1965 was 49–51 percent. By 1987 production under all-Union control accounted for 61 percent and republican and local production for 39 percent.[226]

The entire system operated with input-output models generated by all-Union ministries that set targets and delegated economic output performances for all-Union factories and local production.[227] These models were based on estimates of the resources required to produce certain goods, and did not take world prices of the various inputs into account.

Consequently, in a manner not dissimilar to Russia's trade with the external empire, price distortions occurred that asymmetrically favored some republics over others. Republics that exported underpriced goods in effect subsidized the others. This was particularly the case with energy resources. Given that energy prices were lower than world prices, producers of oil and gas were net losers in interrepublic trade. In real-price terms, Azerbaijan, Turkmenistan, and, most of all, Russia subsidized the other republics.[228]

Russia subsidized many republics not only in trade but in direct budget transactions. By the late 1980s, transfers from the Soviet Union's budget accounted for 16 percent of Belorussia's revenue and for 17 percent of Armenia's. The Central Asian states depended even more on Russian largesse, with Tajikistan relying for almost half of its revenue on such transfers.[229] It could be argued, and indeed Boris Yeltsin was to do just that, that the Soviet Union drained Russian coffers.

But if the republics were, in an objective sense, dependent on good economic ties with Russia, this was not a widely held perception. Many republics argued that centralization of the economy had benefited Russia—relegating the republics to subservient status as deliverers of primary goods. Russia retained the high-value-added sectors of production. Even the Central Asian states, which were highly dependent on budget transfers from other republics, attributed their underdevelopment to Moscow's ineptitude. Uzbekistan tried to renegotiate its cotton production targets and even to bring their cotton to the world market, where it anticipated it would

225. *Report on the USSR,* April 21, 1989, p. 2.
226. *Report on the USSR,* April 21, 1989, p. 4.
227. For an overview, see Zimbalist and Sherman 1984, particularly chaps. 7–8. More comprehensive is Nove 1977, particularly chaps. 1, 2, 10.
228. Noren and Watson 1992.
229. Rubin 1994, 209.

fetch a higher price. Tajikistan, although it derived 47 percent of its revenues from all-Union transfers, nevertheless claimed that it was colonially subjugated to the benefit of the other republics.[230] "Many nationalities in the Soviet Union considered the central leadership in Moscow as the manifestation of the political dominance of the Russians in the country."[231]

Consequently, the advanced republics, such as the Baltic states, saw their immersion in a Western economic union as far more desirable than association with the Russian center.[232] Exemplifying the perspective in some of the Baltic states, Lithuanian nationalist Vytautas Landsbergis invoked analogies to Western decolonization by highlighting two paths to independence: "the model of decolonization: an agreement on moving step by step . . . [or] unilateral political action . . . and in the face of sharp political confrontation."[233]

The center had to question how long it could continue to pursue autarky. As one analysis of the Soviet record put it in 1985: "The most important remaining element of autarky under the present Soviet practice is the high degree of isolation of the economy from world markets."[234] The expanding liberalization of trade and the globalization of trade and financial markets, however, raised the question of opportunity costs. Gorbachev, recognizing the USSR's economic woes, argued:

> The objective process of internationalization of the world economy today calls for a new level of multilateral economic relations. . . . The laws of present-day economic evolution connected with increased interdependence in the world break up the insurmountable barriers between the different economic systems.[235]

At the same time as it entertained opening up the economy, the center confronted the question of whether the Soviet Union constituted a viable economic unit. While interrepublic trade was very high, the concentration was a highly artificial one.[236] Gravity models of trade generated by econo-

230. On the cotton issue, see Sheehy, *Report on the USSR* (February 24, 1989), 19–21; Gleason 1993, 353–54. On Tajikistan, see Rubin 1994, 208; Atkin 1993, 366. Roeder (1991, 215–16) similarly notes that more developed republics subsidized the less developed.

231. Khazanov 1997, 124. The Baltic states, in comparing themselves to the Scandinavian countries, thought they were subsidizing the poor Soviet economy. Lapidus, Zaslavsky, and Goldman 1992, 6.

232. Zaslavsky 1992, 74.

233. Lieven 1993, 233.

234. Ofer 1988, 54.

235. Gorbachev's address to the first session of the USSR Supreme Soviet, August 1, 1989. In Black 1989, 1990, 31. The USSR expressed a desire to join GATT and the IMF in 1988 (Rice 1991, 162).

236. IMF 1992, 7, 37. On the artificial vertical integration of the Soviet economy, see Sakwa 1993, 207; Dawisha and Parrott 1994, 11–13, 48. Indeed, production occurred largely in huge plants: "Seventy-seven percent of products were made by a single enterprise." Suny 1998, 490.

mists in the West suggested that without political constraints to this trade, the evolving pattern would look quite different.[237] Even in the USSR itself input-output models started to emerge in the early 1980s that suggested that a smaller economic unit of only several republics would be far more efficient.[238]

Had the Soviet economy continued to expand, as it had done until the early 1970s, these problems might have proven surmountable. But it became readily apparent that growth rates were declining, and indeed by the 1980s they had sunk to the lower single digits.[239] Taking inflation into account there was no growth at all. Indeed, the eighth Five-Year Plan (1965–1970) was the last that showed considerable expansion.[240] But national income statistics published by Goskomstat did not take inflation into account and thus misrepresented actual economic growth. Indeed, during the Gorbachev reforms, Russian Prime Minister Nikolai Ryzhkov lamented that he had to rely on CIA data for this information. Goskomstat claimed that Soviet national income continued to grow at several percentage points, amounting to 4.4 percent in 1988. CIA figures showed no growth.[241] Such dismal results came on top of very conservative estimates of future growth in the early Gorbachev administration but with the expectation that growth would accelerate in the 1990s.[242]

The Soviet leaders were of course keenly aware that the economy had problems and had tried a variety of reforms to improve individual incentives. However, since the Stalinist era the only reforms that had proved successful delegated responsibility to the local level. In other words, the Communist Party confronted the paradox of maintaining party control while trying to improve local decision making and economic incentives. Radical economic reform could only happen if the party relinquished control over the economy. As one observer phrased it, "The consensus is that decentralization of the economic mechanism is necessary for reforms to be successful. . . . Decentralization is resisted for ideological, political, and bureaucratic reasons."[243]

237. For a discussion of the gravity model of trade, see Baldwin et al. 1995.
238. Granberg 1993, chap. 5.
239. Nee and Lian 1994, 256–57.
240. Kagalovsky 1990, 316. Budget deficits (which multiplied fivefold from 1985 to 1989) and growing barter trade further demonstrated the gravity of the economic crisis. For further figures on the economic collapse between 1989 and 1992, see Sakwa 1993, 203–6, 235, 242.
241. On the issue of growth rates, see Tedstrom, *Report on the USSR*, February 3, 1989. On the absence of inflation figures, see *Report on the USSR*, March 3, 1989.
242. For a discussion of the poor growth rates since 1960 and Gorbachev's expectations, see Stuart 1990.
243. Toumanoff 1987, 129. For a brief discussion of various reform programs, see Tedstrom, *Report on the USSR* 1, no. 16 (April 21, 1989), 1–8.

In sum, Soviet growth rates had shown a downward trend for two decades. A variety of reforms had been tried but only those that had delegated substantial power to local decision makers had proven successful, challenging the party hierarchy. At the same time both the external and internal empires proved to be economic drains on Russia. The particular Soviet mode of account keeping and the Soviet banking system made multiple interpretations plausible.[244] The non-Russian republics could claim exploitation, while the Russian public could claim the reverse.[245] Either way, Soviet leaders increasingly doubted the strategic rationale of keeping the external empire, while to leaders in the Union Republics, and to Russian leaders most of all, the benefits of the internal empire became increasingly dubious as well.

CHANGES IN THE IMPERIAL ENVIRONMENT

The argument of this chapter that changing international conditions disadvantaged empire and large multinational entities after World War II dovetails with arguments made by others. Robert Gilpin contends that "through specialization and international trade an efficient state could gain more than through territorial expansion and conquests."[246] Richard Rosecrance likewise suggests that territorial control diminished as a state objective and that "since 1945 an environment of economic openness and growing interdependence has sustained many small states."[247] James Goldgeier and Michael McFaul submit that "the great powers gain neither more secure borders nor increased wealth by adding more territory."[248] Finally, while the argument of this chapter has primarily emphasized how changes in material factors altered the benefits of territory, it does not conflict with accounts that stress changes in ideology.[249]

These conditions did not change uniformly, nor did they affect the calculations of metropolitan elites in the same way. The smaller powers were more concerned with the economic motives for empire rather than the contributions for home defense. As minor powers their security depended on the support of other greater powers for the defense of the metropole, ir-

---

244. Statistics mattered less than the perception of those statistics; see Lapidus 1992, 54; Samonis 1991; Sakwa 1993, 207.

245. Matlock 1995, 23. Some Russians rejected the idea of Russian colonialism because "the Russians no less than others are its [socialist ideology's] victims." Solzhenitsyn 1981, 97.

246. Gilpin 1981, 132–33.

247. Rosecrance 1986, 160.

248. Goldgeier and McFaul 1992, 484.

249. See, for example, Zacher 2001. Elsewhere, I have suggested that ideational factors played less of a role in the central governments and metropolitan capitals than they did in the nationalist agendas. Spruyt 2000.

respective of their control over peripheral areas. Small states similarly had fewer options for pursuing a strategy of imperial preference, particularly if other, greater powers wished access to the regions under their control. Conversely, smaller metropolitan powers were more vulnerable to shifts in relative power sparked by nationalist movements. As I have argued, one would not have expected small states such as the Netherlands and Portugal to pursue hard-line policies. Yet they did.

Britain and France were both declining great powers. Britain arguably had weathered World War II better than France. Moreover, colonial and dominion troops had provided substantial military support for the defense of Britain and the empire overall. The economic benefits of empire, however, became less obvious with imperial preference schemes no longer permissible. France, occupied and split during the war, benefited less than Britain from its colonial holdings. Fantastic schemes of the colonies shoring up French security had proved illusory. Maintaining French control after the war required metropolitan resources on a grand scale. The economic benefits of empire were alleged but not demonstrated in fact. In short, Britain's relative position and its military and economic interests in the empire put Britain in a better position to stave off territorial adjustment, while French decision makers should have more readily conceded to nationalist demands. The reverse occurred.

The dissolution of the USSR, a superpower equal to the United States in many respects, presents perhaps the most enigmatic case. Despite economic difficulties, the center still had substantial resources under its control. Moreover, Eastern Europe and the internal empire provided a large quantity of troops to the Warsaw Pact. Although military and economic benefits were declining, the relative position of the center might very well have led to a hard-line territorial policy to keep the external and internal empires intact. Yet the USSR dissolved with little bloodshed.

In short, relative position in the international system, strategic value, or economic interests in the subject territories are insufficient explanations of territorial policy. Some states, such as Britain and the Soviet Union, arguably adopted policies that realist theory might expect. Other states, such as the Netherlands, Portugal, and to lesser extent France, adopted policies that are not well captured by strategic realist calculations. Thus, while changes in the international environment put pressure on imperial and multinational territorial orders, the various territorial policies that emerged in the metropoles and central governments were heavily influenced by domestic institutions.

CHAPTER THREE

The Hexagon or the Empire: France and the Algerian Quagmire

We must watch out not to become Montenegro.

EDMOND MICHELET, French minister of defense, 1945

In Algeria we are witnessing the decomposition of the State, and this gangrene is threatening the nation as a whole.

ROBERT DELAVIGNETTE, senior imperial administrator
in the Guy Mollet government, December 1957

Of course independence will come, but they are too stupid there to know it.

CHARLES DE GAULLE, 1957

France came late to the imperial game, obtaining substantial holdings in north and west Africa, equatorial Africa, and Southeast Asia only in the second half of the nineteenth century. Expansion into Algeria proceeded from 1830 on, until France made Algeria an integral part of France with three départements in 1870. France used Senegal as a launching platform to acquire much of west and central Africa in the second half of the nineteenth century. It established full control over Indochina by the late 1880s. Tunisia became a French protectorate only in 1883.[1] Conquest of Morocco started as late as 1907. The First World War brought further gains in the Middle East in the wake of the dissolution of the Ottoman Empire.

But no sooner had France achieved its greatest imperial extension in the interwar period than nationalist sentiments erupted in the French Middle East mandates, Indochina, and North Africa. Its much vaunted "civilizing mission" had failed. Subjects had not come to identify with France proper,

---

1. For a brief overview of this period, see Horne 1978, 30ff.; Hourani 1991, 282–317.

the hexagon of the European homeland. The crushing defeat at Germany's hands in 1940 further exposed the metropole's weakness. Thus, even as jubilation swept the country on victory over Germany on V-E Day in 1945 the Algerians revolted.

France, impoverished by the war and riven by domestic differences that were exposed by the fall of the Third Republic and the Vichy government, had to decide on its postwar imperial course, as did Britain. In chapter 2 I argued that France had good reasons to reevaluate its imperial possessions. Militarily, the overseas territories no longer benefited metropolitan defense to the extent that they once had. Economically, the future of France lay with liberalism and free trade with other Western powers, rather than with neomercantilist imperial preference schemes. The changing environment, in other words, should have precipitated policy change, or at least sparked a careful reassessment of the merits of empire. Unlike Britain, however, the governments of France opted to maintain the empire by force—with calamitous results. France suffered tens of thousands of casualties in its wars to maintain colonial control. The conflict in Indochina drained much-needed financial and military resources and still ended in defeat. The Algerian War felled many governments during the Fourth Republic and brought terrorism at home, attempted coups d'état, and the prospect of civil war.

With hindsight it might be tempting to suggest that no matter what institutions France might have had, no matter which beliefs permeated the public's mind, and no matter who was in office, the result would have been the same. That is, given French weakness and nationalist intransigence, the metropole had no choice but to fight.

That verdict would be wrong. As Tony Smith argues, at several junctures Paris did not act on compromise solutions. With meaningful Algerian representation in 1947 and a compromise in Indochina already in place in 1946, "the Indo-Chinese and Algerian revolutions might have been avoided."[2] Alistair Horne similarly believes there were turning points, such as the fall of Prime Minister Pierre Mendès-France, which forestalled a negotiated solution to Algerian demands.[3] Why were these roads not taken? Why did the French withdrawal from empire look so different from the British readjustment?[4]

The institutions of the Fourth Republic explain the lack of policy change and the failure to adjust to changed circumstances. The lack of civilian control empowered the armed forces, which had corporate interests in keeping the overseas territories, and thus they were able to de facto veto any compromise. The institutions of the Fourth Republic, furthermore, provided

2. T. Smith 1981, 134.
3. Horne 1978, 546.
4. Fry (1997) also contrasts British deliberative readjustment with the French experience.

few incentives for politicians to cater to the median voter. Instead, the multiparty system, transitory coalition governments, and the lack of party discipline provided hard-liners the opportunity to veto any changes in the status quo.

As we focus on the Algerian question and, tangentially, on other postwar colonial areas, such as Indochina, the question before us is whether the political institutions in the metropole created veto opportunities for political groups such as the military, settlers, and business interests and their allies. When such veto opportunities are plentiful the likelihood that the center's policy will cater to the general public declines, as will the likelihood that the center can act on a cost-benefit calculus to the state as a whole.

This chapter is in two parts. The first part discusses the multiple veto opportunities present in the Fourth Republic. The second part discusses the changes implemented by de Gaulle and the new constitution of the Fifth Republic. A comparison of the Fourth and Fifth Republics allows us to conduct a quasi-experiment. Many things, including popular opinion regarding Algeria and France's relative position in the international system, remained constant. However, the constitutional reforms and the crackdown on the military diminished the number of veto players and greatly expanded the power of the presidency.

THE MULTIPLE VETO POINTS OF THE FOURTH REPUBLIC

Lack of Civilian Oversight and the Military's Interests in Empire

The French army consisted of distinct metropolitan and colonial units. French conscripts and professional officers made up the Armée Métropolitaine, which could only be utilized for home defense (defined as France, Algeria, Morocco, and Tunisia). Among the colonial units, the Armée d'Afrique, garrisoned in Algeria, Tunisia, and Morocco, had European units consisting of professional military (including the Légion Etrangère and the Infanterie Légère); indigenous regiments; and mixed units. The Troupes Coloniales (La Coloniale) served largely in black Africa and the Caribbean.[5] Both the Armée d'Afrique and La Coloniale could thus be used in France, but the conscripts of the Armée Métropolitaine could not be used abroad. Because Algeria, Tunisia, and Morocco were not considered "abroad," conscripts could technically be sent there, although this only occurred after 1956 as the situation deteriorated.

This structural separation of the metropolitan army and colonial units created marked differences in strategic rationale and corporate identity. The colonial professionals held distinct perspectives from the metropolitan

5. Clayton 1988, 6–8, 25–27.

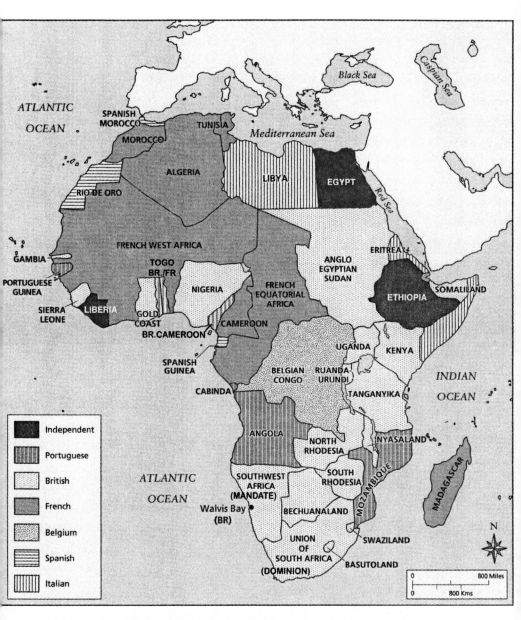

Colonialism in Africa, c. 1930. Produced by Hendrik Spruyt.

army with its conscripts. While the metropolitan home army oriented itself to the defense of France proper, the raison d'être of the overseas units hinged on the continuation of empire.

Moreover, service in the colonies often provided a fast track to promotion for officers. Money mattered as well. "Throughout the 19th century and later Coloniale personnel received various allowances that enabled them to earn more than twice the income of metropolitan officers."[6] Colonial officers and privates enjoyed unique luxuries, servants, and status, even government-sponsored brothels. Individual self-interest coincided with the corporate interests of the overseas forces.

The officers of the crack units, such as the paratroopers and the Foreign Legion, deliberately created a distinctive mystique and esprit de corps around their forces. Tellingly, by 1955 Germans still made up 47 percent of the force, while only 12 percent listed themselves as French, with a dozen or so other nationalities also represented.[7] The legion, in other words, looked quite different than metropolitan contingents. Paratroop regiments similarly developed their own unique reputations.

The colonial environment allowed considerable latitude to officers of such units, given the lack of adequate control from the center and lack of rotation. "Military officers came to see colonies as fiefs."[8] In short, the French civilian government, the principal, faced considerable loss of control over its colonial units, the agents in the field.

The French military's long-standing distrust of civilian governments and the tradition of military disobedience to civilian oversight exacerbated the problem. Indeed, tensions existed between the armed forces and public oversight throughout the Third Republic (1870–1940), surfacing for example, during the Dreyfus affair. Many members of the military placed the ignominy of the 1940 defeat on civilian shoulders. Vichy leaders Pétain, Laval, and others settled all too comfortably into a military government under the wings of the Nazi regime. De Gaulle in turn resisted his nominal superiors in the Vichy government. And de Gaulle, hero of liberated France, repudiated "politics as usual" less than a year after the end of the war. Indeed, when he finally returned to politics in 1958, he returned as the "antisystem" strongman who would rectify the incompetence of the Fourth Republic.

Other factors further diminished the effectiveness of civilian control.[9] For one, military units exercised a variety of functions besides defense of the overseas territories. Administration, police protection, involvement

6. Clayton 1988, 9.
7. Horne 1978, 169.
8. Clayton 1988, 34.
9. Furniss (1964, 2, 3) argues that the army believed that its colonial mission was vital. Overall, "it is difficult to imagine a more thoroughly politicalized [sic] army."

with infrastructural projects, all blended civilian tasks and military functions—in Huntington's analysis, an indication of a lack of civilian control.[10]
Moreover, a well-entrenched colonial army lobby had established itself in
the metropole decades before the decolonization era. Finally, the very fact
that a quarter of all active generals in 1947 came from La Coloniale made
it impossible to reduce their influence in the armed forces.[11]

As if organizational culture, material interests, and functional diffusion
were not problems enough for civilian government, the domestic situation
in France and the international situation exacerbated the problem. As
Michael Desch points out, the lack of immediate external threat, combined
with a high level of internal threat to the state, diminished civilian control.[12] The military explicitly took political instability in Paris as a pretext
for intervention. Moreover, as Deborah Avant notes, the more divided the
principal the more likely the armed forces will be able to circumvent civilian dictates.[13] With government instability in the center, the principal was
in no position to curtail agent defection.

The lack of oversight and the armed forces' corporate interest in continuing overseas control surfaced first in Indochina. When a negotiated solution seemed possible in Vietnam in the immediate aftermath of World War
II, the military dismissed the Vietnamese settlement as a new Munich. Admiral Thierry d'Argenlieu took unilateral action to separate Cochin China
(the southern section of contemporary Vietnam) from Tonkin and Annam
in order to isolate the Vietminh nationalists.[14] The resulting conflict led
France to deploy a force of 200,000 troops at its peak. At the end of seven
years of war, 11,000 Frenchmen had been killed as well as 7,500 legion-
naires, 4,500 black and North African soldiers, and 45,000 Indochinese
troops serving under the French.[15] The severe casualties and metropolitan
indifference only crystallized the military's disdain for civilian authority—
which would subsequently play a role in North Africa.[16]

A similar situation developed in Morocco and Tunisia when local administrators and the military subverted metropolitan decision making. In 1950,
the Socialist and Communist Parties seemed willing to concede the
prospects of ultimate independence. Foreign Minister Robert Schuman described the French delegation as "leading Tunisia towards the full development of her resources and towards the independence that is the ultimate

10. Berstein (1993, 34) notes how the officers in Algeria were unwilling to give up their
"administrative, social, health, and political responsibilities."
11. Clayton 1988, 40.
12. Desch 1999.
13. Avant 1994.
14. Devillers 1974, 279; Rioux 1987, 92–93, 148.
15. Clayton 1988, 160. Rioux (1987, 150) notes a larger number of Vietnamese forces.
16. Horne 1978, 177.

goal for all the territories of the French Union."[17] The military and colons, however, quickly rallied to oppose the initiative and rounded up local nationalists. A hard-line position particularly emerged in Morocco around Resident-General Alphonse Juin, who supported Moroccan traditionalists against the nationalists.[18] When the leader of the Radical Party Mendès-France came to power, he promised peace in Indochina in thirty-three days, as well as a political solution to the problems in Tunisia and Morocco.[19] Although only 11 percent of the metropolitan population believed force would be necessary to settle the demands of the North African nationalists, Paris nevertheless had to deploy 41,000 troops in Tunisia and 106,000 in Morocco—in part to resist unilateral action by French hard-liners.[20] Only the more pressing demands for a solution to the Algerian War made further progress on Tunisian and Moroccan independence possible.

As the Algerian War increased in intensity, the metropolitan efforts increased commensurately. At the outbreak of the war (1954) the army in Algeria numbered no more than 80,000. By late 1957, at the peak of deployment, there were 415,000 men under arms, of which 57 percent were conscripts.[21] Conversely, the nationalist forces numbered somewhere between sixty thousand and one hundred thousand, although, as with all such conflicts, the presence of many irregulars in the ranks makes precise estimates exceedingly difficult.[22]

The Algerian War required not only ever greater sacrifices but Paris increasingly started to lose control over events.[23] The armed forces, particularly the paratroop regiments, refused to implement dictates from the metropole and obstructed civilian efforts at finding a compromise solution. They physically harassed and threatened dispatched civilian officials who did not meet their demands, as happened with Prime Minister Mollet's first choice for minister resident of Algeria. Metropolitan governments could only install officials with the approval of the local armed forces.[24]

The Suez crisis of 1956 not only widened the rift between the United States and France it also eroded the military's confidence in civilian leader-

17. Rioux 1987, 146.
18. Williams 1966, 355, 366–370; Hargreaves 1996, 161–62.
19. Horne 1978, 68.
20. Clayton 1988, 163, 170. For popular opinion in the metropole see Ageron 1976, 258.
21. Clayton 1988, 177; Betts 1985, 204; Lustick 1993, 134–37. Rioux mentions a total force of 450,000 by the summer of 1957, which had doubled in six months by Mollet's decision to send conscripts (Rioux 1987, 268).
22. Horne 1978, 321.
23. For an overview of such events, see Lustick 1993, 258–65; for a full discussion, see Horne 1978.
24. Civilian leaders also abdicated their responsibilities under such pressure. Minister Resident Lacoste "handed over full responsibility and power for the restoration of order to General Massu and his Tenth Paratroop Division" in January 1957. Rioux 1987, 283.

ship.[25] Defeat had been snatched from victory, at least so it appeared to the military, and the episode had strengthened the hand of Egyptian president Gamal Abdel Nasser, who was considered an accomplice in the Algerian revolution.

As the likelihood of metropolitan concessions to the nationalists grew, opposition by the military intensified. The army repeatedly warned that it would not tolerate a government inclined to conciliation. Indeed, the government increasingly came to believe its only choices were a coup d'état by the armed forces or bringing de Gaulle back.[26] Even de Gaulle (who came to power in 1958) became a target.[27] The counterterror by the military and by splinter groups that had broken away from the armed forces in conjunction with hard-line settler militias reached such proportions that even French nationals who were willing to negotiate with the nationalists were treated as hostiles. Until the very end, the OAS (Organisation d'Armée Secrete) continued to torture and assassinate nationalists and French compromisers in Algeria and it engaged in terrorism in France itself.

By pressuring civilian leaders to follow their lead and, extra-institutionally, by disobeying civilian rule the army de facto vetoed possibilities for a negotiated solution.

Multiple Vetoes and Institutional Stalemate

Much of the institutional design of the Fourth Republic was an attempt to deal with the weaknesses of the Third Republic—of which Sir Denis Brogan remarked that it was "a machine so well provided with brakes and safety-valves that it comes slowly to a state of immobility."[28] Unfortunately, that must also be the verdict on the Fourth Republic. The carefully crafted constitutional design and electoral system allowed for so many veto points that a consistent territorial policy never could emerge.

The Third Republic, with its two-round single-member electoral system, had generated a multiparty parliament. But weak party discipline and government instability wreaked havoc on the political process. The Fourth Republic consequently turned to proportional representation of party lists and multimember districts to prevent such an outcome.[29]

The election of the members of the Fourth Republic's Constituent Assembly produced three main parties: the Communists (Parti Communiste Français—PCF), the Socialists (Section Française de l'Internationale

---

25. Horne 1978, 163.

26. Williams 1966, 59–60, 370–72.

27. For a gripping discussion of these episodes, see Horne 1978. For de Gaulle's description of "destiny's decision" to spare him, see de Gaulle 1971, 130.

28. Quoted in Williams 1966, 9.

29. Browne and Hamm 1996.

Ouvrière—SFIO), and the Christian Democrats (Mouvement Républicaine Populaire—MRP), each with roughly 25 percent of the vote. The rest was divided among the Conservatives (an alliance of right-wing members—confusingly, sometimes also described as Independents or Moderates, as they tended to call themselves) and the Radical Party. The MRP preferred a bicameral legislature with a relatively strong executive, while the Socialists and Communists preferred a unicameral legislature and a weaker executive, because the senate in the Third Republic had been a bastion of conservatism.[30] De Gaulle argued against the constitution because it lacked substantial powers for the executive. A first referendum on the new constitution failed, but a second referendum in October 1946 just barely passed, with 9.3 million in favor of it, 8.1 million against, and 8 million abstaining.

The Fourth Republic had few constitutional veto points. It became essentially a unicameral legislative system that could withdraw support from the prime minister. The presidency had minor responsibilities, primarily during the formation phase. Finally, the system lacked judicial review in the American sense.

By contrast, the system created multiple partisan veto points (as delineated in chapter 1) in the Constituent Assembly. First, it used a proportional electoral system. Second, multiple parties with divergent preferences populated the legislature. Third, the legislature dominated the executive. Fourth, executive authority depended on support from multiparty cabinet coalitions.

In the immediate aftermath of the war, a condominium of political interests still seemed possible among the three big parties. The PCF, SFIO, and the MRP covered the spectrum with four-fifths of the 586 seats in the 1945 assembly. And, given their wartime roles in the resistance, they could also hope for the approval of the Gaullists.[31] Tripartisme, however, soon unraveled. The PCF stubbornly clung to Stalinist Marxism, a position increasingly unattractive to the rest of the electorate after 1947. Consequently, they became less viable as a coalition partner, and they retreated to the role of antisystem party.

The Gaullists remained unconvinced of the virtues of the Fourth Republic's institutions. De Gaulle had argued in his Bayeux speech of 1946 for an executive over and above the parties.[32] Failing to achieve their aim, the Gaullists formed their own antisystem organization, the Rassemblement du Peuple Français or "Rally of the French People" (RPF), rather than establishing a traditional party.

30. Neumann 1960, 221ff; Rioux 1987, 59.
31. Williams 1966, 23.
32. De Gaulle 1971, 307.

Consequently, two parties, the Communists and the RPF, made themselves in principle unavailable for coalitions. The remaining parties thus continuously had to operate with weak majorities no matter what coalitions they formed. Cabinet instability became the norm. From September 1944, when de Gaulle formed an interim government, until 1958, when the Fourth Republic fell, twenty-six governments came and went.

In 1951 the "system parties" tried to mitigate the consequences of the Communist and RPF exodus through electoral reforms. The reforms allowed for the linking of party lists (*apparentement*) and the use of the majority principle. If one party gained a majority in a district it would take all seats. More important, if the linked parties could gain a majority, the alliance would receive all the seats in the multimember district. Even if allied parties did not directly take the overall majority, it allowed a more favorable allocation of remainder seats through the d'Hondt method of seat allocation.[33] The Communists and Gaullists lost out because as independents they did not ally with others. "The French 1951–6 system was deliberately engineered against the largest parties and in favor of the medium-sized parties."[34] Indeed, it prevented the majority of seats going to the nonsystem parties, which would have earned 172 seats (Communists) and 143 seats (Gaullists), out of 627, in the 1951 election if the old system still had been in effect. Apparentement had another perverse effect. Because alliances mitigated the electoral problems of small and midsize parties, it led to an increase in the number of parties.

Although the pull of the Communists and Gaullists was diminished, this only solved part of the problem. Because a limited number of parties were available for a ruling coalition, only a finite number of individuals were available for ministerial seats. Parliament divided into *ministrables,* those who had been or could again be ministers in a cabinet and those unlikely to ever gain such a position. Ministers came and went through a revolving door. Cabinets would fall, but ministers would return, whether in their old or new position. Robert Schuman, for example, returned several times as minister of foreign affairs across a variety of coalition cabinets.

The price of bringing down a coalition was, consequently, low. Unlike the Westminster system, voting against party leadership did not entail the possibility of a new government with dramatically new policies. Representatives could switch allegiances when convenient. "Party discipline over its parliamentarians was weak, that over ministers weaker still."[35]

33. Lijphart 1994, 39, 45–46, 134.
34. Lijphart 1994, 70, 135; Williams 1966, 42, 145, 327–29.
35. Rioux 1987, 286. Duncan MacRae argues that the intraparty divisions revolved around the *ministrables,* who supported one another across parties, since they had to form the coalition governments, and the party militants who rejected compromise between parties. MacRae 1967, 5.

Party discipline varied across the spectrum. Ironically, the party with the greatest discipline was the party that functioned outside the system: the PCF.[36] The MRP, the Radical Party, and the Conservatives parties showed greater disloyalty. The MRP feared that imposing discipline would force its members to choose between its left and right wings. The Radicals were divided between Mèndesistes and anti-Mèndes members.

The importance of catering to local interests further weakened party cohesion. True, the parties drew up lists for each electoral district, but despite the lists, elections retained a local flavor. Party control could not bypass a popular local politician, since that would mean abdicating that seat to another party. A parliamentarian had to campaign as an individual entrepreneur. "He had to rely on his own reputation, activity, financial resources, and friends for his campaign."[37] Overall, this system gave local groups and organized interests considerable influence.[38]

With multiple parties in close proximity to one another, party elites contended for voters on their immediate left and right. They did not need to orient themselves to a median voter but instead tried to occupy a particular niche on the political spectrum. Come election time, parties vigorously contested votes on either side of their position. The Socialists could not ally with the Communists, because they were unacceptable to a broader coalition. Yet the Socialists had to be careful not to move too far to the right, since the Communists could still pull 20 percent of the vote. At the same time they feared the erosion of their party by the Radicals and Mendès-France, which occupied the center of the political stage. Mendèsisme in the mid-1950s confronted Socialists as well as the Christian Democratic MRP. The Right too was divided. Antoine Pinay, Joseph Laniel, and René Coty appealed particularly to the agricultural and colonial lobbies that financed them. They, however, feared the Poujadists, a new conservative movement that emerged in 1953, and the hard-liners on the Algerian question that operated even further to their right.[39] Politicians thus sought to gain the floating vote, but this "was not a single group in the centre but a series of grouplets in the interstices between the main parties."[40]

Consequently, no party wanted to be blamed for abandoning the French abroad, especially for losing Algeria.[41] The Christian Democrats were keen

36. Williams 1966, 115, 428–34. The other nonsystem party, the Gaullists, lacked party discipline, however, partially as a result of its informal organization.

37. Williams 1966, 71, 340–42.

38. According to Williams (1966, 411): "It was the weakness of the political system and not their own intrinsic strength that gave most of the groups their opportunities." See also 269–75, 375.

39. For discussions of these divisions before the elections of 1956, see Rioux 1987, 256–58.

40. Williams 1966, 332.

41. For a discussion of the general lack of accountability, see Williams 1966, 351–52, 436, 471.

to show that they could be as tough as the Right. Even Socialist Prime Minister Mollet switched to a harder line when faced by pieds noirs and domestic political opposition.

During election time all system parties also had to appease voters that might defect to antisystem competitors. The latter had in essence a free ride. Not willing to take part in governing the country, the Communists, Gaullists, and later the Poujadists limited themselves to external critique. They could draw votes away in protest of a policy reversal, but they could not be blamed for a policy that did not work out as intended.

During coalition formation, the opposite dynamic prevailed. System parties had to demonstrate a willingness to compromise in order to be viable coalition partners. System parties had to show their opposition to the antisystem parties. Thus, while the Socialists at times seemed more eager to compromise with the Algerian nationalists, they also engaged in hard-line politics to show their ability to function in a broader coalition with a center-right orientation. Although Mollet had received Communist support during cabinet formation, he moved further to the right once in office, since he needed votes beyond the Communists'. "Mollet responded to the demands of Fourth Republic coalition politics."[42]

The Communists, by contrast, hoping for a left front, were eager to appease the Socialists in an attempt to lure them from the Center.[43] When Mendès-France resigned his post as minister of state in the Socialist Mollet cabinet to protest the hardening of his Algerian policy, the Communists, in a telling example of coalitional politics, voiced no opinion. "They still nurtured hopes for a Popular Front with the Socialists, and it was for this tactical consideration, that the Communist deputies decided not to condemn openly what they in fact opposed."[44]

French multipartyism suffered from other complications. In this cluttered system of competing parties and a large antisystem block, small parties (such as François Mitterrand's Union Démocratique et Socialiste de la Résistance—UDSR) could become important players. More important, the MRP and the Radicals were crucial to most coalitions. Indeed, the MRP sat in government for all but two and half years of the Fourth Republic.[45] However, given the particularly weak discipline within those parties, not only did the parties play key pivotal roles but so did small groups of individuals within the parties.

Lack of credible commitment hampered elite bargaining even further. Party leaders under tripartisme could enforce bargains and keep their rank and file in check. When tripartisme fell apart, and individual entrepreneur-

42. Lustick 1993, 246.
43. Rioux 1987, 288.
44. Rioux 1987, 267.
45. Williams 1966, 21, 181, 475–76.

ship began to outweigh party loyalty, leaders "could never commit their troops."[46]

Finally, because parties and individual preferences fluctuated widely, a variety of party alliances became feasible across issues. The MRP would vote with the Socialists, the Radicals, and the Conservatives to maintain the Fourth Republic against the antisystem forces. But the Radicals tended to vote with the Conservatives and the Gaullists on colonial issues. Yet other alliances were formed on the schools issue, clerical matters, and the European Economic Community.[47]

No government could carry through a sustained policy because there was never a consistent majority. The Mèndes-France government might have come the closest to doing so. In 1954, Mendès-France, as premier, had moved Tunisia and Morocco closer to independence—against the opposition of his party's own right wing. Yet he feared that negotiations with the Algerian nationalists would lead the pieds noirs lobby and their Assembly allies to bring down his ruling coalition overnight.[48] Even the 1956 election, in which a moderate center-left majority campaigned against "the majority of Dien Bien Phu," thus suggesting the possibility of a negotiated peace in Algeria, could not provide a clear victor.[49]

This lack of a clear majority befuddled every cabinet of the Fourth Republic.[50] By the middle of the 1950s, Communists, Gaullists, Poujadists, and various members of the Assembly on the left and right had created a permanent opposition of about two hundred deputies. Majorities thus had to be found among the remaining four hundred.[51] Four governments from Mendès-France through Bourgès-Manoury withdrew from possible compromise solutions with the Algerian nationalists out of fear of jeopardizing their majority support.[52]

To make matters worse the public was only sporadically consulted, despite the fluctuation in governments. Aside from four referenda, largely to set up the constitution of the Fourth Republic, there were only six general elections: two in 1945, and one in 1946, 1951 (with the new electoral rules), 1956, and 1958.[53] Public opinion on Algeria thus only imperfectly filtered into the decision making of the governments.

In sum, low costs in bringing down a government and weak party discipline destabilized every government. Party members catered to their local

46. Williams 1966, 491.
47. Williams 1966, 32.
48. Horne 1978, 99.
49. Rioux 1987, 259, 262.
50. For a summary of the problems of the Fourth Republic, see Macrae 1967, chap. 12.
51. Rioux 1987, 285.
52. Lustick 1993, 241.
53. Williams 1966, appendix 5.

constituencies and interest groups. And party leaders sought to fortify their own niche positions rather than try to capture some broad segment of the population.

> Outside government, private pressure-groups found their task facilitated by the indiscipline of parties as well as the weakness of the executive. . . . In France perpetual coalitions obscured responsibility. No party . . . was competing for the rich prize of a central floating vote. There was none.[54]

Incentives for Politicians to Cater to Civilian Interest Groups

With unstable governments, thin majorities in the Assembly, and weak party discipline, organized interests could target individual members across party lines. The army and settlers could count on the Right and rogue members in the SFIO, the MRP, the Radicals, and the Gaullists to protect their aims.[55] "The general indecision of all the political parties toward the Algerian problem . . . favoured the organization of direct pressure on the parliamentarians by the most determined defenders of the French presence."[56]

Public actors had strategic reasons to cater to hard-liners and provide private goods for their niche clienteles, rather than public goods that might appeal to the broader electorate. The threat to bring coalitional governments down gave such parliamentarians considerable leverage on overall policies. As Ian Lustick observed, "The particular way competition of power was structured thus gave a veto over Algerian policy to those parties and parliamentarians who combined strong views on the subject with political eligibility."[57] Michael Fry makes a similar assessment: "Successive British and French governments calculated the political consequences at home of committing to or opposing decolonization. Those consequences were marginal in Britain for both parties, crucial in France for Socialists and Gaullists alike."[58]

Business Stands on the Sidelines. But who availed themselves of these veto opportunities? Although the opposition of the military and its influence on metropolitan decision making has been studied in great detail, and discussed above, less work has been done on the influence of civilian groups such as business associations and settler organizations. British business

---

54. Williams 1966, 373. See also Kahler 1984. For a broad overview of the Fourth Republic, see Rioux 1987.
55. Lustick 1993, 154.
56. Rioux 1987, 290.
57. Lustick (1993, 241) notes the "lowest common denominator approach to the Algerian question."
58. Fry 1997, 126.

interests have received some attention, but the history of French firms and their interaction with the government still shows substantial gaps.[59] No doubt the Parti Colonial lobbied vociferously at the turn of the century, but whether this constitutes evidence of a causal linkage with French imperialism or simply an additional factor remains a subject of speculation.

It is clear, however, that the colonial lobby favored protectionist measures, so as to make the empire self-supporting and to guarantee markets for metropolitan products. During the interwar period its position gained considerable support. The automobile industry, for example, substantially benefited from extending French tariffs in 1930 to the rest of the empire. While 26 percent of French automobiles went to the empire in 1927, by 1932 57.6 percent had such destinations.[60] The colonial lobby also supported modernization and development of the colonies—the mise-en-valeur argument—to make the colonial enterprises more profitable and to enhance the purchasing power of indigenes.

But, as noted earlier, criticism of preferential policies emerged simultaneously. Paul Bernard, an expert on Indochina, noted in a series of publications between 1934 and 1938 that the higher than world market prices and artificial trading patterns would harm the metropolitan economy.[61] Moreover, if colonial products were given privileged access, and if the overseas areas gradually modernized, their products would compete with metropolitan products. Thus, the association of wheat farmers, among others, protested the extension of preferences that would expand colonial imports into France of Indochinese rice and other competing goods. Indeed, whereas 87 percent of Indochinese rice in 1928 went to countries other than France, by 1938 73 percent went to the metropole.[62]

These competing arguments resurfaced after the war. The economic stakes in Indochina were relatively slight compared to those in North Africa. Cambodia and Laos had few plantations. Therefore the absence of such direct investments did not spark business opposition.[63] Their independence came swiftly. Vietnamese development, however, was more advanced, and the country had received a larger share of French direct investment. Some local businesses thus opposed decolonization, but they were relatively disorganized.

Much more was at stake with the colonies in Africa. On the one hand, the arguments within the business community, particularly in declining industries, echoed those of the late 1930s. They feared exposure to foreign competition, hoped for protected markets, and claimed that French well-being

59. Hopkins 1987, 127.
60. Marseille 1984, 198–200.
61. Marseille 1984, 242–47.
62. See Ageron 1982, 10; Marseille 1984, 212–13, 235; 1985, 134.
63. Devillers 1974, 299.

depended on maintenance of the colonies. Pierre Moussa, director of economic affairs at the overseas ministry, argued their cause by claiming that five hundred thousand metropolitan French depended for their livelihood on intra-imperial trade.[64] Business perceptions differed from British economic views. British firms were more competitive on the world market and more accustomed to free trade.[65]

Not all French business, however, took that position. The employers of the Union Française argued in the postwar years against preferential trading blocs with high tariffs. Such systems tended to retard competition and thus much-needed modernization—echoing Bernard's argument of twenty years earlier. French agriculture, particularly in the south, where Mediterranean products were grown, feared competition from North African commodities.[66] By the early 1950s wine exports to France had come to account for almost half of Algeria's exports.[67] Polls indicated that opposition to the Algerian colons was strongest in the south of France.[68] Small landholders in France argued that "empire leads to the destruction of traditional farmers."[69]

French firms after 1945 diminished their stake in the colonies. Between 1915 and 1929, private investment had been roughly seven times that of public investment. In the 1930s they drew almost even, with private investment only one and half times that of government. But, in the 1940–1958 period, public investment, following the mise-en-valeur logic, was five times that of the private sector.[70] Profit margins declined as well. In 1937–39, the profit rates for mines, industry, and plantation agriculture had been roughly 27, 12, and 21 percent, respectively. By 1956–58 their profit margins had declined to 11, 9, and 10 percent. As Miles Kahler demonstrates, profit margins accelerated briefly after World War II and the Korean War, but these were ephemeral.[71]

The stake of French firms in empire also varied by region depending on local property laws and modes of settlement. Algeria consisted of many small holdings and few big business interests. Tunisia and Morocco, however, had relatively large agribusinesses. In Tunisia in 1953, about four thousand European farmers produced about 20 billion francs worth of goods, whereas the five hundred thousand smaller Tunisian holdings produced only 45 billion francs worth.[72] Western and Equatorial Africa

64. Marseille 1984, 30.
65. See Kahler 1981, 388ff., and T. Smith 1981, 109.
66. Marseille 1985, 134–35.
67. Marseille 1984, 62.
68. Ageron 1976, 272.
69. Ageron 1982, 17.
70. Marseille 1984, 104–6.
71. Marseille 1984, 130; Marseille 1985, 138, Kahler 1981, 394ff.
72. Rioux 1987, 487 n. 26.

became the domain of large holding companies, with multiple sectors under their control.[73]

Consequently, some smaller businesses feared decolonization. But with declining profit margins and declining assets in Africa, many of the larger companies had less reason to do so. Even holders of site-specific assets favored some form of compromise. Because their assets were not mobile and could easily be seized, and because these corporations believed that the nationalists would need their technological and marketing expertise, they believed that a negotiated solution would best serve their interests in the long run.[74]

Coquery-Vidrovitch remarks that there emerged a sentiment for decolonization by the Right, "not motivated by democracy, but by money, and the indifference of the French people."[75] Jacques Marseille similarly comes to the conclusion that "it is unlikely that business interests could have been the pressure group behind those politicians hostile to every form of independence."[76] Philip Williams, who suggests that "many of the richest capitalists . . . were in favour of conciliating Moslem nationalism," shares his opinion.[77]

The Colons Dig In. The most intense opposition to decolonization came from the small landholders and settlers in the overseas territories. Why were these settlers so opposed to negotiation, and how did the institutional climate of the Fourth Republic allow them to influence decision making? First, the French empire created large settler populations. North Africa was by far the primary area of settlement, with Tunisia and Morocco having significantly fewer settlers than Algeria.[78] By 1945, almost one million people, or one out of every seven inhabitants in Algeria, were considered French, and more than 80 percent of them had been born there.[79]

Land tenure patterns correlated with degrees of settlement. Morocco saw less alienation of land, perhaps about 750,000 acres. And, although alienation occurred in Tunisia, these were primarily large estates with absentee owners. "By 1915 colons owned about one-fifth of the cultivated land. Comparatively few of them were smallholders."[80] In Algeria, by contrast, al-

73. Fieldhouse 1971; Kahler 1981.

74. See also Kahler 1981, 389.

75. Coquery-Vidrovitch (1975, 610) citing Delavignette.

76. Marseille 1985, 139.

77. Williams 1966, 376. Kahler concurs (1981, 401).

78. Clayton 1988, 139. The European population in Tunisia made up 6.7 percent of the total population of 3.8 million. Rioux 1987, 486 n. 26. Also see Fry 1997, 140.

79. In 1938, figures show that they accounted for 988,000 out of a total population of 7.2 million. This was 39 percent of all French overseas. Marseille 1976, 530; Hourani 1991, 270, 291, 369.

80. Hourani 1991, 295. See also Kahler 1981 on land tenure patterns.

though many of the French lived in the larger cities, many others had also managed to appropriate some of the better agricultural areas. Already by 1891, there were two hundred thousand peasant farmers.[81]

The colons enjoyed privileged legal status, as full French citizens, and owned assets that could not be moved.[82] As small holders with limited education they also enjoyed a lifestyle that they could not hope to duplicate if they returned to the metropole. Consequently, "the core of resistance to decolonization could be found in the agricultural sector."[83]

The colons were institutionally overrepresented. The decision in 1947 to relax the criteria for citizenship and the introduction of a dual electoral system in the colony did little to ameliorate the problem. The two-college system deprived the Muslim Algerians of effective voice in both the local and national assemblies, by giving French colons and Algerians equal representation, despite the numerical superiority of the Muslim population.[84] And when the municipal elections of 1947 demonstrated the depth of popular support for the nationalists, the pieds noirs administration made sure that "the 1948 elections for the new Algerian Assembly . . . turned out to be a masterpiece of rigging."[85] Although the government had been warned that the Messali (nationalist) vote might gain 90 percent of Second College seats, the final tally showed them gaining only nine out of seventy-four seats and the "Beni-Oui-Ouis," the government sanctioned yes-men, gaining fifty-five seats. Between 1948 and 1951 the vast majority of Muslim seats thus went to supporters of the metropole, and the nationalists withdrew from participation in such formal bodies.[86] The situation in other North African states was similar. In the Tunisian local elections of May 1953 only 8 percent of the Tunisian population took part, as opposed to 46 percent of the colons.[87]

Given the institutional weaknesses of the French metropolitan governments and the incentives for politicians to cater to niche clienteles, the settlers could push their objectives forward through supporting parliamentarians who were willing to expound their views. The Radical Party in particular received considerable financial support from the colons, but it was not alone.[88]

When institutional voice proved insufficient the settlers exercised their veto by extra-institutional methods. They openly allied with the intransi-

81. Fieldhouse 1971, 618.

82. Indeed, after the war virtually all of them moved back to France, having no future in an independent Algeria. Betts 1985, 207, 210; Horne 1978, 533.

83. Kahler 1981, 390.

84. Lustick 1993, 132.

85. Horne 1978, 70–71.

86. Clayton 1988, 42, 174.

87. Rioux 1987, 213.

88. Rioux 1987, 210–12; Williams 1966, 374–75.

gent elements in the military and the local administration that resisted any negotiations. Through vociferous protests they forced Socialist Prime Minister Mollet to reverse the appointment of General Georges Catroux—who had brokered the compromise with Morocco—as minister resident in Algeria.[89] They got the hard-line Robert Lacoste instead. Going even further, the hard-liners organized militias and counterterror groups of their own.[90] By late 1959 the pieds noirs militia amounted to 22–25,000 men, embedded within a larger network of 100,000 organized hard-liners.[91] Ultimately, the Organisation Armée Secrète (OAS) attacked Muslims and Frenchmen who compromised with them alike. Thus de Gaulle was undoubtedly correct in his assessment about the intransigent French in Algeria: "For the settlers, the maintenance of the status quo seemed vital, whatever the cost to France."[92]

Silencing the Nationalist Vote

Despite French claims of acculturation and incorporation, non-European indigenes were decidedly second-class citizens in North Africa. Even Algeria, administratively supervised by the Ministry of the Interior since 1870 and thus institutionally equivalent to one of the metropolitan départements, did not enjoy the juridical status of French administrative units. Acquisition of French citizenship, since Napoleon III's decree in 1865, required renunciation of the legal status of the Koran.[93] By 1906, only 1,400 indigenous Algerians had obtained French citizenship. Slight changes were made after 1919 but with little effect. Just before World War II in French West Africa (in seven of the territories) only 72,000 noncolonists were deemed citizens.[94] The distinction between subject and citizen was not insignificant. Subjects could be made to perform forced labor and pay higher taxes.[95]

Indigenous resistance increased. French efforts to draft more troops during World War I led to revolt in Senegal. In the interwar period North African resistance erupted in various places.[96] And in the Middle East, Arab nationalism demanded independence for the French mandates.

The metropole responded to such nationalist demands through repression rather than negotiation, even though there were some champions for

89. Horne 1978, 148–51.
90. Horne 1978, 501–31.
91. Lustick 1993, 279, 291ff.
92. de Gaulle 1971, 41.
93. Hurewitz 1979, doc. 36, pp. 142–45.
94. Ageron 1982, 14.
95. Fieldhouse 1971, 615.
96. On uprisings in Morocco and activism in Algeria, see Hourani 1991, 347–49. On Tunisia, see L. Anderson 1986, chap. 8; Hurewitz 1979, doc. 53.

reform, such as minister without portfolio Maurice Violette former governor of Algeria. The Blum-Violette Bill (1936) promised extension of citizenship without the necessity of renouncing the Koranic legal status.

> But experience has shown that it was impossible to continue treating as subjects without essential political rights French natives of Algeria . . . who for family or religious reasons cannot give up their personal status. . . . It is therefore fitting to resolve the problem . . . without touching their personal status.[97]

Hard-line pressure, particularly from the colons in Algeria, killed the bill before it was ever put on the table.

The collapse of the Third Republic and German occupation gave new life to the nationalists. In Cochin China the Namky uprising of 1940 was put down by force with 155 individuals executed and 175 receiving life imprisonment.[98] In the Middle East nationalists achieved greater success, partially due to Britain, which sought Arab nationalist support against Vichyist French forces in Syria.[99] In Algeria, however, the Sétif uprising, which broke out on May 8, 1945 as Germany was capitulating, received a harsh response.[100]

Rather than cultivating local leaders with whom conditions for a transfer of power could be negotiated, Paris refused to make concessions. In doing so it eroded any basis for local elites who could operate as an intermediary. Jules Gambon, governor-general in Algeria, had presciently recognized the problem as early as 1894:

> We did not realize that in suppressing the forces of resistance in this fashion, we were also suppressing our means of action. The result is that we are today confronted by a sort of human dust on which we have no influence and in which movements take place which are to us unknown.[101]

Little changed over fifty years in the metropolitan mind. The preamble to the Brazzaville conference report of 1944 stated that "the goals of the civilizing work accomplished by France in the colonies exclude any idea of autonomy, all possibility of evolution outside the French bloc of the Empire: the eventual constitution, even in the future of self-government in the colonies, is denied."[102] Hard-line responses had worked before the war and were expected to work again.

97. Hurewitz 1979, doc. 116. See also Horne 1978, 36–37.
98. Chonchirdsin 1997, 288–90.
99. Mickelsen 1976. On the Lebanese issue, see Dallek 1994.
100. French suppression of the revolt might have killed as many as six to eight thousand Muslims. Rioux 1987, 90.
101. Cited in Horne 1978, 37.
102. Cited in T. Smith 1981, 97. Also see Rioux 1987, 86; Emerson 1960, 33.

Moreover, nationalist movements could only be successful, in the eyes of the French government, if external powers supported them. For example, the French government believed that it could root out feeble Indochinese nationalism by neutralizing Soviet support for Vietnam, which France hoped to achieve by distancing itself from the United States.[103] Similarly, the Algerian rebels were estimated to number no more than eight hundred poorly equipped men in 1954.[104] Thus, they could only survive thanks to support from Egypt. A hard-line policy toward Nasser would erode the Algerian nationalist movement.[105] The center continued to misread the depth of nationalist sentiment and the strength of local organization.

Institutional reforms to give indigenous populations some measure of voice did not succeed in curtailing Algerian nationalism. The French Union, for which the groundwork was laid in 1944, attempted to redress the worst excesses of past colonial policies. In subsequent years, laws were passed that abolished forced labor and extended colonial representation. These laws and new institutions, however, did not go far enough in the minds of the nationalists. Instead, they provided rallying points for hard-line sentiments.

Hard-liners thus managed to scuttle the attempt to establish the first Constituent Assembly for the Union.[106] The weakened French Union established by the second Constituent Assembly of 1946, which did pass, created then a union of variegated bilateral ties.[107] The Union established the indivisible French republic: France, Algeria (divided into three départements), overseas territories in French West Africa; associated states (Tunisia, Morocco, Indochina); and associated territories. Rather than a uniform, equal union, the system perpetuated the bilateral hub-and-spoke pattern of traditional imperial ties.

Although the Union also established several institutions—a presidency, a Council, and an Assembly—real power remained with the metropolitan parliament.[108] Most Algerians continued to lack citizenship status, for even the extension of 1945 did not convey citizenship to all Algerians.[109] Algerians did have representation in the National Assembly. But the European community and the Muslim Algerian community were given equal

103. Chesneaux 1969, 119–20.
104. Lustick 1993, 133.
105. Forty-eight percent of the French public believed that Egypt was significantly involved in Algeria; 42 percent supported the Suez action even after its failure in 1956. Ageron 1976, 263–64. However, also see Rioux (1987, 273) who argues that the popular support for Suez ran less deep than in Britain.
106. See Hargreaves 1996, 70–71.
107. Fry 1997, 139.
108. Rioux 1987, 86–87.
109. Clayton 1988, 150ff.

representation even though the latter outnumbered the former by nine to one.[110]

The Loi-cadre of 1956 did set serious reforms in motion, but largely in sub-Saharan Africa.[111] The Algerian question had already proceeded too far for interim solutions. By 1956 Algerian nationalists had withdrawn altogether from the Union organizations.[112] The overseas representatives of the settlers, by contrast, joined the major French parties—initially the MRP, then after 1951 they veered more toward the RPF, while the Radicals also received settler support.

THE FIFTH REPUBLIC'S EXIT THROUGH EXECUTIVE AUTHORITY

De Gaulle's Accession to Power

The institutions of the Fourth Republic thus prevented a strategic reevaluation of France's territorial order, which would have been warranted given changes in its imperial environment. Politicians lacked control over the military, and the multiparty system, with ill-disciplined parties and fragile coalitions, provided hard-line politicians an effective veto over territorial changes.

Consequently, institutional reform and reestablishing civilian control over the armed forces were necessary to bring about a successful end to the protracted Algerian conflict. This required a politician who could perform a high-wire act and at the same time do an end run around the existing veto players—someone who could gain the confidence of the military and yet control it, and someone who could gain public approval while changing the institutional landscape. The answer came from that perennial "antisystem" politician: Charles de Gaulle. De Gaulle reestablished control over the military and limited the impact of multiparty coalitions by constitutional reforms.

The New Military Mission. Initially, few Frenchmen saw de Gaulle as a solution to the stalemate of the Fourth Republic. In December 1955 only 1 percent believed he should head a French government; and even by January 1958 only 13 percent apparently thought so.[113] However, as the army increasingly started to disobey civilian dictates, de Gaulle rose to promi-

---

110. Emerson 1960, 70. Fifteen of the Algerian deputies represented the settler interests (Williams 1966, 220).

111. Lustick 1993, 151; Emerson 1960, 74.

112. Williams 1966, 185–88, 220, 261.

113. Lowi and Shain 1992, 505–6. For similar figures, see Lustick 1993, 254–55. However, by the summer of 1958, 68 percent had confidence in de Gaulle. Rioux 1987, 299.

nence.[114] Indeed, by the summer of 1958 a coup d'état appeared imminent and de Gaulle received special authority to govern with full powers for six months, while he announced a constitutional referendum for the fall.

The armed forces in Algeria initially welcomed de Gaulle. Indeed, they justified their threat of a coup on the grounds that the political stalemate in Paris required a strong executive on whom the armed forces could count. They believed that they had their man in de Gaulle.

One reason for the support had to do with de Gaulle's vacillation on the issue. His positions seemed to change depending on the audience he addressed. (He later declared he had done this deliberately to obfuscate his grand strategy.)[115] Furthermore, the military saw de Gaulle as one of theirs. Indeed, de Gaulle showed disdain for politicians and had rebelled against his political superiors in 1940.

Gradually, however, as de Gaulle started to make concessions to the Algerian nationalists, he too met with military resistance. In the "week of the barricades" in January 1960 the pieds noirs militia and paratroop colonels openly resisted civilian rule in Algeria. With the revolt of the generals a year later, the armed forces challenged the metropolitan government outright.[116]

De Gaulle responded by reestablishing control over the military. He dismissed six hundred officers, while others, who had advocated a coup d'état, received long prison terms or the death penalty.[117] He also instilled a new strategic rationale in the armed forces. Rather than fighting obsolescent colonial wars, the armed forces should refocus on the new means to great power status: a nuclear arsenal. "A great state which does not possess them, while others have them, does not command its own destiny."[118] To be sure, France's nuclear program had started before de Gaulle. It had embarked on its nuclear course under Felix Gaillard in 1957. De Gaulle, however, seized on the opportunity to reorient French strategy.[119] The possession of atomic weapons would replace reserves of African military manpower in both strategic and status-symbolic terms.[120]

The New Constitution of 1958 and Article 16. De Gaulle, furthermore, sought institutional reforms through which he could impose his own views

114. Ageron 1976, 268.
115. Merom (1999) shows there was no such design.
116. Horne 1978; Lustick 1993, 277, 287ff; Berstein 1993, chap. 2.
117. See particularly Furniss 1964. See also Clayton 1988, 194; Horne 1978, 308ff.; Berstein 1993, 35, 39, 49.
118. Speech at Strasbourg, November 1961; see Kohl 1971, 129; Pierre 1994, 279. See also Furniss 1964, chap. 7.
119. Challener 1994, 150; Pierre 1994, 280; Kohl 1971, 50–51.
120. Clayton 1988, 46; Horne 1978, 384.

on decolonization—not that he had always been clear on the matter.[121] To Prince Hassan of Morocco he purportedly remarked in October 1956 that "Algeria will be independent if one wants it or not. It is written in history."[122] But talking to the Algerian settlers, administration, and armed forces in June 1958 he remarked how he had heard their demands: "Je vous ai compris." As late as May 1959 he talked about "a new Algeria bound forever to France."[123]

In practice, though, he let the colonies choose their own destiny, and allowed the west and central African states to decide for themselves. Eleven of the twelve associated territories in central and west Africa chose to remain associated with France (albeit in a looser form). Yet by 1960 all would be independent.[124]

To circumvent the stalemate in the metropole he also pushed for institutional reforms. The referendum of 1958 gave him the power to do that, and he gained additional authority in the next four years. The Fifth Republic thus established the strong presidency that he had sought.[125] Article 11 allowed the president to appeal to the public directly by referendum. And Article 12 allowed the president to dissolve the National Assembly.[126]

Moreover, because he would be elected on a national rather than local constituency basis he would be able to override the pork barrel politics that had immobilized the Fourth Republic.[127] The two-round electoral system in effect produced a second-round runoff between the two strongest candidates and created the formation of two competing blocs rather than a multitude of competing parties.[128] Britain and the United States embraced the constitutional revisions and Secretary of State John Foster Dulles welcomed de Gaulle "with a sense of relief that the long and futile Fourth Republic had ended and at last there was strong leadership."[129]

One may perhaps question whether the Fifth Republic indeed created a presidential-dominant system, as is sometimes argued.[130] However, in foreign policy, particularly in times of emergency, there can be less contro-

---

121. The Gaullists started to vacillate on colonial issues in the early 1950s. Christian Fouchet, chairman of Gaullist deputies, called Indochina the Fourth Republic's "Mexican expedition," referring to Maximilian's invasion of Mexico in the 1860s (Williams 1966, 155).

122. Ageron 1976.

123. Horne 1978, 378.

124. Alexandre 1969; Emerson 1960, 73, 75.

125. De Gaulle 1971, 6ff.

126. Berstein 1993, 9.

127. Williams 1966, 322–24.

128. Lijphart 1994, 18, 143; Berstein 1993, 21.

129. Challener 1994, 151.

130. See, for example, Huber 1998. But for an argument that the Fifth Republic did establish a strong executive, see Loriaux's analysis of French economic policy. Loriaux 1991, chap. 6; Berstein 1993, 50; Blondel 1974a.

versy. Article 16, designed with Algeria in mind, gave the executive considerable autonomy in this area.

Thus, a strong executive, in control of the military and less beholden to niche constituencies, pulled France out of the impasse. Veto groups that attempted to advance their agendas by institutional and extra-institutional means had fewer opportunities to put up barriers to territorial retrenchment. Jacques Marseille put it succinctly: "Undoubtedly only he could declare, without being accused of treason, that Algeria cost more than it brought in . . . [and that] decolonization is in our interest."[131]

Elite Perceptions and Popular Opinion

One counterargument to my line of reasoning claims that public opinion and elite perceptions led to hard-line policies in Algeria. One might follow Tony Smith, who acknowledges that divergent British and French institutional arrangements had important consequences but who believes that the particular character of nationalist elites and public opinion are more critical. In his view, a "stubborn colonial consensus" permeated French decision making.[132] Similarly, Bruce Marshall discusses the pervasiveness of a colonial myth that consisted of "the vision, held by virtually all of the French elite, of an indissoluble link between France and the colonies."[133] There is some merit to this argument.

However, it misreads the data, confuses elite beliefs with broader public opinion, and misconstrues the institutionalist argument. First, institutionalist accounts are not incompatible with the study of elite perceptions and public views. However, institutions do structure the arena of political contestation. The multiparty parliamentary system and the particular coalitional dynamics of the Fourth Republic allowed politicians to emerge who represented preferences across a wide political spectrum.

Second, the data do not show a uniformly held view. One needs to clearly distinguish between elite views and popular opinion. True, one does not have to look far to find evidence of delusions of grandeur among political elites. Indeed, the minister of national economy André Philip turned French dependence on American aid on its head: "France is willing to make concessions to her great ally, the USA. She is willing to help her by relieving her of the overweight of capital that suffocates her."[134] De Gaulle too embellished French standing. Speaking to a reporter of the *London*

---

131. Marseille 1984, 373. See also Berstein 1993, 56.
132. T. Smith thus acknowledges that institutions are important (Smith 1981, 106) but emphasizes other variables (94, 107–8, 124).
133. Marshall 1973, 2.
134. Girault 1986, 49.

Times he remarked that "Great Britain and France are the two principal powers in the world."[135] Political elites, furthermore, tried to convey the message that "France" did not merely connote the territory of the hexagon (European France) but included its overseas départements as well.[136]

But did the French general public and political elites share a national consciousness on the imperial question? And to what extent did such beliefs determine metropolitan policy? It is true that many held inflated views of France's world position in the immediate aftermath of World War II. But this euphoria soon evaporated. As discussed in the previous chapter, France's military and economic position proved weak. London and Washington drove Paris's subordinate position home on the German question. France failed in its objectives of gaining German territories, of preventing rearmament, and of acquiring reparations.

Bruce Marshall, in convincingly arguing for a colonial myth (at that time), limits his analysis to the Constituent Assemblies of 1945–46, the height of tripartisme and consensus. He, furthermore, acknowledges the difficulties in drawing inferences from public statements. Indeed, "because colonial problems were seldom salient issues for the vast majority of French political leaders, those source materials are quite limited."[137] Complicating matters even further, he notes the emergence of divergent positions on the colonial question by the 1946–48 period.

Even Tony Smith suggests that the wars in Indochina and Algeria could have been avoided if policies that allowed for more compromise had been pursued. If he finds this counterfactual plausible, it would suggest that alternative policies were not unthinkable and the colonial consensus was not unanimous or hegemonic, as he at other points seems to claim.[138]

Furthermore, political elites were split on the relative importance of empire, the means to maintain it, and the form such rule should take. The Communists acknowledged a right to separate. The Socialists favored close integration, but distinct from previous autocratic rule. The MRP, by contrast, embodied "the most intransigent position on the colonial question" (at least in the immediate postwar era).[139]

Nor is it quite right to say that only the Communists (after 1947) advocated decolonization. The Socialists vacillated between negotiations and hard-line solutions. Although they were responsible for bringing conscripts to Algeria, they compromised on Tunisia and Morocco. And their general secretary, Guy Mollet, at one time opposed the war in Algeria, as "une

135. Girault 1986, 49. Charles Kupchan (1994) also notes how an imperial strategic culture permeated decision making.
136. Lustick 1993.
137. Marshall 1973, 6.
138. T. Smith 1981, 134.
139. Berstein 1986, 178–80.

guerre imbécile et sans issue."[140] The pro–Mèndes-France Radicals also seemed amenable to compromise. In short, beliefs and perceptions mattered, but elite views were not uniform.

Even more important, the public remained largely indifferent to the colonial question. Already in February 1939, 40 percent of the French public preferred to cede imperial territory rather than fight for it, with 44 percent choosing the opposite.[141] In the postwar period, modernization of the French economy and the religious question—particularly the schools issue—were more important than the overseas question. In 1958, four years into the Algerian War, it still rated as only the sixth most important issue for the public.[142]

Moreover, although many wanted the empire to stay intact, far fewer were inclined to support military means, let alone deployment of conscripts, to hold distant overseas areas. The attempt to instill the belief that France extended beyond Europe—one French politician claimed before the UN that Algeria was as French as the Île-de-France—failed as well.[143] Many French responded to polls on colonial questions with indifference. The number of respondents who had "no opinion" or responded that they "did not know" remained extremely high throughout the decades of decolonization. This was true for both Indochina and North Africa.

Public opinion on the Algerian question also varied over time. By August 1955, about a year after the commencement of hostilities, 47 percent favored the status quo (Algeria as a French département), 26 percent wanted weaker ties, and 27 percent had no opinion. In September 1957, however, only 36 percent still wanted to keep Algeria as a département.[144] A poll in July 1956 showed that 51 percent did not want to raise taxes for the war, and 48 percent opposed the sending of conscripts.[145] Support for the hardline Algérie Française faction declined even before the military revolt and the counterterror of the OAS. In October 1955 almost half the French public supported Algérie Française; by September 1957 barely more than a third did.[146]

In the end, Charles-Robert Ageron's evaluation must stand. The general public was not hostile to independence, because a large number of French were indifferent to decolonization issues. By March 1962, a full 82 percent were satisfied with the termination of the war.[147] Perspectives and ideology,

---

140. Rioux 1987, 256: "An idiotic war without end."
141. Ageron 1982, 18.
142. Ageron 1976, 268.
143. Lustick 1993.
144. Ageron 1976, 261–62; Rioux 1987, 300.
145. Ageron 1976, 261–62.
146. Ageron 1976, 264.
147. Ageron 1976, 277.

of course, matter, but particular institutional arrangements facilitated hard-line elites to act on their preferences.[148] If there was a colonial myth, it was predominant in the immediate postwar years. Rather than political elites following a delusional public, the verdict must be turned around. Political elites considered the public ill informed and tried to manipulate imperial mythology to their own advantage.[149]

This discussion of French policy demonstrates a point that I raised in chapter 1. The fragmentation of the center and the lack of stable coalitions prevented Paris from initiating credible policy proposals. Every time concessions seemed on the horizon, either in the reforms of 1936–37 or immediately after the war, hard-liners managed to scuttle further progress. Credibility of commitment in the subsequent implementation phase did not arise.

Moreover, France's hard-line policies of decades past eroded its ability to commit by others means. Whereas British policy toward India encouraged the African nationalists to think that compromise with Whitehall was possible, French policies in Africa before the war and in Indochina after 1945 suggested to the Algerians that compromise was unlikely.

Finally, the persecution of nationalist elites had eroded the ability of these elites to act as intermediaries. As Jules Gambon had presciently noted fifty years earlier, without recognized indigenous elites Paris had no one with whom to negotiate. Moreover, the erosion of nationalist elites and representative institutions created credible commitment problems for the nationalist side. Which of the various Algerian factions should one negotiate with? If an agreement were reached, would the rank and file, particularly the extreme hard-liners on the nationalist side, abide by the terms of the agreement? This issue was not resolved on the Algerian side without significant bloodletting between the various factions.[150]

Finally, it would be wrong to attribute to the French nation as a whole blind intransigence on colonial issues. Much of the public remained indifferent. Even parliament itself was divided. Indeed, by one account in 1958, only one quarter of the National Assembly consisted of pro-Algeria diehards.[151]

148. As Ian Lustick suggests, ideas require political entrepreneurs willing to champion them (Lustick 1993, 123–24). I would argue that the institutional framework of the Fourth Republic allowed more room for hard-line entrepreneurs than that of the Fifth Republic.

149. Ageron 1985, 400. Merom (1999) similarly notes how the public was not highly involved with the colonial question. Also see Lustick 1993, 180.

150. The conflicts between the Front Libération Nationale (FLN) and the Armée de Libération Nationale (ALN) and other factions are discussed in Horne 1978.

151. Williams 1966, 489–90.

Instead, the institutions of the Fourth Republic allowed the armed forces and political hard-liners in parliament to exercise disproportionate power. In contrast to Britain and the Netherlands, the metropolitan government faced virulent military resistance. Time and again the French military tried to create faits acomplis in direct circumvention of their civilian superiors. The armed forces exercised agenda control until civilian oversight was gradually reestablished under de Gaulle.

The fragmented government of the Fourth Republic created more veto points. Given the multiparty system, politicians could hold niche constituency views rather than pursue the median voter. In contrast to their British counterparts, the French parties captured a smaller percentage of the electorate, were not as well organized, and had less party discipline. Furthermore, the fragility of multiparty coalitions and the permanent opposition of Communists and Gaullists made every government the hostage of any group that refused to countenance a change from the policy equilibrium. Given these conditions, a transformation of the existing territorial order faced too many vetoes. Robert Lecourt, an MRP minister, remarked that in the Fourth Republic "the majority is a de facto provisional association with no formal basis, constituted . . . by the temporary aggregation of the ballot papers of deputies on their way into opposition."[152] That fragmentation and instability condemned the Fourth Republic to ineptitude, whereas the institutions of the Fifth Republic allowed President de Gaulle to set a new course.

152. Williams 1966, 463.

CHAPTER FOUR

Whitehall Tacks to the Wind of Change

> [We need] something like a profit and loss account for each of our colonial possessions, so that we may be better able to gauge whether, from the financial and economic point of view, we are likely to gain or lose by its departure.
>
> HAROLD MACMILLAN

Harold Macmillan's instructions to the Colonial Office to prepare a cost-benefit analysis of empire, eighteen days after he became prime minister in 1957, exemplify the difference between British decolonization and the French and Dutch experiences. Even more tellingly, the Colonial Office did generate the requested profit and loss report, breaking down the overseas territories into seven parts and evaluating their economic and strategic merits and demerits in seventy-six detailed pages.[1]

Within two decades after the end of World War II Britain surrendered virtually all of its key Asian and African colonies, and it managed to do so without protracted military engagements or metropolitan upheaval. Although conflicts erupted in Malaya and Kenya, British deployments hardly matched the more than 150,000 Dutch servicemen sent to Indonesia(on a much smaller population base) or the half a million French troops sent to Algeria. How did the British government succeed in readjusting to the new realities of the postwar era?

The empire undoubtedly faced a different world in 1945 then it did at the outset of the war. Nevertheless, in other respects its predicament did not necessarily compel withdrawal. Relative to France it had fared well. The latter, and some of its colonies, had been occupied by Germany, whereas Britain and most of its key colonies and dominions had escaped such a fate.

---

1. Hyam and Louis 2000, pt. I, no. 2. Report on the "Future constitutional development in the colonies." May 1957.

It could still claim to be a great power, although increasingly the junior partner to the United States. Its special relationship with the United States provided additional benefits. Britain's military position had been compromised in India and East Asia, but its position remained relatively intact in many other areas. The metropolitan government could thus limit concessions and compartmentalize the damage.

Indeed, plans were developed to make East Africa a new source of manpower to replace that lost in India. Kenyan bases would be developed to project British air power throughout East Africa and the Indian Ocean. The plan also envisioned South African support, with the British navy retaining the important facilities at Simonstown. The military plans also foresaw the buildup of the base at Suez, and a renewed emphasis on the key strategic support areas to and from the Suez Canal (Malta, Cyprus, and Aden).[2]

Although Labour prime minister Clement Attlee questioned the value of an imperial grand strategy, his views lost the political battle to his foreign secretary, Ernest Bevin, and the Joint Chiefs of Staff. Voices in the Foreign Office argued that "it is essential that we should increase our strength. . . . This can clearly best be done by enrolling France and the lesser West European Powers, and, of course, also the Dominions, as collaborators with us in this tripartite system."[3] It would, consequently, be wrong to presume after the fact that for the British calibrated withdrawal was the logical and only possible outcome.

Moreover, the colonial mentality, with its gradations of status, race, and rank, did not die overnight.[4] Nor was there a lack of potential settler resistance, particularly in East Africa. Even American pressure to decolonize remained muted, particularly as tensions grew with the Soviet Union. Indeed, the British strategy of reforming and educating, and ultimately empowering, moderate nationalists seemed like the best bet to stem communism.[5]

In short, a hard-line response and colonial wars were not beyond the realm of the possible. If weaker states had opted to fight for their overseas territories, why not Britain? We are left with a paradox. The British Empire had weathered the Second World War better than the other maritime empires, yet it proved willing to compromise with incipient nationalists to a greater extent than the others did.

---

2. Hargreaves 1996, 94.

3. Foreign Office 371/50912, "Stocktaking after VE-Day," cited in Hargreaves 1996, 90. See also Adamthwaite 1985, 225. On Labour's ambivalence about surrendering the empire, see Howe 1993.

4. Lawrence James provides an impressionistic, but telling, example in noting how the ten lavatories at a Suez Canal railway station were allocated according to ten categories of race and rank. James 1994, 541.

5. Hargreaves 1996, 97.

The British engaged in two decades of retrenchment following World War II. The dismantling of empire occurred across the tenure of Attlee's Labour government (1945–51); the Conservative governments of Churchill and Eden until the Suez conflict (1951–57); and the Conservative governments of Macmillan and Alec Douglas-Home (1957–64).[6] Labour, although a more anti-imperial party than the Conservatives, refused to be tainted as the "party of scuttle."[7] Moreover, given postwar economic difficulties, many in the British government still considered the colonies as useful resources. Thus, Labour granted independence only in a limited number of cases. India had essentially been granted greater autonomy during the war under the 1942 concessions. Ceylon and Burma followed suit. Similarly, Britain had already committed itself during the war to remove the Middle East from colonial status. Here Labour simply followed earlier commitments. Italian colonies, such as Libya, that were acquired during the war were also slated for early independence, in that they were considered as distinct cases apart from the older British holdings. Israel, too, constituted a special case.

Winston Churchill's government, which regained office in 1951, proved even more reluctant to disengage. Churchill had grumbled about Indian independence in 1947. African independence hardly registered with him at all. The same held true for his successor, Anthony Eden. Both endeavored to halt the pace of dissolution. The post-Suez government of Conservative Prime Minister Harold Macmillan thus became the principal architect of speedy withdrawal. Within six years after the Suez crisis (1956), Britain granted independence to all its major African and Asian holdings.

How this process could have moved forward so swiftly and without great upheaval must ultimately be explained by the nature of British institutions. The ability of Macmillan's government to expediently withdraw from East Africa warrants specific scrutiny. Here the British, like the French in Algeria, had business interests and settlers to deal with, and here, too, some believed Britain had strategic interests because of East Africa's proximity to the Middle East, Suez, and Aden. Hence, the empirical case of East Africa receives the lion's share of attention in this chapter.

I do not suggest that Whitehall worked with a master plan for extricating Britain rapidly from its overseas possessions. Muddling through and ad hoc decision making operated in London as it did on the European continent. Each colony was considered unique. The British metropole did not have a blueprint for its empire for the decades ahead.[8]

6. For a similar periodization, see Goldsworthy 1990.
7. Howe 1993, chap. 4.
8. As Hargreaves demonstrates (1996, 107).

I do contend, however, that decisions emanating from the government were driven by broad concerns about the overall benefits for Britain rather than parochial interests that might be advanced by the military, certain elements in the business community, or settlers. Although some political elites took up the cause of hard-liners (particularly the settlers in this case), they were unable to veto decisions coming from the top of the political system. Control over the armed forces was never in doubt. Centralized decision making in the Westminster system resided squarely with the cabinet and the strong position of the prime minister and his majority support in Parliament.

CIVILIAN CONTROL OF THE MILITARY

British imperial forces consisted of four components and differed in the degrees of British control.[9] The regular British army consisted usually of all-volunteer forces that served throughout the empire. About one-third of these were posted to India. One division was allocated to Egypt, while other territories received from one to three battalions.[10] The defense of Britain proper fell to the Royal Navy and the reserve territorial army.

The Indian Army likewise served throughout the empire but was financed by India itself, commensurate with the dictate that the colonies had to be self-supporting. It had semiautonomous status and its own general staff. With independence for India on the horizon, this component of course would be phased out.

The African colonial armies were far smaller in size and served only in Africa. Given the colonies' weakly developed economies the armies could not be self-supporting, and British financial contributions had to augment local taxes.

Finally, the main dominion armies were controlled and paid for by the dominions themselves (Canada, Australia, New Zealand, and South Africa).

Functionally and culturally, the British military, unlike the French, was not divided into imperial forces and metropolitan components. In France, the metropolitan army, consisting primarily of conscripts, could only serve in France proper and in Algeria. Professionals largely policed the colonies. The British forces did not evince the professional-conscript divisions that occurred during the Fourth Republic.

British professional forces served with equal ease overseas and in Britain. Unlike in France, British colonial service did not provide any particularly

9. Clayton 1988, 5–6; Clayton 1999, 281–93.
10. The interwar strength of the Indian army amounted to 107 infantry battalions and 21 cavalry regiments, totaling about 180,000 men. Clayton 1999, 283–84.

desirable organizational structure or career opportunities. "It meant nothing to a soldier of the Somerset Light Infantry on leaving India, either personally or in terms of his career."[11] Officers, in general, cultivated a distinct sense of amateurish aloofness. Thus General Archibald Wavell noted in 1936 how "the typical officer will be a public school man who after twenty years of service life can retire to manage his estates and interest himself in the public affairs of his neighborhood."[12] Others commented how few officer cadets in Sandhurst really saw the army as their ultimate career.

British officers, furthermore, did not have the sense of imperial mission that their French colleagues had. In their view, home defense had always come first. Britain had long engaged in strategic calculations regarding the costs of its military deployments overseas.[13] Military expenditures were calibrated against political objectives. Even when the military had to be deployed to deal with "emergencies," the nature of deployment remained limited rather than the prelude to an all-out escalation. The military did not wish to substitute military solutions for what were essentially political problems. As Field Marshall Gerald Templer remarked during the Malayan emergency in 1953, "Shooting only constitutes 25 percent of the business."[14]

Civilian control over the military had been a long-standing dictum in British politics. The functional cohesion of government (through executive and parliamentary unity) and the homogeneity of civilian preferences further aided civilian oversight.[15] Finally, Britain lacked the internal instability that in general tends to precipitate military intervention in civilian government.[16]

Civilian control over the military never wavered in Britain in World War II, even when the British seemed to face imminent defeat. (In 1940 American general George C. Marshall predicted the United Kingdom would fall in a matter of weeks.) That does not mean the military was always happy with its civilian masters. The Chiefs of Staff deemed Churchill unsound, unsuccessful, and unlucky.[17] But even when he concocted feeble plans for military operations (he had a preference for sea-based landings, despite a history of disasters, such as at the Dardanelles in 1915), or when he cajoled them, the chiefs followed his lead.

---

11. Clayton 1988, 8.
12. Quoted in Kier 1997, 122.
13. See, for example, Friedberg 1988.
14. Clayton 1988, 156. See also James 1994, 589. Overall, the Malayan operations involved 35,000 troops and 73,000 police. Clayton 1999, 296.
15. See Avant 1994. Kier notes the unity among preferences (1997, 141).
16. For this general argument, see Desch 1999.
17. Danchev 1996, 191.

Consequently, by the end of the Second World War, politicians and the military could debate the merits of empire without civilians ever losing control over the process. Prime Minister Attlee became one of the early proponents of a modernized, small army with nuclear capabilities firmly embedded in a United States–United Kingdom alliance. Although he lost the political fight within his own cabinet and with the Chiefs of Staff (the latter did not even want a continental commitment), part of his calculations coincided with those of some members of the armed forces. For example, Field Marshall Bernard Montgomery supported continental over imperial commitments and a focus on the army rather than a strategy oriented to the navy. Military men and civilians both regarded much of East Asia, short of Malaya, untenable. The Indian army was no longer perceived to be a cheap asset but had become ever more expensive during the war.[18] Moreover, with India and Pakistan becoming independent, substitutes would have to be found. But the armed forces doubted the use-value of other colonial troops in the cold war, arguing that colonial troops did not provide the same value for the money as British troops.[19]

This did not mean Labour rushed to retreat. Indeed, its military expenditures were large and met with Conservative approval.[20] It did signify, however, that the merits of overseas deployments would have to be evaluated against Britain's economic predicament.

Although Attlee lost the initial fight, subsequent discussions would similarly propel Harold Macmillan to question the use-value of imperial holdings in the new military environment. For Attlee these doubts led him to go ahead with the atom bomb. By 1946, before nuclear development, potential attack plans had been drafted by the Joint Technical Warfare Committee against sixty-seven Soviet cities.[21] Churchill decided to move Britain toward an independent thermonuclear capability by 1954. Churchill, ironically, also drew conclusions from this technology that diminished the rationale for overseas holdings. When criticized by some of his more conservative colleagues for his government's agreement with Nasser in 1954 to withdraw installations from Suez, he noted how the management of potential nuclear conflict stood "utterly out of all proportion to the Suez Canal and the position we held in Egypt." If the members of Parliament would only imagine the consequences of nuclear war, they

18. Low 1991, 38–39.
19. The Colonial Office, not surprisingly given the agency's interest, argued against the Chiefs of Staff that this was easier "to assert than to justify." Hyam 1992, pt. III, nos. 337, 338. Report by Joint Planning Staff to Chiefs of Staff, January 2, 1951, and Colonial Office. See also nos. 339 and 340.
20. Lloyd 1993, 277.
21. James 1994, 529.

would be convinced "of the obsolescence of the base and of the sense of proportion, which is vitally needed at the present time."[22] Later, Macmillan similarly emphasized the thermonuclear arsenal and Britain's V-bomber force, and a smaller, all-professional army with the key mission of defending Europe.

These views came to a head in the Defence White Paper of 1957, championed by the minister of defence, Duncan Sandys.[23] The Defence paper signaled a trend that had emerged after 1945 and would continue until 1967, when Britain withdrew from points "east of Suez." It meant a shift from "palm and pine" imperial missions to NATO tasks and Europe. The imperial mission required light, mobile forces. NATO tasks, however, required a smaller professional army, with heavy armor and advanced multirole strike aircraft.[24] This would also affect allocations to the service branches. For example, Sandys wanted to kill the aircraft carriers (a plan abandoned after heavy lobbying by Chief of Staff Earl Mountbatten). The budgetary allocation would be reduced from £1,600 million in 1956–57 to £1,300 million annually in the following years.

Needless to say, the various services protested vigorously. They objected that the plan, by Sandys's own admission, "would appreciably affect our ability to exert military power in distant parts of the world."[25] Civilian control, however, asserted itself in unambiguous terms, and the armed forces yielded. According to Sir Nigel Fisher, who worked with Sandys when he was at the Commonwealth and Colonial Office, "When he was Secretary of State, policy always came from the top, never from the officials."[26]

In short, the British military had less of an organizational interest in empire than its French counterpart. And where civilians and armed forces had varying preferences, the armed forces had to give way. The new mission for the British forces would be European, not imperial. During his administration, Macmillan continuously drove the point home that overseas commitments had to be measured against other economic needs.[27]

22. Quoted in Gilbert 1991, 930. See also Lloyd 1993, 317–18.
23. Hyam and Louis 2000, pt. I, no. 53. Cabinet conclusions on White Paper, March 18, 1957. Lennox-Boyd, in the Colonial Office, argued against such reductions as "likely to encourage disruptive elements in the Colonies." Hyam and Louis 2000, pt. I, no. 54. See also Clayton 1999, 295.
24. Nailor 1996, 237, 245; Navias 1996, 233.
25. Quoted in Navias 1996, 223.
26. Navias 1996, 217.
27. See, for example, his requests for long-term strategic evaluations. Hyam and Louis 2000, pt. I, no. 8. Future policy in the next ten years, June 10, 1959; Hyam and Louis 2000, pt. I, no. 17. Future policy study, 1960–1970; February 24, 1960.

CIVILIAN PRESSURE GROUPS

The Heterogeneous Attitudes of the Business Community

The Labour government entered the postwar era with a plan for the colonies.[28] It (initially) accepted the prerequisites model inherited from its Conservative predecessors. Independence would be granted if the colony proved to be "fit." However, it deliberately left vague which countries might be deemed to have such traits. Metropolitan interests still came first. It would keep the colonies but develop them. Colonial Secretary Creech Jones referred to Labour's policy as "enlightened self-interest."[29] The Colonial Development Corporation formed part of this effort. Following Labour's overall bent for government intervention to spark economic revival it aimed to improve the development of the colonies.[30]

Development of the colonies also fit with broader aims. Growth in the colonies would enable them to support the mother country. They would particularly serve as sources for food and materials that did not require payment in dollars.[31] Development would also entail forging alliances with moderate business and economic groups, and preventing communist insurgency. The Conservative governments that succeeded Attlee's after 1951 largely had similar interests.

The business community split on the wisdom of such government policies. Some, staunch advocates of empire and a strong commonwealth, believed that more could be done to protect business interests and that concessions to the nationalists should be limited. Others were less convinced about the viability of economic investments, government intervention, or the overall benefits of continuing the imperial project in the first place.

Opponents of decolonization and retreat from imperial preference feared a loss of external markets. This argument for empire was a long-standing one. For example, the Lancashire textile industry had long opposed concessions to India on the grounds that greater autonomy would lead to Indian tariffs and a decline of exports, which by the 1930s still accounted for almost one-third of all British cotton exports. The Manchester Chamber of Commerce had also been a powerful voice for pro-empire industrial interests before the war.[32] Similarly, businesses with key exports to the empire continued such arguments after the war. Pro-empire businesses stressed the harmony of interests between business and political elites in seeking a non-dollar means of exchange. The sterling area and preferential

28. See Hyam 1988, 161–162, 169.
29. Howe 1993, 144.
30. Cowen 1984.
31. Cowen 1984, 63; Hyam 1988, 149, 159.
32. Ghosh 1965, 208, 210.

trading schemes seemed to promise a way out of the postwar malaise. The Ottawa agreements, after all, had proved a reasonable substitute for closed markets elsewhere in the 1930s.

Some of the holders of immovable assets also argued that withdrawal from empire should be slow and protracted with few concessions. Railroads in East Africa, utility companies, mines—all these needed protection. Hardliners opposed concessions in North Rhodesia on the grounds that their control over those assets would be lost.[33] Among their powerful spokesmen they counted Lord Salisbury, who had ties to East African railroads and whose grandfather gave his name to the capital of Rhodesia.

A variety of businesses in Malaya likewise pushed for a harder line during the emergency (1948–1957).[34] Tin, rubber, and trading interests pressured the government for larger military deployments. Their appeal to the Labour government found considerable support, in that Malaya was important for the defense of sterling, given that its natural resources could be exported to boost the national income. They particularly wanted the government to act as insurers of last resort. But big business and Labour coexisted uneasily, with business arguing that not enough was being done.

The Conservative victory brought some natural allies into office. Colonial Secretary Oliver Lyttelton, after all, had been chair of the London Tin Corporation and was close friends with Clive Baillieu, the chair of Dunlop Rubber. Similarly, quite a few members of Parliament who opposed concessions in the Gold Coast had ties to the Ashanti Goldfields Company. Overall, Conservative members of Parliament tended to have company pedigrees, with at one point almost a quarter coming from, or sitting on, board of directorships.[35]

Moreover, if closer economic integration with other industrialized states meant a choice for Europe, pro-imperialists could depict the choice as a stab in the back to commonwealth partners, who feared (rightly) that the European continental powers were reluctant to accommodate the wishes of the British colonies and dominions. Contrasting views emerged regarding the relationship between regional integration with Europe versus commonwealth and empire.[36] One view saw the two as antithetical, involving a choice for either Europe or the commonwealth and empire. A contrasting perspective believed that both regional integration and ties to commonwealth and empire could be obtained. Proponents for a harder line gravi-

---

33. Goldsworthy 1970, 280; Horowitz 1970, 11.
34. White 1998.
35. White 1998, 163; Dragnich and Rasmussen 1974, 96; Hargreaves 1996, 129.
36. In the 1950s commonwealth and empire were treated roughly the same. Schenk 1996, 461. See also Hyam and Louis 2000, pt. II, nos. 362, 363. Cabinet conclusions on joining the Free Trade Area and EEC; March 27, 1958; July 13, 1960.

tated toward the first view and were associated with the Anti-Common Market League, a powerful lobby in the Conservative Party.[37]

But not all business leaders rallied around the imperial flag. Some groups recognized that the more developed parts of the empire, particularly the dominions, had gradually shifted from the British economic orbit. Before the war alternative markets such as the United States and Japan already were becoming more important for Australia and New Zealand. For Canada the American market had been preeminent for some time. Such trends had been exacerbated during the war. South Africa, similarly, had no reason to sell its many resources preferentially to Britain. Imperial preferences had become less relevant.[38]

Even the holders of direct investments did not all favor a hard line. They realized that fixed assets would be difficult to defend regardless of the numbers of troops deployed. Instead, they favored concessions to gain local consent.[39] Similarly, some of the mining corporations in the Central African Federation—an ill-fated attempt to institutionalize a federal government for a unified North Rhodesia, Nyasaland, and South Rhodesia—wished for broad local representation and compromise.[40]

The attempt to foster closer ties between metropole and periphery by modernizing the less developed areas also had its critics. The government's Colonial Development Corporation's support for development projects in Africa met with limited success. Although intended to act as seed financier for profitable projects, it ended up losing money—losses amounted to £37 million in 1953 alone.[41] Other plans, such as the expansion of the East African railroad, proved prohibitively expensive. Thus, the opponents of empire could legitimately question the benefits relative to the costs of closer imperial ties. The Cabinet Economic Policy Committee concluded by 1957 that "a choice had already to be made between the use of resources for essential investment at home and for investment abroad."[42]

Finally, the opponents of the hard-liners argued that the empire could not possibly substitute for Britain in Europe. Proponents of membership in the European Economic Community, "who now believed that Britain's future lay in closer relations with Europe were coming to regard many of its colonial links as economic and political liabilities."[43] They favored pursuing

37. Murphy 1995, 221.
38. Schenk 1996, 446–47.
39. Hyam 1988, 158.
40. Murphy 1995, 232.
41. Cowen 1984, 68.
42. Hyam and Louis 2000, pt. II, no. 301. Minutes of Cabinet Economic Policy Meeting, May 22, 1957.
43. Hargreaves 1996, 207.

European integration with specific accommodations for commonwealth partners and colonies.

In the end, British preferences and Continental desires proved irreconcilable, and entry into the EEC stalled.[44] The European Free Trade Area (EFTA) proved a poor substitute. It did signify, however, that important components of the British business sector believed that Europe was paramount.

Perhaps more important, business elites believed that the best guarantee of their interests lay in establishing moderate nationalist elites in power.[45] Because British policy had been less repressive than French and Dutch strategies in dealing with nationalism, and given their experience with indirect rule, the British believed that such a moderate nationalist elite could be found.

To conclude, British business divided on the wisdom of hard-line policies. Similar to the French situation, debates raged on the need for having colonies to rebuild the metropolitan postwar economy. In France, multiple veto opportunities allowed business interests that favored a hard line to exercise their voice through their political allies. In Britain, by contrast, hard-line business interests and politicians could not advance their preferences against the policy dictated by Whitehall.[46]

The Settlers Push for a Hard-Line Response

The white settlers in East Africa opposed concessions with greater virulence than the business groups. Not only did they hold nonliquid assets, such as land and dwellings, but they also occupied a political and social position far beyond the one they could hope to achieve back in Britain. Like Cecil Rhodes during his occupation of Rhodesia, they wanted support from their homeland when necessary but as little oversight as possible.

The British Empire showed considerable variation in the degree of white settlement. On one end of the spectrum were territories where white settlers eventually became the dominant racial category by displacing and exterminating much of the indigenous population (New Zealand, Australia, Canada). In South Africa whites made up only about one-fifth of the population, but they constituted the politically dominant group. As stated earlier, these cases remain outside the purview of this analysis, because settlers in those states did not see the loss of British tutelage as jeopardizing their

---

44. Schenk 1996.
45. Hyam 1988, 154.
46. Tignor's analysis of decolonization in Egypt, Nigeria, and Kenya bears this out: "Nor were the large-scale modern corporations, whether foreign or locally based, significant actors in the decisions that led to the withdrawal of European power" (Tignor 1998, 387–88).

very existence and, hence, did not put pressure on the imperial government to stay. Settlers would simply become the politically dominant force in those newly independent states. Where settlers constituted a minority, the problem loomed much larger.

On the other end of the spectrum were territories that had received very few British émigrés. West Africa, among other places, was considered too harsh for settlement. East Africa received greater numbers of settlers, although they remained outnumbered by the indigenous population. South Rhodesia by 1950 had about 129,000 Europeans compared to 1.96 million Africans. North Rhodesia counted 36,000 Europeans and 1.85 million Africans. Nyasaland was barely settled by whites with 4,000 Europeans to 2.33 million Africans. Kenya counted roughly 35,000 whites versus 4 million Africans.[47]

Settler opposition thus varied throughout the empire. India, despite being Britain's "jewel in the Crown," had a European presence of roughly 100,000 to 120,000 among hundreds of millions of Indians. Settler resistance to independence in India consequently never took root. Moreover, given the cordial relations between Indian nationalists and British rule, few settlers had reason to fear catastrophic results should the Crown depart. West Africa similarly generated very few problems with settlers, in that there were so few of them and their political mobilization was limited. The settler issue thus emerged primarily in East Africa.

The nature of landholding patterns also affected settler responses. South Africa, of course, provided the most dramatic example. Settlers had over time completely subjugated African landholding. By 1931, some 1.8 million Europeans had appropriated 440,000 square miles of land, while six million Africans had to make do with 34,000 square miles.[48] In West Africa, by contrast, the metropolitan government had curtailed European land ownership. Central Africa (North and South Rhodesia and Nyasaland) looked more like the South African model; whereas Tanganyika, Uganda, and Kenya formed intermediate categories. Further gradation suggests that Kenya demonstrated largely proprietary agriculture, while the plantations in Tanganyika and Nyasaland, which were owned by absentee landlords, catered to the world market. Nyasaland also split between small and large landholders.[49]

As a consequence of the settlement patterns and the differences in landholding patterns, serious settler problems would only emerge in the 1950s in Kenya and the Central African Federation. Indeed, in many respects—in

47. Hargreaves 1996, 83; Good 1976, 610.
48. Fieldhouse 1971, 616–17.
49. Kahler 1981, 392. Good (1976, 603) suggests, however, that some holdings in Kenya were also very large. Nine thousand settlers had exclusive rights to 16,700 square miles of land.

their historical evolution, political position, and attitudes to the metropole—these settlers resembled their Algerian counterparts.[50]

In the Kenyan "White Highlands" landholders started to fear that the successor government would annex their holdings. A variety of responses emerged. One group of conservative hard-liners believed that no compromise with the nationalists could be reached. And if any agreement were brokered, the nationalists could not be trusted to keep it. Consisting of smaller farmers, this group would only compromise if the government would buy them out, making their departure possible.[51] The large estate farmers, by contrast, wanted to stay and maintain their economic relations. This latter segment, the "New Kenya Group," saw greater promise in brokering a multiracial compromise.

If the tide toward greater African participation could not be stemmed altogether, the hard-liners wanted to influence the nature of the emerging African parties.[52] Consequently, they opposed the release of the prominent nationalist spokesman, Jomo Kenyatta, who had been accused of membership in the Mau Mau movement.

The settlers, early on in the nationalist struggle, tried to obtain metropolitan military support to squelch the Mau Mau movement by force. The Mau Mau movement, ethnically predominantly Kikuyu, had emerged in the late 1940s and constituted a mixture of Kenyan rituals, a secret society, and a nationalist program. Complex as the phenomenon was, the white population and the British press could recast the struggle in Kenya as white civilization against African barbarism. In reality, most of the violence targeted blacks, not whites, and only a few dozen whites died in the violence. To the hard-line settlers the incidents demonstrated the impossibility of compromise. To the metropole it indicated that nonpolitical solutions were prohibitively expensive and best avoided. The uprising lasted roughly from 1952 to 1956; it took about 12,000 British and African troops, augmented with Kikuyu irregulars, to end it.[53]

White settlers resorted to the kith and kin argument, trying to mobilize allies within the Conservative Party as well as in the British financial community.[54] It comes as no surprise that the evaluation of Mau Mau and African competence was tainted by racism and claims of cultural superiority. The whole discussion of how India could be accommodated in the white commonwealth suggested that cultural and racial bonds continued to

50. Good (1976, 599–606) makes this argument.

51. Wasserman 1973, 103.

52. Many of the voting schemes that were entertained in this period still heavily favored the white segment of the population. Hargreaves 1996, 143–45.

53. Clayton 1999, 301. The number of casualties was much heavier among Africans (2,000) than whites (32) and Asians (26). Hargreaves 1996, 142.

54. Wasserman 1973, 107.

matter. Indeed, there was even some talk about an independent white high-lands state, separate from Kenya. Although the proposal never took root, it did signify the rift between white highlanders and the Kenyan indigenes.

The Central African Federation proved to be a thorny issue as well. As a means of gradually devolving more powers to African authorities, the British Labour government, followed by their Conservative successors, came up with the idea of creating a federal institutional structure incorporating North Rhodesia, South Rhodesia, and Nyasaland. Rhodesian mineral wealth and the higher level of education of the white settlers in South Rhodesia would then aid the development of the federation as a whole. African opinion, however, opposed the plan as a ruse to continue settler domination.[55] Although only South Rhodesia had a strong white presence, Europeans in all three colonies favored a federal structure that would, they believed, give them greater independence and thus latitude to move freely without oversight from London.

London had to take heed of these hard-liners. Unconstitutional action was considered a distinct possibility, and the metropolitan government feared pushing the settlers too hard.[56] Another reason why Whitehall had to tread lightly was fear that the South African situation might be duplicated. South African reluctance to support Britain during World War II and the institutionalization of apartheid in 1948 were symptomatic of the rift between metropole and former colony. Contacts between the two exacerbated the difficulties for London in dealing with the nonwhite colonies and commonwealth partners. Some politicians feared the possibility of a united white front of Kenyan highlanders, South Rhodesians, and South Africa. (An earlier plan in 1942 intended to make the White Highlands one of five provinces in a new Central African Union. Then Undersecretary of State Harold Macmillan successfully opposed the plan, fearing white separatism.)[57] Given the economic and military importance of these regions— Britain, for example, still maintained the Simonstown naval base in South Africa well after the institutionalization of apartheid—London could ill afford such an outcome.

At the same time, the British government also realized that the more it tolerated settler intransigence, the greater the possibility that the metropole would sink in a colonial quagmire. Ultimately, it had to decide which strategy to pursue, and it chose to neutralize settler opposition.[58]

55. Lloyd 1993, 320; Hargreaves 1996, 179.
56. Good 1976, 611. Hard-line settlers constantly pushed the Conservatives to do more on their behalf. Hargreaves 1996, 173.
57. Hargreaves 1996, 66.
58. In the end, British concessions could not appease all the settlers. The metropolitan government's solution proved so unpalatable that ultimately South Rhodesia broke from the commonwealth altogether in 1965 and established a white minority government that lasted until 1980.

To conclude, throughout this period the metropolitan government recognized constraints on its policy options. The possibility of alliances between these settlers and the South African government and the Portuguese colonies, and unconstitutional action, proved even more threatening. Metropolitan pressure could thus lead to more hard-line resistance rather than calibrated withdrawal. Paternalist arguments still carried considerable currency. Independence would come, but the Africans were simply not ready yet. In 1958 some agencies in London still operated under the presumption that the British would control East Africa for another thirty years.

The settlers were thus not without rhetorical and political means. Yet they, too, as economic pressure groups, failed to dictate the pace and nature of decolonization. Decisions ultimately emanated from the cabinet and the prime minister. Pressure groups and their political allies lacked the institutional means to veto territorial adjustment.

WHITEHALL OVER WESTMINSTER

As suggested at the outset of this chapter, Attlee's Labour government oversaw the divestiture from India and some other "special cases" but refused to be branded the "party of scuttle." Leader of the House of Commons (between 1945–51) Herbert Morrison compared rapid decolonization to giving a ten-year-old child "a latch key, a bank account and a shot-gun."[59] Labour's razor slim majority of six seats after the 1950 elections also left it little room for maneuvering.[60] As with subsequent Conservative governments, policy emanated from the prime minister and the key cabinet members. In the words of one observer, "Decisions in the colonial field were taken under the Attlee government, in all cases where vital British interests were felt to be at stake, not by the Ministers directly responsible but by the Cabinet's dominant figures: Attlee, Bevin and Morrison, Dalton and Cripps."[61]

The subsequent Conservative governments of Churchill and Eden relinquished very few overseas areas as well. Suez marked the apogee of that brand of Conservative policy. It fell to Harold Macmillan, the former Conservative treasury minister, to do away with most of Britain's holdings when he came to power after Eden's downfall; and he did so with remarkable alacrity. Given that the Conservative Party had traditionally been the party of procolonial interests, economic and military arguments for empire had traditionally found a willing ear there; and given the affinity with the "kith

---

59. Quoted in James 1994, 516.
60. Lloyd 1993, 308.
61. Howe 1993, 146.

and kin" abroad, one might wonder how Macmillan could dispense with opposition to his views within the party's own ranks. The policy is all the more surprising given the stature of some of his Conservative counterparts, who believed concessions to the nationalists had gone far enough. Why, in other words, did Macmillan's strategy of calibrated disengagement face few vetoes?

Prime Ministerial Government in a Two-Party System

The British system presents no constitutional veto points. Its government is unitary rather than federal. Moreover, being a parliamentarian system it unifies executive and legislative functions. Laws from Parliament are supreme, and the system thus lacks judicial review. In the legislature the House of Commons dominates the House of Lords.

Nor do the electoral rules create partisan veto points. Indeed, George Tsebelis classifies the United Kingdom as a single veto player.[62] Electoral rules fortify the unitary nature of British government. Single-member districts combined with the "first past the post" system (a plurality suffices to win the seat) limits the number of parties that gain representation in Parliament.[63] Even parties that historically have gained a considerable following among the general electorate might see few of those votes transferred to seats in Parliament. The Liberal Party has often suffered this fate, gaining, for example, 23.5 percent of the votes in the 1929 election but less than 10 percent of the seats. Likewise, Attlee's Labour Party lost control over Parliament in 1951, gaining only 295 seats to the Conservatives' 321, even though it had received a greater share of the popular vote.[64]

Consequently, for most of the twentieth century, the Conservatives and Labour have dominated the legislature. The Liberal Party, while almost as strong as Labour in the early decades, never recovered from the loss it suffered during the Depression era. The largely two-party system (many candidates from multiple parties stand at the local level but gain no seat) has also meant that coalition governments have been few (save the broad coalitions during wartime). The executive thus sits with the confidence of his or her own party.

The electoral rules and a two-party system generate a variety of other effects. Parties inevitably must try to be "catch-all" parties. At the district level candidates must cater to multiple constituencies to gain the relative majority. A narrow issue focus is strategically irrational, unlike the situation in highly proportional electoral systems or in multimember districts (where a

---

62. Tsebelis 2002, 4. See also Crepaz 2002.
63. For a quick overview, see, for example, Moodie 1971, 60–78. Also see Lijphart 1994.
64. Lloyd 1993, 175, 313.

Table 4.1. British electoral results 1945–64

Party	Seats					
	1945	1950	1951	1955	1959	1964
Conservative	213	299	321	345	365	304
Labour	393	315	295	277	258	317
Liberal	12	9	6	6	6	9
Other	22	2	3	2	1	0

Sources: Dragnich and Rasmussen 1974, 81; Lloyd 1993, 269, 308, 313, 334, 357.

party may divide its attention).[65] This does not mean that the national parties are similar but rather that the parties provide a "package" of policies rather than catering to a single, niche constituency.[66]

The Westminster system also encourages party discipline, although backbenchers are not completely docile.[67] Both parties show considerable activity from the backbench during question period and the tabling of Early Day Motions.[68] However, disagreement must be muted when defection might mean a defeat of one's party at the polls. Such defeat might precipitate a radical change in policies, even more odious than the decisions that precipitated one's defection from one's own party. Empirical studies confirm that party discipline is particularly strong for the party in power. Pinto-Duschinsky argues that party discipline derives mainly from deference, from the party whip, and particularly from the prospect of possible electoral defeat.[69] His discussion of the Conservative Party may well be extended to Labour, or to any two-party system of the Westminster mold. While surveys show that the Labour Party members of Parliament vary more in their views than their Conservative counterparts, both show considerable unity in the face of the opponent.[70] Cabinet and prime minister thus enjoy considerable leverage over their own party and thus the legislature. Ronald Butt argues that the prime minister can implement policies against the party's preferences.[71]

The British system, consequently, presents few partisan veto points, and arguably there is but a single decision point. Executive power is based on the support of a single party rather than a coalition; the executive tends to

65. For an example of specialization in multimember districts, see Cowhey's (1993a) discussion of the Japanese political system.
66. Kornberg and Frasure 1971; Frasure 1972.
67. See, for a general discussion, Moodie 1971, 114–17.
68. Barnett 1968–69, 52.
69. Pinto-Duschinsky 1972, 13, 16.
70. Kornberg and Frasure 1971, 701–3.
71. Butt 1966, 373.

dominate the legislature; the system is decidedly two-party; the electoral system is disproportional; and the prime minister controls the party.

Party Discussions and Party Discipline

Although electoral rules provide strategic reasons for party members to adhere to the party line, other features, such as party leadership and shared political background, also work to enhance party discipline. The Conservative Party tends to close ranks slightly more effectively than Labour, although both parties are far more disciplined than their counterparts in other democracies.[72]

Labour and Conservative governments have the prerogative of employing the party whip. When the whip is off, members have greater latitude to vote their own preferences, whereas when it is on, a contrary vote will be registered as an open challenge.[73] Defection with the whip on occurs very rarely.

Studies of the Conservative Party have revealed that party discipline particularly hinges on the prospects of career advancement and the similarity of social backgrounds. Members with reasonable prospects for advancement rarely opposed the leadership, whereas those who had not been advanced for considerable numbers of years, or who faced the final stages of their political careers, tended to be more obstreperous. The considerable homogeneity of social and educational backgrounds led members of the Conservative Party to side with the leadership rather than to cross party lines.[74] "There were tangible incentives for Conservative Parliament members to eschew factional in-fighting and support the government in its many twists and turns. The more able and ambitious within the parliamentary party soon learned the importance of political flexibility."[75]

This is not say that disagreements did not occur within the Conservative ranks during the 1950s, but overall these differences tended to be less pronounced than those among Labour members of Parliament. Both parties experienced internal disputes, even when they held office. Lynskey argues that Labour underwent thirty such disputes between 1945 and 1951, while the Conservatives had twenty-seven in the 1951–57 period.[76] However, with few institutionalized means to express dissent—such as the informal discus-

---

72. One analysis of Conservative Party discipline demonstrated that only one vote in three hundred diverged from party leadership preferences. By contrast, in the U.S. Congress one vote in three showed considerable deviation. Schwarz and Lambert 1971, 399.

73. Historical evidence demonstrates there is less reason to exercise party discipline and apply the whip when the party is out of power. Schwarz and Lambert 1971, 414, n. 32.

74. Schwarz and Lambert 1971, 413.

75. Murphy 1995, 202.

76. Lynskey 1973.

sion groups of the Conservative Party—Labour dissidents were more likely to go public. Labour dissenters tended to vote against party lines (the maximum number of one such vote came to seventy-two) and abstain more (maximum of one hundred) than the Conservative members of Parliament (maximum number of defection votes, twenty-eight, and abstentions, fifteen). Even on the Suez issue the differences within the party led to little overt protest in Conservative ranks, as only fifteen abstained on the decision to withdraw from Suez under American pressure.

Divergent elements in the Conservative Party tended to create private forums to advance particular views.[77] In the immediate postwar years, the Conservative Party encompassed several groups or tendencies.[78] The Conservative Political Centre (1947) and the One Nation Group (1950) were attempts to reconcile the Conservative Party program with the welfare state. The Bow Group, formed in 1951, emerged to counteract the intellectual appeal of Labour.[79]

The Bow Group became the progressive element within the Conservative Party. Contrary to the traditional view within the party that favored evolutionary change, the role of status, and the value of tradition, the Bow adherents supported meritocracy, policy planning, and rapid change. They believed that the colonial problem called for compromise and settlement, driven by an evaluation of benefits over costs, rather than by organic political evolution in Africa.[80] The 1959 election, which expanded the Conservative majority, brought considerable numbers of members of Parliament to power who were sympathetic to the Bow program.[81]

The Monday Club formed as their counterpart, bringing together some of the established Conservatives. Less intellectual in intent, they opposed early independence for the colonies. When Rhodesia broke away after 1965 to set up a white minority government, they opposed sanctions. Like the Bow Group, the Monday Club did not discuss its positions publicly. It circulated memos and newsletters but did not record individual policy statements. Disagreements with the leadership remained in-house.[82] The two main intellectual currents in the Conservative Party, the progressively minded Bow group and the more traditional Monday Club, provided the setting for off-the-record discussions and for the development of policy briefs that could be disavowed when necessary.

77. Rose 1964, 45–46.
78. Rose speaks merely of "tendencies" rather than factions (Rose 1964, 40). Seyd (1972) makes a similar point. Labour, by contrast, did have factions, which were more organized and vociferous, and thus the party leadership did not allow them formal organization.
79. Critchley 1961.
80. For discussions within the Conservative Party, see Rose 1961a.
81. Rose 1961b.
82. Seyd 1972, 468–69.

Macmillan Opts for Exit

The reluctance of the Churchill and Eden governments to decolonize did not stem merely from personal idiosyncrasies. Certainly Churchill had never championed the freedoms of subject people. But objectively as well the overall context seemed to have improved. The Korean War had improved the dollar earnings of some of the resource-exporting colonies. Britain's own economic fate had improved since the dark days of 1945 and 1947. Moreover, the cold war meant that American pressure for decolonization could be tempered by a shared objective to prevent Communist regimes from taking the place of British rule. Indeed, if anything, the Kenyan and Malayan emergencies proved that limited force could still be used to squelch nationalist movements.

Britain could thus dictate the pace and nature of territorial separation. Sui generis cases such as Libya, India, and Israel would not spark contagion effects. The Gold Coast also was considered a special test case for gradual dissolution and dual rule, with considerable powers being exercised by the colonial governor. It did not signify that Britain intended to retreat in other areas. Strategic staging areas, such as Aden, Gibraltar, and Malta, would likely never become independent.[83]

A roll call of ministers demonstrates how these governments saw the situation as hardly requiring scuttle. Lyttelton was colonial secretary from October 1951 until July 1954 and was an opponent of the concessions granted to the Gold Coast. As a former businessman and president of the board of trade during the war, he also supported a harder line in East Africa, given the importance of the copper revenues.[84] His successor, Alan Lennox-Boyd, also anticipated a longer British presence in East Africa. Both were conservative minded, and, given the deference given to ministerial autonomy by their party backbenchers, they managed to firmly imprint their views on colonial policy. There might be redeployment but not retreat.[85] Lord Salisbury became lord president of the Council in the Cabinet from 1952 until 1957. Concessions granted to West Africa would not be extended to East Africa, and any change would be gradual at best. The colonies, said Salisbury in 1953, were but "small countries inhabited by primitive peoples . . . not adult nations."[86]

At the prime ministerial level things were no different. Churchill, after a series of small strokes, gradually retreated from politics; he announced his

---

83. For the argument that the Conservative policy had a multidimensional quality, see Goldsworthy 1990.

84. Hargreaves 1996, 129, 148.

85. Goldsworthy 1990, 101–2; Horowitz 1970, 21, 24–25.

86. Quoted in Goldsworthy 1990, 85.

resignation in July 1955. Foreign Secretary Eden then took on the party leadership.[87] Neither man advocated speedy withdrawal from East Africa.

If Singapore had been a watershed for Britain's position in East Asia, arguably the Suez crisis in the fall of 1956 had similar ramifications. Nasser, who had risen to power in the Free Officers Movement that deposed King Farouk in 1952, became prime minister in 1954. He expounded the virtues of pan-Arab nationalism and the need to aid the still-colonized territories. This was worrisome enough, and the Eden government likened him to Hitler and Goebbels.[88] Egypt's subsequent nationalization of the Suez Canal (for which Nasser offered compensation) triggered British, French, and Israeli military action.

Until Suez, Britain's relative decline could be acknowledged without admitting to fundamental weaknesses—redeployment not retreat. Britain was still a great power and a nuclear one at that. There were even grumblings about American leadership, with Eden believing that U.S. secretary of state John Foster Dulles was a "disaster looking for a place to happen."[89] Nor did Britain have any a priori reason to believe that military options would not work against Nasser. Indeed France, Britain, and Israel achieved virtually all their military objectives with minimal loss of life and in short order.

International pressure, and an American financial stranglehold, however, completely overshadowed any prospects of long-term success. London decided to withdraw its forces. This denouement and loss of prestige led to the downfall of Eden. Although some of the participants denied that Britain had shown any material weakness (Selwyn Lloyd saw it as largely a psychological problem involving British self-doubt), most agree that this was a watershed.[90] "Overall the Suez crisis represented the effective end of the British era in the Middle East . . . and brought home to the British government the reduction of British power and influence."[91]

Macmillan, who assumed office as prime minister early in 1957 (and was ironically a staunch proponent of the Suez mission), inherited a party in controversy. Some conservatives believed that the forces should not have been withdrawn from Suez because that would encourage nationalists everywhere. Exactly when Macmillan moved to support rapid decolonization can be debated. However, he soon drew the conclusion that Suez proved Britain could no longer unilaterally make its own foreign policy. More than ever, American preferences had to be taken into account. He also believed that imperial holdings were becoming more of a burden

87. For a discussion of this episode, see Gilbert 1991, 912ff.
88. See Selwyn Lloyd's views, 1978.
89. Lloyd 1993, 319.
90. S. Lloyd 1978, 210, 252–253.
91. Clayton 1999, 300. For similar assessments, see Hargreaves 1996, 168–70; Navias 1996, 220.

than a benefit. Britain's geostrategic preeminence had been a historical aberration.[92]

He also disagreed with some of his party colleagues about the importance of European integration. Hard-liners preferred to keep the Common Market at arm's length. Closer European integration signaled to them a shift of emphasis from Britain as a world power to a regional role. Moreover, they had doubts about the ability and willingness of Europe to accommodate British colonial and dominion demands. From Macmillan's perspective there was no choice, regardless of commonwealth pressures. The future for Britain lay in closer European cooperation.[93]

Macmillan had started to develop these ideas even earlier, during the Churchill and Eden administrations. He had the mind, as one observer put it, of "someone at the Exchequer," where he had been from 1955 until 1957. Recall that the treasury department in the 1940s and early 1950s had clashed with the Colonial Office and the Colonial Development Corporation in their attempts to develop the colonies with metropolitan financial support. Costs and benefits had to drive decisions. Even the valuable colonial possessions could not possibly substitute for a Britain in Europe.[94]

Initially, however, Macmillan moved with some caution. White settlers and those members of the business community who favored fewer concessions had important political allies. Lord Salisbury and the Monday Club were the more visible of these, but they were not alone. Thus, the chairman of the Conservative parliamentary East and Central Africa Committee (and member of the Monday Club) Patrick Wall could tour Africa as late as 1960 and state with some plausibility that "Britain intends to hold on to power in Kenya . . . for many years to come."[95]

Although Macmillan already possessed considerable means to control the opposition within his own party, given the electoral system and the two-party nature of British politics, his position improved considerably after 1959. In the lead-up to the election the Labour government had argued that "Mr. Macmillan and Mr. Selwyn Lloyd will be regarded by the rest of the world as men with blood on their hands."[96] But domestic issues dominated the scene: "Public opinion polls showed that to most of them concern for their economic well-being came first; foreign affairs came a poor second; colonial and other issues were nowhere."[97] Here, as in other countries, political elites decided the territorial question, not the public.

92. Horowitz 1970, 16.
93. Butt 1966.
94. See this assessment of Macmillan in Butt 1966, 375; Goldsworthy 1990, 86.
95. Wall 1960, 215. See also Hargreaves 1996, 201.
96. Butler and Rose 1960, 55.
97. Butler and Rose 1960, 71.

In the 1959 election the Conservatives gained twenty seats, and the recalcitrance of some hard-liners in the party could be dismissed. One of Macmillan's opponents of rapid decolonization, Lennox-Boyd, had moved to the House of Lords and surrendered as colonial secretary, to be replaced by Iain Macleod, who supported Macmillan's position. From then on Macmillan set out to complete the policy that arguably had gelled earlier but had not been articulated in full. Thus, the rudiments to his famous "wind of change" speech, which announced British withdrawal from Africa in 1960, already appear in a speech in Bedford in 1957.[98] His strong prime ministerial position and the 1959 election, however, showed that he was the uncontested party leader who could now act on his views.[99] Macleod, similarly, supported rapid decolonization and released some of the jailed nationalists, such as Hastings Banda and Jomo Kenyatta, against conservative opposition.

The scholarly literature shows a remarkable consistency in its evaluation that the executive drove British territorial policy. Horowitz's assessment is succinct:

> The policy of rapid decolonization was a government sponsored rather than party sponsored policy. It was the pragmatic viewpoint of Whitehall rather than the more partisan approach of Westminster that inspired this policy, which was in fact never welcomed by the lower echelons of the party.[100]

Nor did an anti-empire business coalition or the bureaucracy drive policies.[101] What had even been true for the Malayan emergency in the early part of the decade—that a harmony of interests might exist between Conservative government and business groups but that such groups did not dictate policy—held even more for decolonization.[102] Overall, government calculations based on national self-interest drove policy.[103]

Macmillan consequently implemented the Conservative Party's policies from the top down, with Macleod leading the charge. First, he provided very little information to backbenchers. Conservative members of Parliament who informed concerned settlers and business interests that they

---

98. "The wind of change is blowing through this continent . . . this growth of national consciousness is a political fact. We must all accept it as a fact, and our national policies must take account of it." Hyam and Louis 2000, pt. I, no. 32. Address to the Parliament of South Africa; February 3, 1960.

99. Butt 1966, 374.

100. Horowitz 1970, 23.

101. Butt 1966.

102. On the Malayan emergency, see White 1998, 153–54. For the general lack of influence of interest groups, see Rose 1964, 42.

103. Goldsworthy 1990, 82.

would not be abandoned, as did Wall, did not do so out of duplicity. They were simply kept in the dark.[104]

Second, he depicted decolonization as a series of ad hoc and unrelated measures. This not only limited the appeal of precedents to nationalists but it also limited the concern of whites in Africa and large businesses. By claiming that the Gold Coast differed fundamentally from East Africa, nationalists in the latter area might moderate their timetable and their lists of demands. At the same time, settlers and business interests in East Africa could feel secure, since surely the abandonment of the Gold Coast had no bearing on them. In reality, Macmillan had come to see the processes in East and West Africa as similar phenomena. Thus, opposition in East Africa and within the more hard-line circles of the Conservative Party only formed slowly, when decolonization was already upon them. By depicting decolonization as a piecemeal and unrelated sequence, Macmillan could present the party dissidents with a fait accompli, which could only be opposed by overt party rebellion—virtually unthinkable given the nature of party discipline.

To gain nationalist support in Kenya, Macmillan's government brokered a massive land distribution, which by July 1962 transferred more than a million acres from European settlers to African indigenes. With British and World Bank support, white settlers received compensation, while fixed prices for commodities helped win over the indigenous middle class. The prime minister could thus retreat from Kenya without too much settler resistance, managing to move liberals and moderates into power.[105] The CAF, however, failed; and Nyasaland, North Rhodesia, and South Rhodesia became separate entities.[106]

NEGOTIATING WITH THE NATIONALISTS: BRITISH REPUTATION AND COMMITMENT

Edmund Burke, a full century and a half earlier, had argued that imperial government should intend to prepare the colonies for independence.[107] Imperial government meant tutelage and education. When certain preconditions had been met that would qualify India as an advanced state, then Britain would willingly hand over power. This "prerequisites model"

---

104. For a discussion of Macmillan's tactics, see Horowitz 1970.

105. See Wasserman 1973, 109–17. Some land transfers had started in 1959. Hargreaves 1996, 209, 216.

106. Lloyd 1993, 365.

107. The doctrine of imperial trusteeship thus emerged; Bridge 1976, 179. For Burke's critique of British maladministration of India, see Whelan 1996.

was resurrected to serve as a basis for British policy in the interwar period and beyond.

India presented the foremost problem of the interwar period. The resolution of the Indian "problem" is illustrative because it became a template for British and nationalist interaction elsewhere in the empire, and because it showed Britain's ability to credibly commit to negotiated solutions.

The British government in the 1930s aimed to curtail nationalist appeals by institutional designs in the White Paper for the All India Federation in 1934 and the Government of India Act in 1935. On the one hand, London favored devolution of powers to the provinces—thus diminishing the appeal of the nationalist, centralist Indian National Congress Party. However, the central government, through the governor-general, was still granted considerable powers to check the centrifugal tendencies of the provinces and ethnic tensions in the heterogeneous Indian society. The princely states, furthermore, were to be used as checks on the Indian congress, by configuring them into a federal structure.[108]

Nationalist movements elsewhere, while not insignificant (particularly in the Middle East), were deemed less critical. India was thought to constitute a special case, not a blueprint for colonial policy elsewhere. The African colonies, it was believed, were not even close to fulfilling the prerequisites model. Hence, Colonial Secretary Malcolm Macdonald confidently declared before the House of Commons in December 1938 that British rule would still be necessary and possible in West Africa for several centuries.[109] In India, however, the British confronted a well-organized nationalist infrastructure, ready to take over the government. And London, despite incidents such as the Amritsar massacre, demonstrated a willingness to negotiate a transfer of power to established national authorities, if British terms could be met.

During the war Indian nationalist demands increased correspondingly with decreasing British military might. Few went so far as Chandra Bose who took refuge in Germany, from where he broadcast Nazi propaganda. However, some elements of the Indian National Army who had been captured when Malaya fell did join the Japanese. Overall, the size of the Indian National Army (forty thousand at most) paled in comparison with the overall Indian effort on the empire's behalf.[110] Most nationalists did not oppose the metropole outright, but they did make clear that their support would only be forthcoming with credible commitments for Indian independence. Consequently, the Cripps Commission recommended in March 30, 1942 (when a Japanese attack on India still seemed a possibility) that steps be

---

108. See the discussions by Bridge 1976; Ghosh 1965.
109. Albertini 1969, 33.
110. Fay 1993, 525–26; James 1994, 502–3.

taken for "the earliest realization of self government in India," much to the dismay of Churchill.[111] This essentially sealed Britain's position in India. Despite Churchill's grumblings that he had not become the king's minister to preside over the dissolution of the empire, the concessions granted to the nationalists during the war could not be repealed.

Moreover, with the dramatic defeat of the Conservative Party at the polls just as the war concluded, the party was in no position to oppose the decolonizing tendencies within the Labour government. Although Churchill had hardly been an advocate of Indian independence, he did support the Labour government in the swift transition.[112] When Lord Mountbatten became viceroy of India to oversee the transition he actually moved up the timetable of Indian independence by ten months.[113]

Finally, the Indian nationalists had rid themselves of any Communist connotation. The Communist Party of India had, after the Soviet Union's entry into the war, thrown its weight behind Britain without having much to show for it. Their subsequent loss of legitimacy left the Congress Party as the primary recipient of nationalist sentiments. It was a party with whom the metropolitan government believed it could negotiate a settlement.[114]

Regarding the Middle East and North Africa, Britain had already resolved during the war that those countries should be given independence. Egypt had already been handed independence in 1922 as had Iraq in 1932. With American support it enforced its decision on the reluctant French, who wished to reimpose French authority in some of the former mandates such as Syria. London believed that moderate nationalists provided the best defense against Soviet encroachment in that area.

The nationalist movements in East and West Africa, while less formalized than Asian nationalist movements, also gradually gained in strength. Indeed, they partially did so in reaction to India's success in freeing itself from British rule. But for the most part Britain faced few problems in Africa in the immediate postwar years. Nevertheless, it was self-evident that the lack of African participation in government bred resentment. Although a British commission might argue in 1948 that 98 senior posts held by Africans in the Gold Coast (out of 1,300 such positions) constituted "a fair increase" since 1927, when only 27 Africans held such posts (out of a total of 500), nationalists could hardly support such a view.[115] A prerequisites

111. Betts 1985, 177–81; Albertini (1969, 27) sees it as an explicit quid pro quo.

112. Lloyd 1993, 283; Gilbert 1991, 884–85.

113. For a brief discussion see MacFarquhar 1997. See also Lloyd 1993, 278–279.

114. Low 1991, 42, 125. One problem that remained was the incorporation of India in the all-white commonwealth. Ghosh 1965, 199. Indian republicanism also presented a problem, in that the king remained technically head of state in the commonwealth system. Lloyd 1993, 282.

115. Report of the Commission of Enquiry into Disturbances in the Gold Coast, colonial report 231, 1948. Cited in Hargreaves 1996, 119.

model held back East African demands for another decade and a half, until there too London gave in.

Britain aimed to create nationalist, noncommunist intermediaries with which the government could continue to interact after the transition. In Kenya the British government actively supported the Kenya African Democratic Union (KADU), the party favored by the proponents of multiracialism and nationalist compromise.[116] Ultimately, the more militant Kenya African National Union (KANU) became the larger party, but the presence of KADU forced it to adopt a more conciliatory stance toward the British position. "The desire to reach agreement with KADU, thus entering the government and preventing exclusion from leading Kenya to independence, also played a role."[117]

It should be clear then that the British strategy of dealing with nationalist agitation differed significantly from the French and Dutch policies.[118] First, the prerequisites model established particular criteria for a transition of power. Transition was thus in principle possible, or at least it could be debated. Of course, nationalists might argue that prerequisites had been met, and London might disagree, but it framed the discussion in terms of timing and the appropriateness of transition, rather than precluding independence outright.

Furthermore, in fostering anticommunist nationalist elites, the British also created a viable negotiating partner that could credibly commit the nationalist side. Whereas the French and Dutch hard line before and after the war had eroded the ability of the nationalists to control their sides, the British dealt with independence movements that were well established, such as the Indian National Congress.

Second, and contrary to the suggestion that governments that can rapidly change policy cannot credibly commit, London was not at a disadvantage. To the contrary, with few veto players to oppose them, British negotiators could *initiate* policy proposals and engage in discussions with the nationalists without fear that agreements would subsequently unravel.

Moreover, and this is why I have discussed British policy in India, London was able to establish a reputation and credibility that they would *implement* the agreements they had reached with the nationalists. Even if it had wanted to renege on agreements, and even if it had few domestic barriers to prevent such reversal of policy, Albion had not proved perfidious. Thus, its follow-through on the Cripps agreement in India gave nationalists in Africa confidence that Britain would live up to the terms of any deal. In-

116. Wasserman 1973, 108–11.
117. Wasserman 1973, 116.
118. Low explicitly contrasts British concessions with the lack of compromise in the Dutch East Indies. Low 1991, 134.

deed, African nationalists saw the Indian movement as a precedent and named their own movements after the Congress Party.[119] Britain established credibility by iterative actions.

Finally, the independence movements believed (correctly) that de facto it would be very difficult for Britain to renege on the implementation of agreements. In other words, like a ratchet, the negotiations and a drawdown of metropolitan military and economic commitments would be very difficult to reverse. Business interests, after all, would alter their behavior and disinvest with the first sign of metropolitan withdrawal. And if the government had considered the subject area not critical for the mother country, in that it had entered into negotiations with the nationalists, then how could that government later expect to generate support to retake the contested territories by an all-out military effort? In short, the nationalists concluded that the door swung only one way.

The British experience stands in marked contrast with that of France. Even though it faced roughly similar international circumstances, it weathered the challenges from its overseas possessions without getting embroiled in protracted nationalist conflicts. Like the French, the British initially believed that empire led to great power status. And like France in Algeria it had significant economic assets as well as settlers in East Africa. Yet Whitehall managed to pursue a dramatically different course.

Civilian control over the military was never in doubt, and even if it had been, the armed forces had less of a stake in empire than their French equivalents. Pressure thus came from some but not all business interests, and primarily from the settlers in East Africa. Their allies in the Conservative Party sought to forestall any swift retreat from East Africa.

However, by 1957 Prime Minister Macmillan had concluded that British imperial strategy needed to be justified by sound cost-benefit calculations. When he and his cabinet came to the conclusion that East Africa (and other areas) contributed little to British security and welfare, he opted for negotiated withdrawal. Despite some business pressure and more active settler opposition, Whitehall pushed its preferences through without much upheaval. The British system provided no constitutional or partisan veto points through which hard-liners could forestall the concessions that Whitehall favored.

Moreover, due to strict party discipline, the Conservative rank and file supported the decisions from the top. Differences of opinion in the Conservative Party were dealt with in informal discussion sessions. Widespread open rebellion never erupted, since backbenchers tended to follow party

119. Chamberlain 1999, 11.

leadership in the interests of their own careers and to prevent the party's electoral defeat.

In realizing that the British public and the median voter had little interest in fighting for their nation's overseas territories, Macmillan could swiftly implement his views over the opponents of territorial adjustment. Hardline politicians lacked the institutional means to exercise a veto when Harold Macmillan decided that Britain's future lay in tacking to the wind of change.

Ranking with Denmark:
The Dutch Fear of Imperial Retreat

> I believe since we have now worked here in Indonesia for three hundred years, that it will take another three hundred years, before Indonesia will be ready for a form of independence.
>
> B. C. DE JONGHE, governor-general of Dutch East Indies, 1936

Within a decade of Governor de Jonghe's confident statement, the seemingly unbreakable bond between the Netherlands and Indonesia was broken. Thousands of Dutch and tens of thousands of Indonesians died in the struggle for independence between August 1945 (when the nationalists under Ahmed Sukarno and Muhammad Hatta proclaimed the independent Republic of Indonesia) and the transfer of power in 1949. In the process the Netherlands antagonized its powerful allies, most importantly the United States; it deployed a large military contingent overseas; it put heavy burdens on its weak postwar economy; and it steadfastly refused to yield even when it became clear it could not win.[1] Even when it granted Indonesia independence on December 27, 1949, the Netherlands refused to relinquish all of the archipelago, but kept control over western New Guinea out of a "pathological" sense of "nauseating self-righteousness, vengeance, and pseudo-morality."[2]

Why did the Netherlands choose to fight for its empire, whereas a great power such as Britain chose to divest itself by negotiated settlement? As I argued in chapter 2, neither security reasons nor relative power can explain the Dutch decision. Indonesia did not aid the security of the mother coun-

---

1. The costs of World War II had been severe, amounting to roughly 230,000 Dutch casualties and 25 billion guilders in damages. Duynstee and Bosmans 1977, 14–15.
2. De Jong attributes this description of Dutch behavior to Arend Lijphart; de Jong 1988, vol. 12, 1077. For a succinct overview of the period, see Drooglever 1997.

try, and the strength of the nationalist movement had increased dramatically during the war. At the time, a case was made for the economic benefits of retaining Indonesia, but on closer examination the case was suspect, to say the least.

Given its status as a small power, the declining benefits of empire, the extreme costs associated with retaking Indonesia from nationalist control, and the opposition of Britain and the United States, one would expect Dutch policy would have been to relinquish their empire conforming with realist expectations. The Dutch case, in other words, provides a tough test of my argument that domestic institutions play an important role in determining territorial policy, even when environmental conditions dictate that the state should pursue a different course.

The Dutch case also presents a good test for the argument that multiparty coalitional governments make policy change more difficult. More specifically, because the civilian leadership maintained oversight and control over the military, one can isolate the impact of institutional arrangements as an independent variable. As we have seen in chapter 3, the French case is overdetermined. The lack of civilian oversight and the fragmented multiparty system with a weak executive all affected French policies. The Dutch case allows us to make a controlled comparison with the British case, in that London too exercised civilian control over the military.

Indonesia (before the war called Dutch East India or the Dutch East Indies), far more than the West Indies, was the key colony for the Dutch. Its population was much larger (close to 60 million compared to the quarter of a million in the West Indies), and it had been economically critical for the Netherlands. Dutch decolonization, in other words, hinged on the Indonesian question.

The empirical evidence substantiates my theory that the presence of multiple veto points will likely prevent policy change and that the likelihood of compromise with nationalist demands will decrease as the number of veto opportunities for hard-liners increases.

Although the military remained faithful to civilian control, the Dutch multiparty system and coalitional dynamics created multiple partisan veto points. Politicians who had similar interests to the settler community and large corporations used these veto opportunities to block compromise solutions. Radical shifts in the international milieu and Indonesian nationalist demands were consistently downplayed, sometimes even ignored outright, by The Hague.[3] The veto opportunities arose because, even though the Catholic People's Party (KVP) and the Socialists represented by the Labor

---

3. Although Amsterdam is regarded as the capital of the Netherlands, The Hague is actually the seat of government.

Party (PvdA) disagreed on colonial policy, they explicitly logrolled on issues about which one or the other coalition partner felt strongly.

THE DUTCH HARD-LINE POLICY AFTER 1945

Despite the changed international conditions and the strength of the nationalist movement in 1945 the Dutch metropolitan government decided to try to retake Indonesia by force. It refused to countenance any change from in its prewar territorial policy. During two "police actions," one in July 1947 and the other in December 1948, the government brought a force of 102,000 troops to bear on Java and roughly 22,500 on Sumatra, with another 27,000 scattered over the other islands, amounting overall to close to 150,000 men.[4]

The decision to try to oust the self-proclaimed Republic of Indonesia by force was neither instantaneous nor unanimous. Many politicians did not favor a hard-line policy. Indeed, particularly during the early post–World War II period, compromise and a negotiated settlement of the dispute seemed possible. In the first postwar Dutch government (June 1945–July 1946) there were several occasions when a solution seemed near. The lieutenant governor-general in Indonesia, H. J. van Mook, seemed willing to go the furthest.[5] In the pre-negotiations held before the Hoge Veluwe conference of April 1946, he brokered a deal with the republic's representative, Sutan Sjahrir (who had not collaborated with the Japanese and was thus more acceptable than Sukarno, who had).[6] In exchange for de facto recognition of the Republic of Indonesia, the republic would consent to a federal structure for Indonesia, with the republic (which controlled Java and part of Sumatra) as only one constituent part. The assessment by van Mook and by Minister of Overseas Territories, the Socialist J. H. Logemann, was realistic in a way that was missing in subsequent years. They recognized that Britain was too weak to come to Dutch aid, while the United States was unwilling to do so, and the Dutch by themselves were militarily too weak to force a solution. The republic could only get stronger as time passed. M. van der Goes Naters (the PvdA party leader) similarly foresaw dire consequences if the Netherlands failed to negotiate. The United Nations would get involved, and the United States would halt loans to the Netherlands, which would mean "the end of everything."[7] Nevertheless, the Dutch

---

4. See Schulten 1987, 29.

5. The Dutch did not appoint a full governor-general after the war, pending a constitutional revision of the status of the Netherlands and the other territories.

6. Low 1991, 135.

7. For these assessments of the situation, see Duynstee and Bosmans 1977, 637–38, 641, 657; Bogaarts 1989, vol. A, 150–51.

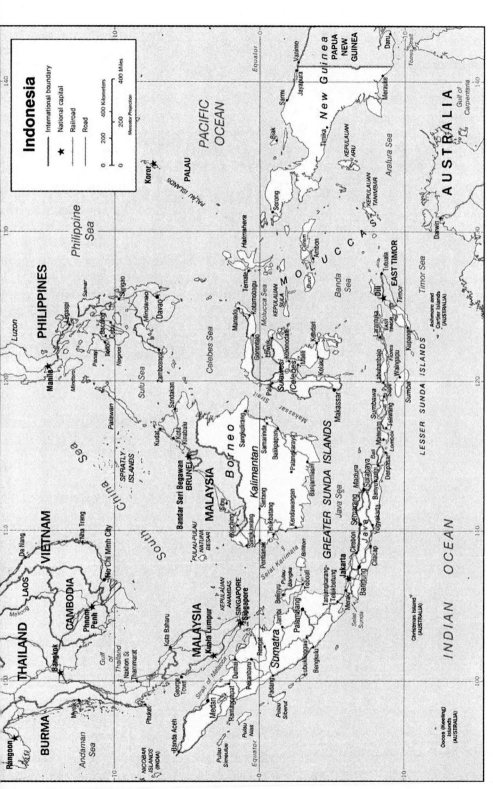

Indonesia, 2002. Map produced by the CIA. With kind permission of the Perry Castañeda Map Collection, University of Texas.

cabinet disavowed the agreement. Catholic Party leader C. P. M. Romme labeled the negotiations with the nationalists "a week of disgrace."[8]

After the elections in the summer of 1946 new negotiations seemed to result in another agreement: the Linggadjati accord of November 1946. But again the Dutch parliament "reinterpreted" the accord after the fact and would only sign the unilaterally reinterpreted accord in March 1947.

This did not meet with Indonesian approval, and the continuing chaos and fighting led to the Dutch decision to try to quell the nationalist movement by force in the first police action of July 1947. The first police action (one important military operation was significantly code-named "Operation Product") aimed at reconquering territories where there were large Dutch corporations that produced oil, minerals, and plantation crops (coffee, rubber).[9] The Dutch achieved many of their objectives but were held short of full territorial reconquest, partially because of pressure from the UN Security Council and the United States's call for a cease-fire.[10] American and Security Council insistence led to the formation of the Commission of Good Services and another agreement in January 1948: the Renville accord. Even though the U.S.-brokered agreement seemed to grant the Dutch government much of what it wanted—a federal state of Indonesia with distinct areas but still affiliated with the Netherlands—it turned out to be a Pyrrhic victory. More important in American eyes was that the agreement led to international recognition of the republic.[11]

The accord did not last, and in December 1948 the Dutch launched their second police action. Like the first operation, this action succeeded in taking many of the territories held by republican troops, although some of the republican military staff escaped into the hinterlands to continue a guerrilla war. In both actions immediate Dutch casualties were light, about two hundred deaths in each action. However, subsequent skirmishing, sniping, and guerilla attacks inflicted a higher toll, in the range of 1,100 dead.[12] The casualty rates for the Indonesians were, however, measured in the tens of thousands. Thus, the total number of dead between 1945 and 1949 amounted to fewer than five thousand Dutch troops; but in 1949 alone there were about fifty thousand Indonesian casualties.[13]

---

8. Duynstee and Bosmans 1977, 642.

9. *Officiële Bescheiden Betreffende de Nederlands-Indische Betrekkingen* (hereafter *NIB*) 1981, vol. 19, docs. 124, p. 153. The operational directives called for occupation of territories in which "economic gains might be made."

10. van den Doel 1996, 289.

11. Giebels 1996, 259.

12. van den Doel 1996, 290, 293.

13. van Doorn 1995a, 70, 73. Schulten (1987, 29) notes that 4,751 Dutch troops died (regular army and KNIL, including disease and accident victims).

Should Dutch policy be seen as strategically realist assessment? Hardly. The government consistently failed to recognize how conditions had fundamentally altered during World War II and the postwar period. The Netherlands lacked support from the great powers, and the nationalists had proved capable of unified political and military action.

Ironically, much of what the Dutch sought might have been achieved had they chosen to negotiate. In the assessment of the historian Louis de Jong, "Much of the calamity could have been avoided had van Mook been given a free hand in 1945–46."[14] Indeed, the earlier Dutch position seemed more flexible than the later position. Compromisers were gradually pushed out and replaced by hard-liners. Domestic reasons prevented compromise with the Republic of Indonesia. The fault, however, lay not with a lack of civilian control over the military but in the veto opportunities provided by multiparty coalitional government.

CIVILIAN CONTROL OF THE MILITARY

Military Preferences

The colonial army was a strong supporter of regaining Dutch control over Indonesia. The Royal Dutch Indian Army (KNIL) had different objectives and a different organizational structure than the Dutch army proper. Its strategic mission focused exclusively on containing rebellions and secessionist movements. Given the distance from the Netherlands and the army's manpower problems, the KNIL could only hope to stall rather than defeat an external enemy.[15] For defense of Indonesia against such foreign encroachment the Netherlands had to rely on the United States and Britain.

The KNIL had at one point aimed at increasing its manpower by local conscription. This proposal, however, failed to acquire settler and political support. The Dutch colonists, after all, had come to Indonesia to make money running plantations and mines, not to serve in the military. Moreover, mobilizing the indigenous population had to be done selectively, given the fact that the more than sixty million natives vastly outnumbered the slightly more than two hundred thousand Europeans. Initially, the Dutch colonial army had little regard for the military ability of the Javanese and Sumatrans, and they disproportionately preferred to use Moluccans.[16]

---

14. de Jong 1988, vol. 12, 1075. De Jong was given the lead in the official "History of the Netherlands during World War II," and his assessment carried considerable weight.

15. Teitler 1979, 71–94.

16. The Ambonese elite troops numbered four to five thousand. Drooglever 1987, 75; 1992, 83. (The terms Ambonese and Moluccan are often used interchangeably.)

Dutch conscripts could not be made to serve abroad until after World War II; it required a constitutional amendment in December 1946.[17] The KNIL thus remained a colonial army whose raison d'être hinged on its internal pacification role. It consisted of professional military and had been relatively successful in repressing secessionist movements.[18]

Not surprisingly, the KNIL favored continuation of its historically evolved strategic mission after 1945. The Indonesian issue justified a sizeable military budget at a time of slim postwar financial resources. Moreover, a well-defined European mission had not yet emerged.[19] Nor did the military objectives seem insurmountable. The police actions had precise, finite objectives and were of limited duration. The military, for corporate as well as strategic reasons, thus supported a hard-line policy.[20]

Persistent Civilian Control

Although the military preferred a decisive military response to the republican demands, the decision to choose that option was in the hands of civilian politicians. The military remained, through all phases of the conflict, under the control of its civilian superiors. In Indonesia the chain of command subjected the area commanders directly to the lieutenant governor-general (van Mook) and later the high representative (Beel).[21]

Objective control of the Dutch military was a long-standing one. Military and political functions had been separated since the advent of Dutch democracy in the nineteenth century. Functional division of labor coalesced with professional attitudes, a merit-based promotion system, and organizational autonomy for the military. Unlike in France, the armed forces had played little role in Dutch politics.

And unlike the Vichy regime, the Dutch army had not been tainted by collaboration with the Nazi occupiers. Nor did the military have any reason to blame civilian government for the German success in 1940. It could hardly be expected that the Dutch could have prevailed, no matter what decisions had been made. Civilian and military elites had no historical traumas and rifts to deal with.

One Dutch scholar has argued that some hard-liners, such as former prime minister P. S. Gerbrandy and former minister of colonies J. I. M.

17. Gerbenzon and Algra 1975, 371. The article had been changed by royal proclamation in 1944 but had not yet been amended in the constitution. Duynstee and Bosmans 1977, 563–67.

18. Drooglever 1987, 74.

19. Much of the military budget was thus dedicated to Indonesia, to the detriment of home defense. Bogaarts 1989, vol. A, 728–44.

20. See Teitler 1990, 12–13. The commander of the army, General Spoor, backed by the navy, argued for the strongest union possible.

21. Duynstee and Bosmans 1977, 618.

Welter, may have considered a coup d'état and that they sought the support of the armed forces.[22] But even if true, not much came of these ideas as most of the army would have no part of it, although high-level officers may have been consulted by the would-be plotters.

This is not to say the armed forces were completely docile. At various junctures they expressed their dissatisfaction with Lt. Governor-General van Mook. Admiral C. E. L. Helfrich, on the eve of the first police action, worried about van Mook's limited aims. Arguing against an ultimatum to the republic (since this in his estimate would tip them off to the impending military action), Helfrich warned his subordinates that van Mook might be inclined to a quick cease-fire after hostilities had started: "This may never happen."[23] General Spoor, the commander-in-chief of the army, likewise held van Mook in disregard and at one point asked to be relieved from his post in protest against van Mook's policies.[24] (He nevertheless stayed on, while van Mook was replaced in 1948.)

Overall, though, the military carried out political orders, regardless of what The Hague handed down. Decision making resided indisputably with the parliament. The hard-line policy chosen by the politicians squared well with the military's preferences in Indonesia. Dutch troops executed their orders, not because of military intransigence vis-à-vis civilian superiors but because civilian superiors had opted for a hard line. Indeed, at junctures, the civilian government seemed to expand on the military's objectives. Thus, when General Spoor argued for action in West Java, Prime Minister Louis Beel advanced several reasons why a larger-scale action would be more beneficial.[25]

POLITICS IN THE MULTIPARTY COALITION

The Dutch political system presents multiple partisan but few constitutional veto points. As was true for the British, the Dutch monarchy had long ago receded from the political scene. The Dutch parliamentary system requires legislative support for the cabinet, without which the executive cannot survive. The legislature consists of two chambers. Although both chambers have considerable powers, the Second Chamber outweighs the First Chamber. However, the "two chambers of the Dutch Parliament have remained congruent in their partisan competition (both elected by proportional methods and hence virtual carbon copies of each other)."[26] In this

22. For a discussion of this rather bizarre episode, see Giebels 1996, 228.
23. *NIB* 1981, vol. 19, doc. 216, p. 464.
24. *NIB* 1981, vol. 19, doc. 338.
25. *NIB* 1981, vol. 19, doc. 68, p. 192.
26. Lijphart 1989b, 151.

sense, even though the Dutch system adds a degree of bicameralism it is a far cry from the bicameralism of the American system with its divergent electoral rules. Finally, the Dutch system lacks judicial review in the American sense.

Thus the Dutch constitution unifies power. The locus of decision making resides squarely with the legislature, and specifically the Second Chamber. But within that chamber, the particular features of the electoral system, and the dynamics of coalitional logrolling, present the opportunity for multiple veto players to engage in the policy-making process.

The Return of Multiparty Government after the War

During the war, the Dutch political elites in exile, as well as some of the elites who were interned in the Netherlands, devised plans to change the rigidly segmented political system after the war. Parties that had traditionally played a minor role in governing coalitions were to be incorporated more fully. Most notably the Catholics would become more active in national government, and the Socialists would surrender their radical left-wing program for more conservative national ambitions.[27] Cooperation and reconstruction were to be the key aims of all the parties.

Despite these intentions, Dutch politics returned to its prewar configuration. Parties split along the old division of religious parties and secular ones. The division between Catholics and Protestants also resurfaced. The prewar Roman Catholic State Party (RKSP) was soon renamed the Catholic People's Party (KVP). Two Protestant parties, the Christian Historical Union (CHU) and the Anti-Revolutionary Party (ARP), reappeared as well. Among the main secular parties once again were the Liberals (nineteenth century in orientation and hence actually conservatives), who were first grouped in the Party of Freedom (the PvdV,) and later with some breakaway Socialists (parliamentarian Oud) restyled as the People's Party of Freedom and Democracy (VVD).

The Left was occupied by the Socialist Labor Party (PvdA, prior to the war the SDAP—the Social Democratic Workers Party) and the Communists (CPN). This plethora of parties was at times intermixed with smaller parties, mainly among the Christian groups of various conservative stripes. In this multiparty environment no one party could win the election outright, and coalition governments became, therefore, the norm in Dutch politics.

In 1945–46 an interim government was formed under W. Schermerhorn (PvdA) and W. Drees (also from the Labor Party) and five other Labor ministers. It incorporated the KVP (three cabinet posts), the Liberals (one min-

27. Bosscher 1986, 39.

ister), Protestants (the ARP with one minister), and three nonparty affiliates.[28] The first election after the war was held in 1946.

Electoral Rules and Coalitional Strategies

The Dutch electoral system gives small parties easy access to the legislature. With proportional representation, large number of members in electoral districts, and the absence of a formal electoral threshold, many parties may gain seats. The system is furthermore highly proportional in that the entire country is counted as one electoral district (the Second Chamber at the time had 100 seats). Hans Daalder calls it a "multiparty system with a vengeance."[29] The use of the D'Hondt system of calculating seats has not prevented the presence of many small parties in Dutch politics.[30]

The nature of the electoral system, and the necessity of forming coalitions, had several consequences for Dutch policy on the Indonesian question. First, all parties had to worry about other parties drawing votes away from either their left or right wings. The religious parties were less concerned with predatorial politics among themselves than with the defection of voters to secular parties. Catholics were unlikely to switch to Protestant parties or vice versa. Both denominations, however, feared that secular parties could encroach on their constituency, and indeed the Socialists intended to do so.[31]

Defection within the ranks was also a possibility. Party leadership enforced discipline by controlling electoral funding and placement on party lists. Individual members would thus usually vote the party line. However, serious disagreements with the party leadership could lead to an individual's exit from the party without necessarily jeopardizing that person's political career, because new parties could be formed relatively easily given the low electoral threshold. Thus, before the 1948 election, the conservative Catholic Welter, who had been minister of colonies just before the war, split from the KVP to form his own Catholic National Party (KNP), which favored an even harder line toward the Indonesian nationalists. The KVP, in other words, had to worry that too many concessions to the nationalists would play into the hands of the Catholic Right.

The Labor Party had to worry about its left wing defecting to the Communists who, because of their resistance during the war, had become quite

---

28. See de Jong 1988, vol. 12, 1104ff. For a brief description of various parties, see Irwin and Holsteyn 1989, and the appendixes in Daalder and Irwin 1989, 154–61.

29. Daalder 1989, 13.

30. For a discussion of electoral systems and how they affect the number of parties, see Cox 1997, particularly chaps. 2 and 3; Lijphart 1994; Taagepera and Shugart 1989.

31. For the argument that this was part of the Labor Party's policy, see Bogaarts 1989, vol. A, 32.

Table 5.1. Results of Dutch parliamentary elections
(second chamber—total 100)

	1937	1946	1948
Catholic People's Party (KVP)	31	32	32
Anti-Revolutionary Party (ARP)	17	13	13
Christian Historical Union (CHU)	8	8	9
Labor Party (PvdA)	23	29	27
VDB*	6	With PvdA	
CDU*	2	With PvdA	
Communist Party (CPN)	3	10	8
Party of Freedom (PvdV)/People's† Party for Freedom and Democracy (VVD)	4	6	8
Political Reformed Party (SGP)	2	2	2
Catholic National Party (KNP)‡	—	—	1
National Socialist Movement (NSB)§	4	—	—

*VDB and CDU merged with the SDAP to form the Labor Party after the war. Note: In 1956 the number of seats in the Second Chamber of parliament was expanded from 100 to the present 150. (Data from Daalder and Schuyt in Daalder and Irwin 1989, appendix 2, 159–61f. Bogaarts 1989, vol. A, 36.)

†The statistics for the PvdV and the VVD have been aggregated since the latter became the reformulated liberal party.

‡The KNP was the Catholic splinter party under Welter.

§The NSB formed the Dutch fascist party, which disappeared after the war.

attractive to voters. Labor, however, did not wish to compete on a pure left-wing agenda with the Communists. It aimed to become a more mainstream party in order to pick up a greater share of the median voters; but in doing so it also had to fear the defection of its left-wing members. Conversely, if it tried to outbid the Communists on socialist issues it would likely lose voters on the right wing of the party. Occasional defections to the Right did occur. For example, Oud switched to the Liberals to create the VVD.[32] Consequently, the PvdA competed against the CPN and tried to discredit the latter because of its links to the Soviet Union.[33] The Socialists, in differentiating themselves from the Communists, separated themselves from the only party that supported the nationalist movement outright (at least until the crackdown on the Communists in Indonesia in the fall of 1948).

The Dutch political system also led to institutionalized logrolling, not between individual members of the legislature but between party elites. Because, in an extreme multiparty environment every party is essentially condemned to a minority position, members of the coalition have to be willing to compromise on ministerial positions during the cabinet-formation phase. During that period ministerial seats are negotiated, and the

32. See Bogaarts 1989, vol. A, 38, 166.
33. Bosscher 1986, 39–41.

future policy of the cabinet is laid out in principle. Electoral results roughly determine the number of seats that partners obtain, while intensity of preferences influences the particular ministerial position that a party desires.

This is exactly what occurred in the cabinet formations of the postwar period. Because the KVP had strong preferences about maintaining control in Indonesia, they, from 1945 until 1949, increasingly took up key ministerial posts on colonial issues. Having finally become a full-fledged member of the political scene, they refused to become the party of retreat. The Left, while concerned with the Indonesian question, had more pressing interests in other areas, namely, Labor wanted its ministers for welfare and housing.

"Both in the Coalition and Neither One Out"

The Dutch multiparty system gave rise to another dynamic: parties were afraid to bring down the existing coalition over any single issue. The price for toppling the government might mean exclusion from the next ruling coalition. The slogan for both KVP and Labor became, therefore, "both in the coalition and neither one out" (*beide erin en geen van beide eruit*). They tolerated each other's policies because they wanted to stay in the ruling coalition, even though substantial differences separated the parties.

Strategic coalitional calculations tended to lead to the inclusion of pro-empire positions. The first postwar cabinet to be formed after German capitulation in May 1945 was the joint cabinet of Schermerhorn-Drees (June 1945–July 1946). Schermerhorn and fellow Labor Party member Logemann, together with Lt. Governor-General van Mook, demonstrated their willingness to negotiate with the republic and even to consider the right of secession (sometime in the future). The KVP objected to the policy but decided not to topple the government but to wait for the upcoming elections.[34] Rather than see the government fall, it decided to change the composition of the next cabinet, as new elections were scheduled for 1946.

After the 1946 election, the KVP and Labor formed a coalition cabinet that ruled from July 1946 until August 1948, the Beel cabinet. However, the Catholic People's Party insisted on personnel changes. The Socialists would still get to man the Ministry of Overseas Territories, but Logemann would have to be replaced by J. A. Jonkman, who was not considered a hard-core party member. Schermerhorn was excluded from the cabinet as well (and moved to a post as president of a special commission in Indonesia). Beel took his position as prime minister. Consequently, dissidents in the right wing of the KVP exercised considerable voice during the formation in opposing concessions to the Socialists on the imperial issue.[35] The KVP

---

34. See Duynstee and Bosmans 1977, 624, 651.
35. Bogaarts 1989, vol. A, 165–70; de Jong 1988, vol. 12, 766.

(thirty-two seats) might have tried to exclude the Socialists from government, by trying to get support from the two Protestant parties (combined twenty-one seats), but then they would have had only a small majority to work with, far short of the two-thirds required for pushing through constitutional amendments. They needed the PvdA with its twenty-nine seats.

Labor for its part had ruled out the Communists as partners (they were still receiving 10 percent of the vote), because any affiliation with them would make Labor unsuitable as a coalition partner for others. At the same time, Labor did not want other parties (Protestants and Liberals) in the coalition, who, because of their more conservative leanings, opposed the Socialists' domestic economic program (government planning and welfare policies). The KVP and the Socialists were thus shackled together. The result was a Catholic-Labor coalition with a KVP prime minister (Beel) and six ministers each for Labor and the KVP, with four unaffiliated ministers.

The newly elected parliament had to redraft the constitution to deal with the anticipated changes in the structure of the kingdom as announced in Queen Wilhelmina's radio address of 1942. While acknowledging some measure of independence in the future for Indonesia, the Dutch government in exile in London had turned down wartime proposals from the Americans that Indonesia be given trusteeship status.[36] Instead, the postwar Dutch government planned to create a federal Indonesia without full independence. Moreover, the new parliament elected in 1946 had to amend the constitution, and specifically Article 192, in order to authorize the sending of conscripts to Indonesia. Because the KVP and Labor together only controlled sixty-one of the one hundred seats in parliament, they required other parties' support for this amendment, which they indeed managed to get from parties on the right end of the spectrum.

When new elections became necessary in the summer of 1948, because of the need for another constitutional amendment to regulate the status of the colonies, the KVP favored greater participation in the new coalition by the Liberals and by the other Christian parties (ARP and CHU). This became the Drees (PvdA) cabinet, which governed from 1948 until 1951. It was the government that oversaw the final episode of the Netherlands' presence in Indonesia. The strategy of the KVP was to neutralize the influence of Labor and to incorporate stronger pro-imperial preferences into the decision-making process. The KVP saw the PvdA wavering on the issue, while the CHU and the ARP had opposed the earlier Linggadjati accord and were thus considered more hard line.[37] Consequently, after the July 1948 elections a new cabinet was formed under a Labor prime minister (Drees) but

---

36. The proposal had been put forward by Rupert Emerson in 1942 and was rejected by the Dutch in 1942 and again in 1945. Maas and van Oerle 1987, 20.

37. Bank 1981, 250–51; Bosmans 1981, 209.

with six KVP ministers, five Labor ministers, one from the reformed CHU, and one from the liberal VVD; two others were unaffiliated.[38] Moreover, KVP member J. R. H. van Schaik became the vice-premier, the Liberal D. U. Stikker was appointed minister of foreign affairs, and KVP member E. M. J. Sassen became minister of overseas territories. The Socialists Schermerhorn and Jonkman were excluded. Beel became the new governor-general in Indonesia, technically the "high representative of the Crown," and pushed van Mook out.[39] In short, the KVP and other proponents of a strong union with Indonesia came to occupy key positions in the government apart from the premiership.

Coalitional Logrolling and Military Action

The consequences of coalitional government and the division of ministerial posts came to the fore when the cabinet had to decide on carrying out the police actions. During the decision making leading up to the first action (July 1947), Prime Minister Beel threatened to resign if the cabinet did not support military action. Socialist refusal to support a military solution would thus bring down the coalition. The discussions in the cabinet dragged on for weeks. Britain and the United States weighed in as well, suggesting they understood the predicament of The Hague, but simultaneously warned against military action.[40] Some ministers, including Drees, suggested a greater involvement for the United Nations or the International Court of Justice. Beel thought this would be counterproductive.[41]

Ultimately, the threat of new elections proved decisive for the Labor ministers in the cabinet. The notes of a meeting between the minister of overseas territories, Jonkman, and his department heads are revealing. Jonkman commented at the time that "the discussions in the [Second] Chamber were quite tranquil. . . . This was to be expected because the PvdA feels responsible for the continuation of this government, and it would create problems to the point that it would not be able to cooperate with the KVP."[42] He went on to note that it was possible that the PvdA membership might split but that the KVP would not accept a deviation by Labor at this point.

Drees (then minister of social affairs) justified Labor's consent to the first police action by arguing that it was to be limited in scope and only to implement the Linggadjati agreement.[43] More important, if the Socialist minis-

38. Daalder and Irwin 1989, 161.
39. Giebels 1996, 239. See Maas (1982) on van Mook's dismissal.
40. *NIB* 1981, vol. 19, doc. 102; doc. 178.
41. *NIB* 1981, vol. 19., doc. 68, p. 187; doc. 158, p. 355.
42. *NIB* 1981, vol. 19, doc. 366, p. 729.
43. de Jong 1988, 919.

ters resigned their posts a new coalition cabinet would likely exclude the Socialists, with the result being an even more hard-line policy. As one Labor parliamentarian phrased it, "The holy coalition with the KVP was on the line, and one did not want to jeopardize that." Seven thousand Labor Party members surrendered their membership in protest, but the Catholic-Labor coalition stayed in power.[44]

The second police action (December 1948) saw a similar dynamic. By early December the government had decided to once again launch military action against the republic and enforce a federal solution.[45] The KVP unequivocally favored military action. Minister of Overseas Territories Sassen saw "no room for negotiation," and Romme, the KVP leader, declared that the party would not accept "a government position that does not initiate a police action before the Security Council has time to come to a judgment."[46] The Socialists initially argued that military action could be a disaster and would jeopardize any international support for the Netherlands.[47]

Just days before the commencement of operations the cabinet was deadlocked with the KVP ministers and CHU minister favoring action and the Socialists, Liberal minister Stikker (who later reversed himself), and one of the nonaffiliates favoring negotiations. KVP minister van Schaik intimated that a new election would likely result in a more conservative cabinet.[48] This deadlock meant cabinet dissolution and new elections. Indeed, the queen was informed that the cabinet had fallen. A last minute "compromise," however, was reached to save the coalition, and the second police action was carried out over the Christmas holidays, when the UN Security Council was in recess.[49] Once again the specter of new elections and cabinet exclusion propelled the Labor Party to concede policy making on the Indonesian question to the KVP.

Two factors influenced the balance between the KVP and Labor to the detriment of the latter. The 1946 election results indicated that the Socialists had declined in strength compared to the pre–World War II period. The 1948 returns showed a loss of two more seats. This raised the very real threat of subsequent Labor Party exclusion, because the KVP, the Protestants, and the Liberals together now controlled sixty-two seats in parliament and could thus form a majority coalition without the Socialists, even if it would complicate matters because constitutional redrafting would require

44. See de Jong 1988, 816, 832–33. (De Jong was, incidentally, one of the seven thousand.)
45. Once again realist assessments were available. Van de Goes Naters of the PvdA, even though he supported a military action if a solution was not reached, suggested that a U.S. boycott and withdrawal of Marshall Plan aid would be the most likely result of military action. *NIB* 1991, vol. 16, doc. 10; doc. 11.
46. *NIB* 1991, vol. 16, doc. 21, p. 42; doc. 59, p. 101.
47. *NIB* 1991, vol. 16, doc. 85.
48. *NIB* 1991, vol. 16, doc. 85, p. 132.
49. *NIB* 1991, vol. 16, docs. 88, 96.

sixty-seven votes. Labor was "led by fear of again losing their hard-won positions [in the coalition], by, for example, flexibility [toward the nationalists] on Indonesia."[50]

Moreover, the Socialists had few alternative partners of their own. The CPN was ideologically incompatible. The Liberals—free trade, noninterventionists—would likely oppose the guided economy that the Socialists had in mind. So a coalition for them without the KVP was essentially impossible. Indeed, for decades thereafter all Dutch coalitions had to include the KVP.

In short, the PvdA gave in on the Indonesian issue in order to obtain some of its preferences on domestic economic matters, and to affect Indonesian policy on the margins. It compromised on an issue on which it had less intense preferences in order to maintain its position in the coalition and direct welfare-state policies. The KVP in turn directed overseas policy.

Pressure from Civilian Interest Groups

The KVP did not make up its mind in a vacuum. Like other pro-empire parties it provided a forum for interest groups wishing to forestall compromise. Given the Socialists' domestic economic programs it stands to reason that the large Dutch corporations found a more receptive audience in the Center and Right of the political spectrum. And given the Socialists' traditional reluctance to endorse empire in general, it is, furthermore, hardly surprising that settlers particularly appealed to the religious parties (considered to be Center and Center-Right) and the Liberal Party (traditionally oriented toward business).

Considering the exposure of the Dutch economy to Indonesia and the particular nature of Dutch investments, most large corporations favored a hard-line response to the republican pronouncement of independence. Indonesia was by far the most important destination for Dutch foreign investments. Just before World War II, 40 percent of Dutch foreign investments went to the Dutch East Indies compared to 50 percent for British investment in all its empire and 30 percent for France.[51]

Indeed, "Operation Product," in the first police action, targeted the capture of essential economic areas, mines, and plantations as a high priority. Similarly, during the second police action, politicians argued that the area of operation should be expanded to liberate important Dutch companies from nationalist control. Dutch firms also attempted to keep control over

50. Bosscher 1986, 41.
51. van Doorn 1995a, 19.

tin exploitation and thus insisted during later negotiations on control over the islands Bangka and Billiton (between Sumatra and Borneo) with their tin mines.[52]

The Production Association of Indonesia, the Association of the Dutch East Indies Sugar Industry, and the Mining Association also argued that economic interests required direct control over Indonesia by the government in The Hague. The corporations thought that Lt. Governor-General van Mook was too prone to compromise with the nationalists.[53]

Private entrepreneurs, furthermore, unilaterally armed themselves for their own protection. By arming their employees and affiliates, and by purchasing weapons from European World War II surplus stocks, they managed to engage in low-level conflict of their own.

There were also direct connections between corporate interests and colonial administration in the crossover of personnel. Various directors of Royal Dutch Shell, responsible for 85 percent of all oil production, went on to high positions in the Dutch government. Hendrik Colijn, who had been director of the Batavian Petroleum Company, a subsidiary of Shell, became minister of colonies and ultimately prime minister before World War II. B. C. de Jonghe (the same one who stated that the Dutch would hold on to Indonesia for three hundred years) became governor-general after occupying a high position in Shell.[54] As governor-general he reversed the policies of his reform-minded predecessor, A. C. D. de Graeff.

Close cooperation between government and economic interest groups was nothing new. The corporatist pattern of Dutch politics meant "that in practice many condominia existed between sections of the bureaucracy and sectoral interest groups."[55] The imperial economic interests simply used well-established patterns of influence and communication to further their grievances and concerns.

The settlers and their families, the expatriate Dutch, and many of the "Indo-Europeans" (people of mixed race but juridically categorized as European) were the most adamant supporters of empire. Although Dutch settlement never reached the proportions of French settlement in Algeria, or of Portuguese settlement in Angola and Mozambique, the size of the community was not insignificant. Though small in number compared with the indigenous population, there were more than two hundred thousand Dutch settlers in Indonesia, with roughly the same number of individuals classified as Indo-Europeans. As was true in other settler communities, these Dutch and Dutch descendants were apprehensive about yielding

52. Bogaarts 1989, vol. B, 1208–9. For the position of the plantation holders, see van Doorn and Hendrix 1987.
53. *NIB* 1991, vol. 16, doc. 82.
54. van den Doel 1996, 234, 243.
55. Daalder 1989, 16.

their privileged positions—in political economic, legal, and racial terms—
for an uncertain future.

Local colonists organized themselves in small but powerful organizations
such as the Fatherland Club (Vaderlandse Club) and resisted surrendering
their careers and holdings.[56] To speak of Indonesian autonomy was for
them tantamount to treason. During various stages of negotiations in the
1945–49 period, the settler community weighed in by pressuring members
of the Dutch parliament, by petition drives, and by self-armament to combat the nationalist forces.

They found a friendly ear with the KVP and other parties that traditionally had favored colonial control. When in 1946 the Socialists in the Schermerhorn cabinet and van Mook seemed to be moving toward recognition
of the republic, members of the KVP were outraged. KVP member M. J. M.
van Poll submitted a motion that an independent commission of inquiry be
sent to Indonesia to appraise itself of the situation and inform the Dutch
population about what was really going on.[57] Parliament accepted the motion, which in effect was a rejection of the PvdA agenda for continued
negotiation. Catholics noted that the Socialist minister Logemann "over-
estimates world opinion and the depth of the nationalist movement."[58]

The resulting "Van Poll Commission" that conducted the inquiry contained no Socialists. Their report gave particular prominence to members
of the Dutch Indonesian community who strenuously objected to any negotiation with the republic. After all, the republic was led by Sukarno and
Hatta, notorious collaborators with the Japanese. The report, furthermore,
suggested that the colonial administration resented van Mook's policies.
The "Brisbane" policies of van Mook (he had spent the war in Australia
rather than in an internment camp as had many colonials) were unacceptable, and van Mook was out of touch with his own colonial government in
Indonesia. The report, furthermore, asserted that large segments of the indigenous population were weary of Javanese domination and favored a federal government with a strong Dutch presence.

Prime Minister Schermerhorn objected to the report, arguing that it
placed undue emphasis on the settler population and colonial administration.[59] He further questioned the impartiality of the commission because it
did not include any Socialists. Nevertheless, the damage was done. Socialist
compromise could now be pictured as abandonment of brethren abroad
and a compromise with wartime collaborators.

The Dutch government's retreat from the Linggadjati accord of March
1947—the agreement for gradual transformation of Indonesia to sover-

56. van den Doel 1996, 242; van Doorn 1990, 115.
57. Bogaarts 1989, vol. A. 150.
58. Duynstee and Bosmans 1977, 622–24.
59. Duynstee and Bosmans 1977, 653–55.

eignty—revealed a similar dynamic.[60] Van Mook favored a United States of Indonesia consisting of Borneo, Java, Sumatra, and the Big-East (made up of western New Guinea and other easterly islands), independent but still within the kingdom. Constitutionally, this would have resembled the status that Suriname already had.[61] In essence it would have looked similar to the position of Australia and Canada within the Commonwealth. During negotiations in the Netherlands, and later in Linggadjati, Schermerhorn (then president of a special commission to deal with the Indonesian question) and Lt. Governor-General van Mook went even further. The United States of Indonesia was to become independent in January 1949. It would not remain a member of the kingdom but would be part of a Dutch-Indonesian union with a Dutch king or queen as its head. (The Dutch were seemingly obsessed with the finer legal nuances of such distinctions.)[62]

A groundswell of opinion erupted against the concessions. The National Committee for the Maintenance of Unity of the Empire submitted a petition with three hundred thousand signatures denouncing the settlement. In the wake of such organized dissent, and virulent opposition from the community abroad, influential politicians from the KVP, such as Romme, came out against the accord. As mentioned earlier, the Dutch government then retreated and unilaterally "reinterpreted" the accord.[63] Ultimately, van Mook was replaced by hard-liners in 1948. The Catholic Beel followed him and was far less congenial to Indonesian demands.[64]

In short, the intensity of KVP preferences (and that of other parties to the Center and Right) was partially propelled by corporate and settler demands. Corporate associations argued that control over Indonesia was crucial for the overall Dutch economy. Dutch settlers and colonial administrators abroad similarly appealed to the general public's interest in keeping Indonesia. Negotiating with the Indonesian Republic was effectively equated with abandonment of the Dutch abroad.

THE DUTCH DECISION AND IDEOLOGY OF EMPIRE

No doubt perceptions and beliefs in the legitimacy of Dutch control over Indonesia influenced decision making. The KVP program in the 1946 election perhaps best exemplified Catholic delusions. It characterized the Netherlands as a middle-range power "on the grounds of its important contribution to winning the war," which was undoubtedly news to the great

60. van den Doel 1996, 282.
61. Mendes 1989, 664.
62. van den Doel 1996, 282.
63. van den Doel 1996, 283.
64. Maas 1982. See Giebels 1996, chaps. 6–8.

powers.[65] Members of the Dutch government misread the international environment and engaged in wishful thinking. And, indeed, nearly all the political parties preferred some form of association with Indonesia. "In actual fact, no one, with the exception of the Dutch Communist Party, ever imagined it would come to a complete break between the two."[66]

But opinions differed significantly as to the type of association the Netherlands should pursue. The parties themselves were internally divided. The KVP had right-wingers eager for military action and a strong union (Welter for example). But it also had more moderate centrists. The PvdA had centrists (Drees) who did not want but could condone military intervention, while others on the left-wing were more amenable to granting independence (Schermerhorn).[67] Some Socialists warned early on about disastrous consequences if international support was lost. They argued that a settlement could be reached, even with wartime collaborators, and that an independent republic should be considered a distinct possibility. Moreover, van Mook and others clearly recognized the strength of the nationalists from the outset.

Sets of ideas, or rather the advocates of those ideas, competed with one another. Shortly after the war, those sets of ideas favoring compromise seemed to sway Dutch policy. But with shifting electoral fortunes, cabinet coalitional dynamics, and interest group agitation, those ideas were set aside because the actors who held such beliefs were pushed out of the critical decision-making circle.

Rather than dispute the arguments of Charles Kupchan, Jack Snyder, and others, who each in a different vein emphasize the impact of imperial beliefs and myths, I must once again emphasize the institutional factors that facilitate the propagation of particular imperial myths.[68] Progressives, such as Lt. Governor-General van Mook, and Socialists, such as Schermerhorn and Logemann, lost the political battle to the more hard-line Catholics such as Beel, Romme, and Sassen.[69] In the cabinet key positions affecting colonial policy were given to hard-liners, and when these hard-liners pushed their political advantage for a military response to the republic, the Socialists acquiesced . . . albeit grudgingly.[70]

65. Bogaarts 1989, vol. A, 153.
66. van Doorn 1995b, 157.
67. Duynstee and Bosmans 1977, 613.
68. See Snyder 1991; Kupchan 1994.
69. This is, for example, Beus's assessment of the second police action. Beus 1977, 168–69.
70. One cannot argue that the Dutch held on to Indonesia in the belief that it was part of the mother country. No Gramscian hegemony existed, as the diversity of opinions already suggests. Moreover, the economic cost-benefit logic applied by the Dutch, faulty as it was, suggests material rather than ideological reasons. For a discussion of Gramscian hegemony as a factor influencing decision making, see Lustick 1993.

Can one make a case that decision makers followed general public opinion and that the policy chosen reflected a broad consensus rather than the vetoes exercised by hard-liners? Certainly some polls suggested that broad segments of the population believed that empire was critical for Dutch welfare and was even morally justifiable. But the data was far less clear when specific questions were asked.

Public support for the government was at its highest when the Dutch government presented a fait accompli, as when it engaged in the controversial second police action in December 1948 (which, however, brought the wrath of the United States and the UN Security Council). The ranks closed in the face of external crisis. A full 61 percent were in favor of the action, only 19 percent against, with the rest undecided.[71] Public approval for hard-liners was far higher than for compromisers. In one survey army commander Spoor topped the public's approval of leaders list, while compromisers such as Lt. Governor-General van Mook, who had been instrumental in pushing for the Linggadjati accord, could not muster a majority of approval.

However, when asked about the importance of the Indonesian question during the 1948 elections, only 22 percent thought it was the primary political issue. Far more (58 percent) thought the economy was of greater importance.[72] The public's answers also depended on the likelihood of personal sacrifices. Thus, in July 1946, only 44 percent favored sending conscripts to Indonesia, suggesting limited public support for a conflictual solution. On the other hand, 74 percent favored military action to regain Indonesia if it was accomplished using professionals and volunteers.

Public opinion data is, therefore, too sketchy to tell us exactly what the populace had in mind. Moreover, it might be argued that the responsibility for shaping public opinion lay with the cabinet (and to Dutch historian de Jong also the media) in its selective reporting of such distant events.[73] One might also add that in the Dutch consociational style of politics, the general public traditionally acquiesced in elite bargaining, and hence elites had the opportunity to form public opinion rather than being guided by it.[74]

UNDERESTIMATING THE NATIONALIST MOVEMENT

To what extent did The Hague's propensity to "reinterpret" agreements and back out of accords hinder its ability to negotiate in general? Fragmented political systems change policies with difficulty, but such systems

71. Bank 1981, 255–57.
72. Giebels 1996, 234.
73. de Jong 1988, 1069–70.
74. On Dutch consociational politics, see Lijphart 1968.

can credibly commit to implementing agreements once they have been reached.[75]

In Dutch minds the credibility of The Hague was not an issue. Instead, they questioned the credibility of the Indonesian nationalists. The Dutch distrusted the nationalists and consistently misperceived their ability to act as a unified political entity. In fact, however, the Dutch inability to commit during the initial negotiation phase was critical. The question of credibility during subsequent implementation did not arise because the parties could not agree on an initial compromise. The nationalists also proved more unified and stronger than The Hague perceived.

The Dutch Create Indonesian Identity

If the misreading of the strategic situation could be regarded as a mistake, the belief that the nationalist movement could be easily dismissed was nothing short of a blunder. Prior to World War II, Colijn, then the minister of colonies, classified the nationalist movement as "futile, not a real people's movement, far more an activity with which in reality only a small layer of the population is involved, like the thin fleece of a grain of rice."[76] The same assessment of the nationalists as a small group of self-aggrandizing entrepreneurs seemed to infuse Dutch decision making after 1945.

The Dutch partially based their assessment that the nationalist movement did not represent a broad segment of the population on the geographic characteristics of the island group (dispersed across three thousand miles); its lack of any previous political unity before Dutch colonization; and the highly diverse ethnic composition of the archipelago. And, indeed, this assessment was not wholly unreasonable. As one Indonesian observer commented in the 1930s, "Each of these ethnic groups then, has its own language, its own well-defined home territory, its own values and normative system (adat), its own political structure."[77] Moreover, the nationalist movements were separated into several secular and Muslim as well as Communist and non-Communist organizations. This also made it easier to crack down on these disparate organizations.[78]

The Hague and the colonial government consistently used local differences in a divide-and-rule fashion. Fearing the influence of Islamic leaders, the government favored the development of *adat* law—local customary law.[79] This had several political repercussions. First, adat law tended to favor the position of secular rulers at the expense of the ulema (the Muslim

---

75. Cowhey 1993a; Martin 2000.
76. As noted in van den Doel 1996, 249; Fasseur 1984, 42.
77. Bachtiar 1972, 434.
78. Low 1991, 130.
79. van Doorn 1995a; Lev 1985.

clergy). Second, the variety of adat systems also accentuated the regional differences among the island groups. Thus, in arguing for respect for the nineteen adat circles, the cultural relativist argument could be used against the nationalist claim of representing the population at large.[80] The Dutch also propped up the position of the low and intermediate aristocracy, the regents, to control higher princes and sultans. This intermediate level of rule also served as a conduit between lesser local rulers and *desa* (village) chiefs.[81]

One final mode of using local differentiation was the racial categorization of Europeans (including those of mixed origin); native Asians; and nonnative Asians (Chinese and Malays—the Japanese were classified as European). Each of these groups had distinct legal systems and obligations. In other words, the Dutch East Indies had a triple set of distinctions: differentiation between Dutch rule and indigenous rule; differentiation of local Indonesian entities by their varied legal systems; and differentiation between various ethnic groups along racial criteria.[82] Indeed, the Dutch expeditionary forces in 1947 and 1948 were told in their training that "Indonesia" did not exist, and they were not supposed to use the name that the nationalists employed for the archipelago, but instead were to refer to "the Dutch East Indies."[83]

But despite the attempts of the Dutch to accentuate, or even create, crosscutting cleavages among the population, a comprehensive nationalist movement emerged.[84] As modernization continued and as the nature of economic development changed, the emphasis on divide-and-rule politics contradicted the desire to efficiently exploit the colony. To increase the benefits from Indonesia, the government had to bring indigenous society into a wider economic realm. Hence, the Dutch paradoxically created the very notion of one country, one "Indonesia."[85] As Indonesian general Nasution commented, "We have become one thanks to the Dutch. If there had not been a Dutch East Indies, if this large geopolitical space was not united by people like van Heutsz, there never would have been an Indonesia."[86] Despite all the local customs and the respect for local differentiation it was

80. Dutch judicial dualism differed from the French or English systems. van Doorn 1995a, 116, 118–19, 127.

81. Kahin 1983.

82. Indo-Europeans were classified as Dutch. About 20 percent of Dutchmen in the colony married Indonesian and non-Indonesian Asians. van Doorn 1995a, 114–15. Bosma (1989) notes how this led mixed Indonesians to oppose the most ardent nationalist demands.

83. van Doorn 1995b, 160.

84. Nationalist sentiment emerged well before World War II. See, for example, McVey 1966, and Brugmans 1977.

85. van den Doel 1996, 301.

86. van Doorn 1995a, 12. Saliently it was van Heutsz, who, as commander of the Atjeh campaign, had waged a ruthless war against the rebels at the turn of the century.

obvious that all natives were subject to the same colonial authority. A new nation could thus be imagined: the community of indigenous peoples that was subject to a colonial overlord.[87]

The use of indigenes in the colonial administration also had the paradoxical effect of creating the means through which the opponents of Dutch rule could unite. It was obvious to such educated locals that, whatever their level of training, they were still considered "native," non-European, in both a judicial and social sense.[88] While the government dictated equal and fair access to the administrative ranks, in practice the criteria for hiring were biased.[89] Official inspections revealed that some criteria such as command of the Dutch language seemed logical enough. Other criteria such as manners and height left all kinds of room for capriciousness. Access to higher positions required schooling in the capital, Batavia (Jakarta), but this was not available to the vast majority of the population. By 1940 there were only 221 Indonesians among the 3,039 officials that occupied high posts in government. Only 128 Indonesians were enrolled in the Western colleges in Indonesia.[90] Fewer still made it to the Netherlands for university education.

And, finally, the Dutch continued to separate—until 1942—the colonial administration by racial criteria. There was a European-staffed internal administration (Binnenlands Bestuur) and a native internal administrative corps (*inheems binnenlands bestuur*). Fasseur critically contrasts this situation with the British Indian administration that had opened up to a far greater extent and had roughly equal numbers of Indians and British civil servants by the end of the 1930s.[91]

The metropole also denied Indonesia representation. The Dutch had institutionalized a local means of representation, the Volksraad, in 1918 but had given it few real powers. The government act of 1927 changed its composition to thirty Dutch, twenty-five Indonesians, and five others. The Dutch parliament, however, retained a right to veto any legislation coming from the Volksraad that went against the Dutch constitution or "the general interest." Given its limited powers, the nationalists refused to serve on the Volksraad.[92]

Given these constraints, political entrepreneurs emerged from the local elites who were exposed to a measure of Western training and education but who were stifled in their advancement. Sukarno, for example, had been educated at a Dutch school in Batavia. Other nationalist elites emerged

87. For an example of how this process operated at a regional level, see Henley 1993.
88. In this sense the alienation of local elites from the Dutch elite resembles some facets highlighted by Benedict Anderson (1991).
89. van Doorn 1995a, 124–25.
90. Yasunaka 1970, 112, 114.
91. Fasseur 1984, 30, and n. 38.
92. Bosma 1989, 27; Low 1991, 133; Keene 2002, 89.

from the group of natives who received education in the Netherlands. Hatta, who with Sukarno proclaimed Indonesia independent, had been schooled at the Rotterdam Commerce College.[93]

During the course of their education these elites were undoubtedly exposed to Western theories of self-determination, national unity, equality before the law, and political participation. Progressive governor-general de Graeff remarked in 1928 that "all the youth that have enjoyed a Western education are without exception ardent nationalists, and their numbers increase each year."[94]

Developments in the Philippines, where the United States had gradually started to divest itself from the islands, also influenced ideas of freedom and self-determination. This directly influenced the 1936 petition of the nationalist Mas Sutardjo (a representative of the internal administrative corps), who, inspired by the definitiveness of the American exit from the Philippines, asked for independence within ten years. The petition was summarily dismissed. There was some recognition that greater independence for Indonesia might occur in the distant future, but, as Fasseur points out, it would have to be "within narrow borders."[95]

In response to the nationalists' increasing demands for greater political say, the Dutch cracked down. They utilized virtually arbitrary police powers and interned people without trial, because "prosecution might cause disturbances."[96] Most noted offenders of the public peace were sequestered in Boven-Digul, a malaria-infested internment camp in New Guinea. Dutch virulence was exacerbated by their claims that the nationalist movement was Communist inspired—a claim not supported in the American assessment.

The Japanese Occupation and the Unification of Indonesia

Japanese occupation proved a catalyst for the development of a stronger and more effective nationalist movement. The Japanese themselves were initially hesitant to embrace East Asian nationalists. The Japanese East Asian command in Singapore warned against relying on nationalist movements, although local commands, such as the Japanese 16th Army in Indonesia, assessed nationalist movements more favorably.[97]

Gradually, however, Tokyo changed its position. It granted several states, such as the Philippines and Burma, nominal independence. The Japanese,

93. Goto 1996.
94. Fasseur 1984, 27. (A. C. D. de Graeff should not be confused with Minister of Colonies Simon de Graaff.)
95. Fasseur 1984, 29.
96. Gouda 1994, 253.
97. Goto 1996.

however, did not envision giving Indonesia or Malaya independence until the very end of the war.[98]

The Japanese recalcitrance was not due to lack of trying on the Indonesian side. Sukarno had early on committed himself to active support of the Japanese, despite his own antifascist leanings. "If you ask me which I would prefer, democracy or militarism, my choice would undoubtedly be democracy. But if the question concerns a choice between Dutch democracy and Japanese militarism, I would prefer Japanese militarism."[99] Hatta was less eager to cooperate, but he had been classified by the Japanese as favorably disposed to the Japanese government based on his interwar visit to Japan.[100]

Despite the overtures of these Indonesian nationalists, Tokyo did not transfer power to the nationalists. Japan, however, did play a significant role in creating several conditions that would influence the struggle for independence after 1945. For one, the Japanese created several paramilitary and auxiliary military organizations in Indonesia.[101] Most of their members were not armed, but their numbers were significant, in the hundreds of thousands. Perhaps more significantly, they created an institutional structure through which subsequent revolt could be organized against the Dutch.

The Japanese had also provided the nationalists in Indonesia with access to the population, which they had not had under the Dutch. Moreover, they removed the intermediate rulers who had been favorable to Dutch rule.

The co-operation between the Dutch civil service and the native chiefs and regents had always been the cornerstone of Dutch authority. . . . The Japanese occupier upset this equilibrium by preferring the nationalist leaders to the priyayi [the traditional chiefs and aristocrats]. When the Japanese left in 1945, the nationalists replaced them.[102]

The last act of the occupying Japanese force was to set up the Investigative Committee for the Preparation of Indonesian Independence (BPUPKI). This committee included Sukarno, Hatta, and fifty-eight others and drafted a preliminary constitution. Sukarno and Hatta propelled themselves with this support to becoming the undisputed leaders of the resistance and proclaimed the independent Republic of Indonesia on August 17, 1945, two days after the Japanese defeat. The draft of the BPUPKI became the constitution of the republic.[103] The nationalists with whom the

98. Goto 1996, 35; van den Doel 1996, 265.
99. This quote was ascribed to Sukarno by his top external advisor, Roeslan Abdulgani. Goto 1996, 281. Also see Hering 1992, 501.
100. Goto 1996, 34; van den Doel 1996, 264.
101. van den Doel 1996, 266; Giebels 1996, 246.
102. van Doorn 1995b, 166.
103. Drooglever 1997, 64–67.

Dutch had to contend in 1945 were infinitely stronger than those in the 1930s.

Dutch Inability to Credibly Commit

The manner in which the Dutch political elites dealt with the nationalists had several consequences. First, as Anthony Low reminds us, "Although the Dutch had created a small Volksraad (assembly), they had never made any significant constitutional concessions to the Indonesian nationalists."[104] Even before the war, the Dutch government had been uncompromising in the extreme. When asked by reporters why he refused to negotiate with the nationalists, Governor-General de Jonghe purportedly remarked that "one does not talk with someone whose throat one wants to slit."[105] Dutch denigration of the nationalists was only strengthened by nationalist collaboration with the Japanese during the war. Over time, Lt. Governor-General van Mook recognized Hatta as the main power broker in the republic, but he was deemed unacceptable by The Hague.[106] Like the French, the Dutch did not have moderate nationalists to work with.

Second, their previous policies and the fragmented nature of decision making in The Hague eroded Dutch ability to credibly commit in the negotiation phase. As discussed earlier, in early 1946 compromise and a negotiated settlement of the dispute seemed possible. Lt. Governor-General van Mook had brokered a deal with the republic's representative, Sjahrir. But the agreement on principles of April 1946 quickly unraveled as a result of the veto by the KVP.[107]

Similarly, the Dutch parliament retracted the Linggadjati agreements reached in the fall of 1946. The Second Chamber refused to sign the agreement and instead unilaterally changed its content. The Indonesian Republic subsequently refused to accept the unilaterally amended accord, which then led to the first police action of July 1947.

Under American pressure, the Dutch signed on to the Renville agreement in January 1948. Particularly important from the American perspective was the repression of the Communists within the Indonesian nationalist camp (the Madiun revolt) in the fall of that year. Again, however, the agreement broke down, and in December 1948 the Dutch launched their second police action.

Consequently, the Dutch government could not parlay dissent at home into a bargaining advantage. Even though in theory a fragmented government should be able to credibly commit once an accord has been reached,

104. Low 1991, 38.
105. Fasseur 1984, 32.
106. *NIB* 1981, vol. 19, doc. 37, p. 69.
107. Duynstee and Bosmans 1977, 642.

the Indonesian nationalists had no reason to believe that agreements reached at the negotiating table would subsequently pass parliamentary muster in The Hague. Dutch inability to credibly commit in the initial bargaining phase rendered credibility in implementation irrelevant.[108] The nationalists also correctly ascertained that bargaining leverage lay with the republic when it came to implementation of any accord. Reassertion of Dutch control, once the troops had been withdrawn, would be impossible.

Moreover, unlike Whitehall, the Dutch government did not demonstrate credibility by other means. Britain's willingness to negotiate in multiple territories created a reputational effect that influenced nationalist movements elsewhere. The Hague did not have multiple areas with which to deal. In essence the Dutch "empire" consisted solely of Indonesia, and there it had consistently repressed nationalist overtures.

Should the Indonesian nationalists have been more forthcoming, given the inability of Dutch negotiators to "sell" the agreements back home? That is, under the logic of a two-level game, could not Dutch negotiators gain greater concessions from the nationalists with the argument that without such concessions the negotiators would not be able to persuade their domestic constituencies?

Again, the problem appeared to the nationalists as dichotomous: ultimate sovereignty would either have to reside in The Hague or Jakarta. Sovereign territorial control was indivisible. Nevertheless, the nationalists did grant certain concessions. They assumed the debt for the police actions (recall the Dutch insistence on billing them for those actions) and allowed Dutch companies to continue operations.[109] Overall though, decolonization did not lend itself to piecemeal disaggregation, and thus it diminished any bargaining advantage that a fragmented system might have given the Dutch.

The decision to launch the second police action in 1948 soon came to haunt The Hague. The UN Security Council swiftly passed a resolution condemning the Netherlands and demanded the release of Sukarno, Hatta, and other nationalist leaders who had been captured. Washington acted decisively as well. Its motives for doing so are revealed succinctly in a memo by the director of the Office of Far Eastern Affairs (Butterworth) to the counselor of the department (Bohlen) on January 7, 1949:

---

108. Ironically, the Dutch consistently accused the nationalists of a lack of credibility; see, for example, *NIB* 1981, vol. 19, doc. 37, p. 64. Besides linking the nationalists to wartime collaboration it also emphasized the existence of Communist elements. *NIB* 1981, vol. 19, doc. 205, p. 450. But it seemed oblivious to its own flaws.

109. They repudiated the debt service in 1951, and in 1956 they annulled the last of their concessions to Dutch multinational companies.

The United States Government should seek the attainment of two objectives: (a) to contribute in every practical way to a solution of the Indonesian problem; (b) to place itself in the best possible light with the Asiatic and Islamic countries. . . . The . . . resort to force has provided the Soviet Union with excellent propaganda. . . .

He continued with a threat: "Congress may feel called upon to take such action in respect of ECA [Economic Cooperation Administration] aid to the Netherlands as to seriously jeopardize progress in North Atlantic security arrangements."[110]

The suspension of Marshall Plan assistance (which eventually totaled $1.125 billion) broke Dutch resistance.[111] Still rebuilding in the wake of the Second World War, it could not do without American aid.[112] Moreover, the Netherlands, given its high dependence on international trade, could not afford to be excluded from the emerging international trading environment. The emerging General Agreement on Tariffs and Trade (GATT) regime promised great returns in trade with the other developed countries that were too lucrative to be ignored.[113]

Given these international pressures, hard-line preferences had to give way. With KVP preferences more closely aligned with those of the PvdA after some of the Catholic hard-liners resigned, the unraveling of empire came swiftly. The Dutch transferred authority in December 1949 to the Federal Republic of Indonesia. In the wake of territorial retreat 380,000 Dutch and Dutch-Indonesians moved to the Netherlands between 1945 and 1958.[114]

In short, Dutch domestic politics forestalled policy change. The Socialists, who had reservations about a hard line toward the republic, required the KVP for a coalition. Association with the Communists was impossible because the CPN could not be part of a ruling cabinet coalition. Socialists and Communists alone would not have had sufficient seats to make up a majority.

Multiparty coalitions provided various veto points to policy change. If the PvdA opposed the police actions, the fall of the government would lead to new elections. The KVP could then exact punishment for Labor's defection by forging a coalition with the other religious parties and the Liberals. To remain in the government coalition and implement its domestic economic policies in the reconstruction of the Netherlands, the PvdA had to concede

110. *Foreign Relations of the United States* 1949, vol. 7 (Far East and Australasia), part 1, p. 136.
111. Bogaarts 1989, vol. B, 1181. Although amounting to only 4 percent of national expenditure, the aid played a key role in consumption and investment activity (Klein 1981, 275).
112. See Reid 1974, 159; Giebels 1996, 300–301; Ansprenger 1981, 257.
113. Bogaarts 1989, vol. B, 1326–27.
114. de Jong 1988, vol. 12, pt. 2, 1050–51.

to KVP hard-liners. Indeed, by allocating the key cabinet seats on colonial and foreign policy to the KVP, the Socialists had already conceded preeminence to the KVP, even before the discussions preceding the second police action.

The hard-line policy was not the result of parties outbidding each other on the colonial issue.[115] Nor was the public fully convinced that Indonesia had to be held at any cost. Indeed, the public, as in the case of France, often held internally inconsistent positions. Most of the time, it did not see colonial questions as particularly salient. Policy was determined by elite negotiations and institutionalized logrolling. Schulten's judgment must, therefore, stand. Politicians were driven by "selective blindness . . . more concerned with tallying votes than with a correct assessment of international developments."[116]

115. Miles Kahler suggests that multiparty competition for voters on the fringes of rival parties tends to lead to imperial outbidding, as in the case of the Fourth Republic (Kahler 1984, 68–69). However, this should not occur if parties are relatively stable, as in the Netherlands.

116. Schulten 1987, 41.

The First Maritime Empire and the Last: Portugal in Africa

> The Army must be honored and revered, as being the scaffolding indispensable to the building up of the New State.
>
> ANTÓNIO SALAZAR, 1939
>
> Beware of the captains. They are too young to be bought.
>
> MARCELO CAETANO, 1974

I have argued in the previous chapters that the multiplicity of veto points in a democratic system increases the probability that politicians who oppose territorial change will be able to forestall compromise with nationalists. Electoral and constitutional rules directly affect the number of such veto points. Fragmented institutions diminish the likelihood of change in territorial policy.

The analysis of the institutionalist literature has for obvious reasons focused on democratic systems. One key feature of democratic polities is, after all, that political contenders adhere to specific rules of the game. In authoritarian regimes, by contrast, the institutional rules are not necessarily representative of the popular will and do not create the same constraints and opportunities as in democratic systems. Nevertheless, in this chapter and the next I will argue that the analysis of veto points can be extended to authoritarian regimes.

Portugal, perhaps more than any other country, presents us with an enigma. Even though great powers such as France and Britain had already withdrawn from their vast African and Asian holdings, and lesser powers such as Belgium and the Netherlands had been ousted from their colonies, Lisbon still clung to its pretensions of Luso-tropical greatness and fought for its empire until 1974.

A realist explanation of this policy is unpersuasive. As I suggested in chapter 2, the strategic reasons for having colonies in the 1920s and 1930s had diminished by the 1960s. Nowhere was this more the case than in the Portuguese overseas territories. By 1961 the African nationalist movements felt strong enough to launch open rebellion. They started in Angola and soon erupted in Guinea (after independence renamed as Guinea-Bissau), Cape Verde, and Mozambique. Although the empire had never been considered a military asset, it rapidly became a major drain on the metropole. Hundreds of thousands of Portuguese served in the military overseas between 1961 and 1974, and this out of a total population of 8.5 million.

The economic argument for retaining the colonies might seem more plausible. But the economic benefits were the result of deliberate policies by the António Salazar regime to artificially orient Portugal toward the African overseas territories. Economic benefits did not motivate the pursuit of empire. Rather, the choice for empire led to economic ties with the overseas territories. This self-arrested development allowed the oligarchy to retain political control by retarding modernization at home.

What explains the lack of adjustment in Portugal's overseas commitments? Settlers, holding companies with colonial investments, and the military proved to be key opponents of withdrawal. The institutional structure enabled pro-imperialists to dominate the political arena and transform their ideas and interests into policy. Portugal forms a classic case in which small groups of pro-imperialists manage to exercise disproportionate power—not dissimilar to the oligarchy of Wilhelmine Germany at the end of the nineteenth century. Portuguese authoritarianism provided multiple vetoes to the members of the ruling coalition, with little regard for the general public's welfare.

More specifically, key actors in the Portuguese corporatist-fascist state, particularly the armed forces and the pro-empire business elites, could bar any change in territorial policy during the Salazar-Caetano regime (1932–74). Strictly speaking, the ruling coalition also consisted of large landholders in the south of Portugal and the Catholic Church. However, while these two latter groups had an interest in maintaining the oligarchy, their stake in empire was less than that of the military and pro-imperial business groups. Although settlers had a vested stake in the overseas territories, the ruling oligarchy—by excluding popular input—gave only a marginal voice to the settler communities. Thus, the armed forces and the business elites turned out to be the key veto players in Portuguese colonial policy.

As long as the veto holders wished to keep the overseas territories, a change in Portugal's colonial policy proved to be impossible. In the 1960s, however, some economic elites started to shift their focus from Africa to Europe, particularly to the European Economic Community. Even more important, the armed forces started to change their mind about the wisdom of the colonial wars. Prime Minister Marcelo Caetano, the last representative of the oligarchy that had ruled Portugal since the military coup d'état of 1926, turned out to be right: the captains were the ones to watch. Once the military no longer saw the defense of the colonies as being in its corporate interest, the armed forces staged a coup and rapidly reversed policy. Essentially the coup reduced decision making to a single veto player. Overriding objections of some pro-empire economic interests and the settlers, the armed forces rushed to the exit. Within a year of the military coup of 1974, Portugal had divested itself from virtually all of its overseas territories.

PORTUGAL IN AFRICA AND
THE RISE OF FASCIST-CORPORATISM

The Portuguese Empire finds its beginnings in the expulsion of the Moors (the *reconquista*) in the late fifteenth century. Maritime breakthroughs, most notably the shift from galleys to caravels and the use of the compass, enabled Portuguese and Spanish mariners to expand their reach.[1] In less than twenty years, the Portuguese flag flew from the East Indies to South America. Nothing symbolizes Portugal's ambitions more than the Treaty of Tordesillas of 1494, which divided the new and yet to be discovered lands in the Western hemisphere between Spain and Portugal.[2]

The Napoleonic era substantially altered the composition of the Portuguese Empire. During the French invasion of the Iberian Peninsula in 1807, the British navy evacuated the Portuguese royalty to Brazil. When the Duke of Wellington ousted the French from Lisbon a period of British rule followed. This rule continued until 1820 when a Portuguese revolution ousted the British. The revolutionists put forward a constitutional monarchy that placed limits on previous royal powers.

The attempt at constitutional monarchy failed. With the support of the army, the Charter of 1826 replaced the Constitution of 1822 and gave the monarchy substantial executive authority. Despite civil war and continued unrest (arguably the revolution only came to an end in 1851), this state of affairs lasted throughout the nineteenth century.[3] Brazil became independent, but Portugal retained control over many of its other holdings—Macao, Goa, and Timor in the Far East—and increasingly turned to the exploitation of its colonies in Africa.

1. Lewis and Runyan 1985.
2. Scammel 1981.
3. Birmingham (1993, 125) notes how the military coup of Saldanha that brought the revolution to an end "epitomized a dynamic tradition of aristocratic military politicians." Arguably that tradition continued well into the twentieth century.

A mutiny in the armed forces felled the monarchy in 1910. The First Republic (1910–1926) turned out to be highly unstable.[4] Leftist turmoil following World War I further exacerbated domestic tensions. In reaction to these democratizing tendencies and emerging leftist sentiments, the military intervened once again.

The armed forces overthrew the republican government in 1926 and established a military regime that lasted until 1933. Gradually, the military elevated a civilian leader who would rule on their terms: António Salazar. Salazar became minister of finance in 1928 and prime minister (technically president of the Council of Ministers) in 1932. A new constitution in 1933 formalized this ruling coalition and incorporated fascist and Catholic-authoritarian elements.

The institutional arrangements established both a prime ministerial position and a presidency. The presidency would fall uninterrupted from 1926 until the end of the regime in 1974 to a high-ranking military officer. The president appointed the prime minister and the cabinet. Both were responsible to the president and not to the National Assembly, thus formalizing the veto powers of the military. In practice this meant that the legislature simply ratified executive decisions that emanated from the prime minister, who took on the day-to-day operations of government.[5] The National Assembly exercised no independent initiative.

Legislative elections served primarily cosmetic purposes. Educational and income restrictions severely limited the size of the electorate. In 1933 only 1.2 to 1.3 million Portuguese were deemed eligible to vote out of a population of 7 million. (Property and education requirements restricted the franchise essentially to the male population.) Tellingly, by the mid-1960s, the number of voters had only increased by about 300,000, whereas the population had increased by almost 2 million.[6] The constitution claimed to be establishing a new state, the Estado Novo, which would steer Portuguese society toward stability and welfare.

Philippe Schmitter's description of the Portuguese regime from 1926 on captures the essence of this government. Large holding companies, the military, the large landholders in the south, and the Catholic Church were the key components of this condominium of interests.[7] It constituted a corporatist regime in that the state funneled all interest representation and claimed to reflect all societal needs. But it constituted state-centered corporatism, rather than societal corporatism, with the government creating and

4. Smith 1974, 657–58; Maxwell 1995, 15–16.
5. Bailey 1969a, 133ff.; Keefe et al. 1977, 198, 202.
6. Keefe et al. 1977, 209.
7. This evaluation of the constitutive actors of the ruling coalition is widely shared. See Blackburn 1974, 7; Schmitter 1975b, 15ff.; Birmingham 1993, 158–61; Martins 1969, 254; Wheeler 1970, 771.

channeling demands rather than responding to societal preferences. The Corporative Chamber only had advisory functions.[8] While the state created employer guilds (*gremios*) to channel business demands, the large industrial elites (through companies such as Champalimaud and the Companhia União Fabril or CUF of the de Melo family) had direct contact with the government.[9] Indeed, economic concentration was such that "ten great families owned 168 firms and controlled 53 percent of the national wealth."[10]

The state also contained fascist elements in its repression of opposition through its secret police. It claimed to be the sole voice of citizen expression. The National Union was the only party in the state. Moreover, state and executive were to be independent from societal demands and instead were to mold civil society to the state's needs. Salazar openly admired Hitler and Mussolini, and some 18,000 Portuguese troops fought for Franco in Spain. The regime lacked, however, other fascist features, such as charismatic leadership; mobilized masses; a drive toward rapid industrialization; and expansionist policies.[11]

As with many political leaders, Salazar revealed a greater adeptness at defining what he opposed rather than what he favored. "We are anti-parliamentarians, anti-democrats, anti-liberals. We are opposed to all forms of internationalism, communism, socialism, syndicalism."[12] Thus, although the National Assembly consisted of two houses elected by direct suffrage, the autonomous executive position and the de facto existence of a one-party state limited any meaningful opposition. While it claimed to represent the common working man, in actuality the new state catered only to the devout Catholics of the small private holdings of northern Portugal. The industrial workers and the landless workers of the large estates in southern Portugal were the avowed enemies of the Estado Novo.

The constitution of 1933 also sought to limit the local autonomy that had emerged in the First Republic.[13] Decision making would be centralized and nationalist and devoid of international commitments and contacts—save with the colonies. Indeed, before the Salazar regime the Portuguese showed little interest in their African colonies.[14] Emigrants and settlers were primarily interested in the more developed Portuguese-speaking countries such as Brazil. Economic interests tended to focus on Europe rather than the colonies.

---

8. Pinto 1991, 70; Schmitter 1975b, 30; Keefe 1977, 194–96.
9. Makler 1979, 126–29; Schmitter 1975b, 20; Wiarda 1974, 26–31.
10. Birmingham 1993, 173.
11. Pinto 1991, 9–11, 13, 22, 25; Schmitter 1975a, 9; Birmingham 1993, 163; Maxwell 1995, 16ff.; Keefe 1977, 374–75.
12. Maxwell 1995, 18.
13. Local authorities held delegated power only. Keefe 1977, 207.
14. Smith 1974, 654–56.

Domestic instability and the Great Depression changed all that. The Salazar government decided to centralize domestic economic planning and the administration of the empire. Colonies had to be managed rationally. The downturn of the 1930s thus served as the catalyst for more rationalized management of the colonies, not dissimilar to what France, Italy, the Netherlands, and other imperial powers were trying to do. Imperial development would be the antidote to the economic downturn at home.

The centralization of government in the metropole extended to the overseas territories. The constitution of 1933 and executive decrees on the overseas territories in 1935 concentrated the decision making in the metropole. The Fundamental Law for Overseas Provinces of 1953, which redesigned some institutional features, reasserted Lisbon's preeminent legislative powers in the overseas provinces.[15] Of the 130 members in the National Assembly, the overseas territories supplied 23.[16] Angola had four representatives and Mozambique six. These representatives came from the local legislative assemblies. A minority of the members of the colonial legislatures was elected by direct suffrage, but the majority was elected by key organizations and interest groups that each were entitled to a fixed number of seats. One may, therefore, question the amount of democratic input in choosing local representatives. Either way, given the limited position of the Portuguese National Assembly, the influence of the colonies on executive decision making was minimal.[17]

In sum, the Portuguese system lacked constitutional and partisan veto players in the democratic mold. Instead, as in other authoritarian governments, a ruling oligarchy controlled the political process. The institutional features of the Estado Novo truncated broader societal demands. Rulers had no incentive to cater to the public welfare. Political survival depended on the provision of private goods to key members of the coalition.

In this authoritarian climate key proponents of empire could capture decision making. In particular, the military and large holding companies with investments in the colonies had direct access to the government. Responding to their demands, the Salazar regime limited foreigners' access to the colonies, established imperial preferences, and controlled exports and imports.[18] The settlers, however, while virulently pro-empire, lacked institutionalized access to executive decision making in much the same way as the general population of Portugal itself.

15. Friedland 1979, 124–26; Ferguson 1963, 127.

16. Bailey 1969a, 135; Newitt 1981, 172.

17. In 1973 Caetano revised the constitution and expanded the National Assembly to 150 deputies, thirty-four of whom would come from the overseas provinces. Keefe 1977, 201.

18. Smith 1974, 666–67.

CHAPTER 6

THE ARMED FORCES AS ELEMENTS
OF THE RULING COALITION

When U.S. secretary of state Dean Acheson met António Salazar in 1952 he considered Salazar to be "a dictator-manager" who was supported by the army but did not rule it.[19] Acheson correctly assessed the prominent position of the armed forces in Portuguese government.

At face value, civilian rule might have seemed well established. After all, former economics professor Salazar had assumed government as a civilian leader in 1926 and did not relinquish his role until he suffered a debilitating stroke in 1968. His successor, Marcelo Caetano, likewise seemed to embody civilian rule.

Civilian leadership also had various means of control over the military at its disposal. The Salazar regime controlled the Republican Guard and the Public Security Police (PSP) as alternative means of exercising control. It also utilized a network of informants and secret police (PIDE) to check on potential opponents within civilian and military circles.[20]

Despite the appearance of civilian control, the armed forces cast a giant shadow. In the eyes of one observer, "The army became the final arbiter of Portuguese politics" in the nineteenth century, and its role in politics had continued.[21] In 1910 the military played a key role in overthrowing the monarchy; it launched the coup of 1917 against the "Democraticos" of the First Republic; and the coup of 1926 established a full military dictatorship. The interwar environment only encouraged the politicization of the military. The rise of authoritarianism in Italy (1922), Spain (1923), Greece (1925), and Poland (1926), and, foremost, in Nazi Germany (1933) indicated how the military could play a prominent role in governing coalitions.

This is not to say that the armed forces simply dictated their preferences to civilian authorities. The secret police could terrorize and control the officer corps, while the government by a decree of May 1945 could "dismiss officers of the armed forces who failed in their duties to the established institutions."[22] Conversely, the civilian government had to find ways to appease and co-opt the military. Any real threat to civilian rule could come only from that corner. Indeed, Douglass Wheeler counts more than twenty-

19. Wheeler 1970, 777.
20. Two years after the 1974 revolution the Republican National Guard still numbered seven thousand members, while the security police had twelve thousand members in its ranks. Keefe 1977, 398–401. Earlier, the International Police for the Defense of the State (PIDE) had been renamed as the Directorate General of Security (DGS) by Caetano, but it remained the same organization.
21. Wheeler 1970, 770.
22. Wheeler 1979, 200.

two coup attempts in the Estado Novo from 1926 to 1974.[23] Most of these were relatively feeble, sparked by disgruntled units or officers, rather than full-fledged uprisings, but, still, the civilian government had to take heed. This was government by *golpismo*, the seizing of power, even if the military gradually started to operate in the background, particularly after 1962.

Civilian leadership thus lacked objective control over the armed forces. First, as shown above, the armed forces historically had intervened many times to thwart civilian ambitions contrary to the military's interests. Promotions were often based on class background and the right connections, rather than on merit.[24] Sons of the ruling oligarchy dominated the officer corps.[25] These officers staunchly defended their corporate interests. Indeed, attempts to democratize the military by providing greater access for the middle class was the cause of several interventions. Additionally, military functions blurred with civilian tasks: officers worked in paramilitary organizations, the secret police, customs duties and immigration, and in the prisons. They also held offices in the cabinet and served in central and local administration, within Portugal as well as in the overseas territories. Particularly after the beginning of the colonial wars in 1961, the upper level of colonial administration was made up of high-ranking officers.[26]

Moreover, as mentioned above, after Salazar's accession as prime minister, the president of the republic had always been a military officer. This politicization of the military also held for other civilian positions. Officers could occupy (nominally) contested political posts.

Finally, the army's strategic doctrine was poorly defined. Externally, the armed forces were expected to defend Portugal and the overseas territories. Arguably, however, Portuguese independence had since long come to rely on great power protection—on Britain before 1945 and on the United States after that. The military also had internal tasks, notably supporting the incumbent regime, preventing leftist agitation, and suppressing whatever other domestic challenges might arise. As Michael Desch points out, the dual role of a military oriented toward both external and internal defense invites military intervention in the political realm. When the external role diminishes while the military sees internal defense of the political status quo as its key mission, political intervention by the armed forces is virtually a foregone conclusion.[27]

23. Pimlott 1977, 334; Wheeler 1979, 210ff. Other counts similarly suggest a high level of intervention. Looking further back, since 1820 the military had intervened on seventy-seven occasions (Harsgor 1980; Bandeira 1976, 4ff.; Maxwell 1995, 16).

24. See Bandeira 1976, 25–28.

25. For the social background of the officer corps, see Blackburn 1974, 11–14.

26. Wheeler 1979, 201.

27. Desch 1999.

Aside from occasionally intervening very directly in the political process, the armed forces also exercised quiet agenda-setting power.[28] The preferences of the military at all times had to be taken into account. The military constituted, consequently, "the only institution that Salazar feared."[29]

The biggest challenge to authoritarian leadership after World War II came from a split within the armed forces that led two candidates from the military to compete for the presidency. The episode illuminates the role of the armed forces in politics and demonstrates how the Salazar regime maintained itself in office. In 1958 the Salazar regime and the high command put Admiral Américo Tomás forward for the presidency. Although the presidency was largely ceremonial, the decision of air force general Humberto Delgado to run against Tomás caused great concern, as it indicated rifts within the military. Moreover, given Delgado's high rank he could not be as easily dismissed as other potential rivals.

Delgado confronted Salazar and the state corporatist system directly. "Corporatism is the socio-economic status-quo in which the rich are always getting richer," he declared.[30] The regime could not let the challenge pass and resorted to subterfuge to defuse the crisis. The existing election system heavily favored the incumbents put forward by the ruling coalition. Opposition groups were forbidden to form political parties and could only form electoral groups.[31] The electoral system further screened candidates based on literacy and property criteria. If necessary, the regime could resort to outright fraud. Out of the total population, no more than 15 percent could, or would, vote.[32]

In short, the elections unsurprisingly revealed a large majority for Tomás, while Delgado got 31 percent of the vote.[33] Delgado was subsequently ousted from the military and went into exile in North Africa. His body was discovered just inside the Spanish border in 1965, after he had been lured back to enter into secret negotiations with the Portuguese government; he was probably killed by the PIDE.[34]

The regime immediately changed the election procedure to prevent such challenges from emerging in the future. The presidential election became indirect, epitomizing the end of limited postwar reform.[35] The electoral college subsequently reelected Admiral Tomás for seven-year terms in

28. On agenda-setting power, see Bachrach and Baratz 1962.
29. Pinto 1991, 59.
30. Raby 1988, 181.
31. Wheeler 1970, 772.
32. Martins 1969, 254. Kohler notes how elections for Salazar between 1934 and 1965 did not attract more than 14.8 percent of the population (Kohler 1981, 20). Bandeira notes even lower figures of 10 percent (Bandeira 1976, 13).
33. Kohler 1981.
34. Maxwell 1995, 73; Bruce 1975, 45–46.
35. Raby 1998, 235; Schmitter 1975b, 30; Bandeira 1976, 14.

1965 and in 1972—and he served until the end of the regime in 1974. Democracy thus remained an illusion. By 1969, the National Union could count on 88 percent of the vote, but based on only 18 percent of the population on voting rolls.[36]

The armed forces' institutional position dovetailed with a strong preference for empire. Why did the military bar any change in territorial policy, and why did it continue to favor a Portuguese presence overseas?

First, the strategic rationale of the armed forces had traditionally included imperial tasks. Officers had routinely served throughout the overseas colonies, and there was no demarcation between home army and colonial service. One could rightly argue that "the whole character of the defence establishment is molded by its mission overseas."[37]

The overseas commitments also justified considerable military outlays. As discussed in chapter 2, Portugal spent proportionately more than any other country in NATO on its armed forces. So, from a narrow corporate perspective, there were reasons to keep the imperial game going. Writing shortly after Salazar's medical incapacitation in 1968, Herminio Martins succinctly captured the preferences of the military:

> The loyalty of these officers is largely assured, if, and only if, the empire is preserved. The armed forces as a whole, busy with the colonial wars, staking everything on the colonial empire, bloated with sinecures (rewarding bureaucratic posts, numerous directorships in various types of business concerns) are probably prepared to accept limited liberalization at the rear [Martins was speculating on the possibility of democratic reform] which may in effect enhance the legitimacy and effectiveness of the war effort.[38]

THE SETTLERS AS PAWNS RATHER THAN PLAYERS IN THE IMPERIAL GAME

The Estado Novo embarked on a deliberate policy of expanding the settlements in Africa in the 1930s. It provided land grants and start-up credit to those who were willing to go abroad. It also engaged in large infrastructural projects to enhance the attractiveness of the overseas territories. Lisbon envisioned several benefits from such migration. For one, the Fundamental Law for Overseas Provinces of 1953 aimed to increase the colonies' level of production. As the colonial conflicts intensified, Portuguese officials also revealed underlying strategic motives. "The land-settlement policy is one of the basic weapons in the struggle we are waging

36. Wheeler 1970, 778.
37. Minter 1972, 101.
38. Martins 1969, 251.

in Africa . . . and at the same time we must make use there of the thousands of young men who are fighting for our cause."[39] Development of the colonies was deemed essential as part of a strategy of "active defense." Who would be more committed to the cause of keeping Portugal in Africa than the colonists?

Angola and Mozambique became the main beneficiaries of this strategy. In the 1950s, while other European empires were winding down, the Portuguese settler population in Africa doubled.[40] By 1960 the white population in Angola had increased to about 175,000, while that in Mozambique rose to 85,000. Settlement in Guinea, however, remained negligible. By 1974 the Angolan settler population rose to 335,000 to 350,000, while it hovered around 220,000 to 250,000 in Mozambique. Of the Angolan settlers, only 20–28 percent had been born there.[41] Migration to Guinea never took root, with only two thousand white colonists settling there.

Nevertheless, even though their absolute numbers were high (certainly compared to the relatively small population base of the home country), the settlers remained a distinct minority within the colonies. In Angola they made up less than 6 percent of the population. In Mozambique their relative share was even lower; and in Guinea, they were negligible.[42]

Portuguese officials, therefore, inflated the numbers. They claimed that Angola had at least six hundred thousand white colonists, thus making retreat more costly in the public's eyes, while at the same time suggesting the viability of maintaining a foothold in Africa.[43] For the long run, Lisbon even foresaw larger European populations. The government aimed to lure hundreds of thousands more Europeans, perhaps even a million (Portuguese and other nationalities) to Mozambique and Angola by 1980 through its development projects.[44]

The daunting prospect of having hundreds of thousands of Portuguese, and mixed descendants, return to the home country also served as a chilling reminder of what would happen should Portugal withdraw. Given the impoverished nature of the Portuguese economy, the nation could hardly incorporate many new competitors for low-paying jobs—at least such was the common perception.

---

39. Hermes de Oliveira at the Land-Settlement Congress of 1970. Cited in Ferreira 1974, 55.

40. Birmingham 1993, 169.

41. Bender and Yoder 1974, 31; Bender 1974, 146–47; Ferreira 1974, 49; Maxwell 1976, 252; Maxwell 1995, 20; Raby 1988, 221–22; Newitt 1981, 164. Birmingham (1993, 176) provides for a lower (and rougher) estimate than these authors, suggesting settlement hovered around 250,000 in Angola and 125,000 in Mozambique.

42. Bender 1972a, 333; Harsgor 1980, 151.

43. Bender and Yoder 1974, 25.

44. Keefe 1977, 99.

Another means of finessing the precarious position in Africa revolved around the myth of Luso-tropicalism—a term popularized by Brazilian sociologist Gilberto Freyre and adopted by the Portuguese elites. According to this thesis, the Portuguese appreciated tropical values and cultures. Assimilation and integration with the indigenous peoples set the Portuguese overseas territories apart from those of the other colonial powers: Portuguese settlers would blend with the local population.

However, in reality, colonial law differentiated among racial categories, and exploitation was commonplace.[45] Although Caetano distinguished Portuguese racial policies from those in South Africa and Rhodesia, he also argued that "in many respects our interests coincide" and suggested that racial equality could be sacrificed for political expediency.[46] South Africa and Rhodesia, as white settler nations battling African nationalists, were useful allies, even if their policies contrasted with Portugal's claims of Luso-tropicalism.

Settlers, of course, supported segregation even more than the metropolitan government because they had a direct stake in raising their economic and legal status.[47] Indeed, metropolitan interests and settler objectives clashed diametrically on this point.[48] Lisbon wished to increase assimilation to diminish the appeal of nationalist rhetoric and demands for independence, while the settlers were far less eager to make concessions to indigenes.

In a democratic system the white settlers might have hoped to sway the metropole against retreat by their votes.[49] However, the regime's authoritarian-corporatist nature disempowered them as much as the average voter in the metropole. Salazar was reluctant to have policy dictated by any societal element that was not directly involved in the ruling coalition, and by 1958 he explicitly excluded the settlers from the policy process.[50] Thus, while they were staunchly pro-empire, the settlers had little role to play in the policy process. The dominant coalition in the metropole dictated colonial policy. As Malyn Newitt succinctly summarizes, "The white settlers, unlike their Rhodesian counterparts, had never controlled the administration or the armed forces; they had never had political parties, and had no leaders."[51]

---

45. Bender 1978b.
46. The Mozambican nationalists accentuated this correspondence between Portugal and the racist regimes at the UN. Barnett and Harvey 1972, 247.
47. Bender 1974; Friedland 1979, 121.
48. Newitt 1981, 170.
49. For the limited ability of the settlers to exercise voice through their votes, see Raby 1988, 190; Friedland 1979, 117.
50. Wheeler 1970, 780.
51. Newitt 1981, 247.

Shifting Business Interests in the Corporatist State

The reliance of the authoritarian state on large landholders and family cartels also gave economic interest groups with stakes in the colonies considerable leverage. This leverage was all the larger because the Portuguese economy lacked international exposure.

The regime feared, not without reason, that internationalization of the economy would lead to greater pressure for reform. Foreign investment and industrialization would strengthen the position of urban workers, who opposed the elite corporatist system. The small farmers in the north, a traditional Catholic constituency, and the large landholders of the south were more loyal supporters than the urban proletariat, and hence, agricultural involution was preferable to industrial development. The small farmers made up 90 percent of all agriculturists, but they owned only 32 percent of arable land. The top 1 percent, by contrast, owned 39 percent.[52] Both opposed the landless agricultural workers in the large estates of the south, who with the urban workforce gravitated to left-wing organizations.[53] Landholders, particularly the large agricultural interests, thus opposed retreat from empire, since they equated that with internationalization and modernization, which would benefit the Left and possibly lead to land reform.

More than a million and a half Portuguese migrated to work in the booming economies of other Western European countries in the 1950s and 1960s. Overseas remittances provided a cash flow for the anemic Portuguese economy, while venting some of the pressure for domestic modernization and democratization.[54]

Salazar's strategy was to keep Portugal out of Europe and to develop the overseas territories instead. Cotton production in Angola and Mozambique, and the mineral resources of those areas proved to be critical in this regard. Given this introverted strategy, some of the holding companies argued, with some justification, that Portugal needed to maintain its economic holdings overseas. As long as Portugal and the holding companies retained a domestic orientation, empire and economic interests intertwined.

52. Schmitter 1975b, 56; Bender 1974, 123. For the general orientation of minifundios of the north and latifundios of the south, see Pimlott 1977, 336.

53. Apart from the traditionally conservative sentiments of the farmers of the north, the northern part of Portugal also contained two-thirds of the population—an added reason to cater to their needs (Kohler 1981). Left-right political cleavages overlay religious cleavages (see Cerqueira 1973, 505) and tensions between city and country (see Pinto 1991, 65). For a discussion of landholding patterns, see Bermeo 1986.

54. In 1972 remittances of overseas workers amounted to 8 percent of GNP (Bender 1974, 124).

Not all economic groups, however, shared Salazar's views. The preferences of the business elites started to diverge once Portugal moved away from rigid isolationism and imperial preferences. Without foreign capital, the Salazar regime could not develop the colonies or finance a protracted war, and thus as the wars of liberation started in 1961, the regime had to open up the local economy and the colonies. Pro-Europeanists gradually started to oppose the pro-Africanists, after considerable foreign investment, attracted by low wages, started to flow into Portugal during the 1960s. Growth rates in Portugal increased along with other economies in the rest of Western Europe that were going through a dramatic expansion. Between 1966 and 1971 the Portuguese economy grew by 6.6 percent annually.[55]

The composition of Portuguese exports also underwent dramatic changes. In 1960 raw materials still accounted for 54 percent of Portuguese exports, while industrial and manufactured goods only made up 14 percent. By 1973, however, raw materials had slipped to 25.5 percent of total exports, while industry and manufacturing now accounted for 29.5 percent of total exports.[56] Furthermore, the destination of exports changed. The EEC and EFTA accounted for 43 percent of exports in 1960 but for 62 percent in 1970. The trend to the colonies showed the reverse. In 1960, 26 percent of exports had the overseas territories as their destination, but in 1970 this had declined to 14 percent, and by 1973 to 10 percent.[57]

There is some disagreement about the exact figures, but the conclusion remains the same: European economic ties had started to displace the African holdings in importance.[58]

Some economic interests thus became more interested in gaining access to the EEC. The internationally oriented firms also came to the conclusion that state corporatism was incompatible with their needs.[59] The large holding companies with much more diversified assets had increasingly gained a stake in participating in the European economy along less interventionist lines. Influential companies, such as those of the de Melo family and Champalimaud, had started to support the demands for decolonization and democratization. General António Spínola, who would assume power in the coup of 1974, epitomized their sentiments: "We shall not survive if we cast

55. Pimlott 1977, 337; Blackburn 1974, 8–10.
56. Bender 1974, 124.
57. Raby 1988, 221ff.
58. Bandeira 1976, 33. Blackburn says exports to the colonies were 34 percent of Portuguese exports in 1960 but only 15 percent by 1973. Colonial imports only accounted for 10 percent of the metropolitan total (Blackburn 1974, 8–10). Pimlott (1977, 338) gives similar figures. He adds that by 1973 48 percent of Portugal's exports, and 45 percent of its imports, were with the EEC.
59. Makler 1979, 151. See also Schmitter 1975b, 26. The schism between industrial elites also pitted the internationalized industrial elite against the agricultural elites. Maxwell 1995, 28.

Europe aside, and we are cast aside by her for economic and political reasons."[60]

These economic players also foresaw that if changes were to come in Africa and in Portugal itself, they should dictate those changes rather than be preempted by more left-wing forces, such as the Communists. Europeanism corresponded with democratization and decolonization.

Those holding asset-specific investments in the colonies, however, tended to oppose greater internationalization of the Portuguese economy and retreat from Africa. Franco Nogueira, foreign affairs minister under Salazar, opposed withdrawal. His views were at least partially influenced by his chairmanship of the board of the Benguela Railway and his membership on the board of directors of the Espiritu Santo Bank.[61] For the Africa lobby, authoritarianism at home and continued overseas control were interdependent.

These differences became more salient as the economy faced high inflation in the world economic downturn of the early 1970s. Inflation rose to 30 percent a year and may have risen as high as 60 percent in the first quarter of 1974.[62] By one estimate, about half of the elite opposed integration with Europe, while 60 percent opposed integration with Africa.[63]

The pro-empire economic interests could win this argument as long as the armed forces also remained committed to the overseas territories. However, once the military started to change its views, the imperialists' days were numbered. Tellingly, the military made no attempt to negotiate a settlement with the nationalists on Portuguese investments. Thus, in contrast to the Dutch (who assumed that they had brokered a deal to protect Dutch assets in Indonesia, which indeed held up until 1956), the Portuguese government, when the time came, withdrew unilaterally.

THE FALSE PROMISE OF LUSO-TROPICALISM

When the African wars of liberation started in earnest, they seemed to ride a tide that was immersing the entire African continent. France had granted independence to most of its African holdings, and even Algeria was

60. Quoted in Pimlott 1977, 338, citing Spínola's book, *Portugal and the Future*, p. 4. Maxwell similarly argues that Spínola drew support from the "more advanced sectors of the Portuguese business community." Maxwell 1976, 259. Bragança (1988, 434) also notes Spínola's connections to large industrial groups.

61. Maxwell 1995, 28. The Espirito Santo Bank had interests in, among other things, Angolan oil (Blackburn 1974, 14).

62. Calculations of inflation in 1973 range from 21 percent (Makler 1979, 124; Blackburn 1974, 10; Bandeira 1976, 30) to 30–35 percent for the 1973–74 period (Kohler 1981, 39 n. 22; Pimlott 1977; Makler 1979, 124).

63. Makler 1979, 152.

on the verge of gaining its sovereignty. Britain, similarly, had closed the book on its imperial legacy. Belgium, anticipating in 1955 that Congolese independence was still thirty years away, was notoriously unprepared for the Congo's breakaway and had been forced to retreat in less than five years. Nationalists were carrying the field.

Although the armed struggle for independence in Portuguese Africa started in 1961, nationalist movements had emerged well before that. In Mozambique, nationalists had started to organize as early as 1920. Their demands gained in momentum in 1935 when the Salazar regime implemented greater centralization throughout its colonies. Indigenes were denied access to public meetings and legal representation.[64]

Portugal managed to suppress these early nationalist movements relatively easily, if brutally, as France and the Netherlands had done in the interwar period. But the postwar drive for independence was of quite a different character. Starting with attacks in Angola, Portugal soon faced armed nationalist forces in Guinea and Mozambique as well. In Angola three major forces were to emerge. Holden Roberto led the Frente Nacional de Libertação de Angola (FNLA). Constituting, by the early 1970s, a force of about two thousand in Angola and about twelve thousand in Zaire, its main base of operations lay in the north. The Marxist Movimento Popular de Libertação de Angola (MPLA) under Agostino Neto concentrated on Angola's urban and central zones. Jonas Savimbi's União Nacional para a Independência Total de Angola (UNITA), numbering about eight hundred, operated in the east. In Mozambique, the Frente de Libertação de Mocambique (Frelimo) constituted the primary nationalist organization. In Guinea the nationalists led by Amílcar Cabral included the small Cape Verde islands within their demands for independence and thus became the Partido Africano de Independencia de Guiné e Cabo Verde (PAIGC).[65]

These nationalist movements emerged despite Lisbon's claims that the racial, ethnic, and class differences that divided metropolitans from indigenes in many other colonial empires did not exist in the Portuguese case. Portugal, so the argument went, strove for assimilation with the overseas territories into a greater Luso-tropical empire. Given this situation, nationalist demands would only appeal to a small extremist minority. Indeed, Salazar expounded exactly that position in 1963. African local elites were yet incapable of assuming power; Portuguese control benefited European and African alike; and the attack on the Portuguese presence was inspired by outside (Communist) influence.[66] Even though his successor, Marcelo Caetano (1970–74), showed himself more open to democratization and

64. Friedland 1979, 126.
65. Ebinger 1976, 671–82; Maxwell 1995, 20, 100–103, 124–26; Birmingham 1993, 178.
66. Africa Institute 1963, 294, 304.

CHAPTER 6

reform in Portugal and the overseas territories, he too defended that perspective until the very end:

> The two great provinces of Angola and Mozambique, which Portugal created out of a mosaic of poor and generally decadent tribes . . . are populated by blacks, whites, and Asians who love their motherland. There races are blended, cultures are altered. . . . We therefore consider it our duty to defend those who trusting in Portugal are loyal to its flag.[67]

Lisbon further submitted that the colonies were "overseas provinces." Thus, the colonial wars were matters of internal, rather than international, jurisdiction. Hence, these conflicts were not subject to oversight by international organizations such as the United Nations.[68]

Moreover, despite some criticism from the Kennedy administration, Portugal expected Western support in suppressing the African movements for independence. True, Kennedy had put colonial powers on notice that the United States "shall no longer seek to prevent subjugated peoples from being heard."[69] But once in power, the Democratic administration, spearheaded by Secretary of State Dean Rusk and others, instructed the African Bureau and the American mission to the United Nations to cease all contacts with African nationalists.[70] Portuguese colonial policies, and South African apartheid for that matter, were to be evaluated against the backdrop of Soviet, Cuban, and Chinese influence in the region. The vital Azores air base provided added support for Washington's instrumental evaluation of Portuguese ambitions.[71]

Finally, Lisbon argued that political and ethnic differences divided the nationalist movements. Particularly, the Angolan opposition divided along tribal and regional lines with no unified opposition emerging in the course of the wars with Portugal.[72] The FNLA found its ethnic roots among the Bakongo, and received support from Zaire. The MPLA, by contrast, sought its support from the People's Republic of China and Cuba. Zambia initially assisted UNITA.

---

67. Caetano to the National Assembly, March 5, 1974, cited in Bender 1978b, xix. Earlier, as minister of the colonies visiting Mozambique in 1945, he had been far less sanguine about assimilation: "On one point only should we be rigorous with respect to racial separation: namely marital or casual sexual mixing of blacks and white, the source of serious disturbances in social life, and of the serious problem of race mixing." Cited in Minter 1972, 19.

68. Birmingham 1993, 169.

69. Mahoney 1983, 187. He also rejected the blanket equation of all nationalism with communism.

70. Mahoney 1983, 218; Minter 1972, chap. 4.

71. Maxwell 1976, 267; Maxwell 1995, 46–47, 50; Ebinger 1976, 671; Szulc 1975, 20–21; Birmingham 1993, 173, 175.

72. Keefe 1977, 262ff.

192

The Salazar-Caetano regime could thus argue that a hard line vis-à-vis the nationalists was strategically sound. The Portuguese assessment of the nationalist movements, however, seriously understated their strength, as subsequent military successes by the nationalist forces demonstrated. Although the Angolan theater was stalemated, other areas saw a more united and more effective opposition.[73] In Mozambique, the Portuguese were engaged in a protracted withdrawal. With time, as the military recognized, Portuguese presence would be untenable. In Guinea, the metropolitan armed forces faced imminent disaster.

Similarly, the much-vaunted assimilation with the local population turned out to be chimerical. Ethnic biases favored metropolitan settlers over native born. In Guinea, for example, the government—using the legal distinction between civilized and noncivilized indigenes—only listed 1,478 natives as civilized in 1950.[74] That some of the settlers were almost as poor as the local colonial subjects was not evidence of economic equality but of the settlers' impoverished backgrounds. They nevertheless enjoyed a privileged legal and political status and occupied most of the government posts. White Portuguese officers similarly dominated the officer corps.

The administrative reforms that were instigated to stem the rising tide of nationalism had some success. The legal distinction between "civilisado" and "indigena" had been dropped in 1961.[75] In theory, Portuguese Africans gained equal status to that of metropolitans. Nevertheless, in Angola in 1965, among 182 high administrators there were only thirty-four local people.[76] As Gerald Bender convincingly argues, the mere absence of overt racist policies and segregationist measures does not mean the absence of racial discrimination and categorization.[77] Assimilation and Luso-tropical integration remained illusions.

The nationalists also increasingly received external support. A UN Security Council resolution of July 31, 1963 called for an arms embargo on Portugal and independence for the overseas territories. Even though the United States, Britain, and France abstained, international support for the nationalists was mounting. This support did not just come from Communist states, and it increased during the colonial wars. By October 1973, fifty-four states had recognized Guinea-Bissau as an independent nation.[78]

---

73. Maxwell 1995, 102.

74. Forrest 1992, 22. Others give higher numbers (Newitt 1981, 142; Minter 1972, 20). Whichever figures one uses, it is clear the overall number of "integrated" Africans was low compared to the size of the indigenous population.

75. Newitt 1981, 186.

76. Bailey 1969b, 150.

77. Bender 1978b.

78. See Africa Institute 1963, 284; Maxwell 1995, 332.

The refusal of the Portuguese government to face up to reality is perhaps best exemplified by its refusal to accept the Indian takeover of the Portuguese State of India (Goa and a few small enclaves) in 1961. It continued to classify these as "temporarily occupied territories," and continued to assign them seats in the National Assembly up until 1974.[79]

THE LACK OF CREDIBLE COMMITMENT IN METROPOLE AND PERIPHERY

The Portuguese wars in Africa were intractable for various reasons. One reason was the symbiotic connection between the ruling oligarchy and the deliberate, self-arrested development of the mother country and the overseas territories. The second reason was the negotiating environment in which both Portugal and the nationalist movements were unable to credibly commit themselves to negotiated solutions.

To reiterate our earlier theoretical discussion: standard political science literature suggests that polities with multiple veto points face difficulties initiating and concluding negotiated solutions, but once those solutions are accepted, polities with multiple veto players cannot easily back out of those agreements. They are thus poor in credible commitment in the initiation phase of negotiations but are strong in credibly committing to implementation of agreements once they have been achieved.[80]

Two important caveats apply. First, the credible commitment argument applies to democratic systems where elites can be held accountable. The authoritarian system in Portugal clearly did not fit that bill. Thus, even if a compromise solution could have been reached, the nationalists had little reason to trust that Lisbon would implement it.

Second, the lack of credible commitment in the initiation phase once again proved critical. Indeed, Portugal fared even worse than democratic systems with multiple veto players, such as the Netherlands and the French Fourth Republic. The Portuguese oligarchy did not back out of negotiated solutions, it simply never presented any. The ruling coalition saw its fate so closely intertwined with the overseas areas that the situation presented itself as dichotomous. Yielding territorial control would mean the end of the ruling coalition's position in the metropole.

The metropole's repression of the nationalist movements further eroded its standing in negotiations. The metropole lacked credibility because of its years of repression, its avowed but not implemented Luso-tropicalism, and its lack of concessions in other areas of the empire.

79. Keefe 1977, 258.
80. Cowhey 1993a; Martin 2000.

Overall, the nationalists—as in the cases of the other maritime empires—were not that concerned with the metropole's ability to commit. Reading the shifting circumstances after World War II more accurately than the central government did, the nationalists concluded that once the metropole had retreated it could not reinsert itself. The tide was running out on empires, and independence movements were winning everywhere.

It is fair to say that the nationalists also lacked the ability to credibly commit, particularly in Angola. Given the politically and ethnically divided movements, Lisbon had no unified negotiating partner. But this was less the case in Mozambique, and even less so in Guinea. Had Lisbon started with negotiations there its credibility might have been enhanced so that it could later negotiate in other areas.

Could Portugal have gained greater concessions from the nationalists? After all, if retreat came at such a great cost to the metropolitan elites, Frelimo, the MPLA, and other groups might have been more accommodating in order to see Portugal retreat at an earlier date. In other words, why could not the metropole translate its multiplicity of domestic veto players into an external bargaining advantage?

For one thing, Portugal did not have much to offer. Underdeveloped itself, it held little in terms of resources, know-how, or financial connections that might have made the nationalists more inclined to try to come to an understanding with the metropole. The nationalists correctly understood that if Portugal withdrew, other Western powers would step in. For example, the United States had already moved into oil field exploration in Angola.

Moreover, the lack of credibility in the initial phase of negotiations influenced the metropole's subsequent ability to gain bargaining leverage. That is, while a fragmented polity might be a bargaining advantage—as two-level game theory suggests—the advantage hinges on the metropole's ability to credibly commit.[81] Because Lisbon could not put forward a credible package for negotiations, the nationalists were not inclined to discuss the details of a possible compromise. Thus, the territorial issue once again became a dichotomous one, in which only one party would gain full sovereignty.

MILITARY PREFERENCES AND THE COUP OF 1974

Initially, the corporate interests of the armed forces made them one of the staunchest advocates of a hard-line response to nationalist demands. Military outlays, career advancement, and strategic doctrine all reinforced

81. On two-level games, see Putnam 1988.

this position. The armed forces concluded that without the empire their position and budgetary allocation would come under closer scrutiny. (Indeed, within two years of the revolution, decolonization would lead to a sharply reduced military force. From its peak strength of 220,000 in 1974, it was reduced to 46,000 by 1976.)[82] That prospect had to be opposed by whatever means necessary. Given their position in the ruling coalition of the authoritarian system, they had the institutional means to realize their preferences.

To hold the colonies Portugal deployed hundreds of thousands of troops on tours of duty of up to six years.[83] Considerable numbers of indigenous people served along with the Portuguese, as conscription had been introduced to the colonies in the 1960s. In Mozambique as much as 60 percent of the army was black. In Angola thirty thousand local militia members augmented the Portuguese military.[84] Overall, roughly three quarters of the men in the field were metropolitan draftees with the rest being conscripted in the overseas territories. The officer corps, however, remained largely a white Portuguese force.

But corporate interests and preferences can change. While we may wish to postulate preferences a priori for the sake of parsimony, the complexities of history often defeat such endeavors. As Robert Jervis reminds us, although the military may often be guided by narrow corporate interests, for example, in its choice of particular strategies that guarantee large budgets and military autonomy, ultimately armies need to win the war.[85]

In the Portuguese case, more and more elements within the army started to question the wisdom of continuing a war that led, at best, to stalemate (as in Angola), protracted withdrawal (in Mozambique), or imminent defeat (in Guinea). Influential elements within the armed forces started to come to the conclusion that the military's corporate interests were no longer served by fighting for a lost cause. Concerns about the overall colonial policy meshed with narrower individual concerns. The fortunes of war, however, provided the canvas against which all other events unfolded.

In Angola, where the fighting had first started in 1961, the military's predicament did not look that bad. Portugal had deployed most of its troops there, and it did so with several logistical advantages. First, as already noted, Angola had the largest settler population. The armed forces could count on considerable support from Portuguese on the ground, and because of conscription in the colonies, Angola provided a source of manpower for the colonial war. Second, Angola's size and sparse population

82. Keefe 1977, 373, 383.
83. Maxwell 1995, 23, 29ff.
84. Bender 1974, 147, 150.
85. Jervis 1995, 48.

also worked to the metropolitan advantage. Guerrillas could infiltrate from neighboring states, such as Zaire and Zambia, but they found it difficult to advance far beyond the border, which served also as an escape route. Third, the Portuguese had some measure of success in Angola with emulating French counterinsurgency strategies in Algeria and U.S. strategies in Vietnam.[86] Fortified settlements allowed the armed forces to relocate the local populations away from nationalist influence in the countryside. Because of the significant economic interests involved in Angola, it was also relatively easy to mount metropolitan support for a hard-line solution. Holding companies with plantations and mines needed to be protected. But the divided nature of the opposition conveyed perhaps the largest advantage on the Portuguese. The MPLA, FNLA, and UNITA fragmented along political and tribal lines. As long as the rebels did not have a unified strategy, the armed forces could deal with them piecemeal.[87] As a consequence of all these factors, the colonial army was holding its own in Angola.

Such advantages only existed to a lesser extent in Mozambique and not at all in Guinea.[88] The settler population in Mozambique was substantial but smaller than that in Angola. Economic interests were also less pronounced. Guinea lacked a substantial settler population, and its resources were negligible. The opposition movements in Mozambique and Guinea also displayed greater unity than those in Angola. In Mozambique, Frelimo, despite some minor opposition, constituted the main nationalist force. In Guinea, the PAIGC had unified the drive for independence of Guinea-Bissau and the Cape Verde Islands.[89]

In Mozambique, the Portuguese military initially held its own but gradually started to give ground. While defeat was not imminent, it seemed inevitable in the long run. The situation in Guinea was altogether critical. Here, a considerable Portuguese force had fought vainly against a well-organized, well-trained foe. By the early 1970s, the PAIGC forces were on the verge of taking the entire country, even though the Portuguese armed forces and militia totaled more than seventeen thousand.[90]

With the increasing nationalist military successes, Portuguese casualties started to mount. At the high end, some calculations suggest that the armed forces suffered sixty thousand casualties (dead and seriously wounded) between 1961 and 1974. Other estimates suggest lower numbers: 7,700 dead,

86. For a discussion, see Bender 1972a, 356; Newitt 1981, 231.

87. For a bottom-up account of the MPLA, see Barnett and Harvey 1972.

88. For assessments of the overall military situation in these three territories, see Raby 1988, 245; Bragança 1988, 429.

89. There was some dissension regarding the dominance of the Cape Verdeans in the movement, but the PAIGC remained the dominant force.

90. Davidson 1974, 12. Other estimates put the Portuguese presence as high as thirty thousand, while PAIGC regulars totaled roughly five thousand. Forrest 1992, 35.

28,000 wounded.[91] Relative to the small population base, however, Portugal sustained heavier casualties than the United States in Vietnam.

The precarious military situation intertwined with challenges to more narrowly defined corporate interests of the armed forces. One cleavage emerged as a result of changes in promotion and retention criteria. Most officers at the beginning of the war were professionals from well-to-do families. As the war progressed, however, army careers became far less attractive. Attrition in the field, falling recruitment levels, and early retirement all led to a precipitous shortage of officers. Longer deployments overseas extended the presence of officers already in the field, but it also diminished incentives to join the officer corps. In 1961 the military academy admitted 257 new candidates for the officer corps. By 1972, the number had dropped to 72.[92] By 1973, less than 10 percent of military academy positions were being filled.[93]

Because of these declining numbers, the military had to open up the higher ranks of the military. Increasing the number of officers entailed attracting more candidates to army careers and accelerated promotion for noncommissioned officers and draftees. This meant that requirements for promotion went down. Exam levels were lowered so as to facilitate the entry of candidates with less formal education and from less prestigious backgrounds. It also meant that officers in the field would be given credit for time served, which could be substituted for certain officer-level examinations.

Decree Law 353/73, which enhanced the position of the militia officers, directly challenged the privileged position of the older semi-aristocratic officer corps.[94] They resented that newcomers had easier access to the academy and that they were promoted at a rapid pace. Moreover, the newcomers came from middle-class or lower-class backgrounds. Those most affected by these changes were the middle-ranking officers who had taken years to pass the exams and rise through the ranks. Dissatisfaction with the civilian government thus first arose from the middle-ranking officers on this relatively narrow issue.

The "captains' movement," as it was soon called, was hijacked by different agendas, however. Whereas the early movement had simply served as a convenient tool to voice dissatisfaction, other officers started to use the movement to advance much broader objectives.[95] The changing composition of

91. High-end estimates are given by Blackburn 1974, 6ff.; Pimlott 1977, 336. Raby (1988, 244) gives lower numbers. Keefe suggests a total number of 7,873 dead with roughly 5,000 coming from direct action, and another 2,900 noncombat deaths. Keefe 1977, 376–78.

92. Blackburn 1974, 11–14.

93. Bender 1974, 134.

94. Bandeira 1976, 40; Wheeler 1979, 207ff.; Kohler 1981, 38; Raby 1988, 244ff.; Maxwell 1995, 35–38; Schmitter 1975a, 24–27.

95. See Maxwell 1995, 57.

the officer corps meant that more lower- and middle-class political views started to permeate the military.[96] The new corps was far more amenable to socialist and Marxist sentiments than the authoritarian officers of an older generation. Consequently, they started to amalgamate their opposition to the colonial wars with opposition to the regime in general. The Armed Forces Movement (Movimento das Forças Armadas—MFA) became a radical movement against the Caetano regime.

Other elements in the army, while not as far left as some elements within the MFA, similarly lost confidence in a military solution to the war. Indeed, they invoked an analogy with the Indian takeover in Goa in 1961, where the garrison capitulated as 30,000 Indian troops moved in. Governor-General Vassalo e Silva of Goa was subsequently court-martialed for not fighting to the finish.[97] Some elements in the army feared that once again the army would become the scapegoat—this time in Africa. In its manifesto of February 1974 the MFA submitted that the army is "presented to the country as if those mainly responsible for the disaster."[98]

Still, the army could not move without at least some elements from the upper echelons signing on to the protest. Earlier attempts by breakaway military elements had been suppressed relatively easily. Rival branches within the military, the secret police, and their armed affiliates had quickly quelled such attempts.[99] Indeed, only shortly before the 1974 coup, an earlier attempt to seize power by democratic elements in the military had been forestalled.

The MFA gained momentum when some of the highest-ranking officers in Africa started to take their side. Chief of Staff General Costa Gomes and General Spínola, commander in chief in Guinea from 1967 to 1973, began to change their minds about the likely outcome of continued colonial war. General Spínola had initially taken a hard-line position on nationalist demands. He believed that suppression of the insurgents and colonial reforms, combined with administrative changes in the military, could still save the day. And, indeed, thanks to his reforms, the war in Guinea had at first swung in Portugal's favor. His success, however, did not last. Already by 1968 he had come to believe that a military solution was no longer feasible.[100]

Still, General Spínola did not favor severing all ties. He wrote a book in which he argued for a commonwealth of states to replace the old colonial structure, with close ties between the mother country and the erstwhile

96. Szulc 1975, 22–23.
97. Raby 1988, 211–12; Bandeira 1976, 34; Soares 1975, 133.
98. Wheeler 1979, 191.
99. For a discussion of various such attempts, see Raby 1988, 202–3, 211–12, 242–43; Martins 1969, 254–55.
100. Maxwell 1995, 31; Davidson 1974, 7–9.

colonies. "Without the African territories the country would be reduced to a small corner in a growing Europe."[101] Although some members in the armed forces wanted to go considerably further, it was clear that Spínola and Gomes had become useful allies for the MFA.

It is unclear how far Caetano had started to shift toward negotiated withdrawal and a commonwealth model. On the one hand, he asserted that he would brook no retreat. Even if Guinea could not be held, there was no reason to abandon the other areas. He claimed that "armies are made to fight and must fight to win, but it is not power which wins. If the Portuguese army is beaten in Guinea . . . their defeat would allow us to initiate legal-political steps to continue the defense of the rest of the overseas provinces."[102] He thus argued that negotiations in Guinea would simply encourage further nationalist demands in Angola and Mozambique. Furthermore, in his first address as prime minister in 1968 he stressed how Portugal had to maintain the overseas territories.[103]

On the other hand, he did tolerate the publication of General Spínola's inflammatory book. Surely, with censorship securely in place, Caetano must have known of its content before publication. Caetano, on other occasions, had also advocated reforms within the colonies to appease secessionist demands. He had released some metropolitan opponents from prison, such as Mário Soares, a Socialist who later would become prime minister.[104] He further had initiated some rudimentary reforms in the overseas territories, perhaps opening a route to a commonwealth model.

Either way, he was well aware that the military was divided. Indeed, the right wing within the armed forces threatened a military coup because they opposed Caetano's limited reforms and tolerance for Spínola.[105] Against Spínola, Costa Gomes, and the MFA, stood high-ranking metropolitan officers who sided with Admiral Tomás. Thomás, as president, was technically the commander in chief. With him stood Generals Kaúlza de Arriaga and Silvério Marques. For them the overseas territories were nonnegotiable.[106] General de Arriaga even opposed attempts at assimilation, arguing that "blacks . . . of all peoples in the world . . . are the least intelligent."[107] Costa Gomes and Spínola were summarily dismissed from office by the conservative forces in the military for their defeatist statements.

101. Bender 1974, 139. Birmingham 1993, 178; Bragança 1988, 432.
102. Quoted in Maxwell 1995, 31.
103. Wheeler 1970, 775. See also Martins 1969, 250.
104. Wheeler 1970, 776.
105. Raby 1988, 247.
106. Maxwell 1995, 34–35, 44; Kohler 1981, 30–31; Szulc 1975, 19.
107. Bender 1974, 134.

Given Caetano's unwillingness to engage in negotiated withdrawal, and given the divisions within the military, the MFA came to the conclusion that only a military coup could resolve both the colonial issue and authoritarianism at home. General Spínola now intervened to save the nation from further dissension, by consciously emulating de Gaulle's actions a decade and a half earlier.[108]

On the night of April 24, 1974 a song was played on one of Lisbon's radio stations.[109] The song, a previously agreed upon code, activated the units sympathetic to the MFA to move on Lisbon and capture key installations and neutralize possible resistance. Caetano and key opponents of reform were quickly arrested, and subsequently exiled. The military surrounded the barracks of the secret police, the PIDE, and jailed its main leaders. The armed forces took total command and rescinded the previous territorial policy.[110]

Portugal then rapidly pulled out of the colonial wars. By June 1974 it reached a settlement with the PAIGC in Guinea-Bissau. By September 6 it had struck a similar deal with Frelimo in Mozambique.

Along with some of the business interests with site-specific assets in the colonies, the settlers resisted retrenchment. Like the pieds noirs in Algeria they had resorted to armed resistance to nationalist demands and took to the streets of the colonial capitals to pressure the local administrations. When the decision to abandon finally came in 1974, some settlers revolted outright and had to be suppressed by the Portuguese military and the nationalists now working together. In Mozambique, an attempted coup was carried out by the Front for Independence and Continuity with the West (FICO), a right-wing organization catering to the conservative white settler population, with the intention of creating a government along the lines of the white separatists in Rhodesia. Frelimo and the Portuguese army quelled the revolt.[111]

Ultimately, more than five hundred thousand settlers returned to the metropole. In the turbulent years after the April 1974 coup, they became ardent supporters of the far right, and indeed the danger of a countercoup in Portugal remained for several years.[112] Many settlers also went to South Africa.

The socialists and Communists soon ousted General Spínola from the presidency on September 30, 1974. The Armed Forces Movement had by

---

108. Pimlott 1977, 334.
109. For a quick overview of these events, see Blackburn 1974, 15–18.
110. Maxwell 1995, 81; Blackburn 1974, 29.
111. Keefe 1977, 269; Blackburn 1974, 29.
112. Harsgor 1980, 146; Szulc 1975, 17; Birmingham 1993, 188.

then come to encompass at least five distinct groups. Portugal was racked by political turmoil, with more than six governments coming and going within a two-year span. Within this political arena, the former settlers took their position on the right end of the spectrum.[113] Their role, and their imperial dreams, however, had come to naught.

This look at Portugal and it colonies has extended to authoritarian regimes the fundamental insight that numerous veto points retard policy adjustment. More specifically we started with the hypothesis that an authoritarian, cartelized system would diminish the state's responsiveness to international change. A hierarchical authoritarian system with few veto points, by contrast, would more likely alter its strategy. Portugal's overseas policies bear this out.

The Portuguese case presents a classic case of an authoritarian, cartelized government that gives members of the ruling coalition disproportionate power, while excluding direct input from the general population. The military, property owners (large holders in the south and smaller ones in the north), the Catholic Church, and traditional business elites were key components of the Estado Novo. Some of these, specifically the military and the industrialists with site-specific assets in the colonies, had vested interests in maintaining Portuguese control over the overseas provinces. The settlers who had been encouraged to migrate to the African colonies by the Salazar regime also had a strong preference for empire, but they lacked access to the corporatist-authoritarian structure of the regime. The key veto points to change in the existing territorial policy thus lay with the large holding companies and the armed forces.

Salazar and Caetano, and the politicians supported by the armed forces and business interests, had reasons of their own to maintain the overseas territories. Keeping Portugal in a state of arrested development—by focusing on Africa rather than Europe, and sacrificing modernization of the metropole—kept the authoritarian government in power.

In the 1960s some economic interests started to change their minds about the benefits of empire, partially due to the changing position of Portugal in the international and European economies. But without the military on their side, the pro-Europe economic interests could not move. Schmitter thus rightly points out that the change in position in the armed forces was the key.[114] Once the military's corporate interests dictated withdrawal and they usurped power—reducing the political system to a united authoritarian regime rather than a cartelized one—the imperial game was

113. For a discussion of events after decolonization see Blackburn 1974, 29ff.; Maxwell 1976; Maxwell 1995.
114. Schmitter 1975a, 23, 27. Newitt (1981, 243) makes a similar point regarding the importance of regime change.

over. As soon as the armed forces reversed course, they retreated with alacrity from the overseas territories. The new regime granted Guinea-Bissau independence by September 1974; Mozambique gained sovereignty in June 1975; the Cape Verde Islands, Sao Tome, and Principe in July 1975; and Angola became independent in November of that year. Goa, annexed by India in 1961, was retroactively given independence. Macao remained in Portuguese hands until 1999. But for all intents and purposes the five hundred-year-old empire had come to an end in just over a year.

CHAPTER SEVEN

Russia Retreats from the Union

We must think, and think hard, about how in fact to transform our federation. . . . The use of force is excluded. It has been ruled out in foreign policy and is absolutely inadmissible against our own people.

MIKHAIL GORBACHEV, May 1989

We are the world's last disintegrating empire.

GALINA STAROVOITOVA, member of the USSR Congress of People's Deputies, later adviser to Yeltsin on ethnic issues

I am convinced that we should look for answers to all the questions that concern us not in the destruction—not in the destruction—of unity, but in the path of the firm renewal of the federation.

MIKHAIL GORBACHEV, July 1989

When Mikhail Gorbachev assumed power in the Soviet Union in 1985, most Western analysts foresaw only marginal changes in the Soviet future. As a protégé of Yuri Andropov, the former head of the KGB and general secretary of the Communist Party, the expectation was that he would probably push similar policies. Whatever reforms there would be, they would be well within the established institutional framework of the Soviet Union; the Communist Party would reign supreme, as it had for the past seventy years, and its hegemonic domination over its external empire would be unquestioned.[1] Within six years, however, the party was forced to relinquish its preeminence in Soviet political life; Moscow consented to substantial conventional and nuclear force reductions; the Soviet regime retreated from its external empire; and, most startling of all, in December 1991 the Union of Soviet Socialist Republics itself ceased to exist.

---

1. Some dissidents in retrospect seemed blessed with remarkable prescience. See, for example, Amalrik 1970; Medvedev 1975; Solzhenitsyn 1981.

The Soviet Union shared some of the traits of Western colonial empires. It had a hierarchical organization; subject areas were held by force (exit was nominally possible but de facto denied); the center ruled the various areas by a hub-and-spoke pattern of bilateral relations; and some areas were more favored than others in the asymmetric federalist structure of the Soviet Union.[2]

But the Soviet "empire" differed from the Western empires in that it combined hierarchical demarcation of center and periphery in the territorial sense with a functional, nonterritorial aspect of domination. These two perspectives of empire coexisted uneasily.[3] Viewed geographically, for non-Russians Russia was the dominant territorial entity in a classical imperial relation. The prevalence of Russians in the officer corps, the ubiquity of Russians in science and managerial leadership roles, and the dominance of Russian cultural symbols and language (despite the attempt to create an all-Soviet identity) exemplified this relation of superordinate and subordinate.

From an organizational perspective, Mikhail Gorbachev described the Soviet Union as a "supercentralized unitary state" within which "the central government, the so-called Center—that is, essentially the party—did as it pleased."[4] Thus, the center dominated Russia itself. From the Russian (non-party) perspective, the empire consisted of the dominant Communist Party of the Soviet Union (CPSU), which repressed Russian and non-Russian alike. Russian resources were siphoned off to maintain and subsidize the empire, and Soviet acculturation sought to erase Russian identity as well as that of peoples in the periphery. Indeed, Russia alone among the union republics lacked a republican party organization of its own. Its interests were deemed to be represented by the all-Union CPSU. (Interestingly, as Gorbachev denuded the party of its power, he referred back to the territorial understanding—speaking of a federation in which "different relations will result between the republics and the Center," using "the Center" to refer to Russia.)[5]

The dissolution of the internal empire (the USSR itself) involved a double move. On the one hand, it entailed a diminution and shunting aside of the party and the groups that through the party pursued their imperial

2. See Laitin 1991.
3. Marc Beissinger (1997) argues that because the all-Union institutions of the empire subordinated Russia itself, the imperial label is inappropriate. I argue that it nevertheless demonstrates certain taxonomic elements of an imperial polity. See Spruyt 1997a, 1997b. Others who label it an empire include Hough (1997, 373–74), who draws attention to comparisons with other empires, as does Motyl 1993. See also Suny 1993, 112–13; Bunce 1993; Matlock 1995. Dunlop (1993b, 45) notes that the USSR did not constitute a Russian empire because of the asymmetrical structure that disadvantaged the Russian Republic. Nevertheless, the party-state empire did occasionally resort to Russian patriotism to bolster its power.
4. Gorbachev 2000, 85.
5. Gorbachev 2000, 106.

preferences. On the other hand, it entailed a retreat by Russia from its hierarchical relation with the other republics.

In chapter 2 we saw how empires and multinational states generally speaking had become increasingly a burden to the central governments of those polities after World War II. Looking at the Soviet Union's military outlay and the economic drain of the external and internal empires one might conclude that the dissolution of the USSR would be a foregone conclusion. Nothing would be further from the truth. Such teleological and post hoc accounts distort empirical reality.

Indeed, in the first decades after the war, an imperial policy could be strategically justified. The external and internal empires still provided economic gains for Russia and the USSR as a whole and, more important, were key military assets. They provided forward bases, buffer zones, and manpower. While the economic benefits of empire arguably started to decline by the late 1960s, the military benefits lasted until the early 1980s.

Even in the mid-1980s, the Soviet position was more favorable than the situation in which the Western empires found themselves in the immediate postwar years. Despite its problems, the Soviet Union still possessed a formidable military capability.[6] Slow growth bedeviled the economy, but it need not have led to a breakup of the Soviet Union, as economic problems had not done so in the past. Furthermore, few of the union republics could risk severing economic ties with Russia, given Moscow's considerable support and subsidized resources. And a (still) authoritarian system could largely ignore popular demands.

Moreover, influential political elites and interest groups, such as many in the upper echelons of the CPSU, the armed forces, and the Russians in the union republics, continued to favor a strong Soviet Union. A transfer of assets to the non-Russian union republics would present significant political and economic losses to the actors at the top of the highly integrated Soviet economic structure. The more than 25 million Russians who were outside of the Russian union republic would also resent any diminution of Soviet dominance; Soviet institutions had traditionally given many of these groups considerable influence.

What then explains the relatively peaceful and unexpectedly swift breakup of the external and the internal Soviet empire? This chapter focuses on the internal empire, since *Ending Empire* analyzes across the various cases how political institutions might allow the armed forces, settlers, and vertically integrated business groups to veto territorial adjustment. However, since the retreat from the external empire (Eastern Europe) influenced the disintegration of the USSR itself, the discussion will occasionally touch on the disintegrative process in the external empire as well.

6. See Menon and Spruyt 1997, 1999.

I argue that the changes in the overall environment provided necessary but not sufficient conditions for the changes in Soviet territorial policy. The structural challenges to the Soviet Union sparked a search for solutions to military and economic stagnation, and demands for greater local autonomy. To carry out such reform, General Secretary Gorbachev encouraged institutional reforms that had the effect of empowering dissolutionists at the expense of the pro–Soviet Union hard-liners.

Gorbachev or others in the upper echelons of decision making did not have a blueprint for divestiture, as Macmillan had after 1957 in the British case. Indeed, Gorbachev arguably condoned the military intervention in Baku (1990), Tbilisi (1989), and the Baltic republics (1991), and he perhaps even tacitly supported the August coup attempt in 1991.[7] He did not seek the dismantling of the existing system but merely reform. More radical individuals (such as Boris Yeltsin and Stanislav Shatalin), who were ousted from the center, were the ones who changed their objectives to favor reform and dissolution. Even after the coup of 1991 that made Yeltsin the heir apparent, Gorbachev tried to have a Union treaty drafted that would provide for a common economic union and common defense policy.

Nevertheless, the importance of the specific decisions made by Gorbachev cannot be denied. The institutional changes he implemented gave him virtually unprecedented powers through which he managed to sideline many of his rivals in the Politburo. Had Gorbachev chosen to pursue a hard line in 1989 or 1990, the forces in favor of keeping the Soviet Union intact would have succumbed far less easily to nationalist pressures.

In chapter 1 I argued that a reduction in veto players makes policy change more likely. This chapter shows how the reduction in veto points in the Soviet decision-making process, particularly between 1989 and 1991, allowed a strong executive government to circumvent hard-line opposition to territorial change. Civilian control over the military meant that ultimate decision-making authority resided with civilian leaders. The strong executive powers acquired by Gorbachev to push for reforms had the effect of diminishing the influence of the party and the instruments through which the party wielded influence—its control of information, its use of outright repression, and its control over lower cadres.

A divided Russian legislature delegated Yeltsin (particularly from late 1991 on) perhaps even stronger presidential powers than Gorbachev had and in the context of a weak party system, similarly diminished the veto opportunities of potential hard-liners in the Russian Republic. The long-term structural problems of the USSR, together with the particular institutional modality of the reform process, explain the dissolution of the USSR. Structural factors intermeshed with proximate, institutional causes.

7. Dunlop 1993a.

Commonwealth of Independent States, 1997. Map produced by the CIA. With kind permission of the Perry Castañeda Map Collection, University of Texas.

CIVILIAN CONTROL OVER THE ARMED FORCES

It would seem logical to expect that the military, as in other cases of imperialism, would be a strong proponent of empire. The Gorbachev reforms challenged the autonomy of the Soviet military through arms and troop reductions and by accepting nuclear doctrines originating in the West.[8] Such agreements also threatened the military's budget. Consequently, high-ranking officers openly challenged Gorbachev's foreign policy. Chief of Soviet Air Defense Forces Gen. Ivan Tretyak warned of the dangers of being "lured by apparent benefits" of force reductions.[9] Withdrawal from the external empire, let alone dissolution of the Soviet Union, would have even more serious repercussions for manpower and military bases.[10]

Why then did we not see a determined effort by the Soviet military—then still one of the most powerful in the world—to influence the course of policy, as in France and Portugal? Why did civilian objective control hold under these pressures, even if the armed forces showed dissatisfaction with Gorbachev's reforms and feared the possible end of the Soviet Union?[11]

The military played only a minor role in the events surrounding the dissolution of empire for several reasons. Some of these indicate that objective control measures were in place, others, more unique to the Soviet case, show a military in disarray and divided on policy issues. First, the Soviet army's mission had largely centered on external defense of the Soviet Union, not the maintenance of internal order. The latter task fell to the internal security forces, the KGB (the Committee for State Security) or the MVD (the Ministry of Internal Affairs and its special troops).[12] Consequently, the Soviet military had little taste for repressing internal nationalist demands, most especially those from Russia itself.

Second, the army, even though personnel changes were subject to approval at the highest level had a degree of autonomy. It could largely determine the contents of military doctrine but not the policy on arms talks or foreign policy. A division of labor between civilians and the military rele-

8. Gorbachev announced in December 1988 that the USSR would unilaterally cut five hundred thousand men and ten thousand tanks. Trehub in *Radio Free Europe/Radio Liberty* (hereafter cited as RFE/RL) 1, no. 1 (January 6, 1989), 1–3.

9. Peterson and Trulock 1988, 20.

10. Gelman 1991, 39.

11. The scholarly literature uniformly agrees that civilian control did not waiver during this period, see Colton 1990; Desch 1993; 1999; Lepingwell 1992; Meyer 1991–92. Odom (1998, 218–22) argues for a convergence model and compatibility of interests of party and military. Cleavages in the party mirrored cleavages within the military, preventing sustained military resistance against the reforms.

12. Desch 1993, 455–56; Lepingwell 1992, 551. As Desch points out, high external threat (which was reduced during the Gorbachev era but still present) facilitates civilian control (Desch 1999).

gated the latter tasks to civilian decision makers.[13] Civilian and military tasks were functionally distinct.

Third, some of the high-ranking officers in the army supported the Gorbachev reforms.[14] As seen in chapter 2, the technological and logistical revolution taking place in modern warfare had bypassed the Soviet military. Individuals in the highest echelons of the military argued that "such an army as we have today, an army that practically preserves its postwar structure, is no longer needed. The new circumstances require a radical perestroika of all army structures."[15]

Many high-ranking officers also agreed with Gorbachev that Soviet expansionist policies could not be sustained.[16] These policies not only generated high costs but also created quagmires from which the Soviet Union could extricate itself only with considerable difficulty.[17] On becoming general secretary Gorbachev almost immediately decided to pull out of Afghanistan. While he gave Gen. Mikhail Zaitsev one or two years to win the war, he already issued a secret directive in June 1985 to reduce the Soviet forces there.[18]

Needless to say, not all high-ranking officers agreed with Gorbachev's policies. Indeed, the Rust affair, when a German pilot landed a small private plane close to the Kremlin, set the stage for an acrimonious debate. Had the military aimed to embarrass Gorbachev and his reforms? Or was the military just bloated and incompetent, as the reformers claimed? Either way, 150 officers were tried in court and removed from their posts. The minister of defense, Marshal Sergei Sokolov, had to step down as well. Arguably, these senior officers were replaced by "mediocre careerists who would follow orders, any orders."[19]

Fourth, the economic costs of the stagnating Soviet system were disproportionately borne by the younger generation of officers.[20] The Gorbachev reforms promised them improvements in their dismal living conditions and higher wages. Whereas the old guard, the heroes of the Great Patriotic War, continued to expound the virtues of orthodox Communism, the younger cohort of officers was far less convinced of its virtues. The generational split

13. Rice 1987, 74; Desch 1993.

14. For the resistance to such reform, see Foye, *Report* on the USSR 1, no. 15 (April 14, 1989).

15. Maj. Gen. Nikita Chaldimov. Cited in Alexiev, RFE/RL 1, no. 1 (Jan. 6, 1989), 10. See also Foye, RFE/RL, 1, no. 8 (February 24, 1989), 7–11.

16. Odom 1998, 115; Wohlforth 1994–95, 114.

17. On the impact of the war in Afghanistan, see Mendelson 1993.

18. Odom 1998, 103.

19. This is William Odom's assessment. Odom 1998, 111.

20. For discussions of these generational splits, see Gelman 1991, 36, 44; Lepingwell 1992, 554–55; Meyer 1991–92, 28–30.

logically entailed a cleavage in the ranks. High officers, those with the rank of colonel or higher, staunchly supported the CPSU. Middle-ranking officers, majors primarily, vacillated. And the younger cohort, mostly captains and lower, opposed the party outright.

Such splits manifested themselves in the public debates surrounding the elections of 1989. For the first time officers denounced the party, the higher command, even the political system altogether. Polls taken among the card-carrying officers, that is, CPSU members, reveal that only about half supported the party. Keeping in mind that only two-thirds of the officers were party members, this suggests that the majority of the officers might have voted against the party.

Fifth, civilian leaders used alternative institutions for effective oversight over the military. Arguably, the "most important factor working against a military attempt to remove Gorbachev" was the KGB.[21] Indeed, Gorbachev used the support of the KGB, such as from KGB head Victor Chebrikov, to supervise the ousting of high-ranking military personnel who disagreed with Gorbachev's policies.[22] Hence, it wasn't the loyalty of the military but that of the KGB that was a key reason for concern. Gorbachev repeatedly replaced KGB directors: from August 1988 until March 1989, seven of the fourteen chairmen of the republican committees of state security were replaced, and the overall head of the KGB, Chebrikov, had to make way for Vladimir Kryuchkov.[23] Like some of his counterparts in the regular armed forces, Kryuchkov warned of the increasing technological and economic gap with the West, which would only increase with European unification in 1992. Reform was therefore imperative.[24]

Sixth, the military had learned in decades past that political involvement was a dangerous thing. The whims of the civilian superiors had destroyed many an officer who ventured into the political arena.[25] The Stalinist purges were of course the most dramatic example of this. But even after the war as great a hero as Marshal Georgy Zhukov, victor over the Nazi Reich, could be politically eliminated. More recently, some elements in the military also believed that in suppressing the riots in Tbilisi in 1989 and Baku in 1990, they had been made the scapegoats for decisions made in political circles.[26] Jack Matlock argues that, in the wake of Baku, "military intervention as a future means of 'bringing order' to the republics began to look more and more problematical. The Russian public was less and less willing

---

21. Gelman 1991, 51.
22. Rahr, Report on the USSR 1, no. 15 (April 14, 1989), 22.
23. Knight, Report on the USSR 1, no. 10 (March 10, 1989), 7–9.
24. Rahr, RFE/RL 1, no. 1 (January 6, 1989), 4.
25. Holloway 1983, 10; Rice 1987, 81.
26. Gorbachev tended to blame the use of military force on others, such as Yegor Ligachev, who had retreated from the reformist camp. See Gorbachev 2000, 94–103.

to pay the price the Soviet empire was exacting."[27] Indeed, a poll conducted in the RSFSR (Russian Soviet Federated Socialist Republic) after the hard-line faction had attempted a coup in Lithuania in January 1991 showed that only 29 percent approved of the military's actions, whereas 55 percent condemned its behavior.[28]

Seventh, ethnic divisions overlay age and rank cleavages. Whereas ethnic Russians dominated the officer corps, some ethnic groups were overrepresented among the enlisted men—more than a third of the conscripts were Muslims from Central Asia (which had a high birthrate).[29] Some regiments comprised as many as thirty nationalities, with 10–30 percent unable to speak Russian.[30]

Finally, organizational clashes between the KGB and the army, between the various services of the army, and between the various regional commands prevented unified resistance.[31] This showed up, for example, in the ill-fated coup attempt of August 1991 and the lack of coordination of the various segments of the KGB and military forces.[32] Eventually, the support of the Leningrad command and the support of the airborne forces saved the day for the reformers and turned the tide against the hard-line plotters. Gorbachev had also consistently appointed outsiders (particularly from the Far Eastern command) to important military positions, because they were less likely to owe their positions to the Brezhnev administration, and this aided the opposition to the putschists.[33]

In other words, although some elements in the armed forces clearly preferred to keep the Soviet Union intact, ultimately civilian control over the military held. Valerie Bunce, similarly, sees the lack of an interventionist military in the USSR as a critical reason why the dissolution of the Soviet Union transpired so differently from that of Yugoslavia. "The role of the military was clearly defined in international and not domestic terms. . . . This mission and the ways in which the war in Afghanistan and the Gorbachev reforms produced a divided and immobilized military . . . allowed the Soviet military to function as a bystander."[34]

27. Matlock 1995, 304. See also Odom 1998, chap. 12.
28. Dunlop 1993b, 64.
29. Alexiev, RFE/RL 1, no. 1 (January 6, 1989), 11. The quality of the personnel had also deteriorated. According to one report in *Red Star* (Krasnaya zvezda) 40 percent had been convicted prior to entering the service; Alexiev, n. 15. The Central Asian birthrate was roughly 3.5 to 4 times as high as that in the Baltic republics. Hill 1993, 119 nn. 20, 22, 35.
30. Meyer 1991–92, nn. 41, 61, 62, and p. 22.
31. On the command structure, see Berman and Baker 1982.
32. Dunlop 1993a, chap. 5; Shevtsova 1992, 6–7.
33. Zamaschikov, RFE/RL 1, no. 3 (January 20, 1989), 14–17.
34. Bunce 1999, 120.

INSTITUTIONAL REFORMS ESTABLISH
AN AUTHORITARIAN HIERARCHY

The key question facing us is how executives in the center, foremost, party general secretary (and later president) Gorbachev and Russian president Yeltsin, could ultimately let the Soviet Union dissolve without pro-Unionists in the party carrying more sway? Clearly, there were many party hard-liners who opposed any thought of dissolution. Even Gorbachev wanted to keep the Soviet Union intact, although he did not want to do so by the massive use of force. Why, in other words, could not the Russian settlers in the other union republics and the hard-liners in the party halt the Soviet Union's demise?

Part of the answer lies with the institutional structures in which political leaders operated. Both Gorbachev and Yeltsin managed to forge strong, independent executive posts, through which they could sidestep the pro-Unionist groups who favored a harder line on the territorial question.

Gorbachev against the Party

When Gorbachev first assumed power in 1985 his accession to the general secretaryship had hardly been uncontested. Indeed, if it were not for the absenteeism of several Politburo members, Gorbachev might not have been elected.[35] As other party secretaries before him had done, he had to consolidate his rule. Initially the Politburo conservatives still held considerable sway.[36] However, he swiftly moved to create a more solid independent basis for his power. He replaced many of the party secretaries at the regional levels. Because these regional secretaries voted for deputies to the party congresses, who in turn voted for the party Central Committee, who ultimately voted on Politburo candidates, control over lower cadres ultimately lead to a firmer foundation for the general secretary. By March 1986 about a third of the party first secretaries were new, and the return rate of the Central Committee was down to 60 percent from a previous 90 percent.[37] The lower cadre appointments were well aware that their posts derived from the general secretary and that they were expected to support his candidates for office. One of Gorbachev's assistants describes this "circular flow of power" from the top down and then back up: "Most Politburo members simply did not know who would be elected and who would be dismissed. This secret, which was the basis of the leader's immense power,

35. Matlock 1995, 46.
36. Gustafson and Mann 1986.
37. Mendelson 1993, 347, 350. Odom (1998, 137) notes that during the first two years of perestroika 60 percent of the oblast (relatively large regional organizations) and *raion* (small regions) party secretaries had been replaced.

enabled him to decide the fate of the Central Committee and the Politburo as he wished."[38] Gorbachev thus first worked to entrench himself at the top of the Communist Party hierarchy by creating a solid lower cadre support base.

It became readily apparent, however, that his desire for political and economic reform faced considerable opposition from within the party. "His advisers, Georgy Shakhnazarov, Anatoly Chernyayev, and Alexander Yakovlev told Gorbachev repeatedly, beginning in early 1987, that the party would never carry through on reform. The alternative was political reform that would allow Gorbachev to work around the party."[39] Gorbachev from then on started to engage in institutional reforms to sidestep opponents of reform. In the fall of 1988 he surrounded himself with a group of personal advisors who were not attached to the general secretary's office. Gradually, he also started to transfer powers from the party apparatus to a reformed Supreme Soviet. A state political institution, not the party organization, thus became the new locus of power. "The September plenum [1988] marked a pre-emptive strike against the CPSU Central Committee."[40]

The institutional reforms of 1989 proved to be a watershed. The new system provided for the election of 2,250 members to the Congress of People's Deputies. Of these deputies, 1,500 were elected in districts, while 750 were appointed by selected organizations. For example, the Communist Party appointed 100 members, and other groups similarly appointed their allotted total. These deputies then in turn elected a new Supreme Soviet body (542 members) to perform the day-to-day legislative tasks.[41]

Two features in this system further eroded the power of the Communist Party. First, the Congress of People's Deputies, not the Supreme Soviet, directly elected the president. The president would, after constitutional amendments, have the power to appoint top executive and judicial posts, including a cabinet of ministers and the chairman of the Soviet Council of Ministers (the prime minister), subject to the approval of the Supreme Soviet and Congress of People's Deputies. The president acquired full control over the economy. "The new parliament had no control over the budget and resources. The executive branch 'owned' and ran the economy."[42] The president also would have the authority to dissolve the Supreme Soviet and dismiss the chairman of the Council. As one observer noted at the time, Gorbachev's election by the Congress would give him "a safer position institutionally than before and [he] will be less dependent on . . . his Politburo

38. Valery Boldin, as cited in Hough 1997, 83.
39. Odom 1998, 173.
40. Rahr, RFE/RL 1, no. 5 (February 3, 1989), 3.
41. Voronitsyn, RFE/RL 1, no. 12 (January 13, 1989), 16–18. For a description of this process, see Hough 1997, chap. 5; Matlock 1995, 130–34; Suny 1998, 465–68.
42. Odom 1998, 175.

colleagues."[43] Ronald Suny similarly argues that "the election of the Congress of Peoples' Deputies and the Supreme Soviet radically shifted power at the top of the state structure from the party to the state and gave Gorbachev, now chairman of both, a new base of power outside the party."[44]

Second, the district candidates now faced competitive elections; indeed, of the 1,500 district positions, 1,320 fielded more than one candidate.[45] This changed the nature of the strategic calculations made by party members. Previously, party members merely had to be concerned with placating the party hierarchy. Now, they also had to cater to local constituencies. This, notes Gail Lapidus, "gave unprecedented leverage to organized local groups and accelerated the fragmentation of the Party along national lines."[46] Gorbachev's election by the Congress threatened the party from above, while local elections created perverse incentives for party members from below. If party members received their positions from their local constituents, rather than from the higher levels of the party, then they no longer had to reciprocate by supporting the party's upper echelons. Gorbachev had interrupted the circular flow of power.[47]

There can be little doubt that the party continued to favor a strong Soviet Union. One segment of the party argued that the resurgent nationalist tendencies should be met with a reemphasis on the old policy of merging (*sliianie*) the different ethnic groups through economic development. Another segment of the party argued, at the Leningrad Initiative Congress, for greater emphasis on the Russian preeminence within the Soviet Union: Russian hegemony would counter nationalist revivals.[48] The institutional reforms, however, changed the influence of the party hierarchy on political decision making. Indeed, by March 1990, Article 6 of the constitution, which proclaimed the party as the leading and guiding force of the regime, was repealed.[49]

At the same time, the electoral system gave titular Communist leaders incentives to tack toward their local constituencies. Communist Party leaders who wished to maintain their indigenous support had to adopt a nationalist mantle. Even if they preferred to maintain some form of the Soviet

---

43. Rahr, RFE/RL 1, no. 5 (February 3, 1989), 2. See also Rahr, Report on the USSR 1, no. 15 (April 14, 1989), 19–24. Several of the reformers around Gorbachev were influenced by the presidential system in France; Hough 1997, 157.

44. Suny 1998, 474.

45. Mann, RFE/RL 1, no. 10 (March 10, 1989), 5–7. Shakhnazarov argues that the election of the new Supreme Soviet marked the point at which perestroika could no longer be reversed. Odom 1998, 447, n. 62.

46. Lapidus 1992, 57.

47. Hough 1997, 261.

48. Lapidus, Zaslavsky, and Goldman 1992, 13.

49. See the depiction of these events in Medish 1994, 79.

Union, political expediency forced them to adopt ethnic and nationalist rhetoric.

In the latter part of 1990, Gorbachev worked to further expand his presidential powers. He argued specifically for the replacement of the Council of Ministers with a cabinet of ministers, roughly comparable to the presidential cabinet in the United States. In December 1990 constitutional amendments provided him with the desired institutional changes.[50]

In sum, the general secretary eroded the power base of the Communist Party, and at the same time sought his support from outside the party. "The officials of Politburo and Central Committee apparatus in the legislature foundered with no role to play."[51] The primary proponent of empire, the Communist Party, was gradually taken out of the decision-making loop, and Gorbachev, although not in favor of dissolution, had, through his political and institutional reforms, weakened the center's ability to withstand challenges from the republics.[52]

Yeltsin and the Russian Challenge

Gorbachev originally brought Yeltsin in as one of the leaders of his reform effort. Yeltsin's charismatic, even boisterous, advocacy of reforms arguably served as a good barometer for Gorbachev. In pushing the limits of Politburo and Central Committee tolerance, he served as a lightning rod for the general secretary. Ultimately, when Yeltsin challenged some of the Politburo members outright, Gorbachev disavowed his connections with Yeltsin, who was then relegated to a lesser position as deputy head of the Soviet state construction committee.[53]

Yeltsin then moved his basis of support from the Soviet Union to the union republic level. He turned Russian dissatisfaction with the party and desire for reform into a nationalist-separatist program. In the 1989 elections for the Congress of People's Deputies he ran for the entire Moscow district and received 90 percent of the vote. In May 1990, as chair of the Russian Republic's legislature, he challenged the conservatives and Gorbachev's ambivalence on reform, and he resigned from the party. Within months he argued that the republics had the right to secede from the Soviet Union and that bilateral treaties between the republics should replace the all-Union organizations. Gorbachev, by contrast, had previously, in April 1990, pushed through a law aimed at preventing such secession, and

---

50. Matlock 1995, 422–24.

51. Hough 1997, 173. See also pp. 249–50.

52. Arguably, the specific relation between authoritarian leadership and the selectorate also prevented adaptation by the party; see Roeder 1993.

53. On the dissension within the Communist elite, see Lane 1996.

he had imposed periodic economic embargoes on the Baltic republics to weaken separatists' will to secede.

In one of the more dramatic steps of Russian detachment from the Soviet Union, the Russian government then withheld its contribution to the all-Union budget and declared its sovereignty in the summer of 1990. This in turn empowered the actions of the other republics. "The stance of the Russian Republic's leadership provided an umbrella of legitimacy and protection to all the others, and created novel opportunities for coalition building among republics directed against the center."[54]

In this sense, the Russian Republic and its president, Boris Yeltsin, disavowed not only the position of the party as the legitimate authority to rule the all-Union territory but also the idea that Russia stood at the apex of a multinational state. Russia would not maintain its position through forceful intervention in the other territories. Russia itself—if perceived as the territorial metropole in control of a peripheral empire (the other republics)— chose to retreat from the periphery. With the dissolution of the Soviet Union and an end to Gorbachev's authority, many of the former center's resources fell to the Russian Republic, and Yeltsin remained as its head.[55]

Russian support provided Yeltsin with a power base to push for greater autonomy for the union republics. But clearly within Russia itself there were voices against secession. Indeed, in the wake of the August 1991 putsch attempt, Russian concerns with ethnocentrism in the other republics as well as concern for further disintegration of Russia itself (through secessionist movements from territories within Russia) propelled Yeltsin's advisors, such as Sergei Stankevich, Ruslan Khasbulatov, and Gavriil Popov, to adopt a more centralist agenda.[56] What allowed Yeltsin, despite this, to push for Russian secession, and argue that the Soviet Union in fact presented a drain on Russian economic viability?

Like Gorbachev, Yeltsin proceeded to craft a strong executive position. He managed to attach to the all-Union referendum of March 1991 (more on this below) a second referendum in the Russian Republic. The referendum called for the creation of a Russian presidency. The referendum passed, and three months later Yeltsin became president of the Russian Federation with 57 percent of the vote. Conservative opposition to reforms, economic collapse, and factionalism required a strong executive, argued Yeltsin. Like de Gaulle's return in 1958, so Yeltsin's presidency was an attempt to circumvent political chaos. To that end, the Fifth Russian Congress of People's Deputies gave Yeltsin emergency powers on November 2, 1991. It authorized him to appoint ministers and pass economic decrees

---

54. Lapidus 1992, 59; Bunce 1999, 108.
55. Bunce 1999, 122.
56. Drobizheva 1992, 111.

without reference to the parliament. Even this did not seem enough. Jerry Hough notes that "Yeltsin found the powers of the office too limited . . . he did not adopt the policy of cohabitation with the legislature that was implied in the system and that Francois Mitterrand accepted in France."[57]

In subsequent months Yeltsin expanded his authority further. Tellingly, after the dissolution of the Soviet Union in December 1991 and the emergence of a truly independent Russia, he failed to call new elections or construct a party of his own. He created various consultative bodies, but then transformed or even dismantled those same committees. His old democratic supporters—Yuri Afanasyev, Gleb Yakunin, and Boris Ponomarev—feared that presidency had turned to dictatorship.[58] Like Gorbachev, he had transferred power to a strong executive that was devoid of substantial parliament oversight, but consequently also unable to be captured by any special interest groups favoring the Soviet Union. Hough concludes that:

> The key event in 1991 in the disintegration of the Soviet Union was the election of Boris Yeltsin as president of Russia. . . . This gave him a legitimacy that Gorbachev lacked, and it gave him an executive post from which he could take drastic (and unconstitutional) actions without worrying about hesitation by the Russian legislature.[59]

RUSSIANS IN THE "NEAR ABROAD" STAND ON THE SIDELINES

The Russians living outside the Russian Republic, or those living in autonomous republics where other ethnic groups predominated, had a vested interest in the continuation of the Soviet Union. With almost 26 million Russians living outside Russia they were the ones most threatened by laws that privileged local languages, anti-Russian sentiments, and the retreat of Soviet authority.[60]

Indeed, Gorbachev expected that nationalists would moderate their demands out of fear of intervention by Moscow because of the large numbers of Russians in the other republics.[61] Nevertheless, these settlers carried little weight. Yeltsin commented in March 1991 that "it is impossible to defend people with tanks. . . . It is necessary to put our relations with those republics on a juridical foundation, one of international rights."[62] In short, Yeltsin would not oppose dissolution because of the Russians abroad. In-

57. Sakwa 1993, 47–48. Hough 1997, 269.
58. See the description of events by Easter 1997; Sakwa 1993, 51.
59. Hough 1997, 405.
60. Shevtsova 1992, 13.
61. Hough 1997, 331.
62. Dunlop 1993b, 53.

stead, he preferred to resolve the issue by international treaties between sovereign states. Why did the settlers carry so little weight?

The Russians abroad, unlike the Dutch settlers in Indonesia or the pieds noirs in Algeria, lacked political organization. The Soviet project after all was an attempt to instill a hegemonic perception of the Soviet Union as an integral entity. Republican differences and nationalist sentiments were supposed to diminish with modernization and the benefits of Marxism. In that project there could be no room for Russians organizing themselves as imperial colonists abroad; hence the party downplayed Russian nationalism.

Toward the end of the Soviet Union's existence, some groups attempted to take matters into their own hands, as, for example, the paramilitary organizations that sprang up in the Baltic states. But these were not the institutionalized channels that marked French colonial representation in Paris. Even several years after the dissolution, Russian communities in the former republics remained poorly organized. According to Igor Zevelev, "Political or any other mobilization, solidarity and cooperation along ethnic lines are entirely new concepts for the formerly dominant people."[63]

The Russian communities also faced different environments. Only 1 percent of Russians in Kyrgyzstan and Kazakhstan listed the titular languages as their second language, yet they occupied 70 percent of the positions in the sciences. They were thus poorly integrated but functionally indispensable. In Armenia the reverse was true. Thirty percent of the Russians knew Armenian, but only 6 percent of the positions in the sciences were held by Russians.[64] Russians in the Baltic states feared an ethnic backlash, but conversely they lived in the most affluent of all the union republics.

Their concentration in the union republics varied as well. In Armenia, Russians only made up 1.6 percent of the population. But in Kazakhstan 38 percent of the population was ethnically Russian; in the Ukraine 22.1 percent, in Kyrgyzstan 21.5 percent; and in Estonia and Latvia, Russians made up more than 30 percent of the total.[65] These varying contexts complicated collective action among the various settler communities.

The very speed of dissolution also played a role. Even in 1989 Gorbachev had publicly declared that dissolution of the USSR remained inconceivable. In the worst case scenario the central government would devolve considerable autonomy to the union republics and autonomous republics, but some form of association would endure. Had not most citizens supported continuation of the Soviet Union in the March 1991 referendum? Were not the leaders of the various republics going to sign a declaration of continued association by August 1991? In other words, few foresaw the rapid pace that

63. Zevelev 1996, 279.
64. Zevelev 1996, 278.
65. These figures are from the 1989 census. See Khazanov 1995, 247; Kaiser 1994, table 4.3; Levita and Loiberg 1994, 15.

dissolution would take, and fewer still had the experience to establish organizations to prevent such imperial retreat.

Furthermore, most union republics, despite the development of ethno-national myths and the promulgation of language laws, embraced relatively benign policies. Except for the Baltic republics (which by 1997 still denied citizenship to ethnic Russians) most states wanted to continue some form of association with Russia, even if they did not want to make it a strong commonwealth. Moreover, of the total Russian diaspora, almost 21 million lived in four states: Ukraine (11.4 million), Kazakhstan (6.2), Uzbekistan (1.7), and Belorussia (later Belarus) (1.3).[66] These four were relatively benign environments for Russians, as compared to the more vociferously nationalist Baltic states.[67]

Consequently, the greatest agitation from settler communities came in the Baltic region and Moldova. "The leaders of the 'Interfront' movements in the Baltic states were thus closely tied to the military and KGB."[68] The Russian community in the Trans-Dniester region similarly opposed Moldovan separation. Nevertheless, mass migration of Russians from those areas did not occur. Even if they were discriminated against, the economic situation on the Baltic was still better than it was in Russia.[69] In Moldova, a continued Russian military presence (the 14th Army) forestalled the development of virulent ethnic tensions.

Surveys reveal a dramatic change in attitudes among Russians in the other union republics regarding the prospects of dissolution—even in the Baltic republics where nationalist sentiments ran high. In April 1989 54 percent of non-Estonians thought that the status quo should be maintained, while only 5 percent believed Estonia should be an independent state and about a quarter favored some form of confederation.[70] Less than a year later, in January 1990, only 20 percent of non-Estonians opted for the status quo, while 17 percent favored complete independence, and 52 percent thought a confederate structure the best. In Latvia, in the February 1991 plebiscite, 73.6 percent favored Latvian independence. But with Latvians making up only 54 percent of the population and Russians 34 percent, it was clear that many Russians voted for independence as well. A poll taken in late fall 1990 indicated that most Russians remained satisfied with living in those union republics. Dissatisfaction ran the highest in Tajikistan (the poorest union republic), with 25 percent of Russians saying they were dissatisfied.

---

66. Khazanov 1995, 247. On the importance of concentration also see Zevelev 1996, 271.
67. See the comments by Lapidus 1996, 286.
68. Lapidus, Zaslavsky, and Goldman 1992, 12.
69. Lapidus (1996) makes the argument about economic opportunity.
70. Dunlop 1993b, 65–67.

In sum, the Russians in the "near abroad" could not exercise a veto. Given the authoritarian character of the Soviet system, they lacked the direct routes of influence available to the settlers in the Western democracies. Equally important, the Russians abroad lacked incentives and the institutional means for collective action.

THE FRAGMENTATION OF THE VERTICALLY INTEGRATED ECONOMY

The upper echelons of the heavy industrial sector and the military industrial complex were undoubtedly among the losers in the dissolution process, given the distribution of transaction-specific assets across the union republics. And indeed the military-industrial complex was one of the groups that supported the August 1991 coup.[71] Nevertheless, they did not succeed in their push for a harder line vis-à-vis nationalist demands.

As argued above, the political neutralization of the party attenuated the primary means of institutional access for the holders of Union-wide assets. The party leadership had de facto been the corporate elite in charge of a vast network of resource extraction, transportation, and production. Gorbachev's political strategy to neutralize the party leadership by devolution of the party's authority to lower cadres also neutralized the party's ability to run the vertically integrated Soviet economy.

Moreover, Gorbachev's economic reforms required more local autonomy in management as well as self-financing. But such economic reforms created incentives for union republic leaders and the lower strata of decision makers to disavow central control altogether. As Andrew Walder argues, economic reform brought about political change by creating "alternatives to the rewards and career paths formerly controlled by the party organization."[72] If the transfers from the center were declining (partially because of the economic downturn, partially because other republics—such as Russia—were contributing less to the central budget) then why keep paying tax revenue to the all-Union organizations? "Ever greater responsibilities were devolved upon them while at the same time they were increasingly deprived of the resources needed to deal with them."[73]

In addition, with the evolution of competitive markets, the union republics wondered whether a reorientation to international trade would be more advantageous than catering to markets within the Soviet Union.

71. Dunlop 1993a, 34.
72. Walder 1994, 303. See also Lapidus, Zaslavsky, and Goldman 1992, 4, 10.
73. Lapidus, Zaslavsky, and Goldman 1992, 5.

According to one set of calculations, at world prices, Russia would have a positive trade balance of thirty billion rubles, while Turkmenistan would break even. Azerbaijan would have a minor negative trade balance. The others would have negative balances of between 1.1 and 6.6 billion rubles.[74] Even if the figures suggested that Russia would benefit the most from opening up, other union republics drew the conclusion, not incorrectly, that the patterns of trade were artificial and did not take into account the opportunities for trade and profit that had been foreclosed by the Soviet trade system. The Baltic states thus started to orient themselves to Scandinavia. Energy producers (Russia, Azerbaijan, and Turkmenistan) envisioned outlets on the world market. In Russia, the Burbulis-Gaidar faction—which favored the free market—argued for a package that modernized production, opened the economy to world market prices, and exported raw materials to gain hard currency. Indeed, "the Burbulis-Gaidar economic policy implied that the Soviet Union was unnecessary."[75]

Further, with the exception of the Baltic states, it seemed reasonable for Russian decision makers to presuppose that most of the other union republics would continue to seek some form of association with Russia. Indeed, many of these republics supported maintaining some form of territorial integrity. The March 1991 referendum on the Soviet Union demonstrated the reluctance of the Russian population to maintain the Union, while populations in Belorussia and the Central Asian republics showed the reverse, although they envisioned such a Union with much greater autonomy for the various republics. The Ukraine, however, was divided, and six republics did not bother to participate.

Finally, institutional reform changed the informational environment facing the Soviet population. Previously, even if international changes imposed high opportunity costs on the Soviet economic system, such effects were shielded by Communist institutions. Contrary to Jeffry Frieden and Ronald Rogowski's argument that the globalization of the world economy created domestic incentives to change the Soviet structure, Matthew Evangelista argues that "international economic changes did not have a direct impact on holders of assets in the Soviet Union . . . because control of those assets was so highly concentrated in the political elite and because institutions mediated and buffered international transactions."[76]

However, without such institutional barriers, economic actors could reassess, or at least speculate about, whether they might win or lose from opening up the closed Soviet economy. While Evangelista persuasively suggests that economic opportunity costs did not dictate reform or dissolution

74. Kaiser 1994, 337.
75. Hough 1997, 463. See also p. 460.
76. Evangelista 1996, 178; Frieden and Rogowski 1996.

of the USSR, once the political structure changed, the economic opportunity costs argument became more salient.

In short, those elites that wished to maintain a strong Soviet Union lacked
the institutional means to veto the dissolution by hard-line tactics. At the
same time, economic decentralization created incentives for members of the
former economic establishment to capture parts of the production process
for local (and considerable personal) gain. Economic decentralization and
political nationalism thus went hand in hand. "Increases in the power of
lower-ranking economic agents . . . vis-à-vis the central authorities meant that
the former relations of subordination between the higher ranking and the
lower ranking hierarchic links turned into bargaining relations."[77]

Indeed, the emergence of a private sector encouraged entrepreneurship
and rent-seeking behavior for which previous Communist cadres were ex-
ceptionally well positioned due to their patronage networks and control of
information. Imperfect and developing markets only enhanced their ability
to use information asymmetries and weakly defined property rights to their
advantage. Thus, argue Victor Nee and Peng Lian, "many communists
come to love the market" under conditions of partial reform.[78] Indeed,
with the prospect of dissolution becoming a real possibility, defection by
local cadres took on the form of an inverse bank run.[79]

THE INCREASING SALIENCE OF NATIONALISM

Of all the empires in this book, the Soviet Union arguably came closest to
building a multinational state. It aimed explicitly at integrating Russians
and other nationalities into a new Soviet citizenship. This did not come
to pass. Instead, nationalist sentiments lingered throughout the Soviet
Union's existence and erupted explosively in the 1980s. The particular dynamics of the ethno-federalist system and the emergence of nationalist sentiment played a considerable role in the dissolution of the USSR. They
influenced not only decision making in the center but also the ease of the
transition to fifteen independent states.

The Attempt to Merge the Nationalities

Tsarist conquests incorporated a great diversity of non-Russian peoples in
the empire. A population census of 1897 put the number of inorodtsy

77. Kagalovsky 1990, 320.
78. Nee and Lian (1994, 262, 267) clarify how former Communist cadres gained disproportionately with subsequent market reforms. Similarly, Richard Sakwa argues that the old
nomenklatura seized the lion's share of state property; Sakwa 1993, 233.
79. For this logic, see Solnick 1996.

(nonnatives) at 126 million, about 55 percent of the empire's total population.[80] The central government attempted to gradually integrate these disparate peoples into the greater empire. "The final objective of education to be provided to the non-natives . . . is undoubtedly their Russification (*obrusenie*) and their fusion with the Russian people."[81]

After the First World War and the end of the Russian Empire, the Bolsheviks were confronted with many of the same problems as their predecessors. For Lenin, modernization and nationalism were antithetical. To prove his point he noted how assimilation and modernization coincided in New York City.[82] Although he recognized the right to secede—indeed, in September 1914 he had spoken of dismantling the empire—he also argued that the party would have to decide on the legality of secession, since such action would only occur in areas dominated by the bourgeoisie.[83] Socialists should support the right of repressed nations to secede, but at the same time they should work for the integration of all workers.[84]

However, Lenin's principle of self-determination threatened to leave the young Bolshevik regime potentially denuded of many of the previously held territories. By force and compromise it managed to reintegrate many of the nationalities into the Union between 1919 and 1920. In exchange, many of the nationalities were formally recognized and given particular indigenous rights. Territorial political administration was explicitly linked to the titular nationality of that region and was meant to indigenize the local elites (*korenizatsiia*). Titular nationals thus received preferential treatment by the central state.[85]

These union republics formed the key components of the federation that was established by treaty in 1922 and in the constitution of 1924.[86] These were direct subcomponents of the overall Soviet Union, on the geographic edge of Russia, facing external powers. In theory these union republics were even permitted to leave the union.[87] Below these, the federation established autonomous republics (subcomponents of the union republics) with more limited powers of their own, and autonomous provinces or regions

80. See D'Encausse 1992.

81. So stated the minister of public education D. Tolstoi in 1870. Quoted in D'Encausse 1992, 6.

82. Kaiser 1994, 96.

83. Lenin feared that "national and state differences . . . will continue to exist for a very, very long time even after the dictatorship of the proletariat had been established on a world scale." Quoted in Connor 1992, 32. See also D'Encausse 1992, 65–69.

84. See Kaiser 1994, 96–98; D'Encausse 1992, 31, 43; Suny 1992, 29.

85. Zaslavsky 1992, 76.

86. For a discussion of the institutional structure, see Hill 1993, 104–6; Zaslavsky 1992, 71; D'Encausse 1992, 134–35.

87. D'Encausse 1992, 69.

(the autonomous *okrugs* and oblasts). The multinational state was thus organized as a staggered federal system, with a variety of levels of autonomy.[88]

Why did the Bolsheviks concede to this organization? Recognizing the potentially fissiparous tendencies of giving nationalities political structures of their own, Lenin believed that the unifying element in all this would be the Communist Party. While each republic had its own Communist Party (except Russia), in reality the party was centrally controlled. The hierarchical party structure would be the glue holding these various territorial entities together by influencing the local leadership and providing selective access to the center's resources.[89] Moreover, with modernization and industrialization of the Soviet Union as a whole, the nationalist tendencies of the non-Russian peoples would dissipate.

Stalin had less patience with nationalist sentiment. Tellingly, when the 1926 census identified 194 nationalities, Stalin's simplified accounting reduced this to 60.[90] He equated nationalism with bourgeois sentiment. To overcome nationalism, he advocated the indigenization of the local party and state organizations, while effectively denying the right to secede.[91] If necessary, the Soviet regime would use force to prevent secession.

But rather than emphasizing force, the Soviet strategy was to control these diverse populations by selective incentives to become part of the Soviet project. The regime gave local elites access to the center, and they could become part of the nomenklatura, the select group of influential party officials. Stalin himself was a Georgian. Essentially this amounted to affirmative action for the benefit of titular power brokers.[92]

While local languages were retained, the road to career advancement required Russification. The Soviet government also built universities in the republics, but Russian was the lingua franca. Museums and monuments similarly downplayed national differences, emphasizing a party-oriented and Russian reading of history. "In principle the Soviet regime aimed at a very high extent of political activation of the periphery, but at the same time at total control by the center of the channels and expressions of such activization."[93]

---

88. The variation in autonomy and the hierarchy of status was de facto a divide-and-rule policy, even though the official position professed adherence to the principle of a civic, multinational nation. Khazanov 1997, 127. For a general discussion of the multiple contradictions in Soviet nationality policy, see Suny 1993, 106–7, 154ff.

89. D'Encausse 1992, 151–52. For a discussion of the principle of "democratic centralism" in the federation, see Churchward 1975.

90. Hill 1993, 118, n. 11. For Stalin's definition of a nation (*natsia*), see D'Encausse 1992, 173; Kaiser 1994, 102.

91. Kaiser 1994, 106. For the contrast between Lenin and Stalin, also see Suny 1992, 29; D'Encausse 1992, 130.

92. Suny 1993, 155. D'Encausse notes how this affirmative action gradually expanded non-Russian participation in local party cadres. D'Encausse 1992, 153.

93. Eisenstadt 1995, 214.

Nationalist tendencies were also repressed by the economic, administrative, and military organization of the Soviet Union. The distribution of the Soviet military throughout the empire and the fact that much of the officer corps remained Russian limited the ability of the republics to utilize the military for their own purposes. Economically, the forced integration of the Soviet economy imposed costs on greater autonomy, while at the same time transfers from the center to the periphery made association with the center attractive for local elites. Thus, local elites, while ethnically affiliated with their own populations, became dependent on the center for the resources they needed to maintain their position and to deliver goods to their local constituencies.

While the central government recognized the reality of nationalist sentiment, it created an incentive structure to induce adherence to central control. Titular elites who followed Moscow's guidelines might rise to the very pinnacles of power. At the same time, the center could punish elites, and relocate entire groups, should it choose to do so. So how did the nationalist upheaval of the 1980s emerge?

Resurgent Nationalism

The tsarist and the Soviet empires faced, like all empires, a paradox.[94] The greater the center's desire to control and develop its subject peripheries the more it unites the periphery against it. Intrusiveness begets opposition. D'Encausse describes this tendency in tsarist Russia: "The crises brewing in the periphery multiplied: dominated peoples, previously divided by cultural and statutory differences, began to express their solidarity."[95] Particularly when great power competition intensified, the center clamped down on cultural pluralism and tolerance for local institutions.[96] The Soviet empire underwent a similar process.[97]

First, as a consequence of modernization, less-developed areas came to see themselves as political units—distinct from the Russian center but also distinct from earlier modes of association such as clan, tribe, and kin. Modernization in the USSR, as Suny points out, correlated with a rise in nationalism.[98] Areas of the USSR that underwent limited modernization, consequently, showed only limited nationalist sentiments. In Kyrgyzstan, as

---

94. Spruyt 2001.
95. D'Encausse 1992, 5.
96. Dawisha and Parrott 1994, 7.
97. The 1989 census still listed more than a hundred national groups. Connor 1992, 30.
98. Suny 1993. Mark Beissinger similarly notes how high levels of education correlate positively with ethnic awareness. Beissinger 1992, 144. See also Gitelman 1992, 227.

Gene Huskey states, even in the 1990s "clan and tribal loyalties continue to temper Kyrgyz nationalism."[99]

The Soviet empire also confronted a second problem. During World War II it incorporated the existing well-developed Baltic states. It also gained control over nationalities, which, if not endowed with their own states, had historically been affiliated with other states, such as Moldova.[100]

These potentially fissiparous tendencies in the USSR were made worse by its ethno-federalist structure. By officially equating titular nationalities with certain areas it provided nationalities with logical focal points to express and act on their nationalist desires. They were, in other words, "states ready to go." Federalism also provided potential secessionists with an administrative apparatus that could take over the tasks of previously all-Union administrative organization.[101] Indeed, the all-Union organization of councils—the Supreme Soviet, Presidium, Council of Ministers, and such—had been duplicated in the separate union republics. This existing institutional machinery mitigated collective action problems.

This identification of nationalities with a given territorial space did not necessarily correspond with the demographic composition of the polity. The manner in which nationalist groups sought their independence in the wake of the crumbling Soviet Union demonstrates how the resulting entities were not based on the identification of ethnic groups with some primordialist homeland but more on artificial territorial divisions and institutional arrangements imposed at the beginning of the USSR.[102]

But while ethno-federalist institutions created the opportunities for nationalist mobilization, this does not explain why individuals chose to lead nationalist movements against the metropole. Personal risks, after all, were involved. Without such political entrepreneurs concerted political action would not occur.[103] Suny's perspective is worth quoting at length:

> Understandings of ethnic and social differences, themselves always in the process of construction and contestation, are available to the intellectuals and activists who in turn privilege a particular perception of society and history. . . . They find, borrow, or invent the social and ethnic "traditions" they need.[104]

---

99. Huskey 1993, 409.

100. Szporluk (1994) notes how Poland similarly became problematic for the tsarist empire. Marc Raeff makes a comparable observation: "With the conquest and assimilation of peoples and nationalities whose level of civilization was equal to, if not greater than Russia's, problems arose." Raeff 1984, 217.

101. On the consequences of the ethno-federalist structure, see Roeder 1991; Laitin 1991.

102. Connor 1992, 39.

103. Beissinger similarly argues that it is an elite-driven process. Beissinger 1992, 141.

104. Suny 1993, 10.

The challenges to the Soviet Union's territorial integrity initially came from local counterelites, nonparty politicians, artists, and scientists who were hamstrung by the party and the all-Union administration. Given their lack of access to resources, they could not forge political alliances based on material exchanges. Instead, appeals to nationalist sentiments provided mobilization on the cheap.

This mobilization caught the titular elites in a bind. By toeing the party line they could advance their own careers. Support from the center allowed titular elites to engage in patronage politics in the republics. Outright defection could also mean an end to one's career or worse—imprisonment, even execution.

At the same time, titular officials also had incentives to create local support bases to maintain their advantage over political rivals in the republics.[105] One had to be careful not be outmaneuvered by rivals who played the nationalist card.[106] Thus, the Lithuanian Communist Party started to assert its independence from Moscow in the wake of greater nationalist demands by the Lithuanian Restructuring Movement (Sajudis).[107] Moscow had long understood these countervailing incentives facing the titular nationalities and had, to prevent capture of these titular elites by nationalists, consistently appointed Russians as second secretaries of the party in the republics.[108]

The loyalty of the titular elites thus depended on the benefits flowing from the center to the republics and on the ability and willingness of the center to punish the defectors. Both these features were increasingly drawn into doubt from the late 1970s onward.[109] With Poland leading the way, other countries were quick to follow. In the USSR itself, Gorbachev refrained from pursuing a hard line toward nationalist demands. The center, in other words, no longer wielded a big stick. The inability, or unwillingness, to punish defection coincided with diminished material incentives to follow party dictates.

Contagion effects also occurred.[110] Nationalist leaders seeking greater independence from Moscow drew conclusions regarding the central government's probable behavior based on its actions in other areas. Given that the Soviet Union did not exercise force to stop the tide of rising demands for autonomy in the external empire, leaders of union and autonomous re-

105. For contradictions in their incentives, see Suny 1993, 139.

106. For example, the Uzbek leadership, while relying on two billion rubles of subsidies per year from Moscow, simultaneously promoted cultural nationalism. Critchlow, Report on the USSR 1, no. 6 (February 10, 1989), 7–10.

107. Girnius, Report on the USSR 1, no. 7 (February 17, 1989), 18–20.

108. Miller 1977.

109. Solnick 1996.

110. Bermeo 1992b.

publics concluded that the party leadership would likely not retaliate against nationalist movements within the Soviet Union itself. When rising nationalist agitation met with some success—as in the Baltic states—they were further emboldened. Indeed, it became increasingly obvious that the Russian Republic itself opposed centrist attempts to maintain the empire.[111]

Moreover, the lack of rotation of indigenous elites further exacerbated the principal-agent problem that had begun during the Brezhnev administration. In exchange for local elites' support for Brezhnev's accession to office, they received greater autonomy and less formal oversight. As a result, titular elites entrenched themselves in powerful patronage networks rife with corruption, as in Uzbekistan.[112]

The Center's Lack of Credibility

Could agreements between the center and the nationalist movements have arrested the final phase of disintegration? Results of the 1991 referendum suggested that most of the population within the Soviet Union did not support a complete breakup. Gorbachev also worked to maintain a strong center by creating a tight commonwealth. By December 1991, however, that plan had come to naught. The Commonwealth of Independent States, which took the place of the former Soviet Union, was but a loose set of bilateral treaties between independent states, not a federation.

The lack of credibility of the center (by fall 1991 represented by Gorbachev), and nationalist elites' lack of interest in brokering such a compromise, barred the emergence of a strong commonwealth institution. Gorbachev's strong executive position allowed him to change policy with relative ease, but it also eroded his ability to credibly commit. His replacement of the party apparatus with a state beholden to him and his control over the military gave him the means to oppose CPSU and military hard-liners, but it also gave him the means to reverse course. Indeed, his periodic reversals eroded his credibility with both reformers and conservatives alike. Most often he opposed military action against nationalists, but he occasionally tolerated such action, such as in Tbilisi. Sometimes he sided with economic and political reformers like Yakovlev; sometimes he switched to a more conservative course, as he arguably did in the spring of 1991. Consequently, he could not credibly claim to be able to keep all the hard-liners in control, certainly not after the attempted coup and his apparent house arrest in the summer of 1991.

111. This accentuates the classical principal-agent problem. Given the limited will and capability of the principal (the party) to punish defection in test cases, agents gain information about the future behavior of the principal. See, for example, Solnick 1996; Stone 1996.

112. Critchlow, *Report on the USSR* 1, no. 12 (March 24, 1989), 20–22.

On the other side, nationalist elites had little incentive to try to broker a deal with the center. Unlike the situation in the Western maritime empires, the issue of credible commitment by the center to the continued independence of the former Soviet republics mattered a great deal. With the Western colonial empires, the nationalists might be concerned with indirect, post-imperial hegemony by the erstwhile metropole, but in the former Soviet space, the newly independent states had to be seriously concerned with a revival of outright Russian or Communist dominance.[113] In the maritime empires, a return of formal empire seemed highly unlikely, whereas that situation in the former Soviet Union could not be ignored given the continued presence and geographical proximity of large military contingents and the previous use of force during the Soviet era.

Some republics, such as the Baltic states, also anticipated a quick insertion into the capitalist economies of the West. Others, Belorussia for example, anticipated bilateral deals with Russia, rather than a broad union. All the republics were concerned that a strong Union treaty would simply be the pretext for continued control by the center. Most important, perhaps, Russia, which had been the territorial but not the functional center of the USSR, did not wish for a strong territorial union on the old model. (Gorbachev later saw the declaration of Russian sovereignty in June 1990 as the key event preventing an accord that could have maintained the Soviet Union.)[114]

Rather than seek closer ties with Russia or with each other, the incipient elites—the new nationalist cadres, reformed Communist cadres under different guise—stood to gain from the fragmentation. Indeed, elites faced an extended prisoner's dilemma. Even if a negotiated dissolution with a loose confederal structure might have been beneficial for all parties concerned, the danger of negotiating with the center while other groups seized resources created strategic incentives for every party to seek dissolution before compromise.

Needless to say, the dissolution of the Soviet Union had many causes. The ideological bankruptcy of Marxist-Leninism; nationalist revival within the USSR; the waning of the old Stalinist generation; vast expenditures on the arms race; renewed democratic sentiments; and many other factors all contributed to its demise.[115] I make no claim that a single variable can provide a full account of the sequence of events that transpired in the USSR since

113. On the possibility of renewed Russian imperialism, see Menon 1995; Menon and Spruyt 1997, 1999; Spruyt 1997b.

114. Gorbachev 2000, 102, 110–11.

115. For example, Petro (1995) suggests that the collapse of the regime was due to the reemergence of a preexisting democratic culture among Russian citizens. For an overview of other causal arguments, see Dawisha and Parrott 1997.

the Second World War or even of the events during the Gorbachev era. As with any other historical set of events, the Soviet case presents unique features: unintended consequences confront strategy, serendipity travels with accident.

The questions before us are more restricted. Given international and domestic pressures, how did the center manage to change territorial policy? And why did the change in territorial policy occur without the level of conflict that permeated other cases?

In this and in chapter 2 I have shown that the Soviet Union faced a deteriorating set of conditions in its imperial environment. Territory and empire had declined in military value. The economic benefits of empire had receded. More importantly, the socialist economy had stagnated and proved incompatible with the international capitalist order. Finally, nationalism proved more resilient than imagined and, indeed, increased in the face of diminishing benefits from the center and declining repression.[116]

These changes precipitated a drive for political, economic, and institutional reforms. These reforms, particularly after 1988, unified decision making and gave the executive greater latitude to deal with territorial issues than would have been the case in a cartelized-authoritarian coalition.[117] While centrist, pro-Union forces existed in parts of the military, among the Russians outside the Russian Republic, and in the higher echelons of the industrial complex, they lacked the institutional ability to veto a change in the existing territorial configuration. Civilian oversight of the military even allowed Gorbachev to order the gradual withdrawal from the external empire. Yeltsin, as elected president of Russia, similarly benefited from the basic neutrality of the armed forces.

In creating strong executive positions to engage in political and economic reforms, Gorbachev and Yeltsin also neutralized powerful segments in the Communist Party that catered to hard-liners. In creating alternative institutions that lacked substantial legislative control over the executive they also created new constituencies that had only diffuse interests in maintaining the Soviet Union. Instead, low- and mid-range cadres and elites in the union republics stood to gain from its dissolution.

116. Peter Liberman's argument, that the costs of the Soviet external empire were not as debilitating as some suggest, on closer inspection does not contravene what I have just claimed. Indeed, he states that "nuclear deterrence had long decreased the importance to Soviet security of East European territory," and that central planning led to economic stagnation in these areas. He also recognizes that "the chief liability of the Soviet Empire . . . was that it provoked the hostility of a much more powerful Western coalition." Liberman 1996, 125, 143–44.

117. Daniel Deudney and John Ikenberry's assessment shows considerable similarity with my own. In a nutshell, they claim that "the transformation of the Soviet Union was made possible by the transformation of the international system." Changes in the imperial environment led to domestic reform. Deudney and Ikenberry 1991–92, 76–77.

It remains a moot issue whether one sees this as an example of a central-ized authoritarian system (since Gorbachev was never popularly elected and Yeltsin had vastly expanded powers) or whether one sees this as strong presidential leadership in an (emerging) democracy. The theoretical proposition that strong executives who face few veto points can more read-ily change territorial policy holds either way. Once again I stress that strong executives in centralized authoritarian systems might be motivated by dif-ferent sets of preferences than strong executives in democratic systems. The institutionalist account does not allow us to make educated guesses re-garding the preferences of leaders in such authoritarian systems, since, un-like strong executives in democratic regimes, they are ultimately not beholden to the general electorate. In this sense, the policies emanating from hierarchical authoritarian leadership with few veto points remain dif-ficult to predict.

I reiterate that this argument does not presume that Gorbachev, or Yeltsin for that matter, started with a blueprint for dissolution of the exter-nal and internal empires. Gorbachev did not have the fragmentation of the USSR in mind, even though Eduard Shevardnadze and Yakovlev later stated that they understood from the very beginning that the reforms might lead to the collapse of the Soviet Union—although it fell apart quicker than they anticipated.[118] However, the problems facing the Soviet Union could only be solved by domestic reforms. The institutional choices made during the reform process, unintentionally or not, set forces in motion that weak-ened the power of the Communist Party, the primary actor with a stake in the continuation of the Soviet Union. Thus, while it is correct to argue that Gorbachev started perestroika (reconstruction) with economic reform in mind rather than concerns with either the external or internal empire, it rapidly became apparent that reform had direct consequences for both.

What about the public in all of this? Were Gorbachev and Yeltsin democ-rats before their time, responding to their citizens for dissolution of exter-nal and internal empire? Once again, leaders led rather than followed the public. First, the public's message was ambiguous. In the referendum on the Soviet Union of March 1991, about 90 percent of the Central Asian vot-ers favored continuation of the Soviet Union, while only 53.5 percent in Russia wanted to do so.[119] Opinion polls also showed that 65 percent of Russians associated the Soviet Union with shortages, lines, and the overall

118. Odom 1998, 439, n. 5. William Wohlforth supports this view. Sergei Tarasenko, an aide to Shevardnadze, reports that by August 1989, Shevardnadze believed that the situation in the external empire, such as in Poland, would have direct consequences for the integrity of the internal empire. Wohlforth 1994–95, 119.

119. Dunlop (1993b, 65) suggests that about 70 percent in the Russian Republic favored the Soviet Union, but he too notes the logical inconsistencies in the public's attitudes.

malaise of the economy.[120] Second, while, overall, 77 percent in the nine participating republics voted for the Soviet Union, some of the greatest nationalist tensions occurred in the states that wished to secede and had not participated in the referendum in the first place: the Baltic states, Georgia, Armenia, and Moldova.[121] Third, the language of the March referendum was deliberately vague, asking voters: "Do you consider necessary the preservation of the Union of Soviet Socialist Republics as a renewed federation of equal sovereign republics, in which the rights and freedom of an individual of any nationality will be fully guaranteed?"[122] Was one voting for the Soviet Union, the sovereignty of republics, or the rights of ethnic groups? Finally, in an attached referendum, 70 percent of the Russian population voted for an elected presidency against the wishes of party centrists.[123] So, while voting in favor of the Soviet Union, Russians were also objecting to the institutional arrangements favored by the party.

It is clear, however, that the public shifted attitudes in response to events on the ground. In the fall of 1989, 63 percent of citizens in the Russian Republic thought that the preservation of the Soviet Union should be given high priority.[124] But just before Yeltsin became chairman of the Russian Supreme Soviet, 35 percent believed that Russian political and economic rights should be expanded and 43 percent wanted Russian independence. Indeed, by the fall of that year, 56 percent of respondents in RSFSR believed the autonomous areas in Russia should be allowed to secede if the majority in those areas wanted to do so.

Without regressing to the view that "great individuals make history," this account comports well with arguments that stress the impact of individual leaders such as Gorbachev and Yeltsin. However, without the antecedent conditions of military and economic stagnation, and rising nationalism, they would have had no need to engage in reforms. And most important, they could act on their individual preferences because they succeeded in creating institutions that gave them considerable autonomy.

In sum, as with the other cases of our analysis, changes in the international environment, and the rising tide of nationalism, explain the impetus for changes in the existing territorial configuration. However, in order to explain why opponents to change could not dictate the agenda for the state as a whole requires us to focus on the institutional changes of the late Soviet system.

---

120. Lapidus, Zaslavsky, and Goldman 1992, 14.
121. Suny 1998, 479.
122. Matlock 1995, 476–78.
123. Dunlop 1993a, 33.
124. Dunlop 1993b, 62–63.

CHAPTER EIGHT

The Fourth Republic in Jerusalem

> I favor facts that will bind hands; not only ours—also those of the other side, and the hands of reality.
>
> MOSHE DAYAN, on the settlements in the occupied territories

> These divisions in society have grave consequences for diplomacy. A divided political order places a heavy burden on the conduct of foreign affairs, and factional struggles make systematic planning or consensual national policy difficult to achieve.
>
> SASSON SOFER, Hebrew University

Significant changes in the international realm in the 1990s raised hopes that a final settlement might be reached in the long-standing Arab-Israeli conflict. The end of the cold war eradicated the last vestiges of superpower competition in the region, while the United States and its allies crushed Iraq's regional aspirations and one of Israel's most formidable foes. Israel had already diminished the existential threat to its security emanating from its Arab neighbors. Several disengagement agreements with Egypt culminated in the peace accord of 1979. Jordan disengaged from the West Bank and signed a formal treaty with Israel in 1994. Even an accord with Syria seemed within reach.

The changes in the international environment also coincided with American pressure on Israel to move forward. The George H. W. Bush administration pressured Yitzhak Shamir's government to curtail its settlement policy and enter into negotiations with the Palestinians by holding up Israel's request for $10 billion in loan guarantees.[1] The Clinton administration likewise pressured Palestinians and Israelis to seek an accord.

Domestically, the Labor Party gained at the polls in 1992 and installed a three-party coalition with the leftist Meretz and the Orthodox Shas Parties.

1. Steinberg 1995.

With support from the Arab parties, the coalition would seemingly have sufficient support in the Knesset (parliament) to advance the peace process. Unlike the earlier Likud governments of Begin and Shamir, the Labor Party had been far more amenable to entering into a potential land-for-peace deal. A similar opportunity seemed to present itself when Ehud Barak's Labor-led coalition supplanted the hard-line Likud government of Benjamin Netanyahu in 1999.

Moreover, the Palestinians, in seeing their support from the Arab world diminish due to their support for Iraq, appeared amenable to negotiations.[2] Diplomatic overtures in Madrid (1991) and the Oslo agreement (1993) held up the possibility of settling the most complicated issue of all: the conflict over the territories Israel acquired during the 1967 Six-Day War. Nothing signified such optimism more than the 1994 Nobel Peace Prize shared by Yitzhak Rabin, Shimon Peres, and Yasser Arafat.

Just a few years later those expectations seem like a distant chimera. This raises several questions to which this chapter will provide partial answers. Why did not the two Labor-led coalitions—that pushed respectively for the Oslo agreements (1993, 1995) and the negotiations in Camp David (2000)—succeed in concluding a comprehensive agreement on the West Bank and Gaza? Why could not the Likud-led government of Benjamin Netanyahu, which half-heartedly sought to implement parts of the Oslo agreement, control the members of its coalition? And, related to this last question, why is it that international pressure on Israel has had limited success in pressuring Likud to come to the bargaining table?

Many factors contributed to the demise of the peace process. Arguably, Hezbollah's actions in southern Lebanon and Israel's withdrawal from that region emboldened more radical groups among the Palestinians. Many Israelis, as well as international observers, also questioned the extent to which Palestinian leader Yasser Arafat was really committed to a comprehensive peace agreement.[3] Palestinians in turn attributed the failure to a consistent lack of willingness on the part of Israel's leaders to move toward peace.[4] In Edward Said's view, Shimon Peres and Benjamin Netanyahu were birds of a feather.[5] Extremists on both sides sought to scuttle the negotiations. And finally some analysts suggested that the involvement of the United States was inadequate and inept.

While recognizing the interplay of these various factors at the domestic and international level, this chapter submits that domestic politics have

2. See Lister 2002.

3. Ehud Barak ascribed the failure of Israeli-Palestinian talks to the lack of will and integrity on the Palestinian side; see Morris 2002a and the reaction by Agha and Malley 2002. See also their subsequent discussions: Morris 2002b, which includes a reply by Agha and Malley.

4. For an overview of various explanations, see Quandt 2001; Slater 2001; Pundak 2001.

5. Said 2000, 60.

played an independent causal role. The multiparty system and the multi-party coalitions that are required to gain a majority in the Knesset curtail the latitude of action for Israel's prime ministers to alter the territorial status quo.

The Israeli-Palestinian conflict shows a similarity to the Algerian War. More specifically, Israel's fragmented political system resembles the institutional stalemate that beset the French Fourth Republic (1944–1958), which combined multiparty coalitions with a lack of party discipline. Israel's leaders themselves have on occasion suggested such parallels. Former Prime Minister Ehud Barak referred to a possible agreement with the Palestinians as "a peace of the brave," invoking Charles de Gaulle's description of his pact with the Algerian nationalists.[6] Prime Minister Ariel Sharon apparently kept a copy of Alistair Horne's account of the Algerian War, *A Savage War of Peace*, at his bedside.[7] Although Israel has not been confronted by outright military rebellion as France was, it has suffered the similar fate of settler intransigence, internal turmoil, and even assassination of its prime minister by one of its own citizens. Scholars, as well, have noted that the parallels between postwar Western decolonization and Israel's quagmire are more than superficial.[8]

Israel's political system has traditionally been fragmented. However, the problem became exacerbated during the 1990s. This fragmentation and Israel's domestic institutional arrangements have limited the options for the executive to change policy. This has been true for both Likud and Labor prime ministers. Ehud Barak's Labor coalition could not count on support from the more right-wing coalition partners. And while Yitzhak Shamir's 1990–92 Likud coalition went to the bargaining table under American pressure, it too fell because the right-wing would not condone aspects of the Madrid talks. Netanyahu's hard-line Likud-led government could not resist the pressure from groups further to Likud's right that opposed concessions in Hebron (January 1997) and the Wye agreement (October 1998).

Domestic institutional arrangements have made it difficult for any Israeli government to change territorial policy, regardless of the particular preferences of the prime minister or broad segments of the population. With multiple veto points available, hard-liners can easily find some political allies in order to forestall concessions.[9]

6. John Burns, "Barak Proposes Pact with Likud if Arafat Balks," *New York Times*, August 25, 2000.

7. Elon 2002.

8. Lustick 1993; Kahler 1984, 381; Levine 1984.

9. While the national, religious, and ethnic differences among the Israeli populace are well recognized, Andersen and Yaish argue that class differences also affect policy preferences (Andersen and Yaish 2001).

Internal politics have always played a role in Israel's foreign policy. In the early 1970s both Prime Ministers Golda Meir and Yitzhak Rabin feared defection from their coalition governments by the National Religious Party (NRP), and dissent within the Labor Party itself. Consequently, they felt constrained from entering into negotiations with Jordan, or from discussing the status of Gaza and the West Bank.[10] The ending of the war of attrition (1970) with Egypt led to the collapse of the national unity government, when Menachem Begin—then leader of Gahal (the precursor to Likud)—withdrew his support.[11] At virtually every stage of Israeli negotiations with Egypt, Syria, Jordan, and the Palestine Liberation Organization (PLO) in these past decades, Israel's leaders have had to be concerned with being able to keep their multiparty coalitions in tact. However, the increasing fragmentation of Israeli society and the high degree of proportionality make it more difficult than ever to initiate a change in the status quo of the occupied territories. Thus, while the international environment improved considerably, the internal constraints on Israel's executives rose to new heights.

The chapter begins with a brief overview of Israel's acquisition of the occupied territories in Gaza and the West Bank. It then turns to a discussion of civilian control of the military. In the following section I discuss how societal pressure groups, particularly settlers rather than business interests, have had intense preferences on the territorial question. The chapter then turns to the crux of the argument and focuses on the institutional fragmentation of Israeli politics. The multiple partisan veto points created by the highly proportional electoral system present serious obstacles to policy change. The electoral reform of 1992, by separating the vote for the executive, the prime minister, from the vote for the legislature, the Knesset, added a new constitutional veto point. While the chapter emphasizes the period from the end of the Shamir government (1992) to the end of the Barak coalition (2000), it occasionally touches on events since Ariel Sharon took over as prime minister in 2001.

Israel and the Occupied Territories

From the very beginning of Israel's control over the territories gained during the Six-Day War, various Israeli government officials questioned the wisdom of keeping these areas.[12] Incorporating Arabs into the Jewish state

10. Lustick 1993, 366.
11. Bar-Siman-Tov 2001, 31.
12. Here, too, terminology is a contested terrain. The Likud-led governments of the 1980s tried unsuccessfully to erase the terminology of occupation and attempted to enforce a designation of the West Bank and Gaza as simply part of Israel (See Lustick 1993, 359). Many Israeli scholars continue to use the terminology "occupied territory."

237

before 1967 had proven difficult enough, and indeed the "new historical school" in Israel argues that incorporating a large number of Muslims was never intended.[13] After 1967 how could the Zionist project be reconciled with the presence of more than a million Arabs that came with the conquest of the Golan, Sinai, Gaza, and the West Bank?[14]

While Israel surrendered the Sinai following the 1978 Camp David accord, its control of large segments of Gaza, the West Bank, and the Golan Heights continued. After decades of Israeli control, various groups developed a stake in retaining many of these territories, despite Arab and UN pressure to implement UN Security Council Resolution 242, which calls for a peace agreement and a return to the borders of 1967. (Indeed, as part of the Egyptian-Israeli cease-fire agreement of 1970, Golda Meir's government signed 242 with the understanding that this would entail a withdrawal from all territories.)[15]

Jewish settlement following the Six-Day War started with the Labor governments that dominated the political scene until 1977, but it greatly accelerated with Likud prime minister Menachem Begin's administration, even as a land-for-peace agreement on the Sinai was being negotiated with Egypt. The Likud-Labor national unity governments of 1984 and 1988 continued further settlement under the direction of Ariel Sharon, who had taken on the post of minister of industry and trade. With Labor's departure from the coalition in 1990, Likud's Yitzhak Shamir had strategic reasons to cater to the extreme-right member parties of his alliance (such as Moledet and Tehiya) that favored further settlements. Indeed, their opposition to discussing any territorial concessions in the October 1991 Madrid talks led to their defection and the fall of Shamir's government.[16]

The subsequent victory of Labor brought to power Yitzhak Rabin who decried "the mad delusion of Greater Israel."[17] But, although he halted 6,500 construction contracts, he condoned the fulfillment of another 9,000 contracts that had previously been approved.[18] Although he deplored "political" settlements, settlements constructed by Likud to torpedo the peace process by creating irreversible "facts on the ground," he nevertheless toler-

13. One representative of the new historical school is Avi Shlaim (1998). For a discussion of the new school of Israeli historians, see Slater 2002.
14. Foreign Minister Abba Eban thought the time was right to trade territory for a lasting peace. Even Ben-Gurion thought that continued control would raise demographic problems. For the discussions in the cabinet about whether to retain the territories acquired during the Six-Day War (with the exception of Jerusalem, which all believed should be kept as part of Israel), see Oren 2002, 314.
15. Lustick 1993, 365.
16. Marcus 1992, 694.
17. Marcus 1992, 697.
18. See Slater's critique of this policy (Slater 2001, 177–78); Marcus 1992, 702. Edward Said (2000), therefore, argued that Labor and Likud leaders were similar.

ated "security settlements," which are deemed important for Israel's overall defense. Nevertheless, Rabin managed to sign the Oslo accords with his Palestinian counterparts, and a durable peace seemed within reach. His assassination by a right-wing settler in 1995, however, led to new elections that brought a Likud-led coalition to power.

Settlement increased under the Likud-led coalition of Benjamin Netanyahu (1996–1998). Netanyahu was far less enthusiastic than Rabin about the Oslo accords. Nevertheless, he tried to implement some of its components to which Israel had committed itself. His coalition, however, proved unstable, and the government soon fell.

Even the subsequent Labor-led coalition of Ehud Barak (1999–2000) could not stem the tide of Israeli settlement in the occupied territories. Consequently, today the number of settlers stands at 200,000 on the West Bank and Gaza and the same number in East Jerusalem and its suburbs. The Israeli settlers on the Golan number about 20,000.

THE ARMED FORCES AND CIVILIAN CONTROL

The armed forces traditionally justified control over the occupied territories as a critical element needed for Israel's "defense in depth." The occupied territories added valuable buffer zones and early warning to Israel with its small territory and narrow shape. Golan allowed the Israeli military to monitor developments deep inside Syria, while the West Bank and Sinai provided more room to meet an attack emanating from Jordan and Egypt.

Such strategic rationales have become increasingly less relevant. The 1978 Camp David accord eliminated the need to hold the Sinai. A de facto peace with Jordan since 1967, and a formal peace treaty in 1994, has mitigated the likelihood of attack from the east. Of all the areas, the Golan Heights was considered the most important security asset, providing Israel early warning and a means of projecting power far into Syria. But even the military value of the Golan Heights has diminished, provided Syria agrees to certain conditions that would make it a demilitarized buffer zone.[19] Israel's nuclear weapons (estimated to number at least several dozen warheads) and developments in high-technology warfare have given it a substantial security guarantee.

Indeed, arguably an Israeli-Syrian agreement has been within reach several times.[20] The Rabin-Peres government gradually came to the conclusion that parts of the Golan could be surrendered, and it was purportedly

19. See, for example, the discussion by Yorke 1990; Shalev 1994; Lee Hockstader, "On the Horizon: Giving Up the Golan," *Washington Post* (National Weekly Edition), January 17, 2000.
20. For an account that assigns responsibility primarily to Israel for the failure of such an agreement, see Slater 2002.

willing to concede most of the Golan Heights for a peace treaty with Syria. Even Benjamin Netanyahu, who generally opposed territorial concessions, seems to have offered Syria such a withdrawal, according to documents released by the Barak government.[21] Barak openly declared himself willing to cede virtually all of the Golan with a return to the June 4, 1967 line, as Syria has demanded. He subsequently, however, took that offer off the table. Presumably, these prime ministers' views corresponded closely with the military perspective—Rabin and Barak, after all, were extremely high-ranking officers before entering politics.

Consequently, if the argument for retaining territories for defense in depth does not hold for the Golan, it a fortiori cannot be argued for Gaza or the West Bank. Indeed, the threat to Israel emanates exactly from trying to control Gaza and the West Bank. Certainly, after the formal peace agreement with Jordan in 1994, and Jordan's own interest in maintaining the peace so as not to destabilize the monarchy, the defense-in-depth argument seems less plausible.[22]

Nor is it obvious that holding the occupied territories serves the military's narrow corporate interest. Indeed, with some divisions emerging within the Israeli military about the wisdom of holding these areas under control, its continued presence in the area might be harmful to the best interests of the armed forces. Any alleged security gains from holding these areas as security zones have to be weighed against the loss of life, the costs of combating terrorism, and the decline in morale.[23] Surveys conducted among members of the military who are from the kibbutzim—who have supplied numerous high-command posts in the Israel Defense Forces (IDF) and elite units—show that many are critical of the territorial policies.[24] Other research shows declining morale among Israel's reserve units, which make up 65 percent of the IDF. Surveys reveal strong polarization among the reserve troops, with 45 percent admitting they tried to avoid service.[25]

It is, moreover, unlikely that a withdrawal from the contested areas would precipitate a dramatic reversal of its budget and thus jeopardize the armed forces' more narrowly defined corporate interests. Even though the existential threats to Israel have declined, the volatile political situation in the Middle East suggests that political and financial support for the military will continue.

But whatever the preferences of the military, civilian control so far has not been in jeopardy. Although there is considerable crossover between military elites and political leaders, the civilian government has set terri-

21. Lochery 2000, 234.
22. On Israel's overall strategic environment, see Inbar 2002.
23. See the discussion by Alpher 1994, 232.
24. Dar et al. 2000.
25. Ben-Dor, Pedahzur, and Hasisi 2002, 245.

torial policy. Much of this might be attributed to the shared interests in meeting external, existential threats. With external threats clearly defined and with few internal roles for the military, civilian control has been relatively easy.[26]

Another reason the military has not opposed civilian authority has to do with its heterogeneous composition. "Although the heterogeneity among the senior staff does not reflect that among the civilian public, it is sufficiently broad so that the IDF General Staff and senior officers rarely formulate a unified position on any substantive military-strategic issue."[27] The military, in other words, has not advanced a unified position that differs from that of its civilian superiors.

This is not to say that there has been no blurring of boundaries. The military has played a considerable role in discussions with the Palestinian Authority regarding the implementation of the Oslo agreements. Conversely, political elites (often themselves high-ranking military officers at one point in their careers) have set objectives in military strategy. In this sense, the Israeli model of civilian-military affairs differs somewhat from the conventional model, in which blurring of functions is taken as an indicator of weak civilian oversight. Overall, although there have been changes in civil-military relations, the "subordinate position of the military with regard to the political system" remains unaltered.[28]

SOCIETAL PRESSURE GROUPS

Unlike the settlers, business groups have not been adamant supporters of continued control over the occupied territories. With a more advanced economy than any of its neighbors, Israel's insertion among the advanced capitalist states of the world is economically far more important than retention of the West Bank. Israel's security relationship has directly affected its foreign risk rating, which in turn has influenced the level of foreign direct investment. When Israel's security environment improved in the early 1990s, Standard and Poor's raised its risk rating for government bonds from BBB to A. Although certain economic policies also had a positive effect (such as privatization in certain sectors), the normalization of ties between Israel and many countries as a result of the peace process had a significant independent impact. Thus, "from 1982 to 1990, foreign direct investment in Israel remained stagnant between US$50 and US$230 million dollars per annum with a peak in 1987/88. After 1990, investment

26. High external threats facilitate civilian control; see Desch 1999.
27. Lissak 2001, 249.
28. Lissak 2001, 235.

began to increase steeply, reaching half a billion dollars in 1993 and a billion dollars in 1995."[29]

Moreover, the heavy involvement of the state in the economy has led to large public expenditures for military purposes and for state-owned corporations. A peace agreement would likely lead to less intervention, a lighter tax burden, and greater privatization.[30]

Finally, the continuation of violence and the various lockdowns of the Palestinian areas hamper the movement of cheap labor from the Palestinian territories to Israel. A comprehensive agreement would open the door for economic integration with a Palestinian state and Israel's Arab neighbors. When the Oslo accords and the Cairo agreement of 1994 still seemed viable, discussions were conducted regarding possible modes of economic cooperation.[31] In short, the economic gains from holding the 1967 territories seem opaque at best.

The demand for holding onto the contested areas has largely come from settlers and religious groups. As settlers elsewhere, these Jewish Israelis have been the most zealous opponents of any territorial compromise. Although most settlers have pursued their objectives through political parties that represent their interests, some of the hard-liners among them, like the Algerian colons, have used terrorism to set the agenda and influence public opinion. Since the beginning of housing construction in conquered territories, the advocates of "Greater Israel, and the settler movement Gush Emunim seamlessly incorporated members from the earlier Jewish terrorist underground."[32] Extremists among the Gush Emunim have occasionally used terrorist tactics against Israeli citizens.[33] The assassination of dozens of Muslim worshipers in a mosque in 1994 provoked a spiral of ensuing violence. More dramatic still, the assassination of Prime Minister Yitzhak Rabin in 1995 by an extremist Jewish law student set the stage for the less compromise-prone government of Netanyahu when he defeated Rabin's successor, Shimon Peres.

For material reasons as well as ideological ones, these groups and their supporters have advocated the creation of a Greater Israel, particularly the annexation of the biblical lands of Judea and Samaria. (The religious Right has not made such forceful claims for the Golan.)[34] Some of these groups have advocated not merely the formal incorporation of the West Bank into Israel proper but even the expulsion of the Palestinian population, so as to assure that Israel retains its Jewish majority. Like settlers elsewhere they

29. Lavy 2001, 154.
30. Sharkansky 1999.
31. Hofnung 2001, 183.
32. Morris 1996, 71.
33. For examples, see Lustick 1993, 368.
34. Lochery 2000, 233; Morris 1996, 72.

have enjoyed a privileged legal position compared to the local population. They have found particularly strong support from 1977 onward, when Likud displaced Labor from its preeminent position in Israeli politics.[35] Even the Cairo agreements of 1994—that aimed to delineate prospective legal regimes among the two authorities under the Oslo accords—were biased in favor of Israelis. For example, Israelis would not be subject to Palestinian criminal jurisdiction even if they performed a criminal act in Palestinian territory.[36] Transportation networks and infrastructural improvements in the occupied territories also deliberately favored Israeli settlers over Arabs.[37]

Settlement has been a deliberate policy to create "facts on the ground." While the 1949 armistice line had become the accepted border for Israel, the swift victory of 1967 reignited support for a Greater Israel. Defense minister and later foreign minister Moshe Dayan, initially a member of the Labor Party but gradually switching to Likud affiliation, favored a policy of changing Israeli perceptions by demographic changes in the occupied territories. The policy became fully ensconced with Likud's rise in the late 1970s. (Paradoxically Dayan later became a proponent of unilateral withdrawal.)

Many of the hard-line demands of the settlers fly in the face of popular opinion. Polls have shown that during the negotiations of the past decade a large majority of the Jewish population favored some form of a land-for-peace deal. Surveys conducted in 1987, 1988, and 1990 reveal that the public valued "retaining a Jewish majority in Israel" and "peace" far more than "democracy with equal rights for all" and "Greater Israel."[38] Following the Oslo accords, between 50 and 65 percent of the public expressed support for a land-for-peace deal.[39] Although Netanyahu faced considerable opposition within his own Likud Party when he signed the agreement to redeploy troops from Hebron (January 1997), 67 percent of the population in January 1997 favored it. Similarly, polls in 1999 showed that 75 percent of the population supported the October 1998 Wye agreement (which committed Israel to implementing the Hebron and Oslo accords and to transferring certain areas to the Palestinian side), with 55 percent stating they believed the Palestinians deserved their own state. A full 69 percent viewed such a state as inevitable.[40]

Nor has the international environment been conducive to the hard-line, pro-settlement perspective. As noted earlier, the first Bush administration

35. Lustick 1993, 356.
36. Hofnung 2001, 179–81.
37. Lustick 1993, 358–61.
38. See Shamir and Arian 1994, 253–57.
39. Alpher 1994, 232.
40. Aronoff 2000, 112.

linked billions of dollars in U.S. loan guarantees to the settlement policy. Rabin used Shamir's jeopardizing of such aid as an issue in the 1992 election campaign.[41]

The question thus arises why Israel has not reached an agreement in which it might trade land for peace. Neither narrow corporate military interests, geostrategic calculations, nor economic benefits dictate that Israel needs these territories. Moreover, it has achieved stable agreements with Egypt and Jordan, and it might have concluded a deal with Syria. With the PLO renouncing the use of terrorism, acknowledging Israel's right to exist, and even being willing to concede parts of the West Bank to Israeli settlements, one would expect some progress toward an agreement. Yet by the end of the 1990s the prospects for an agreement seemed more remote than ever.

THE FRAGMENTATION OF ISRAELI POLITICS

The Israeli political system contains very few constitutional veto points. Indeed, from a constitutional perspective, scholars sometimes compare Israel to Britain's parliamentary system. The 120 members of the Knesset are the key locus of authority. The president performs largely ceremonial tasks (the president plays a minor role during coalition formation), and executive power resides with the prime minister. The prime minister and the cabinet require support from the legislature, which is unicameral. The Israeli system does not provide for judicial review, and it lacks a formal constitution. The 1992 reforms created a new constitutional veto point by separating the vote for the prime minister from the vote for the legislature. However, these reforms were repealed in 2001.

The number of partisan veto players is quite another matter. Multiple parties necessitating coalition governments have always occupied the political landscape. Israel's electoral system is highly proportional. The entire country is counted as one electoral district. Since the size of electoral districts correlates strongly with the degree of proportionality, Israel's system provides any faction easy access to the Knesset.[42] This electoral system has allowed multipartyism throughout Israel's existence, with minor changes over time in how votes were allocated.[43] The low electoral threshold, raised to 1.5 percent of the vote in 1988, has done little to remedy the situation. Although it pushed the number down from twelve to ten lists (fourteen par-

41. Marcus 1992, 702. Quandt (2001, 26–40) blames the Clinton administration's lack of pressure on the Israeli government on the settlement issue for complicating the negotiations.
42. Dow 2001, 111; Sartori 1999, 15.
43. For a discussion of changes in electoral formulas, see Hazan and Diskin 2000, 630; Doron and Harris 2000, 57–64.

ties) with seats in the Knesset in 1992, the number subsequently rose again.[44] In 1996, eleven lists (fifteen parties) managed to gain seats, and by 1999 a total of fifteen lists managed to do so (representing twenty-one parties).[45] The January 2003 election, which returned to the 1992 electoral system, similarly saw thirteen lists gain representation.[46]

Assuming voters are rational and wish to see their votes translated into parliamentary seats this means the various parties have little incentive to cater to the median. (The multidimensionality of Israeli political space, with secular-religious, Left-Right, and ethnic cleavages, further complicates the search for a median.) Israel's parties have carved out niche clienteles across the political spectrum and defend their position against possible encroachment from the left or the right or from ethnic groups and religious parties. Conversely, there are few disincentives that dissuade voters from choosing parties that cater to their specific interests. With the highly proportional system it is unlikely their votes will go to waste.

Until the electoral reform of 1992, which introduced the separate vote for the prime minister, the legislature determined who became premier. Since no party has ever gained a majority outright (Mapai, the predecessor of Labor, almost did so in the early 1960s), coalition governments have been the norm. Individuals could thus see their votes translate into seats in the Knesset as well as government policy should their party join the ruling coalition.

Despite the extreme fragmentation of the political spectrum caused by the electoral rules, the postindependence consensus provided Labor sufficient votes to play a key role until 1977. Labor (previously Mapai and then Ma'arach) could align on the left with Achdut Ha'Avodah or Mapam, and on the right with the Progressives or General Zionists. By 1977, however, Likud had become the largest party.[47] With Labor and Likud of roughly equivalent strength, unity governments with various supporting parties became the norm in the 1980s. The 1981 coalition contained five parties; the 1984 and 1988 coalitions each incorporated six. These coalitions were oversized. Labor commanded 47 seats in 1981, 44 in 1984, and 39 in 1988. Likud matched Labor's strength at the polls. In 1981 it gained 48 seats; in 1984 it obtained 41; and the 1988 elections yielded 40.[48] Strictly speaking, Likud and Labor could rule without additional parties to the unity government, but by oversizing the coalition they could threaten to rule without the other. This occurred in 1990. When Shimon Peres failed

---

44. Marcus 1992, 699. The higher threshold for the 1992 elections did not deter thirty factions from competing for the voters' attention.

45. Aronoff 2000, 102.

46. CIA, *World Factbook* <www.odci.gov/cia/publications/factbook> and <www.mfa.gov.il>.

47. Harris and Doron 1999, 23.

48. Ottolenghi 2001, 117.

to countenance Shamir's lack of progress toward peace, Labor left the coalition, while a Likud-led right-wing alliance continued on.[49] After Shamir's government fell, each of the two major parties in turn tried to rule with the support of myriad coalition partners, while excluding the other. Ariel Sharon's election in March 2001 opened the door to another broad-based unity government, albeit briefly.

The Growing Impact of Religious and Ethnic Cleavages

Various factors have complicated this already fractured domestic political scene in the last decade and a half. First, demographic changes and the influx of immigrants have altered the political landscape, which was already divided along religious-secular lines and ideological differences of opinion on the peace process. Sephardic Jews from North Africa and the Middle East have grown in number and have found increasing expression in the Shas Party. Championing Orthodox religious causes and ethnic claims of discrimination against the Sephardim by the Western Jews, the Ashkenazim, Shas leapt from 4 seats in 1984 to 6 in 1992, and 17 by 1999.[50] It lost seats in the January 2003 election but still elected 11 members of the Knesset.

Following the unraveling of the Eastern bloc, the number of Russian immigrants to Israel also rose considerably, ultimately climbing to seven hundred thousand. They too organized themselves in various political parties, most notably in Anatoly Sharansky's Yisrael B'aliyah. Although more than half of the Russian immigrants voted for Labor in 1992, they started to exercise their independent strength as the decade wore on.[51] A more nationalist immigrant party, Yisrael Beiteinu, gave further voice to their demands.

Demographics have also altered the relative balance of constituencies and parties. On one side, the Orthodox Jewish population has grown at a considerable rate. Indeed, birthrates among some Orthodox groups, such as the Hasidim, have been almost twice as high as those among secular Jews. The National Religious Party, Shas, and the United Torah Party have catered particularly to these segments of the population. On the other side of the political spectrum, Israel's Arab population has also grown. Although poorly integrated into Jewish society, Israeli Arabs do have the vote, and with their demographic growth Arab parties have gained more seats. In 1988 the Progressive List for Peace (PLP) and the Arab Democratic Party

49. For an overview, see Marcus 1992, 693.
50. Aronoff 2000, 102–3; Elazar and Mollov 2001, 5.
51. With the Russian vote, Labor gained enough seats with Meretz and the Arab parties to block any right-wing coalition.

Table 8.1. Election results for the Knesset

1988			
Unity Coalition	Seats	Opposition	Seats
Likud	40	Meretz (Shinui, Ratz, Mapam)	10
Labor (in opposition, 1990)	39	Hadash (DFPE)	4
Yahadut Ha Torah	7	Tehiya	3
Shas	6	Progressive List (PLP)	1
NRP	5	Arab Democratic Party	1
Moledet	2		
Tsomet	2		
Coalition: 101 (-39) seats		Total: 120 seats	

1992			
Rabin Coalition	Seats	Opposition	Seats
Labor	44	Likud	32
Meretz	12	Tsomet	8
Shas (in opposition, 1993)	6	NRP	6
		Yahadut Ha Torah	4
		DFPE	3
		Moledet	3
Coalition: 62 seats		ADP	2

May 1996			
Netanyahu Coalition	Seats	Opposition	Seats
Likud-Gesher-Tsomet (joint list)	32	Labor	34
Shas	10	Meretz	9
National Religious Party (NRP)	9	Hadash	5
Yisrael B'aliyah	7	Ra'am	4
Yahadut Ha Torah	4	Moledet	2
Third Way	4		
Coalition: 66 seats			

May 1999			
Barak Coalition	Seats	Opposition	Seats
One Israel (Labor, Gesher, Meimad)	26	Likud	19
Shas	17	Shinui	6
Meretz	10	Ra'am	5
Yisrael B'aliyah	6	National Unity	4
Center	6	Yisrael Beiteinu	4
NRP	5	Hadash	3
Yahadut Ha Torah	5	Balad	2
Coalition: 75 seats		Am Ekad (One People)	2

February 2001*			
Sharon Coalition	Seats	Opposition	Seats
One Israel	26	Meretz	9
Likud	19	Shinui	6
Shas	17	Center	6
Yisrael B'aliyah	6	NRP	5
National Unity	4	Yahadut Ha Torah	5
Yisrael Beiteinu	4	Ra'am	5
Am Ekad	2	Hadash	3
Coalition: 78 seats		Balad	2

Sources: Elazar and Sandler 1995, 344–48; Hazan and Diskin 2000, 633; www.knesset.gov.il/elections/asp/ereresults.asp; see also www.electionworld.org/election/israel.htm.
*The Knesset that was elected in 1999 did not have to step down due to Barak's resignation.

(ADP) commanded only 2 seats, but by 1999 Ra'am (the United Arab List) and Balad (the National Democratic Alliance) had 7.[52]

Electoral Reforms and Their Consequences

The deleterious effects of the electoral reforms of 1992 were even more consequential than earlier reform attempts. Decades earlier, Israel's first prime minister, David Ben-Gurion, argued for reforms to make the Israeli system more closely resemble the British and American systems.[53] The 1980s witnessed further proposals to raise the electoral threshold, to diminish the district magnitude, and to institutionalize a constructive no-confidence vote that would require the opposition to come up with an alternative government coalition that could command a majority.[54] None of those proposals carried the day, except for some minor changes in how votes were allocated. Consequently, since 1948 Israel has experienced only two significant electoral reforms: the raising of the threshold to 1.5 percent, which was applied in 1992, and the change in the electoral system in 1992 that was first applied to the 1996 elections.[55]

The 1992 reform of The Basic Law: The Government (Israel has no constitution) created a two-ballot system. Voters would from then on vote separately and simultaneously for a prime minister and for a party list. A prime minister would be elected if she or he managed to get an absolute majority in the first round. Failing that, a runoff between the two front runners would be held in a manner analogous to the French system. However, the prime minister, although separately elected, would still need a simple majority approval in the Knesset. A no-confidence vote by 61 members of the Knesset could precipitate new elections for the Knesset and the prime minister. The prime minister could also resign with a lack of support and call for new elections for the premiership only—as Barak did in 1999.[56]

The reforms were intended to fortify the executive position of the prime minister vis-à-vis the multiparty legislature. By giving voters the opportunity to simultaneously vote for the prime minister and a party, the executive would gain an autonomous mandate and thus more authority. Moreover, the vote for the prime minister would likely create a coattail effect, allowing the prime minister's party to fortify its numbers in the Knesset.[57]

The reforms proved to be a disaster. In 1992 Labor still obtained 44 seats. But in 1996 it could command only 34 seats and by 1999 only 26 (on a joint

52. Elazar and Sandler 1995, 344–48; Hazan and Diskin 2000, 633; Ottolenghi 2001, 117.
53. Harris and Doron 1999, 22.
54. Ottolenghi 2001, 111ff.
55. Doron and Harris 2000, 64–66.
56. See Elazar and Mollov 2001, 8; Aronoff 2000, 97; Hazan and Diskin 2000, 630.
57. Doron and Harris 2000, chap. 5.

list with Meimad and Gesher). The Likud suffered a similar fate. In 1992 it had 32 members in the Knesset. In 1996 it again received 32 seats but operated on a joint list with Gesher and Tsomet that actually had 10 of those 32, thus bringing Likud down to 22. In 1999 it mustered no more than 19 seats.[58]

While the two front runners for the premiership continued to be from Likud or Labor, their respective parties, on which they depended for parliamentary support, declined precipitously. Instead of the desired coattail effect, the reforms produced the reverse: votes for the prime minister did not translate into votes for the prime minister's party. In 1996, roughly 45 percent of the voters engaged in split-ticket voting; by 1999 almost two-thirds of the electorate did so.[59]

The elections of 1996 gave Benjamin Netanyahu a slim majority with 50.5 percent, barely edging out Shimon Peres with 49.5 percent, thus making a second-round runoff unnecessary.[60] But his Likud Party lost 10 seats, with many of the votes going to the religious Right. Since Labor dropped 10 seats as well (going to 34), a unity government centering on Labor and Likud alone had become impossible. They would need the support of smaller parties to govern, contrary to the logic of the unity governments of the 1980s that were partially formed to avoid blackmail by the smaller parties.

The elections of 1999 proved even more damaging. Barak won the election for prime ministership with a decisive margin of victory of 56 percent, against Netanyahu's 44 percent, but Labor commanded less than 20 percent of the votes, giving it 23 seats (with Meimad and Gesher contributing 3 to their combined list). Likud lost to such an extent that Shas (17 seats) threatened to surpass its 19 members of the Knesset. In 1981 Likud and Labor could form a unity government with 95 seats under their control. By 1999 such an alliance would have mustered a mere 45 seats.

Ariel Sharon crushed Ehud Barak even more dramatically in the elections for prime minister on February 6, 2001. Sharon gained 62.4 percent to Barak's 37.6 percent. But since Barak had stepped down rather than go through a vote of no-confidence, the Knesset that had been elected in May 1999 stayed on. Despite his prime ministerial mandate, Sharon had to govern with a Likud parliamentary base of only 19 seats.[61]

The reforms of 1996 also nullified what the earlier threshold reform had sought to achieve. Dozens of factions once again vied for contention. The earlier change in the electoral threshold (from 1 percent to 1.5 percent)

58. For discussions of the electoral reforms and their consequences, see Harris and Doron 1999; Aronoff 2000; Ottolenghi 2001; Hazan and Diskin 2000; Goldberg 2001.
59. Aronoff 2000, 97–101.
60. Hazan and Dishkin 2000, 631; Harris and Doron 1999, 31–32.
61. For these results, see <www.electionworld.org/election/israel.htm>.

had decreased the twelve parties then in the Knesset to ten after the 1992 elections. But by 1996, thirteen parties had seats. And in 1999, once again fifteen parties populated the legislature (counting joint parties on one list as one party).[62] With Likud and Labor in no position to form a unity government (had they chosen to do so), their respective coalitions ended up being a tapestry of diverse interests. Netanyahu needed six parties (counting the parties on his list as one) to form his coalition. Barak had to pull together seven parties to form his government (again counting the list parties as one). Ariel Sharon's subsequent government similarly incorporated seven parties.[63]

The Fragility of Coalitions and the Need for Coalitional Payoffs

Given the fragmentation of the Knesset, creating government coalitions has been a high-wire act. Three key tensions have tended to divide the political spectrum: the religious-secular tension; ethnic cleavages of Ashkenazim, Sephardim, and Russian immigrants; and the divergent perspectives regarding Greater Israel.

Clashes between Orthodox and secular parties centered on the subsidies for religious schools and demands by Orthodox Jews for stricter adherence to the Sabbath and other aspects of religious life. In response, the secular Shinui Party vowed to limit the growing influence of Orthodox Jews. Some Orthodox Israelis also refused to serve in the army while arguing for a Greater Israel. Yet other Orthodox groups opposed the Zionist national project altogether, leading to further tensions with secular Zionists.

Numerous ethnic and racial tensions also erupted. Sephardic Jews from North Africa and the Middle East argued that the political system has consistently favored the Western Ashkenazim. Russian immigrants in turn lamented that the government favored the Sephardic Jews through Shas's control over such key ministries as housing. Russian immigrants themselves split between Yisrael B'aliyah and Yisrael Beiteinu, with the latter more nationalist and farther to the right. Racial tensions erupted as well with, for example, Ethiopian Jews accusing Labor of discrimination, leading to yet another breakaway faction.

Israeli Arabs organized themselves in Ra'am, which, thanks to demographic growth, gained 5 seats in the 1999 elections, and Balad, which garnered 2 seats. Hadash, the Communist Party, also represented some of the Arab constituency and obtained 3 seats in 1999. However, these parties, and thus means of Arab representation, have been systematically excluded

62. See also Hazan and Dishkin (2000, 632–33) for a discussion of the increase in effective parties, which are those parties that gain seats rather than parties that contend. Thirty-three parties competed for seats in the 1999 elections (Harris and Doron 1999, 30).
63. Ottolenghi 2001, 117 <www.electionworld.org/election/israel.htm>.

from any coalition, although individually a few Arab members of the Knesset have risen to some prominence. At times during the peace process, however, their support for possible land-for-peace deals has been critical for the survival of some cabinets.

Finally, on the territorial dimension, religious parties have fallen across a spectrum between moderate Meimad and the hard-line NRP. Secular parties such as the Communist Hadash and the liberal Meretz have traditionally been amenable to a land-for-peace agreement. Secular hard-liners, such as the National Unity list (consisting of Moledet, Herut, and Tekuma), have unabashedly favored an extended Jewish state without Palestinians.[64]

Building coalitions across such diverse constituencies was further complicated by the lack of loyalty among coalition partners. Examples are not hard to find. Labor withdrew after two years in the (1988) unity coalition of Yitzhak Shamir. Shas pulled out shortly after joining the (1992) Rabin government. Gesher appeared with Likud and Tsomet on a combined list in 1996. Three years later, however, it combined with Labor and Meimad. Shas and NRP conspired with other parties to bring down Netanyahu's Likud-led government and joined the Barak Labor-led coalition in 1999. They then withdrew support from the Barak camp, bringing down his coalition. Shas subsequently joined the unity government of Likud prime minister Ariel Sharon in the spring of 2001, but then soon created problems for that coalition.

The need to pay off desired coalition partners has constantly required the prime minister to make concessions, particularly to those parties with special interests such as Shas or United Torah. Such concessions have come in the form of public revenue for religious schools or in the form of coveted cabinet posts. For example, Shas, during the Netanyahu government, wanted the Interior Ministry cabinet post so that it could distribute benefits such as housing to its constituents. These distributions raised the ire of those parties who sought similar benefits for their own constituents. Yisrael B'aliyah claimed that Shas discriminated against Russian immigrants.

Prime ministers have engaged in balancing acts between ministerial posts, sometimes even distributing posts within the same ministry to divergent political perspectives. Barak gave the Ministry on Education post to secular Meretz. But to appease Orthodox Jews, he gave the deputy minister's post to the NRP. Sharansky, the leader of the immigrant Israel B'aliyah party, became minister of the interior, while the deputy minister's post went to a Shas Party member.[65] Such arrangements gave various parties not only

---

64. The Haichud HaLeumi (National Unity) platform calls for "Jewish settlement in all areas of the Land of Israel" and explicitly repudiates the Wye, Hebron, and Oslo agreements <www.knesset.gov.il/elections/knesset15/eichudleumi_m.htm>.

65. Elazar and Mollov 2001.

an effective veto on policies they opposed through leverage on the coalition in the Knesset but a veto within single government ministries.

Consequently, to lure parties away from rival coalitions, prospective prime ministers have had to offer complicated packages to diverse constituencies. Coalition packages have been explicit in their allocation of ministerial seats, deputy ministerships, and even the details of legislation (such as mortgage levels).[66] By way of illustration, in the lead up to the 1999 elections, Labor had alienated Shas by highlighting the plight of Russian immigrants and by attacking the religious parties in general, in an attempt to lure Israel B'aliyah away from the Netanyahu camp. Subsequently, however, Barak had to appease the parties of the religious right such as the NRP, United Torah, and Shas to create his own coalition.[67]

A lack of party discipline complicated the prime minister's task even further. With a plethora of parties across the political spectrum, switching party loyalties hardly required a fundamental transformation. Because the fringes of the parties tended to overlap, any member of the Knesset could find an alternative venue. Moreover, with low electoral thresholds and a large district size, defectors have been able to create their own parties. Parties have thus constantly split. Individuals who broke with their own party need not fear an end to their political career. For example, five new parties managed to gain 18 seats in the 1999 election alone, indicating that newness was no critical impediment to success.[68] Factionalization has been the norm, not the exception. Indeed, since the creation of the State of Israel, only one term of the Knesset ended its session with the same number of parties with which it started.

Party leaders and prime ministers not only have had to contend with the potential defection of coalition members but with opposition from within their own parties. Shimon Peres had to contend with Yitzhak Rabin and, more recently, Ehud Barak in Labor. Netanyahu had to square off with Ariel Sharon in Likud. Infighting within Likud could partially explain Netanyahu's failure in the 1999 election. Dan Meridor and Yitzhak Mordechai broke away from Likud to form the Center Party. Mordechai subsequently even ran as candidate for the prime minister position. Benny Begin similarly broke with Likud and ended up running for the office of the premiership as well. David Levy, the foreign minister and leader of Gesher (on the

66. See, for an example, the text of the detailed agreements between Labor, Meretz, and Shas in *Journal of Palestine Studies* 22, no. 1 (1992): 143–45.

67. In this respect, a party such as Shas has acquired pivotal status, meaning that its support has become necessary for the survival of the coalition when either Labor or Likud is not part of the coalition. On the role of pivotal parties, see Laver 1997, chap. 7. See also *The Economist*, May 13, 2000, 47; December 16, 2000, 51–52.

68. Aronoff 2000, 102; Harris and Doron 1999, 30.

Likud list), even switched to Labor.[69] Few cases were as extreme as the member of Knesset who switched party affinities five times in one month, but still, from January to March 1999, twenty-eight members switched their party identity.[70]

Effects on the Peace Process

Israel's coalitional dynamics have limited the options for the executive in the peace process, because every prime minister has had to take the demands of territorial hard-liners into account. The Third Way, a breakaway faction from Labor, has explicitly aimed to keep the Golan under Israeli control, but it is considered flexible on peace negotiations overall. Other secular parties, such as Moledet and the National Unity Party, have refused to relinquish the West Bank and, indeed, favor its annexation. Religious parties, too, have largely opposed territorial concessions. The NRP and United Torah continue to favor the re-creation of the borders of the biblical homeland, refusing to surrender Judea and Samaria. Shas has also largely favored continued control over the contested areas, although it has tended to focus more on domestic material benefits for the Sephardim. Because the votes of these parties have been critical to the Labor and Likud coalitions of the last decade, such hard-line parties have had a de facto veto on the peace process.

Indirectly, the crosscutting and overlapping issues have made institutionalized logrolling the norm, further limiting the options in cabinet decision making. Some secular parties on the left, such as Meretz, have tended to favor a more conciliatory approach to Arab demands. But, to gain support from the religious parties for territorial concessions, the prime minister has had to attend to their demands on the schools question, in turn jeopardizing the support of the secular parties and even secular members of the prime minister's own party. Rabin's cabinet thus incorporated Meretz (with secularists of Shinui) and Shas, which maintains the direct opposite of Shinui's position.

Institutionalized logrolling has led to a division of labor in which the parties with the most intense preferences on specific issues have garnered key cabinet positions. The incorporation of such special-interest parties is, however, a double-edged sword. On the one hand, such parties make good coalition partners. Because they are single-issue oriented, they are willing to logroll on other issues that are less close to their hearts. Shas, for example,

69. Both Mordechai and Begin withdrew just before the election, allowing Barak to win in the first round. Elazar and Mollov 2001, 4, 7; Goldberg 2001, 23.

70. Hazan and Diskin 2000, 630.

has on occasion condoned territorial concessions provided it gets its way on housing and education. At the same time, such single-issue parties do not conform to the usual expectations of coalition loyalty based on their position on the left-right political spectrum. Because they focus only on the particular, private goods they can obtain from the coalition, they can credibly threaten to leave any coalition—left or right—and move across the spectrum if the opposition promises more benefits. Shas, United Torah, and the NRP have thus seamlessly moved from the Likud coalition, to Labor, and back to a Likud-led coalition.

These coalitional dynamics and domestic vetoes played a particularly crucial role in the Arab-Israeli negotiations of the 1990s. Given the new constellation of power in the Middle East, the United States under President George H. W. Bush pressed for a comprehensive agreement and put Yitzhak Shamir's government under pressure by 1991. At that point, however, his cabinet was already working with a slim majority of two seats because of Labor's withdrawal with its 39 Knesset members from the unity government in 1990. Shamir's government thus required the support of the Right and religious parties, but several of these balked at peace talks in Madrid, and his government fell.

This is not to say that Likud favored substantive peace talks, and that the failure to achieve more progress was simply due to the extreme Right. Had Shamir modified his policies to converge with those of Labor, a unity government might have been a possibility, given the parties' strength. The key point in my argument is that with divergent preferences, the opportunities for vetoes for coalitional allies (and hard-liners) increase.

Rabin's 1992 cabinet seemed to stand a better chance of being able to deal with the Palestinian issue without coalitional complications. Labor could then still command 44 seats in the Knesset. Together with Meretz's 12 seats and Shas's 6 seats it formed a coalition that included only three parties. With fewer parties to appease there was a reasonable hope that an Israeli government might make headway with the peace process. Indeed, should Shas defect the expected support of the Arab and Communist parties (2 plus 3) would still give Rabin's cabinet the 61 votes needed to continue functioning.

And, indeed, the Rabin government made considerable progress during this period. The Oslo accords of September 1993, pushed by Yossi Beilin and Shimon Peres, ceded considerable territory to the Palestinians. The Likud and other parties on the Right attacked Labor for abandoning the (then) 120,000 settlers. Despite defections from the Rabin coalition, 61 members of the Knesset voted for the accords, while 50 voted against and 9 abstained.[71] The follow-up Oslo II agreements were supposed to lead to

71. Shlaim 1994, 34; Bar-Siman-Tov 1997, 175.

Israel's withdrawal from many West Bank cities, although the question of Hebron with 3,000 settlers in Kiryat Arba and 450 settlers in Hebron proper (amid 160,000 Arabs) was not fully settled.[72] The Palestinian Authority on its side recognized the right of Israel to exist in peace and denounced terrorism.[73] Oslo II similarly garnered only 61 votes; 59 members opposed it, including 2 from Labor.[74] The assassination of Rabin in October 1995 brought this process to an end.

The subsequent elections utilized the new two-ballot system. Given the two-round system adopted for the prime ministerial election, strategic calculation dictated that prime ministerial candidates adopt a centrist position. Even if multiple candidates stood for the first round, a second round between the two front-runners would require each candidate to cater to the median voter. (Neither the 1996 nor the 1999 election required a second round, since fringe candidates withdrew before the vote.) Netanyahu in 1996 thus tried to soften his hard-line stance to defuse Shimon Peres's critique. In like manner, Barak, going into the 1999 elections, backpedaled in his attacks on the religious Right and distanced Labor from Meretz and the labor unions.[75]

But such logic did not hold for the parties. They had strategic reasons not to compete for the median (see chapter 1). Commenting on the 1996 and 1999 elections, Emanuele Ottolenghi observes that:

> while the majoritarian principle underlying direct election of the PM impelled the electorate to choose between two seemingly moderate options, the proportional principle at work in the parliamentary elections pulled the same voters in precisely the opposite direction.[76]

Paradoxically then, the prime ministerial candidates tried to project themselves as centrist, while the parties on which they depend for parliamentary support increasingly avoided a centrist position. Likud, in particular, tried to defend its right flank, given the growing strength of the religious Right. The combination of fragile coalitions, extreme multipartyism, weak party discipline, and multiple cleavages proved a witches' brew. In the words of Michael Harris and Gideon Doron, "Minor parties exerted pressure on the major parties: in essence, holding the major parties hostage to their par-

---

72. Morris 1996, 78.

73. The Palestinian side was hardly united either. More extreme groups such as Hamas denounced the Oslo accords, and intellectuals such as Edward Said viewed Oslo as a surrender to Israel (Said 2000).

74. Bar-Siman-Tov 2001, 46.

75. Goldberg 2001, 26, 29.

76. Ottolenghi 2001, 116.

ticularized demands and rendering the government incapable of responding to many of the pressing problems demanding attention."[77]

With Rabin's assassination and the subsequent defeat of Peres in the first direct elections for the premiership, the implementation and follow-up negotiations to Oslo ended in the hands of a Likud-led bloc (1996–98). Consequently, although Netanyahu had openly disavowed land-for-peace agreements with the Palestinians, he found himself obliged to implement elements of earlier accords—partially due to American and international pressure.

But Netanyahu's cabinet was fraught with internal contradictions from the outset. Netanyahu's coalition contained six parties (with Likud, Gesher, and Tsomet counted as one) and could count on 66 seats in the Knesset. Most of these parties uniformly condemned the Oslo accords. Shas, the NRP, and United Torah (Yahadut Torah) wanted to protect the interests of their religious followers and had, to varying degrees, biblical claims for a Greater Israel. The Third Way focused on retaining the Golan. It also included Yisrael B'aliyah, which wanted benefits for its Russian immigrant constituency, and which had clashed earlier with Shas on the allocation of housing contracts and other benefits. Netanyahu thus led a coalition that was hostile to Oslo (as he himself was) and yet felt international pressure to move forward. He also had to manage potentially divergent strands in his coalition by selective allocation of ministries and other goods. But with Likud's decline from 32 to 22 seats, it had less leverage on the coalition, and it controlled fewer committee chairs, giving it less influence on legislative proceedings.[78]

Netanyahu's own victory had been hard fought; he barely edged out Shimon Peres for the premiership. He benefited from a turn to the right among Russian immigrants. Whereas 60 percent of them had voted for Labor in 1992, a similar number now voted for Likud. Votes from the religious constituency also proved key, particularly because of the very high turnout of such voters. Almost 90 percent of inhabitants in some of the settlements turned out to vote—preponderantly favoring Netanyahu over Peres.[79] Consequently, Netanyahu could ill afford to neglect those constituencies.

Likud also had to make concessions to its partners on the Knesset list. It promised several members of Gesher and Tsomet high positions on the joint list, at the expense of some prominent Likud members. This set the stage for subsequent intraparty conflicts. In January 1998 David Levy resigned as foreign minister (replaced by Ariel Sharon), which led to the

77. Harris and Doron 1999, 17.
78. Lochery 2000, 222–223.
79. Morris 1996, 72, 74.

withdrawal of support from most of the Gesher Party. Because Labor had declined overtures from Likud to form a unity government, and with Likud now having only a majority of 62 seats, this "gave each of the seven remaining parties veto power over any decision."[80]

Needless to say, Netanyahu's own position on the Oslo accords and the peace process did not help matters. He introduced new conditions to the peace process: a demand for greater reciprocity and democratization. At the same time, he believed he could retain a larger percentage of territory and reconcile that with Oslo. Moreover, to gain the support of the religious parties he continued with settlement housing construction, including in East Jerusalem.[81] Nevertheless, at the same time he recognized U.S. pressure to move forward and the previous international obligations that Israel had incurred.

Let me be clear. Had Likud chosen to pursue the avenues laid out by the Rabin government, Likud (with Gesher and Tsomet) with their 32 seats would have likely gained support from Labor, Meretz, and the Arab parties, thus assuring a majority for following up on the Oslo accords. In fact, Likud's policy was more hard line than that of Labor, and many in Likud were critical of Oslo. I, therefore, do not contend that Netanyahu's own preferences were irrelevant but rather that even limited concessions were difficult because his coalition only gave him marginal room for maneuver. Bound by Oslo II, Netanyahu entered into an agreement with the Palestinians on Hebron, consistently weighing the need to garner American support against the need to keep his coalition intact. However, only eleven of his ministers voted in favor while seven opposed it. In the Knesset 17 members voted against, with 15 refusing to participate and 1 abstention.[82] It passed thanks to opposition support.

The negotiations surrounding the Wye agreement (October 1998) led to the collapse of his administration. At the Wye River Plantation in Maryland, Netanyahu agreed to implement Israel's obligations in Hebron and to follow through on the Oslo accords. But the religious groups did not support these concessions and so they withdrew from the coalition. Labor, although not a party to the coalition, supported the administration on this particular issue, and the agreement was accepted by 75 votes to 19. However, only 29 members of Netanyahu's own coalition voted in favor, and without the support of the Right, the coalition could not persist and it fell a month later.[83]

The fall of Netanyahu's Likud coalition demonstrates how small single-issue parties can credibly threaten to bring down any government on the

80. Hazan and Diskin 2000, 629. (They count Likud and Tsomet separately.)
81. Morris 1996, 76; Lochery 2000, 227.
82. Bar-Siman-Tov 2001, 50.
83. For discussions of this episode, see Elazar and Mollov 2001, 2–4; Aronoff 2000, 103; Hazan and Diskin 2000; Lochery 2000, 232.

left or the right. Given Netanyahu's razor-thin majority (it fluctuated from several seats to no more than one vote above a majority), the government required the support of parties who had committed themselves to the Golan (the Third Way with 4 seats) or who focused on keeping the West Bank and Gaza (Moledet with 2 seats and the National Religious Party with 9 seats).[84] Given their single-issue orientation, these parties were willing to bring down a center-right government, even though a left-wing and more compromise-prone government might be the result—as indeed emerged with the subsequent Barak coalition. The exit threat of these parties is always credible given the intensity of their preferences on the territorial question, demonstrating their ability to veto policies as they choose.

Similar dynamics befell Barak's self-proclaimed "peace coalition" that assumed office after the 1999 election. Barak entered office to settle the issue of the occupied territories, conclude peace with Syria, and withdraw from the Lebanese quagmire. His margin of victory over Netanyahu (56 to 44 percent), his military standing as a highly decorated officer, and his large Knesset coalition boded well. Indeed, even some Palestinians who opposed the Oslo accords thought that Barak would push through a peace agreement.[85]

Political observers in Israel thought that Barak's seven-party coalition—counting the three-party One Israel list (Labor, Gesher, and Meimad) as one—with 75 Knesset seats could not be held hostage by any individual party, unlike Netanyahu's fragile majority. Besides his One Israel he included three religious parties—Shas with 17 seats, NRP (Mafdal) with 5, and the United Torah with another 5. On the left and center he incorporated Meretz with 10 seats and the Center Party that had 6 members. Yisrael B'Aliyah with 6 members rounded out the coalition. The secular leftist Shinui and the Arab parties were not included (the latter figured in no Knesset coalition), but they were expected to support any peace overture.[86]

Despite the early optimism, Barak's coalition soon ended up in the same predicament as his predecessor's. Consequently, he succeeded only in withdrawing troops from Lebanon. His overtures to Syria, with considerable concessions on the Golan, went nowhere. When he turned to the Camp David negotiations with the Palestinians on the future of the West Bank and Gaza his coalition fell apart.

Early on Barak had campaigned against Shas in order to lure the Russian immigrants to his side. But then he had to make broad concessions to the three religious parties (with their combined 27 seats being larger than One

84. Arian 1998, 23.
85. Said 2000, xi. He thought the resulting agreement would be a dictated peace rather than a negotiated outcome.
86. For optimistic perspectives on what Barak might accomplish, see Lochery 2000, 236; Hazan and Diskin 2000, 636.

Israel). To appease the various conflicting demands of religious versus secular, Shas versus Russian immigrants, and hard-liners versus doves, he had to expand the cabinet from eighteen to twenty-three ministers. Shimon Peres and Yossi Beilin, the architects of the Oslo accords, were pushed to the background.[87]

The high-wire act of balancing conflicting demands could not be sustained. The United Torah left the coalition after only four months. By the summer of 2000, when he entered into the Camp David negotiations, only three parties unambiguously supported his position, leaving him with a minority government.[88] With support from Shinui and other secular parties Barak narrowly avoided a no-confidence vote with 50 votes going against him, 8 abstentions, and 12 members of the Knesset disappearing without casting their votes.[89] Thanks to the Knesset's summer recess and a side deal with Shas, his cabinet limped on, lasting until December. He then had to call for a new prime ministerial election. Barak's willingness to concede large portions of the West Bank despite the ongoing violence aroused the ire of the hard-line parties. With their key swing votes they wanted to control the substance and pace of any negotiations. A decade of peace negotiations essentially came to naught.

LACK OF CREDIBLE COMMITMENTS ON BOTH SIDES

With governments beholden to niche clienteles, no Israeli executive could initiate or credibly commit to the various stages of the complicated accords that were reached at Madrid, Oslo, and Camp David. As in the other cases we have examined here, one needs to distinguish between the impact of political fragmentation during the initiation and the implementation phases.[90] Because Israeli governments from Shamir to Barak constantly faced rebellion in their coalition and sometimes within their own party, they could not credibly *initiate* territorial negotiations. For example, the concessions made by Barak at Taba (in December 2000) went further than those of any prior Israeli government.[91] But by then Barak was already a lame duck executive.

Moreover, and contrary to what bargaining theory would predict for fragile governments, one may even question whether the multiple vetoes in

87. Aronoff 2000, 106; Goldberg 2001, 34; Elazar and Mollov 2001, 9; Hazan and Diskin 2000, 636.

88. Ottolenghi 2001, 119.

89. See the aptly titled article by John Kifner, "Political Survival with a Slap in the Face," *New York Times*, August 1, 2000.

90. See Cowhey 1993a; Martin 2000.

91. See Lister 2002.

Israel made *implementation* any more likely. That is, once an agreement has been reached, such as with Oslo I and II, the subsequent stages of implementation invite even further negotiation and bargaining. Oslo left the most controversial items open for future negotiations. Rather than leading to a stable equilibrium (because the multiple-veto-player framework would make it difficult to reverse the agreement), in fact, the various stages of implementation created new opportunities for veto actors.

This inability of executives to acquire substantial support in the Knesset has not translated into greater concessions by the Palestinians. With fragile coalitions on the Israeli side, the Palestinians have been less inclined to believe that concessions would lead to the conclusion of a final agreement. Reversals of political fortune—the assassination of Rabin, the disinclination and difficulties of his successor, Netanyahu, in implementing Oslo—have made Palestinian leaders doubt the will or ability of Israel's leaders to conclude a final deal.

Furthermore, sovereignty over the occupied territories has presented itself to the protagonists as a dichotomous choice. Hard-liners on either side were not satisfied with an agreement that provided for less than their goal: full control over Judea and Samaria (for the advocates of a Greater Israel), or full Palestinian control over the West Bank, including Jerusalem, and Gaza.

It is instructive to note that the Palestinian side has also been rife with internal conflicts. Palestinian spokespersons, as Edward Said, have criticized the Palestinian Authority for its lack of transparency, low level of democratization, and outright corruption.[92] With a lack of democratic accountability, leaders have had less incentive to engage in broad-based calculations of public goods and have catered to their political allies.

Consequently, with a fragmented authority structure, and with the Palestinian Authority being challenged by more radical elements, such as Hamas, the ability to make credible concessions was slim. There was significant reason to doubt whether Palestine Authority and Palestine Liberation Organization (PLO) leader Yasser Arafat could credibly commit the Palestinian side, whether he had the support of a majority of the Palestinians, or even whether he could control rival factions.

This problem had bedeviled the peace process from the beginning. As Yaacov Bar-Siman-Tov notes regarding Labor's difficulty in reaching an agreement in Oslo (in 1993 and 1995) on a pullback from Gaza, the Israeli negotiators realized, "This could only be effectuated through an agreement with an authorized Palestinian body that could take responsibility for the

92. Said suggested the Palestinian Authority "is at bottom a kind of Mafia" (Said 2000, 22). Pundak argued that the loss of confidence in the Authority and internal fragmentation hindered the Palestinians' ability to negotiate at Camp David (Pundak 2001, 35, 42).

areas after its evacuation."[93] However, Rabin's government thought the PLO was on the verge of collapse and that Hamas would take over.

The fragmentation of the Palestinian camp continues to this day. Given Arafat's preeminent position in the PLO for forty years, and given his reluctance to share power, the Palestinian Authority, which was established in 1994, has faced considerable difficulties in creating a more transparent and accountable government.[94] Arafat even squared off with his hand-picked potential successor, Mahmoud Abbas (Abu Mazen), and with the Palestinian Legislative Council.[95]

Needless to say, this analysis is only a partial explanation of the persistence of the Arab-Israeli conflict over the occupied territories. It focuses on one dimension of the conflict: the domestic institutional arrangements in Israel. I do not gainsay the importance of international factors, including the foreign policies of other Arab states, pressure from the United States, or the importance of religious and ideological differences.

However, Israel's institutions mediate how contending perspectives have translated into political outcomes. More specifically, I maintain that the nature of Israel's domestic institutional arrangements have significantly limited the latitude of the executive to pursue certain options that might change the existing territorial order. This perspective corresponds quite closely with Bar-Siman-Tov's assessment: "External rather than domestic factors were responsible for initiating conflict reduction or resolution." However, once initiated, "a lack of consensus arose . . . not only between coalition vs. opposition parties, but sometimes even within the coalition itself."[96]

I also reiterate that this line of analysis is based on the divergence of preferences. It was not just the extreme Right in Israel that opposed a land-for-peace deal. Likud itself has been at best ambivalent and at times directly opposed to territorial concessions. Begin only gradually came to the negotiating table with Egypt. Netanyahu opposed Oslo. If Labor and Likud's preferences converged and had the support of allies to their left and right, then policy change would be possible, regardless of the institutional architecture.

Nevertheless, the two major parties' political positions continue to diverge. On the one hand, this can be attributed to different ideological positions and deviating evaluations of their Arab counterparts. On the other hand, the electoral system facilitates and encourages the divergence of preferences. If Likud moves to the Left it must fear erosion of its position

93. Bar-Siman-Tov 2001, 45.
94. See Lister 2002.
95. For coverage of this episode, see *New York Times*, March 13, 2003; *Ha'aretz*, April 15, 21, 22, 25, 30, 2003 (English edition).
96. Bar-Siman-Tov 2001, 29–30.

CHAPTER 8

on its Right. Similarly, if Labor moves to the Right it must dread erosion on
its left to parties like Meretz. Institutional configuration rewards ideological
diversity. Veto players acquire influence because of this institutional structure and the diversity of preferences.

At some point, the Israeli government may wish to devise an exit strategy
for the occupied territories. The question is whether the executive could
control the fallout within the executive's own party and within the multiparty coalition. How might, therefore, the domestic situation in Israel unfold in the future? Even before Ariel Sharon took office in 2001, the Knesset
voted to return to the old 1992 electoral system without separate elections
for prime minister. Together with the repeal of the two-vote system, which
was first implemented in 2001, the Knesset introduced the requirement of
a constructive no-confidence vote requiring the opposition to demonstrate
the existence of an alternative coalition that could command 61 votes.[97]

Initially, though, Sharon faced the same problems as all his predecessors.
Since Barak had stepped down rather than be voted out, the 2001 elections
were called for the prime minister only, not for the Knesset. Even though
Sharon won by a landslide vote of 63 percent, he had to find support in the
Knesset that was elected in 1999. Consequently, he had to build a coalition
of seven parties and expand the cabinet to a record size (twenty-six ministers) to give each party a minister or deputy minister. Although he constructed an oversized coalition, Shas soon put the coalition under
pressure.[98] One observer remarked that "Sharon's first year as prime minister has been characterized by indecisiveness and constant zigzagging between Right and Left."[99] By the fall of 2002, One Israel withdrew its
support. Without Labor's support and unable to build a center-right coalition, Sharon was forced to call new elections in 2003.

Despite the return to the one-vote system that was last used in 1992, voters still supported a multitude of small parties. Compared to other polities,
Israel continued to demonstrate a much larger spread across the political
spectrum than majoritarian systems, or even other highly proportional systems such as the Netherlands.[100] True, Likud gained significantly, doubling
its 19 seats in 1999 to 38. Labor-Meimad was reduced to only 19 members.
Shinui rose to 15, with Shas declining to 11. Nine other lists divided the rest
of the seats.[101] Sharon subsequently created a coalition including centrist

97. Ottolenghi 2001, 114, 120.
98. <www.guardian.co.uk/israel/story/> (May 21, 2002).
99. Benn 2002, 65.
100. Dow 2001; Harris and Doron 1999, 20, 26.
101. Analysts suggested that the return to the electoral system of 1992 had not remedied
factionalism in the Knesset. See Shahar Ilan, "Parliamentary Anarchy of the Small Parties,"
Ha'aretz, January 26, 2003, and Uzi Benziman, "Was Return to Single Ballot a Mistake?"
Ha'aretz, January 29, 2003,.

Shinui (which is not opposed to a Palestinian state, provided the violence is halted), the 6-member NRP (catering to Jewish settlers), and the ultranationalist National Union—itself a combination of three parties (7 seats). It thus controlled 66 of the 120 Knesset seats.[102] NRP and National Union thus held a veto on any concessions that Likud might contemplate.

Israel's current predicament demonstrates George Tsebelis's argument that while proportionality guarantees a high degree of representation, it may come at the expense of governability. The electoral reforms of 1992 aimed to bolster the latter by the separate prime ministerial election. Their failure suggests that a more drastic change is required. Historically, however, very few states have tried to move from proportionality to majoritarianism. The French Fifth Republic stands out as one of the few cases.[103]

De Gaulle's remedy for the Algerian War was harsh. To get the army on his side, he reassigned and arrested hundreds of the most recalcitrant hardliners in the officer corps. The pieds noirs were unceremoniously cut loose, and many Algerian loyalists were abandoned. Whether Israel has the stomach for such a dramatic change of its institutions, or whether there is a de Gaulle waiting in the wings, is open to question.[104]

Needless to say, the costs to Israel of its current predicament are high. Since the start of the second intifada in the fall of 2000, more than 3,000 Palestinians and more than 900 Israelis had died by July 2004.[105] The fragmented party system and the fragility of coalitions provide multiple opportunities for hard-liners on the Israeli side to veto even modest concessions. Paradoxically, they also provide hard-liners on the Palestinian side an indirect veto on decision making within Israel. Acts of terrorism by Palestinian extremists need not sway the majority of Israeli opinion. By targeting exposed settlers or the population within Israel itself they give hard-liners additional reasons and added legitimacy to their argument that concessions will not bring a lasting peace—which the Palestinian extremists do not want either. In this sense, the hard-liners on both sides are locked in a perverse, if unconscious, alliance.

102. See Associated Press release, "Sharon Sets Tough Terms for Palestinians," *New York Times,* March 6, 2003.

103. Sartori (1999, 17–18, 23) argues that majoritarian remedies should be sought when proportionality leads to paralyzed coalition governments. Lijphart, a strong proponent of multipartyism and proportionality, has nevertheless suggested that Israel's consensus democracy should be improved to make the smaller parties more responsible. He suggests a higher threshold or diminishing the size of the electoral district (Lijphart 1993, 121).

104. The Israeli press has, on occasion suggested that Israel requires a leader who can extricate the country from the occupied territories in a similar manner to de Gaulle. See the interview of Ariel Sharon by Ari Shavit in *Ha'aretz,* May 8, 2003.

105. Figures provided by Israel's Ministry of Foreign Affairs and Palestinian Red Crescent.

Conclusion:
Contesting Sovereignty in a Global System

EXTERNAL CHANGES AND DOMESTIC RESPONSE

Significant changes in military technology, communications, and commerce since the late Middle Ages have led to the development of a system of consolidated territorial states.[1] These changes reduced the number of polities in Europe from five hundred in the early sixteenth century to two dozen by the beginning of the twentieth century. Gradually, the world was also divided into two spheres: one made up of sovereign, juridically equal entities, and one made up of subject territories.

This trend reversed in the course of the twentieth century, particularly after the end of World War II. With the dissolution of multinational states and empires since 1945, the number of states has increased fourfold. The advent of the nuclear age and high-technology warfare, the spread of capitalism and a liberal economic order, normative shifts in favor of sovereign equality, and nationalist mobilization have changed the international environment of the postwar era.[2]

Ending Empire has analyzed political reactions to these systemic transformations by scrutinizing central governments in empires and multinational states. However, the analysis is not merely a historical exercise. These environmental conditions arguably play a role in many nonimperial polities that face challenges to the existing territorial status quo. For example, the liberal trading environment created by the U.S.–Canada Free Trade Agreement (1987) and the North American Free Trade Agreement (1994)

1. North and Thomas 1973; Spruyt 1994; Tilly 1990.
2. For accounts noting the impact of ideational factors, see Jackson 1993; Lustick 1993; Kupchan 1994, Spruyt 2000.

arguably facilitate Quebec's demands for independence, which would be prohibitively costly in a mercantilist environment.[3] Some scholars have raised questions regarding the territorial integrity of China, which in its long history has faced pressures of centralization and fragmentation.[4]

I have argued in these pages that the number of veto points in the imperial metropole (the territorial core of the empire) or the central government affects how the center will react to challenges to the existing borders and sovereign control. The preferences of social and political actors, and the institutional configuration in which they operate, determine the range of policy choices. Institutions thus set the context in which diverse opinions and perspectives are advanced and reconfigured.[5] Settler communities, business interests with investments in the subject areas, and the military are among the most likely advocates for the territorial status quo. Particular institutional configurations give political elites incentives to cater to these demands and block the possibility of territorial change. Institutions in which political oversight of the military is weak, or institutions that provide multiple partisan and constitutional veto points, will forestall concessions to secessionist and nationalist demands.

The French, Dutch, and Portuguese cases provide evidence that this logic operates across regime type. The multiple veto players in their systems posed serious obstacles to any move away from the territorial status quo. Colonial quagmires were the result. The Soviet and British political systems presented fewer veto opportunities. Their territorial adjustments occurred with far less bloodshed than one might have feared. At present, the multiple veto players in Israeli coalitions thwart the government's ability to deal with the occupied territories.

We might "test" our claims counterfactually.[6] Would the British case have evolved differently if Britain had a multiparty system? It seems quite plausible to suggest that this situation would indeed have complicated matters. Imagine if parties existed to the left of Labour and to the right of the Conservatives. Labour and the Conservatives would then have had to defend their flanks, staying further from a median position on the political spectrum. Labour would be more inclined to support swift retreat, defending itself from (say) a Communist Party that opposed any form of Western colonialism. But if Labour had thus been forced to become the party of scuttle, it would have lost support from the median voters. If the Conservative Party had to defend its flanks against a party on its right that favored a hard line on the colonies, say a party based on the pro-Suez and Lord Salis-

3. Meadwell and Martin 1994.
4. The People's Republic of China consists of fifty-six officially recognized nationalities, with about 91 million non-Han Chinese (Gladney 1994, 171).
5. Thelen and Steinmo 1992, 23; Hall 1992, 109. Also see Hall 1989.
6. Przeworski 1995, 21.

bury position, the resulting harder line would be difficult for Labour to support, thus giving the pro-empire group to the right of the Conservatives an effective veto in the Conservative and pro-empire party coalition.

The study of veto points and policy change, and the analysis of downstream effects of institutions, arguably work best in explaining decisions of democratic regimes. Abiding by the institutional rules of the game, after all, forms the crux of democratic government. We can deductively derive propositions regarding the causal effects of institutions and veto points.

Nevertheless, I have extended the study of fragmented policy networks and veto opportunities to nondemocratic governments. I have done so by distinguishing authoritarian coalitional forms of rule (as in Portugal) from more unified forms (as in the Soviet Union). The assessment of veto opportunities is, admittedly, more inductive than deductive in these cases. The logic of analysis, however, remains the same.

It is interesting to note that across these cases business interests with site-specific investments proved to be less intractable than the settler populations. While in the initial phases of territorial conflict such business elites supported hard-line responses to territorial demands, often their preferences diminished in intensity over time. Given the vertical nature of their production processes, such elites assumed that the incipient new states would still require foreign companies for investing, production, and marketing. Moreover, given that they foresaw a long-term iterative relation with the new host countries, and given that their first preference—formal governance in these territories—was rapidly becoming unfeasible, they instead engaged in attempts to channel the nature of the emerging regime rather than fight independence outright.

Settlers, by contrast, almost uniformly objected to changes in the territorial status quo and continued to do so as the conflict dragged on. The settlers feared (and the migration of French colons, Dutch settlers, and Portuguese from the overseas territories confirms) that a change of status meant a dramatic end to their position. Similarly, Israeli settlements—true to Dayan's intent—have created "facts on the ground," vastly complicating Israel's extraction from the territories.

I stress again that my explanation does not preclude a lack of change in territorial policy and a hard-line response even if institutions present few veto points. Favorable structural conditions, or a majority opinion supporting a hard-line response, may propel leaders facing few domestic barriers to forgo territorial adjustment. I argue, however, that executives in such an institutional setting will be more likely to behave according to realist tenets, while governments facing domestic barriers to reconfiguring their boundaries will be constrained from behaving like unitary strategic actors. Thus, the Dutch and Portuguese cases should be relatively "easy cases" for realist explanations of foreign policy that focus on states as strategic, unitary actors.[7] As small states, they should have been particularly attuned to the demands of the international environment; yet they engaged in perilous foreign policy, even at the risk of alienating much-needed allies.

Britain, by contrast, despite problems in the postwar years, had fared better than France and was obviously more powerful than the smaller maritime empires. Nor was there anything in 1985 that foreshadowed the dissolution of the USSR. In other words, on realist grounds one might have expected Britain and the USSR, among all these cases, to have pursued the very policies adopted by weaker powers.

A realist perspective rightly focuses on the changes in environment that have challenged empires and multinational states. One requires, however, a domestic institutionalist explanation to account for why some governments acted in ways that realists would not expect. Between structural environment and policy choice, institutions provide the material and cognitive context in which decisions are embedded.[8]

THE PARADOXES OF INSTITUTIONAL CHOICE

Logrolling and Outbidding in Multiparty Parliaments

The argument that multiparty parliamentary systems impede territorial adjustment, particularly when they lead to multiparty coalitions, is not altogether new. Miles Kahler's path-breaking analysis of decolonization in France and Britain suggests that territorial demands create strains in multiparty systems because the competition for shared constituencies will push leaders to "outbid" each other on the territorial question. Kahler, however, places an important caveat: multiparty systems with party discipline should look more like the two-party Westminster variety because leaders do not fear defection.

Moreover, even though Kahler does not raise this possibility himself, electoral "outbidding" in a multiparty system could hypothetically even lead to a "run for the exit." That is, if leaders thought that their constituents preferred territorial withdrawal, they might outbid their political rivals by arguing that they were the voters' best bet in achieving such retreat under the slogan "no more quagmires."

In short, party discipline might prevent outbidding from occurring despite multipartyism. And even if it did occur it might not have negative con-

---

7. Note that realist accounts that emphasize the nature of domestic politics often focus on great powers (e.g., Snyder 1991). By contrast, see M. Elman 1995.

8. The approach taken here resembles that of John Ikenberry (1988): societal perspectives shed considerable light on policy, but the state's institutions set the terrain for how the policy struggle evolves between proponents and opponents.

sequences but instead lead to a speedy exit. Kahler's views could lead to a more optimistic conclusion regarding the ability of (some) multiparty parliamentary systems to deal with territorial conflicts.

Why then do multiparty coalitional governments, nevertheless, diminish the likelihood of policy change? In the 1948 Dutch elections 83 percent voted for the same party that they voted for in the 1946 elections. According to some analysts of Dutch politics, "Structured competition is hardly competition at all, since voters are so tied to a particular party that few votes are actually contested."[9] Kahler's hypothesis would thus predict that this system should behave like a two-party one. Why did not this occur?

For one thing, political elites may run scared in multiparty systems, even when they should be more confident about loyal support. They may do so out of fear that splinter parties may break away (and this in turn will depend on expected voter support, the degree of proportionality in the electoral process, electoral thresholds, and so on) or that voters may defect on the margins. Exit of party members and competition on the wings might occur even in relatively segmented societies.

I have also argued that other factors besides party discipline and outbidding complicate the decision-making process in multiparty democracies, as we have seen in the French and Dutch experiences. The segmentation of parties across the political spectrum rather than hovering around the median, coalitional logrolling, and the division of ministerial positions all weigh in the balance. Multiparty systems do not behave like two-party systems on territorial issues.

Furthermore, if outbidding occurs it will more likely favor the hard-liners than the territorial compromisers. The constituencies that favor the territorial status quo are more likely to be well organized—in a better position to overcome transaction costs and information barriers and to override collective action problems—than the proponents of change. They are well aware of the specific benefits that accrue from their holdings or residence in those territories that are in dispute. For the population at large these territories might impose a collective cost, but the public nature of these costs will lead to free riding. Moreover, because these groups will often be single-issue constituencies (particularly the settlers and their supporters in the home country), politicians will have strategic incentives to cater to them.

Coalitional dynamics do the rest. Parties will trade their support on issues they find of minor importance for reciprocal support for their cherished objectives. Parties that have strong preferences for continuing the existing territorial order are likely to trade their support for nonterritorial issues in return for a hard-line vote on the territorial question. It is even possible that a small party with a strong policy preference may exercise significant

9. Irwin and Holsteyn 1989, 22, 31.

influence in a coalition, particularly if it has the option of joining an alternative coalition.

Consociationalism, Institutionalized Vetoes, and Territorial Compromise

Ending Empire's analysis also has implications for how states might deal with conflicting multinational and multiethnic demands. One important tradition has explicitly linked institutional design with the politics of accommodation among diverse groups. Arend Lijphart stands as probably the most well-known advocate of this view, but the theory has had many adherents.[10] Accommodation requires institutional designs based on a grand coalition of all the principle groups, proportionality in the electoral system, segmental autonomy, and a recognized veto for each group.[11]

The requirement of proportionality will likely yield a multiparty political system with coalitions. Indeed, the institutional design explicitly aims to create and even formally recognize a multiplicity of veto actors. The officially recognized right to veto policy is meant to prevent religious or ethnic tensions from arising by preventing a powerful group, or alliance of groups, from dominating other sections of the population. Extreme proportional systems may be a recipe for domestic stability in fractionated societies. The veto right prevents territorial demands from emerging, because few extreme policies will emerge to exclude one group from benefits or rights.

But, conversely, my argument here is that if such demands for secession and territorial redress do, despite everything, emerge, then a consociational polity might be ill equipped to deal with them. Lijphart does not shirk from addressing separation as one possible solution to ethnic and racial divisions. "Secession into sovereign statehood goes a significant step beyond segmental autonomy, of course, but it is not incompatible with the basic assumptions underlying the consociational model."[12] That is, if segments of the population are geographically concentrated and these segments find themselves unwilling to coexist within the consociational polity, then secession should be an option.

Nevertheless, this does not resolve the paradox. In multiparty coalitional governments with many veto players, the central government will find it difficult to extricate itself from the area that wishes to secede. In particular, if there has been some mixing of populations (creating the equivalent of settler communities), cross-segmental economic interaction, or if the separation jeopardizes corporate interests of the previous multiethnic or multi-

---

10. Lijphart's theory was originally developed to explain Protestant and Catholic accommodation in the Netherlands (Lijphart 1968), it but has been applied far more broadly (Lijphart 1996, 258).
11. Lijphart 1977, 25.
12. Lijphart 1977, 45.

national military, the government might likely face vetoes to territorial compromise. In short, it might be that giving multiple actors a voice at the table would squelch secessionist demands. Policies will be stable because they are the result of complicated compromises. However, should secessionist demands nevertheless arise, then multiparty parliamentary systems can become a double-edged sword. The very logic of giving every group a voice also means that special interests will have a veto when it comes to territorial compromise. Consociational systems thus come with a paradox.

Institutions and Foreign Policy

The preceding argument suggests that strong executives can more readily initiate policy change, and that they are less likely to be subject to vetoes by politicians and groups who favor the territorial status quo. On territorial issues, one could investigate whether strong presidential systems such as those that have emerged in the wake of the Soviet Union's demise might have diminished the likelihood of territorial conflict.[13] Arguably, Yeltsin's presidency kept the more virulent imperial elements in the Russian parliament, such as Vladimir Zhirinovsky and the Communists, at bay. Even the conflict in Chechnya does not provide prima facie evidence that the presidential system has failed in this regard. The theoretical model advanced here does not preclude that an executive facing few veto points might choose a hard-line policy. It simply suggests that changes in territorial policy will be more likely when politicians face few incentives to cater to niche clienteles.

Moreover, counterfactually, one need not presume that a multiparty system would have handled the situation more deftly. To the contrary, given the multiple hard-line and Communist factions in the legislature, one might wonder whether numerous conflicts besides Chechnya might have emerged within Russia, or with the other newly independent states.

While *Ending Empire* has explored whether some institutions make territorial policy change more likely or not, we might ask whether governments with few veto points will be more likely to adjust foreign policies when international conditions warrant. Nothing so far precludes us from extending this work in that direction.

Ronald Rogowski argues that polities with proportional electoral systems generate more stable policies than majoritarian systems and seldom reverse policy.[14] Similarly, Stephan Haggard and Robert Kaufman submit that strong executives can more easily implement economic reforms than lead-

---

13. Post-Soviet regimes, as well as much of Eastern Europe, have had a marked proclivity for presidential governments (Taras 1997).

14. Rogowski 1987. A similar argument is advanced in Frieden and Rogowski 1996, 43–44.

ers in systems where power is more widely distributed. However, they add that fragmented party systems are beneficial for locking in those reforms.[15] Andrew MacIntyre shows that countries in East Asia with many veto points act too rigidly to deal with crises, while countries that lack any veto points are too volatile.[16] David Auerswald argues that strong executives are more likely to show initiative (and to use force). This squares with my observation that governments with few veto points will face fewer obstacles in initiating a new policy.[17] Miriam Elman similarly demonstrates how strong presidential systems provide for activist foreign policy.[18]

However, even if governments with few vetoes are more flexible on issues of territorial contestation, or on foreign policy in general, this does not imply that strong presidencies are per definition superior to other forms of government. I merely suggest that executives who face few veto points and who are beholden to broad segments of the population are more likely to initiate policy change in response to changed structural conditions. Moreover, given that political leaders in two-party systems will cater to a median voter they will tend to be more receptive to the demands of the national electorate than to narrower groups across the political spectrum.

All this presupposes an executive beholden to an electorate, rather than a hierarchical authoritarian system, or a presidential system without a meaningful choice of candidates. Where a presidency has evolved beyond control of popular preferences the executive naturally has the latitude to change territorial policy (as does any strong executive with few vetoes), but the direction of policy change will be difficult to predict. In this sense hierarchical-authoritarian systems, although they can change the direction of their policies, may violate realist expectations.

Multiple Veto Points, Credible Commitment, and Two-Level Games

Scholars who are familiar with the institutionalist literature in international relations might suggest that fragmented political systems could also have beneficial effects. Although unified systems can change policy quickly, that very flexibility also makes them unreliable negotiating parties. As Lisa Martin argues, "Unconstrained executive-branch actors can indeed bargain more flexibly . . . but their lack of *ex-ante* domestic constraints also gives them the capacity to act arbitrarily, making them unreliable partners in international cooperation."[19] To put it within the framework of this analysis: If a unified central government (one facing few veto points) is willing to ne-

15. Haggard and Kaufmann 1995, 9–15.
16. MacIntyre 2001, 2003.
17. Auerswald 2000, chap.2.
18. M. Elman 1995.
19. Martin 2000, 5; Keohane 1984, 117.

gotiate and change the territorial status quo, why would nationalists believe that commitment to be credible? And if they did not believe it to be credible, why bother to negotiate? If this were the case it would erode the connection I have drawn between the willingness of the metropole to change territorial policy and the outcome of negotiated, calibrated withdrawal.

The answer lies in realizing there is a difference between the *initiation* of commitments and the *ability to reverse* them. As Peter Cowhey succinctly states, "Divided powers make it harder to initiate commitments and also harder to reverse them."[20] Conversely, the easier it is to initiate policy change, the easier it is to reverse policy as well; hence, the credible commitment problem. Fragmented decision making results in difficulties in initiating new policies, but it is more credible than centralized decision making in carrying out agreements once they have been reached.

This expected relation, however, did not hold on questions of territorial policy. Because a fragmented government will find it difficult to generate a policy proposal that diverges dramatically from the existing status quo, the multiple veto players will forestall the proposal going forward. A proposed change in territorial policy will not be likely to make it through the initiation phase, thus precluding the subsequent question of credible commitment during implementation.

As I have demonstrated in the empirical case discussions, governments facing multiple veto points failed to advance possible agreements in the negotiation phase. The Dutch negotiators early on (before the police actions) reached an accord with the Indonesians (the Linggadjati agreement), but this was subsequently annulled by a parliamentary veto in the Netherlands (by the Catholic People's Party in particular). Similarly, in the French case, Paris failed to advance a consistent policy on Algeria. When compromise solutions seemed to emerge, as in the Blum-Violette proposals before the war and the proposed reforms of 1947, they were quickly scuttled. There, the lack of credible commitment lay in the initial negotiation phase.

Moreover, lack of commitment in the implementation phase of an agreement only causes concern if a policy is potentially reversible. Although an actor might face few domestic constraints to reverse policy, such a reversal might come at considerable cost to that actor. Territorial withdrawal arguably constitutes such a one-directional environment. Once one has pulled out of a given territory, reasserting one's control might be extremely difficult. And, indeed, this is what nationalists thought in all the cases discussed in *Ending Empire*. Nationalist elites believed that once the metropolitan power had handed over sovereignty, it would be very difficult, if not impossible, for it to reverse the process. Only in the Soviet case was there

20. Cowhey 1993, 302. Martin (2000, 18, 41) similarly draws a distinction between the bargaining stage and the implementation stage.

considerable apprehension of a possible return of a neo-imperial relationship where Russia would reassert its hegemony over the "near abroad." Russian relative power thus cast doubt on its commitment in the early phases of the dissolution of the USSR.[21]

Further, even governments with few veto points at home can create credible commitments by other means. Thus while British credible commitment might seem problematic (in that it faced few veto points), in fact its domestic institutions were not seen as detrimental to its credibility. Whitehall established credibility by abiding by its earlier commitments (withdrawal from India, its move away from imperial preference) and by public opinion at home.

If fragmentation of the imperial center created an inability to initiate bargains, the same has held true for fragmented nationalist movements. Although this present analysis is admittedly a study of metropolitan decision making, similar effects can be discerned in instances where nationalist movements were not unified. For example, divisions among the Algerian nationalists complicated French-Algerian negotiations. Similarly, the lack of unity among the various Palestinian factions undoubtedly diminishes their ability to put forward credible proposals.

One might also conjecture that fragmented political systems provide another advantage. If executives in the metropole face multiple vetoes and can plausibly argue they have little room for maneuvering, wouldn't the nationalists be more accommodating? And if so, then the flexibility of the nationalists in reaching an agreement should erode the connection between multiple veto points in the metropole and a lack of a compromise agreement.[22]

In the cases presented here, central governments facing multiple veto players were not able to parlay their fragmentation into diplomatic advantage with the nationalists for various reasons. First, territorial questions were largely indivisible. The nationalist project hinged on gaining ultimate sovereignty over a given territory and its resources. Unlike, say, trade concessions, territorial sovereignty was difficult to break down into parts.[23] For example, the control over Jerusalem presents itself currently as an either-or situation to Israelis and Palestinians. Nationalists were reluctant to grant metropolitan powers continued control over parts of the contested territories.

21. Spruyt 1997b.

22. This is the logic of the two-level game. Politicians that face constraints at home might be able to parlay these constraints into bargaining advantages at the international level, provided the negotiating partner is aware of the constraints. Putnam 1988.

23. However, see the work of Alex Cooley, who suggests that if credible agreements can be reached, intermediate degrees of sovereign rights can be negotiated. Cooley 2000/2001.

Second, and related to the argument above, when nationalists did make concessions, subsequent reversals by the metropolitan powers not only eroded confidence in the center's credibility but eroded the position of compromising nationalists. That is, a failure to reach agreement in the initiation phase of negotiations created a ratchet effect. Compromisers among the nationalists were discredited and replaced by hard-liners.

In short, multiple veto points in the center proved an impediment to policy change and territorial compromise, not an advantage. Multiple veto points did not create credibility of commitment but rather the converse. The inability to initiate policy negotiation prevented the metropoles from parlaying fragmentation at home into concessions from the nationalists.

Ending Empire weaves a tapestry from the intersections of agency, institutional constraint and opportunity, and broad systemic change. With all the attention we as historians, political scientists, and sociologists devote to studying international and domestic configurations, we are often reluctant to recognize how individual agency has a knack of defying the most elegant theory. During moments of crisis and revolution even institutional architectures (and thus the veto points in the system) mutate. Whereas they operate as structural constraints most of the time, institutions at those junctures can be altered despite the costs associated with such change.

The birth of the Fifth Republic that gave de Gaulle powers that the Fourth Republic had denied him, constituted such a watershed. Similarly, the institutional changes initiated by Gorbachev during the Soviet reforms gave him the ability to outmaneuver hard-liners in the Politburo. Military stalemate and economic stagnation empowered the reformist forces. But in the end, de Gaulle, Gorbachev, Macmillan, and others made choices within the room for maneuver that was given them. Accident and serendipity played a role as well. Gorbachev, after all, had not set out to break apart the USSR, but no doubt his choices influenced the eventual outcome of the reform process.

All theories and accounts must, therefore, be partial and imperfect. Nevertheless, I hope to have at least illuminated some aspects of the great macrohistorical events of the twentieth century that continue to unfold in the twenty-first. We surely have not experienced the last of attempts to reallocate territorial sovereignty.

Bibliography

References to short research reports, newspaper articles, and many primary documents are included in the footnotes, not in the bibliography.

Where multiple chapters have been used from an edited volume, the individual contributions are abbreviated. The full volume information is listed under the editors' names.

Primary Sources and Document Collections

Black, J. L. 1989, 1990. *USSR Documents Annual.* Gulf Breeze, Fla.: Academic International Press.

Dennett, Raymond, and Robert Turner. 1947–49. *Documents on American Foreign Relations.* Vols. 9–11. Princeton: Princeton University Press.

Foreign Relations of the United States (FRUS). 1947, vol. 6 (The Far East); 1948, vol. 3 (Western Europe); 1949, vol. 7 (Far East and Australasia). Washington, D.C.: U.S. Government Printing Office.

Hyam, Ronald, ed. 1992. The Labour Government and the End of Empire, 1945–1951. Part I–IV. British Documents on the End of Empire, ser. A. London: Her Majesty's Stationery Office.

Hyam, Ronald, and William Roger Louis, eds. 2000. The Conservative Government and the End of Empire, 1957–1964. Part I, II. British Documents on the End of Empire, ser. A. London: Her Majesty's Stationery Office.

Officiële Bescheiden Betreffende de Nederlands-Indische Betrekkingen 1945–1959(NIB). 1971–91. 20 vols. 's-Gravenhage, Netherlands: Martinus Nijhoff.

Books and Articles

I use the following abbreviations:

APSR   *American Political Science Review*
BMGN   *Bijdragen en Mededelingen Betreffende de Geschiedenis der Nederlanden*

BTLV   Bijdragen to de Taal-, Land- en Volkenkunde
IO   International Organization
JICH   Journal of Imperial and Commonwealth History
RFHOM   Revue Française d'Histoire d'Outre-Mer

Abshire, David, and Michael Samuels, eds. 1969. *Portuguese Africa*. London: Pall Mall.
Adamthwaite, Anthony. 1985. "Britain and the World, 1945–49: The View from the Foreign Office." *International Affairs* 61, no. 2: 223–35.
Africa Institute. 1963. "Portugal in Africa and Portuguese Overseas Policy." *International Bulletin* 1, no. 10: 284–94.
Ageron, Charles-Robert. 1976. "L'Opinion française devant la guerre d'Algerie." *RFHOM* 63, no. 231: 256–85.
———. 1982. "La Perception de la puissance française en 1938–1939: Le Mythe impérial." *RFHOM* 69, no. 254: 7–22.
———. 1985. "La Survivance d'un mythe: La Puissance par l'empire colonial, 1944–1947." *RFHOM* 72, no. 269: 387–403.
Agha, Hussein, and Robert Malley. 2002. "Camp David and After: An Exchange (A Reply to Ehud Barak)." *New York Review of Books*. June 1.
Albertini, Rudolf von. 1969. "The Impact of Two World Wars on the Decline of Colonialism." *Journal of Contemporary History* 4, no. 1: 17–35.
Alesina, Alberto, and Enrico Spolaore. 1994. "On the Number and Size of Nations." Paper presented at Columbia University.
Alexandre, Pierre. 1969. "Francophonie: The French and Africa." *Journal of Contemporary History* 4, no. 1: 117–25.
Almond, Gabriel, and Stephen Genco. 1977. "Clouds, Clocks, and the Study of Politics." *World Politics* 29, no. 4: 489–522.
Alpher, Joseph. 1994. "Israel's Security Concerns in the Peace Process." *International Affairs* 70, no. 2: 229–41.
Amalrik, Andrei. 1970. *Will the Soviet Union Survive until 1984?* New York: Harper and Row.
Amsden, Alice. 1989. *Asia's Next Giant: South Korea and Late Industrialization*. New York: Oxford University Press.
Andersen, Robert, and Meir Yaish. 2001. "Social Cleavages, Electoral Reform, and Party Choice: Israel's 'Natural' Experiment." Working paper, Oxford University.
Anderson, Benedict. 1991. *Imagined Communities*. New York: Verso.
Anderson, Lisa. 1986. *The State and Social Transformation in Tunisia and Libya, 1830–1980*. Princeton: Princeton University Press.
Ansprenger, Franz. 1981. *The Dissolution of Colonial Empires*. New York: Routledge.
Arian, Asher. 1998. *Israeli Public Opinion on National Security*. Tel Aviv: Jaffee Center for Strategic Studies.
Arian, Asher, and Michal Shamir, eds. 1995. *The Elections in Israel 1992*. Albany: State University of New York Press.
———, eds. 1999. *The Elections in Israel 1996*. Albany: State University of New York Press.
———, eds. 2002. *The Elections in Israel 1999*. Albany: State University of New York Press.
Aronoff, Myron. 2000. "The 'Americanization' of Israeli Politics: Political and Cultural Change." *Israel Studies* 5, no. 1: 92–107.
Ascherson, Neal. 1992. "Africa's Lost History." *New York Review of Books*. June 11.
Aslund, Anders. 1995. *How Russia Became a Market Economy*. Washington, D.C.: Brookings Institution.
Atkin, Muriel. 1993. "Tajikistan: Ancient Heritage, New Politics." In Bremner and Taras, eds., *Nations and Politics*.

Auerswald, David. 2000. *Disarmed Democracies*. Ann Arbor: University of Michigan Press.

Avant, Deborah. 1994. *Political Institutions and Military Change*. Ithaca: Cornell University Press.

Bachrach, Peter, and Morton Baratz. 1962. "The Two Faces of Power." *APSR* 56: 947–52.

Bachtiar, Harsja. 1972. "Bureaucracy and Nation Formation in Indonesia." *BTLV* 128, no. 4: 430–46.

Bailey, Norman. 1969a. "Government and Administration." In Abshire and Samuels, eds., *Portuguese Africa*.

———. 1969b. "The Political Process and Interest Groups." In Abshire and Samuels, eds., *Portuguese Africa*.

Baldwin, Richard, Pertti Haaparanta, and Jaakko Kiander. 1995. *Expanding Membership of the European Union*. New York: Cambridge University Press.

Baljé, Chr. L. 1977. "Dekolonisatie in Dokumenten." *BMGN* 92, no. 3: 462–73.

Bandeira, Antonio R. 1976. "The Portuguese Armed Forces Movement: Historical Antecedents, Professional Demands, and Class Conflict." *Politics and Society* 6, no. 1: 1–56.

Bank, Jan. 1981. "Rubber, Rijk, Religie: De Koloniale Trilogie in de Indonesische Kwestie, 1945–1949." *BMGN* 96, no. 2: 230–59.

———. 1985. "Exercities in Vergelijkende Dekolonisatie: Indonesië in Zuidoost-Azië, Nederland in West-Europa." *BTLV* 141, no. 1: 19–35.

Barkey, Karen, and Mark von Hagen, eds. 1997. *After Empire*. Boulder, Colo.: Westview.

Barnett, Don, and Roy Harvey. 1972. *The Revolution in Angola*. Indianapolis: Bobbs-Merrill.

Barnett, Malcolm. 1968–69. "Backbench Behavior in the House of Commons." *Parliamentary Affairs* 22: 38–61.

Bar-Siman-Tov, Yaacov. 1997. "Peace-making with the Palestinians: Change and Legitimacy." In Efraim Karsh, ed. *From Rabin to Netanyahu*. London: Frank Cass.

———. 2001. "Peace Policy as Domestic and Foreign Policy." In Sofer, ed., *Peacemaking in a Divided Society*.

Bates, Robert. 1981. *Markets and States in Tropical Africa*. Berkeley: University of California Press.

Bates, Robert, Avner Greif, Margaret Levi, Jean-Laurent Rosenthal, and Barry Weingast, eds. 1998. *Analytic Narratives*. Princeton: Princeton University Press.

Baudet, H. 1975. "Nederland en de Rang van Denemarken." *BMGN* 90, no. 3: 430–43.

Becker, Josef, and Franz Knipping, eds. 1986. *Power in Europe?* Berlin: Walter de Gruyter.

Beissinger, Marc. 1992. "Elites and Ethnic Identities in Soviet and Post-Soviet Politics." In Motyl, ed., *Post-Soviet Nations*.

———. 1995. "The Persisting Ambiguity of Empire." *Post-Soviet Affairs* 11, no. 2: 149–84.

———. 1997. "State Building in the Shadow of an Empire-State." In Dawisha and Parrott, eds., *The End of Empire?*

———. 2002. *Nationalist Mobilization and the Collapse of the Soviet State*. New York: Cambridge University Press.

Bender, Gerald. 1972a. "The Limits of Counterinsurgency: An African Case." *Comparative Politics* 4, no. 3: 331–60.

———. 1972b. "Angola: History, Insurgency, and Social Change." *Africa Today* 19, no. 1: 30–36.

———. 1974. "Portugal and Her Colonies Join the Twentieth Century." *Ufahamu* 4, no. 3: 121–62.

———. 1978a. "Angola, the Cubans, and American Anxieties." *Foreign Policy* 31: 3–30.

———. 1978b. *Angola under the Portuguese*. Berkeley: University of California Press.

Bender, Gerald, and Stanley Yoder. 1974. "Whites in Angola on the Eve of Independence: The Politics of Numbers." *Africa Today* 21, no. 4: 23–37.

Bendix, Reinhard. 1978. *Kings or People*. Berkeley: University of California Press.

Ben-Dor, Gabriel, Ami Pedahzur, and Badi Hasisi. 2002. "Israel's National Security Doctrine under Strain: The Crisis of the Reserve Army." *Armed Forces and Society* 28, no. 2: 233–55.

Benn, Aluf. 2002. "The Last of the Patriarchs." *Foreign Affairs* 81, no. 3: 64–78.

Berman, Robert, and John Baker. 1982. *Soviet Strategic Forces: Requirements and Responses*. Washington: Brookings Institution.

Bermeo, Nancy. 1986. *The Revolution within the Revolution*. Princeton: Princeton University Press.

———. 1987. "Redemocratization and Transition Elections: A Comparison of Spain and Portugal." *Comparative Politics* 19, no. 2: 213–31.

———. 1992a. "Surprise, Surprise: Lessons from 1989 and 1991." In Nancy Bermeo, ed., *Liberalization and Democratization*. Baltimore: Johns Hopkins University Press.

———. 1992b. "Democracy and the Lessons of Dictatorship." *Comparative Politics* 24, no. 3: 273–91.

Berstein, Serge. 1986. "French Power as Seen by the Political Parties after World War II." In Becker and Knipping, eds., *Power in Europe?*

———. 1993. *The Republic of de Gaulle, 1958–1969*. New York: Cambridge University Press.

Berthélemy, Jean-Claude. 1980. "L'Économie de l'Afrique Occidentale Française et du Togo, 1946–1960." *RFHOM* 58, no. 248: 301–37.

Betts, Raymond. 1985. *Uncertain Dimensions*. Minnesota: University of Minnesota Press.

Beus, G. 1977. *Morgen bij het Aanbreken van de Dag*. Rotterdam: Donker.

Birchfield, Vicki, and Markus Crepaz. 1998. "The Impact of Constitutional Structures and Collective and Competitive Veto Points on Income Inequality in Industrialized Democracies." *European Journal of Political Research* 34: 175–200.

Birmingham, David. 1993. *A Concise History of Portugal*. New York: Cambridge University Press.

———. 1995. *The Decolonization of Africa*. Athens: Ohio University Press.

Blackburn, Robin. 1974. "The Test in Portugal." *New Left Review* 87–88: 5–46.

Blacker, Coit. 1991. "Learning in the Nuclear Age: Soviet Strategic Arms Control Policy, 1969–1989." In Breslauer and Tetlock, eds., *Learning in U.S. and Soviet Foreign Policy*.

Blondel, Jean. 1974a. *The Government of France*. London: Methuen.

———. 1974b. *Contemporary France*. London: Methuen.

Bogaarts, M. D. 1989. *Parlementaire Geschiedenis van Nederland na 1945: De Periode van het Kabinet Beel*. 4 vols. The Hague: SDU.

Bootsma. N. 1978. "Nederland op de Conferentie van Washington, 1921–1922." *BMGN* 93, no. 1: 101–26.

———. 1995. "The Discovery of Indonesia: Western (non-Dutch) Historiography on the Decolonization of Indonesia." *BTLV* 151, no. 1: 1–22.

Bosma, U. T. 1989. "De Indo-Europeaan en de Autonomie voor Indië." *BMGN* 104, no. 1: 17–38.

Bosmans, J. 1981. " 'Beide er in en geen van beide er uit': De Rooms-Rode Samenwerking, 1945–1952." *BMGN* 9, no. 2: 204–29.

Bosscher, D. F. 1986. "De Partij van de Arbeid en het Buitenlands Beleid, 1945–1973." *BMGN* 10, no. 1: 38–51.

Boulding, Kenneth, and Tapan Mukerjee, eds. 1972. *Economic Imperialism*. Ann Arbor: University of Michigan Press.

Boxer, C. R. 1965. *The Dutch Seaborne Empire*. London: Penguin.

Brada, Josef. 1988. "Interpreting the Soviet Subsidization of Eastern Europe." *IO* 42, no. 4: 639–58.

Bradley, David, Evelyne Huber, Stephanie Moller, Francois Nielsen, and John Stephens. 2003. "Distribution and Redistribution in Postindustrial Democracies." *World Politics* 55, no. 2: 193–228.

Bragança, Aquino de. 1988. "Independence without Decolonization: Mozambique, 1974–1975." In Prosser Gifford and William Louis, eds., *Decolonization and African Independence*. New Haven: Yale University Press.

Bremmer, Ian. 1994. "Nazarbaev and the North: State-Building and Ethnic Relations in Kazakhstan." *Ethnic and Racial Studies* 17, no. 4: 619–35.

Bremmer, Ian, and Ray Taras, eds. 1993. *Nations and Politics in the Soviet Successor States*. New York: Cambridge University Press.

Breslauer, George. 1987. "Ideology and Learning in Soviet Third World Policy." *World Politics* 39, no. 3: 429–48.

Breslauer, George, and Philip Tetlock, eds. 1991. *Learning in U.S. and Soviet Foreign Policy*. Boulder, Colo.: Westview.

Brett, Michael. 1994. "Anglo-Saxon Attitudes: The Algerian War of Independence in Retrospect." *Journal of African History* 35, no. 3: 217–35.

Bridge, Carl. 1976. "Conservatism and Indian Reform, 1929–39: Towards a Prerequisites Model in Imperial Constitution-Making?" *JICH* 4, no. 2: 176–93.

Brown, Judith, and William Roger Louis, eds. 1999. *Oxford History of the British Empire*, vol. 4: *The Twentieth Century*. Oxford: Oxford University Press.

Browne, Eric, and Keith Hamm. 1996. "Legislative Politics and the Paradox of Voting: Electoral Reform in Fourth Republic France." *British Journal of Political Science* 26: 165–98.

Brubaker, Rogers. 1992. *Citizenship and Nationhood in France and Germany*. Cambridge: Harvard University Press.

——. 1994. "Nationhood and the National Question in the Soviet Union and Post-Soviet Eurasia: An Institutionalist Account." *Theory and Society* 23: 47–78.

Bruce, Neil. 1975. *Portugal: The Last Empire*. New York: John Wiley.

Brugmans, I. J. 1977. "De ontwikkeling van de Nationalistische Beweging in Nederlands-Indië." *BMGN* 92, no. 2: 300–307.

Bunce, Valerie. 1985. "The Empire Strikes Back: The Transformation of the Eastern Bloc from a Soviet Asset to a Soviet Liability." *IO* 39, no. 1: 1–46.

——. 1993. "Domestic Reform and International Change: The Gorbachev Reforms in Historical Perspective." *IO* 47, no. 1: 107–38.

——. 1999. *Subversive Institutions*. New York: Cambridge University Press.

Burk, James. 2002. "Theories of Democratic Civil-Military Relations." *Armed Forces and Society* 29, no. 1: 7–29.

Butler, D. E., and Richard Rose. 1960. *The British General Election of 1959*. New York: St. Martin's.

Butt, Ronald. 1966. "The Common Market and Conservative Party Politics, 1961–62." *Government and Opposition* 2: 372–86.

Campo, Joep à. 1980. "Orde, Rust en Welvaart: Over de Nederlandse Expansie in de Indische Archipel omstreeks 1900." *Acta Politica* 15, no. 2: 145–89.

Caulfield, Max. 1995. *The Easter Rebellion*. Boulder, Colo.: Roberts Rhinehart.

Cell, John. 1980. "On the Eve of Decolonization: The Colonial Office's Plans for the Transfer of Power in Africa, 1947." *JICH* 8, no. 3: 233–57.

Cerqueira, Silas. 1973. "L'Église Catholique et la dictature corporatiste portugaise." *Revue française de science politique* 23, no. 3: 473–513.

Challener, Richard. 1994. "Dulles and De Gaulle." In Paxton and Wahl, eds., *De Gaulle and the United States*.

Chamberlain, Muriel. 1998. *European Decolonization in the Twentieth Century.* New York: Longman.
——. 1999. *Decolonization.* Oxford: Blackwell.
Chesnaux, Jean. 1969. "The Historical Background of Vietnamese Communism." *Government and Opposition* 4, no. 1: 118–35.
Chonchirdsin, Sud. 1997. "The Indochinese Communist Party and the Nam Ky Uprising in Cochin China, November-December 1940." *South East Asia Research* 5, no. 3: 269–93.
Churchward, L. G. 1975. *Contemporary Soviet Government.* London: Routledge and Kegan Paul.
Cipolla, Carlo. 1965. *Guns, Sails, and Empires.* Manhattan, Kan.: Sunflower Press.
Clayton, Anthony. 1988. *France, Soldiers, and Africa.* London: Brassey's Defence Publishers.
——. 1999. " 'Deceptive Might': Imperial Defence and Security, 1900–1968." In Brown and Louis, eds., Oxford History, vol. 4.
· Colton, Timothy. 1990. "Perspectives on Civil-Military Relations in the Soviet Union." In Timothy Colton and Thane Gustafson, eds., *Soldiers and the Soviet State.* Princeton: Princeton University Press.
Colton, Timothy, and Robert Tucker, eds. 1995. *Patterns in Post-Soviet Leadership.* Boulder, Colo.: Westview.
Connor, Walker. 1992. "Soviet Policies toward the Non-Russian Peoples in Theoretic and Historic Perspective: What Gorbachev Inherited." In Motyl, ed., *Post-Soviet Nations.*
Cooley, Alexander. 2000–2001. "Imperial Wreckage: Property Rights, Sovereignty, and Security in the Post-Soviet Space." *International Security* 25, no. 3: 100–27.
Coquery-Vidrovitch, Catherine. 1975. "L'Impact des interets coloniaux: S.C.O.A. et C.F.A.O. dans L'Ouest Africain, 1910–1965." *Journal of African History* 16, no. 4: 595–621.
Cowen, Mike. 1984. "Early Years of the Colonial Development Corporation: British State Enterprise Overseas during Late Colonialism." *African Affairs* 83, no. 330: 63–75.
Cowhey, Peter. 1993a. "Domestic Institutions and the Credibility of International Commitments: Japan and the United States." *IO* 47, no. 2: 299–326.
——. 1993b. "Elect Locally–Order Globally: Domestic Politics and Multilateral Cooperation." In John Ruggie, ed., *Multilateralism Matters.* New York: Columbia University Press.
Cox, Gary. 1997. *Making Votes Count.* New York: Cambridge University Press.
Crepaz, Markus. 2002. "Global, Constitutional, and Partisan Determinants of Redistribution in Fifteen OECD Countries." *Comparative Politics* 34, no. 2: 169–88.
Critchley, Julian. 1961. "The Intellectuals." *Political Quarterly* 32, no. 3: 267–74.
Daalder, Hans. 1989. "The Mould of Dutch Politics: Themes for Comparative Inquiry." *West European Politics* 12, no. 1: 1–20.
Daalder, Hans, and Galen Irwin, eds. 1989. Special issue on "Politics in the Netherlands." *West European Politics* 12, no. 1: 1–188.
Dabrowksi, Marek, and Rafal Antczak. 1996. "Economic Transition in Russia, Ukraine, and Belarus: A Comparative Perspective." In Bartlomiej Kaminski, ed., *Economic Transition in Russia and the New States of Eurasia.* Armonk, N.Y.: M. E. Sharpe.
Dallek, Robert. 1994. "Roosevelt and De Gaulle." In Paxton and Wahl, eds., *De Gaulle and the United States.*
Danchev, Alex. 1996. "Waltzing with Winston: Civil-Military Relations in Britain in the Second World War." In Smith, ed., Government and the Armed Forces in Britain.
Dar, Yechezkel, Shaul Kimhi, Nurit Stadler, and Alek Epstein. 2000. "The Imprint of the *Intifada:* Response of Kibbutz-Born Soldiers to Military Service in the West Bank and Gaza." *Armed Forces and Society* 26, no. 2: 285–311.

Davidson, Basil. 1974. "Victory and Reconciliation in Guinea-Bissau." *Africa Today* 21, no. 4: 5–20.

Dawisha, Karen. 1997. "Constructing and Deconstructing Empire in the Post-Soviet Space." In Dawisha and Parrott, eds., *End of Empire?*

Dawisha, Karen, and Bruce Parrott. 1994. *Russia and the New States of Eurasia.* New York: Cambridge University Press.

———. eds. 1997. *The End of Empire? The Transformation of the USSR in Comparative Perspective.* Armonk, N.Y.: M. E. Sharpe.

de Gaulle, Charles. 1971. *Memoirs of Hope: Renewal and Endeavor.* New York: Simon and Schuster.

de Jong, L. 1988. *Het Koninkrijk der Nederlanden in the Tweede Wereldoorlog.* 12 vols. The Hague: SDU.

D'Encausse, Hélène Carrère. 1992. *The Great Challenge.* London: Holmes and Meier.

Desch, Michael. 1993. "Why the Soviet Military Supported Gorbachev But Why the Russian Military Might Only Support Yeltsin for a Price." *Journal of Strategic Studies* 16, no. 4: 455–89.

———. 1999. *Civilian Control of the Military.* Baltimore: Johns Hopkins University Press.

Deudney, Daniel, and G. John Ikenberry. 1991–92. "The International Sources of Soviet Change." *International Security* 16, no. 3: 74–118.

Devillers, Philippe. 1974. "La Fin d'une 'guerre d'Indochine' (1954)." *Revue française de science politique* 24, no. 2: 295–308.

Diamond, Larry, and Marc Plattner, eds. 1996. *The Global Resurgence of Democracy.* Baltimore: Johns Hopkins University Press.

Doron, Gideon, and Michael Harris. 2000. *Public Policy and Electoral Reform.* Lanham, Md.: Lexington Books.

Dow, Jay. 2001. "A Comparative Spatial Analysis of Majoritarian and Proportional Elections." *Electoral Studies* 20: 109–25.

Downs, Anthony. 1957. *An Economic Theory of Democracy.* New York: Harper and Row.

Doyle, Michael. 1986. *Empires.* Ithaca: Cornell University Press.

Dragnich, Alex, and Jorgen Rasmussen. 1974. *Major European Governments.* Homewood, Ill.: Dorsey Press.

Drobizheva, Leokadia. 1992. "Perestroika and the Ethnic Consciousness of Russians." In Lapidus, Zaslavsky, and Goldman, eds., *From Union to Commonwealth.*

Drooglever, P. J. 1987. "Mars in Beweging: Denkbeelden Over Legerhervorming in het Tijdvak van de Dekolonisatie." In Teitler and Groen, eds., *De Politionele Acties.*

———. 1992. "De Vrijheid Vanuit Ambons Perspectief." In G. J. Knaap, W. Manuhutu, and H. Smeets, eds., *Sedjarah Maluku.* Amsterdam: Van Soeren.

———. 1997. "The Genesis of the Indonesian Constitution of 1949." *BTLV* 153, no. 1: 65–84.

Duffield, John. 1992. "The Soviet Military Threat to Western Europe: U.S. Estimates in the 1950s and 1960s." *Journal of Strategic Studies* 15, no. 2: 208–27.

Dunlop, John. 1993a. *The Rise of Russia and the Fall of the Soviet Empire.* Princeton: Princeton University Press.

———. 1993b. "Russia: Confronting a Loss of Empire." In Bremmer and Taras, eds., *Nations and Politics.*

Duverger, Maurice. 1980. "A New Political System Model: Semi-Presidential Government." *European Journal of Political Research* 8: 165–87.

Duynstee, F. J., and J. Bosmans. 1977. *Parlementaire Geschiedenis van Nederland na 1945: Het Kabinet Schermerhorn-Drees.* Amsterdam: van Gorcum.

Easter, Gerald. 1997. "Preference for Presidentialism: Postcommunist Regime Change in Russia and the NIS." *World Politics* 49, no. 2: 184–211.

Ebinger, Charles. 1976. "External Intervention in Internal War: The Politics and Diplomacy of the Angolan Civil War." *Orbis* 20, no. 3: 669–99.

Eckstein, Harry. 1975. "Case Study and Theory in Political Science." In Fred Greenstein and Nelson Polsby, eds., *Handbook of Political Science.* Vol. 7. Reading, Mass.: Addison-Wesley.

Eisenstadt, S. N. 1995. "Center-Periphery Relations in the Soviet Empire: Some Interpretive Observations." In Motyl, ed., *Thinking Theoretically.*

Elazar, Daniel, and Ben Mollov. 2001. "Introduction: Elections 1999—The Interplay between Character, Political Culture, and Centrism." *Israel Affairs* 7, no. 2–3: 1–17.

Elazar, Daniel, and Shmuel Sandler, eds. 1995. *Israel at the Polls, 1992.* Lanham, Md.: Rowman and Littlefield.

Elman, Colin. 1996. "Horses for Courses: Why Not Neorealist Theories of Foreign Policy?" *Security Studies* 6, no. 1: 7–51.

Elman, Miriam Fendius. 1995. "The Foreign Policies of Small States: Challenging Neo-Realism in Its Own Backyard." *British Journal of Political Science* 25, no. 2: 171–217.

——. 1997. *Paths to Peace: Is Democracy the Answer?* Cambridge: MIT Press.

Elon, Amos. 2002. "No Exit." *New York Review of Books.* May 23.

Elster, Jon. 1989. *Nuts and Bolts.* New York: Cambridge University Press.

——. 1997. "Afterword: The Making of Postcommunist Presidencies." In Taras, ed., *Postcommunist Presidents.*

Emerson, Rupert. 1960. *From Empire to Nation.* Cambridge: Harvard University Press.

Evangelista, Matthew. 1996. "Stalin's Revenge: Institutional Barriers to Internationalization in the Soviet Union." In Keohane and Milner, eds., *Internationalization and Domestic Politics.*

Fasseur, C. 1984. "Nederland en het Indonesische nationalisme: De Balans Nog Eens Opgemaakt." *BMGN* 99, no. 1: 21–44.

Fay, Peter. 1993. *The Forgotten Army.* Ann Arbor: University of Michigan Press.

Feaver, Peter. 1996. "The Civil-Military Problematique: Huntington, Janowitz, and the Question of Civilian Control." *Armed Forces and Society* 23, no. 2: 149–78.

——. 1999. "Civil-Military Relations." *Annual Review of Political Science* 2: 211–41.

Ferguson, A. J. 1963. "Constitutional Development in Portuguese Africa." *International Bulletin* 1, no. 5: 126–30.

Ferreira, Eduardo de Sousa. 1974. "The Present Role of the Portuguese Resettlement Policy." *Africa Today* 21, no. 1: 47–55.

Fieldhouse, David. 1971. "The Economic Exploitation of Africa: Some British and French Comparisons." In Prosser Gifford and William Roger Louis, eds., France and Britain in Africa. New Haven: Yale University Press.

Forrest, Joshua. 1992. *Guinea-Bissau: Power, Conflict, and Renewal in a West African Nation.* Boulder, Colo.: Westview.

Frank, Robert. 1986. "The French Dilemma: Modernization with Dependence or Independence and Decline." In Becker and Knipping, eds., *Power in Europe?*

Frasure, Robert. 1972. "Backbench Opinion Revisited: The Case of the Conservatives." *Political Studies* 20, no. 3: 325–28.

Friedberg, Aaron. 1988. *The Weary Titan.* Princeton: Princeton University Press.

Frieden, Jeffry. 1994. "International Investment and Colonial Control." *IO* 48, no. 4: 559–94.

Frieden, Jeffry, and Ronald Rogowski. 1996. "The Impact of the International Economy on National Policies: An Analytical Overview." In Keohane and Milner, eds., *Internationalization and Domestic Politics.*

Friedland, Elaine. 1979. "Mozambican Nationalist Resistance, 1920–1940." *Transafrican Journal of History* 8, no. 2: 117–28.

Fry, Michael G. 1997. "Decolonization: Britain, France, and the Cold War." In Dawisha and Parrott, eds., *End of Empire?*

Furniss, Edgar. 1964. *De Gaulle and the French Army.* New York: Twentieth Century Fund.

Furnivall, J. S. 1941. *Progress and Welfare in Southeast Asia.* New York: Institute of Pacific Relations.

——. 1967 [1939]. *Netherlands India.* New York: Cambridge University Press.

Gaddis, John. 1986. "The Long Peace." *International Security* 10: 99–142.

Galbraith, John. 1968. "The 'Turbulent Frontier' as a Factor in British Expansion." *Comparative Studies in Society and History* 2: 150–68.

Geertz, Clifford. 1963. *Agricultural Involution.* Berkeley: University of California Press.

Gellner, Ernest. 1983. *Nations and Nationalism.* Ithaca: Cornell University Press.

Gelman, Harry. 1991. *Gorbachev and the Future of the Soviet Military Institution.* Adelphi Papers 258. London: Brassey's.

George, Alexander. 1979. "Case Studies and Theory Development: The Method of Structured, Focused Comparison." In Paul Lauren, ed., *Diplomacy: New Approaches in History, Theory, and Policy.* New York: Free Press.

George, Alexander, and Richard Smoke. 1974. *Deterrence in American Foreign Policy.* New York: Columbia University Press.

Gerbenzon, P., and N. Algra. 1975. *Voortgangh des Rechtes.* Groningen: Tjeenk Willink.

Ghosh, S. C. 1965. "Decision-Making and Power in the British Conservative Party: A Case Study of the Indian Problem, 1929–34." *Political Studies* 13, no. 2: 198–212.

Giebels, Lambert. 1996. *Beel: Van Vazal tot Onderkoning.* The Hague: SDU.

Gilbert, Martin. 1991. *Churchill.* New York: Henry Holt.

Gilpin, Robert. 1981. *War and Change in World Politics.* Cambridge: Cambridge University Press.

——. 1987. *The Political Economy of International Relations.* Princeton: Princeton University Press.

Girault, René. 1986. "The French Decision-Makers and Their Perception of French Power in 1948." In Becker and Knipping, eds., *Power in Europe?*

Gitelman, Zvi. 1992. "Development and Ethnicity in the Soviet Union." In Motyl, ed., *Post-Soviet Nations.*

Gladney, Dru. 1994. "Ethnic Identity in China: The New Politics of Difference." In William Joseph, ed., *China Briefing, 1994.* Boulder, Colo.: Westview.

Gleason, Gregory. 1993. "Uzbekistan: From Statehood to Nationhood." In Bremmer and Taras, eds., *Nations and Politics.*

Goldberg, Giora. 2001. "The Israeli Left in the 1999 Elections." *Israel Affairs* 7, no. 2–3: 21–36.

Goldgeier, James, and Michael McFaul. 1992. "A Tale of Two Worlds: Core and Periphery in the Post-Cold War Era." *IO* 46, no. 2: 467–92.

Goldstein, Judith. 1993. *Ideas, Interests, and American Trade Policy.* Ithaca: Cornell University Press.

Goldsworthy, David. 1970. "Conservatives and Decolonization: A Note on the Interpretation by Dan Horowitz." *African Affairs* 69, no. 276: 278–81.

——. 1990."Keeping Change within Bounds: Aspects of Colonial Policy during the Churchill and Eden Governments, 1951–57." *JICH* 18, no. 1: 81–108.

——. 1991. "Britain and the International Critics of British Colonialism, 1951–56." *Journal of Commonwealth and Comparative Politics* 29, no. 1: 1–24.

Good, Kenneth. 1976. "Settler Colonialism: Economic Development and Class Formation." *Journal of Modern African Studies* 14, no. 4: 597–620.

Goodin, Robert. 1982. "Banana Time in British Politics." *Political Studies* 30, no. 1: 42–58.

Gorbachev, Mikhail. 2000. *Gorbachev: On My Country and the World*. New York: Columbia University Press.

Gordon, Alec. 1983. "National Income of the Netherlands Indies." *Journal of Contemporary Asia* 13, no. 2: 243–49.

Goto, Ken'ichi. 1996. "Cooperation, Submission, and Resistance of Indigenous Elites of Southeast Asia in the Wartime Empire." In Peter Duus, Ramon Myers, and Mark Peattie, eds., *The Japanese Wartime Empire, 1931–45*. Princeton: Princeton University Press.

Gouda, Frances. 1994. "Visions of Empire: Changing American Perspectives on Dutch Colonial Rule in Indonesia between 1920 and 1942." *BMGN* 109, no. 2: 237–58.

Gourevitch, Peter. 1986. *Politics in Hard Times*. Ithaca: Cornell University Press.

Granberg, Alexander. 1993. "The Economic Interdependence of the Former Soviet Republics." In John Williamson, ed., *Economic Consequences of Soviet Disintegration*. Washington, D.C.: Institute for International Economics.

Green, Andrew. 1969. "Portugal and the African Colonies." In Abshire and Samuels, eds., *Portuguese Africa*.

Greenfeld, Liah. 1992. *Nationalism*. Cambridge: Harvard University Press.

Grieco, Joseph. 1988. "Anarchy and the Limits of Cooperation: A Realist Critique of the Newest Liberal Institutionalism." *IO* 42, no. 3: 485–507.

Gustafson, Thane, and Dawn Mann. 1986. "Gorbachev's First Year: Building Power and Authority." *Problems of Communism* 35, no. 3: 1–9.

Haggard, Stephan, and Robert Kaufmann. 1995. *The Political Economy of Democratic Transitions*. Princeton: Princeton University Press.

Hall, Peter, ed. 1989. *The Political Power of Economic Ideas*. Princeton: Princeton University Press.

———. 1992. "The Movement from Keynesianism to Monetarism: Institutional Analysis and British Economic Policy in the 1970s." In Steinmo, Thelen, and Longstreth, eds., *Structuring Politics*.

Hallerberg, Mark. 2002. "Veto Players and the Choice of Monetary Institutions." *IO* 56, no. 4: 775–802.

Hallerberg, Mark, and Scott Basinger. 1998. "Internationalization and Changes in Tax Policy in OECD Countries: The Importance of Domestic Veto Players." *Comparative Political Studies* 31, no. 3: 321–52.

Halpern, Nina. 1993. "Creating Socialist Economies: Stalinist Political Economy and the Impact of Ideas." In Judith Goldstein and Robert Keohane, eds., *Ideas and Foreign Policy*. Ithaca: Cornell University Press.

Hargreaves, John. 1996. *Decolonization in Africa*. New York: Longman.

Harris, Michael, and Gideon Doron. 1999. "Assessing the Electoral Reform of 1992 and Its Impact on the Elections of 1996 and 1999." *Israel Studies* 4, no. 2: 16–39.

Harsgor, Michael. 1980. "Aftereffects of an 'Exemplary Decolonization.' " *Journal of Contemporary History* 15, no. 1: 143–67.

Hazan, Reuven, and Abraham Diskin. 2000. "The 1999 Knesset Elections and Prime Ministerial Elections in Israel." *Electoral Studies* 19: 615–46.

Henley, David. 1993. "Nationalism and Regionalism in Colonial Indonesia: The Case of Minihasa." *Indonesia* 55: 91–112.

Hering, Bob. 1992. "Soekarno, the Man and the Myth: Looking through a Glass Darkly." *Modern Asian Studies* 26, no. 33: 495–506.

Herz, John. 1976. *The Nation-State and the Crisis of World Politics*. New York: David McKay.

Hill, John S. 1994. "Germany, the United States, and de Gaulle's Strategy for Economic Reconstruction, 1944–1946." In Paxton and Wahl, eds., *De Gaulle and the United States*.

Hill, Ronald. 1993. "The Soviet Union: From Federation to Commonwealth." In John Coakley, ed., *The Territorial Management of Ethnic Conflict*. London: Frank Cass.

Hind, Robert. 1984. " 'We Have No Colonies': Similarities within the British Imperial Experience." *Comparative Studies in Society and History* 26, no. 1: 3–35.

Hinsley, F. H. 1969. "The Concept of Sovereignty and the Relations between States." In W. Stankiewicz, ed., *In Defense of Sovereignty*. New York: Oxford University Press.

———. 1986. *Sovereignty*. Cambridge: Cambridge University Press.

Hirschman, Albert. 1980 [1945]. *National Power and the Structure of Foreign Trade*. Berkeley: University of California Press.

Hobsbawm, E. J. 1980. *Nations and Nationalism since 1780*. New York: Cambridge University Press.

Hobson, J. A. 1961 [1902]. "Imperialism: A Study." In Harrison Wright, ed., *The New Imperialism*. Lexington, Mass.: D. C. Heath.

Hofnung, Menachem. 2001. "The Peace Process and the Internationalization of Internal Legal Arrangements." In Sofer, ed., *Peacemaking in a Divided Society*.

Holloway, David. 1983. *The Soviet Union and the Arms Race*. New Haven: Yale University Press.

Holsti, Kalevi. 1991. *Peace and War: Armed Conflicts and International Order, 1648–1989*. New York: Cambridge University Press.

Homan, Gerlof. 1983. "American Business Interests in the Indonesian Republic, 1946–1949." *Indonesia* 35: 125–32.

———. 1984. "The United States and the Netherlands East Indies: The Evolution of American Anticolonialism." *Pacific Historical Review* 53: 423–46.

Hopkins, A. G. 1987. "Big Business in African Studies." *Journal of African History* 28: 119–40.

Horne, Alistair. 1978. *A Savage War of Peace: Algeria, 1954–1962*. New York: Viking Press.

Horowitz, Dan. 1970. "Attitudes of British Conservatives towards Decolonization in Africa." *African Affairs* 69, no. 274: 9–26.

Hough, Jerry. 1997. *Democratization and Revolution in the USSR, 1985–1991*. Washington, D.C.: Brookings Institution Press.

Hourani, Albert. 1991. *A History of the Arab Peoples*. Cambridge: Harvard University Press.

Howe, Stephen. 1993. *Anticolonialism in British Politics*. New York: Oxford University Press.

Huber, John. 1998. "Executive Decree Authority in France." In John Carey and Matthew Shugart, eds., *Executive Decree Authority*. New York: Cambridge University Press.

Huntington, Samuel. 1957. *The Soldier and the State*. Cambridge: Harvard University Press.

Hurewitz, J. C. 1979. *The Middle East and North Africa in World Politics: A Documentary Record*. Vol. 2. New Haven: Yale University Press.

Huskey, Gene. 1993. "Kyrgyzstan: The Politics of Demographic and Economic Frustration." In Bremmer and Taras, eds., *Nations and Politics*.

Hyam, Ronald. 1988. "Africa and the Labour Government, 1945–51." *JICH* 16, no. 3: 148–72.

Ikenberry, G. John. 1988. "Market Solutions for State Problems: The International and Domestic Politics of Amerian Oil Decontrol." *IO* 42, no. 1: 151–77.

———. 2001. *After Victory*. Princeton: Princeton University Press.

Immergut, Ellen. 1992. *Health Politics: Interests and Institutions in Western Europe*. Cambridge: Cambridge University Press.

Inbar, Efraim. 2002. "Israel's Strategic Environment in the 1990s." *Journal of Strategic Studies* 25, no. 1: 21–38.

International Monetary Fund. 1992. *Common Issues and Interrepublic Relations in the Former USSR*. Washington, D.C.

Irwin, Galen, and Joop Holsteyn. 1989. "Decline of the Structured Model of Electoral Competition." *West European Politics* 12, no. 1: 21–41.

Jackson, Robert. 1987. "Quasi States, Dual Regimes, and Neo-Classical Theory: International Jurisprudence and the Third World." *IO* 41, no. 4: 519–49.

——. 1993. "The Weight of Ideas in Decolonization: Normative Change in International Relations." In Judith Goldstein and Robert Keohane, eds., *Ideas and Foreign Policy.* Ithaca: Cornell University Press.

James, Lawrence. 1994. *The Rise and Fall of the British Empire.* New York: St. Martin's.

Jentleson, Bruce, Ariel Levite, and Larry Berman. 1993. "Protracted Foreign Military Intervention: A Structured, Focused Comparative Analysis." In Dan Caldwell and Timothy McKeown, eds., *Diplomacy, Force, and Leadership.* Boulder, Colo.: Westview.

Jervis, Robert. 1976. *Perception and Misperception in International Politics.* Princeton: Princeton University Press.

——. 1989. *The Meaning of the Nuclear Revolution.* Ithaca: Cornell University Press.

——. 1995. "Navies, Politics, and Political Science." In John Hattendorf, ed., *Doing Naval History.* Newport, R.I.: Naval War College Press.

——. 1997. *System Effects.* Princeton: Princeton University Press.

Kagalovsky, Konstantin. 1990. "Economic Crisis in the USSR." *Communist Economies* 2, no. 3: 315–23.

Kahin, Audrey. 1983. "Brokers and Middlemen in Indonesian History." *Indonesia* 36: 135–42.

Kahler, Miles. 1981. "Political Regime and Economic Actors." *World Politics* 33, no. 3: 383–412.

——. 1984. *Decolonization in Britain and France.* Princeton: Princeton University Press.

——. 1997. "Empires, Neo-Empires, and Political Change: The British and French Experience." In Dawisha and Parrott, eds., *The End of Empire?*

Kaiser, Robert. 1994. *The Geography of Nationalism in Russia and the USSR.* Princeton: Princeton University Press.

Katzenstein, Peter, ed. 1978. *Between Power and Plenty.* Madison: University of Wisconsin Press.

——. 1985. *Small States in World Markets.* Ithaca: Cornell University Press.

——. 1987. *Policy and Politics in West Germany.* Philadelphia: Temple University Press.

Katznelson, Ira. 1997. "Structure and Configuration in Comparative Politics." In Mark Lichbach and Alan Zuckerman, eds., *Comparative Politics: Rationality, Culture, and Structure.* New York: Cambridge University Press.

——. 1998. "The Doleful Dance of Politics and Policy: Can Historical Institutionalism Make a Difference?" *APSR* 92, no. 1: 191–97.

Keay, John. 1997. *Empire's End.* New York: Scribner's.

Keefe, Eugene, et al. 1977. *Area Handbook for Portugal.* Washington, D.C.: U.S. Government Printing Office.

Keene, Edward. 2002. *Beyond the Anarchical Society.* New York: Cambridge University Press.

Kennedy, Paul. 1985. "The First World War and the International Power System." In Steven Miller, ed., *Military Strategy and the Origins of the First World War.* Princeton: Princeton University Press.

Keohane, Robert. 1984. *After Hegemony.* Princeton: Princeton University Press.

——, ed. 1986. *Neorealism and Its Critics.* New York: Columbia University Press.

——. 1987. "Power and Interdependence Revisited." *IO* 41, no. 4: 725–53.

Keohane, Robert, and Helen Milner, eds. 1996. *Internationalization and Domestic Politics.* New York: Cambridge University Press.

Keohane, Robert, and Joseph Nye. 1977. *Power and Interdependence: World Politics in Transition.* Boston: Little Brown.

Khazanov, Anatoly. 1995. *After the USSR.* Madison: University of Wisconsin Press.
——. 1997. "Ethnic Federalism in the Russian Federation." *Daedalus* 126, no. 3: 121–42.
Kier, Elizabeth. 1997. *Imagining War.* Princeton: Princeton University Press.
Kimball, Warren. 1991. *The Juggler.* Princeton: Princeton University Press.
Kindleberger, Charles. 1973. *The World in Depression, 1929–1939.* Berkeley: University of California Press.
King, Gary, Robert Keohane, and Sidney Verba. 1994. *Designing Social Inquiry.* Princeton: Princeton University Press.
Klein, P. W. 1981. "Wegen Naar Economisch Herstel, 1945–1950." *BMGN* 96, no. 2: 260–76.
Kohl, Wilfrid. 1971. *French Nuclear Diplomacy.* Princeton: Princeton University Press.
Kohler, Beate. 1981. *Politischer Umbruch in Südeuropa.* Bonn: Europa Union.
Kokoshin, Andrei. 1998. *Soviet Strategic Thought.* Cambridge: MIT Press.
Kornberg, Allan, and Robert Frasure. 1971. "Policy Differences in British Parliamentary Parties." *APSR* 65, no. 3: 694–703.
Kupchan, Charles. 1994. *The Vulnerability of Empire.* Ithaca: Cornell University Press.
Laitin, David. 1991. "The National Uprisings in the Soviet Union." *World Politics* 44, no. 1: 139–77.
Lake, David. 1988. *Power, Protection, and Free Trade.* Ithaca: Cornell University Press.
——. 1996. "Anarchy, Hierarchy, and the Variety of International Relations." *IO* 50, no. 1: 1–34.
——. 1999. *Entangling Relations.* Princeton: Princeton University Press.
Lane, David. 1992. *Soviet Society under Perestroika.* New York: Routledge.
——. 1996. "The Gorbachev Revolution: The Role of the Political Elite in Regime Disintegration." *Political Studies* 44, no. 1: 4–23.
Lapidus, Gail. 1992. "From Democratization to Disintegration: The Impact of Perestroika on the National Question." In Lapidus, Zasklavsky, and Goldman, eds., *From Union to Commonwealth.*
——. 1996. "A Comment on 'Russia and the Russian Diasporas.' " *Post-Soviet Affairs* 12, no. 3: 285–87.
Lapidus, Gail, Victor Zaslavsky, and Philip Goldman, eds. 1992. *From Union to Commonwealth: Nationalism and Separatism in the Soviet Republics.* New York: Cambridge University Press.
Laver, Michael. 1997. *Private Desires and Political Action.* Thousand Oaks, Calif.: Sage.
Laver, Michael, and Norman Schofield. 1998. *Multiparty Government.* Ann Arbor: University of Michigan Press.
Lavy, Victor. 2001. "Regional Conflict, Country Risk, and Foreign Direct Investment in the Middle East." In Sofer, ed., *Peacemaking in a Divided Society.*
Lee, J. M. 1977. " 'Forward Thinking' and War: The Colonial Office during the 1940s." *JICH* 6, no. 1: 64–76.
Legvold, Robert. 1991. "Soviet Learning in the 1980s." In Breslauer and Tetlock, eds., *Learning in U.S. and Soviet Foreign Policy.*
Lenin, V. I. 1939 [1916]. *Imperialism: The Highest Stage of Capitalism.* New York: International Publishers.
Lepingwell, Joseph. 1992. "Soviet Civil-Military Relations and the August Coup." *World Politics* 44, no. 4: 539–72.
Lev, Daniel. 1985. "Colonial Law and the Genesis of the Indonesian State." *Indonesia* 40: 57–74.
Levine, Alicia. 1994. "The Breakup of Multinational States: Why Do Democracies Fight?" Ph.D. diss., University of Chicago.

Levita, Roman, and Mikhail Loiberg. 1994. "The Empire and the Russians." In Vladimir Shlapentokh, Munir Sendich, and Emil Payin, eds., *The New Russian Diaspora*. Armonk, N.Y.: M. E. Sharpe.

Lewis, Anthony. 2000. "Is There a Solution?" *New York Review of Books*. April 25.

Lewis, Archibald, and Timothy Runyan. 1985. *European Naval and Maritime History, 300–1500*. Bloomington: Indiana University Press.

Liberman, Peter. 1996. *Does Conquest Pay?* Princeton: Princeton University Press.

Lieberson, Stanley. 1992. "Small N's and Big Conclusions: An Examination of the Reasoning in Comparative Studies Based on a Small Number of Cases." In Charles Ragin and Howard Becker, eds., *What Is a Case?* New York: Cambridge University Press.

Lieven, Anatol. 1993. *The Baltic Revolution*. New Haven: Yale University Press.

Lijphart, Arend. 1968. *The Politics of Accommodation: Pluralism and Democracy in the Netherlands*. Berkeley: University of California Press.

——. 1971. "Comparative Politics and the Comparative Method." *APSR* 65, no. 3: 682–93.

——. 1977. *Democracy in Plural Societies*. New Haven: Yale University Press.

——. 1989a. "Democratic Political Systems: Types, Cases, Causes, and Consequences." *Journal of Theoretical Politics* 1, no. 1: 33–48.

——. 1989b. "From the Politics of Accommodation to Adversarial Politics in the Netherlands: A Reassessment." *West European Politics* 12, no. 1: 139–53.

——. 1993. "Israeli Democracy and Democratic Reform in Comparative Perspective." In Ehud Sprinzak and Larry Diamond, eds., *Israeli Democracy under Stress*. Boulder, Colo.: Lynne Rienner.

——. 1994. *Electoral Systems and Party Systems*. Oxford: Oxford University Press.

——. 1996. "The Puzzle of Indian Democracy: A Consociational Interpretation." *APSR* 90, no. 2: 258–68.

Lindblad, Thomas. 1989. "Economic Aspects of the Dutch Expansion in Indonesia, 1870–1914." *Modern Asian Studies* 23, no. 1: 1–23.

Linz, Juan. 1996. "The Perils of Presidentialism." In Diamond and Plattner, eds., *The Global Resurgence of Democracy*.

Lipson, Charles. 1985. *Standing Guard*. Berkeley: University of California Press.

Lissak, Moshe. 2001. "The Unique Approach to Military-Societal Relations in Israel and Its Impact on Foreign and Security Policy." In Sofer, ed., *Peacemaking in a Divided Society*.

Lister, John. 2002. " 'Middle' Politics: Looking Again at the Peace Process." *Middle East Policy* 9, no. 3: 22–33.

Little, Daniel. 1991. *Varieties of Social Explanation*. Boulder, Colo.: Westview.

Lloyd, Selwyn. 1978. *Suez 1956*. New York: Mayflower.

Lloyd, T. O. 1993. *Empire, Welfare State, Europe: English History, 1906–1992*. New York: Oxford University Press.

Lochery, Neill. 2000. "The Netanyahu Era: From Crisis to Crisis, 1996–99." *Israel Affairs* 6, no. 3–4: 221–37.

Loriaux, Michael. 1991. *France after Hegemony*. Ithaca: Cornell University Press.

Louis, William Roger. 1999. "Introduction." In Brown and Louis, Oxford History, vol. 4.

Low, Anthony. 1991. *Eclipse of Empire*. Cambridge: Cambridge University Press.

Lowi, Theodore, and Martin Schain. 1992. "Conditional Surrender: Charles de Gaulle and American Opinion." *PS: Political Science and Politics* 25, no. 3: 498–506.

Lukauskas, Arvid. 1997. *Regulating Finance*. Ann Arbor: University of Michigan Press.

Lustick, Ian. 1993. *Unsettled States, Disputed Lands*. Ithaca: Cornell University Press.

Lynskey, James. 1973. "Backbench Tactics and Parliamentary Party Structure." *Parliamentary Affairs* 27: 28–43.

Maas, P. F. 1982. "Dr. H. J. van Mook, Onze Laatste Landvoogd, tot Ontslag Gedwongen (Augustus/October 1948)." *Acta Politica* 17, no. 3: 367–84.
Maas, P. F., and J. E. van Oerle. 1987. "Het Leger te Gelde." In Teitler and Groen, eds., *De Politionele Acties.*
MacFarquhar, Roderick. 1997. "India: The Imprint of Empire." *New York Review of Books.* October 23.
MacIntyre, Andrew. 2001. "Institutions and Investors: The Politics of the Economic Crisis in Southeast Asia." *IO* 55, no. 1: 81–122.
———. 2003. *The Power of Institutions.* Ithaca: Cornell University Press.
Mack, Andrew. 1975. "Why Big Nations Lose Small Wars: The Politics of Asymmetric Conflict." *World Politics* 27, no. 2: 175–200.
MacRae, Duncan. 1967. *Parliament, Parties, and Society in France, 1946–1958.* New York: St. Martin's.
Maddison, Angus. 1989. "Dutch Income in and from Indonesia, 1700–1938." *Modern Asian Studies* 23, no. 4: 645–70.
———. 1990. "Dutch Colonialism in Indonesia: A Comparative Perspective." In Anne Booth, W. J. O'Malley, and Anna Weidemann, eds., *Indonesian Economic History in the Dutch Colonial Era.* New Haven: Yale University South East Asian Studies.
Mahoney, James. 2003. "Strategies of Causal Assessment in Comparative Historical Analysis." In James Mahoney and Dietrich Rueschemeyer, eds., *Comparative Historical Analysis in the Social Sciences.* New York: Cambridge University Press.
Mahoney, Richard. 1983. *JFK: Ordeal in Africa.* New York: Oxford University Press.
Mainwaring, Scott, and Matthew Shugart. 1997. "Juan Linz, Presidentialism, and Democracy: A Critical Appraisal." *Comparative Politics* 29, no. 4: 449–71.
Makler, Harry. 1979. "The Portuguese Industrial Elite and Its Corporative Relations: A Study of Compartmentalization in an Authoritarian Regime." In Lawrence Graham and Harry Makler, eds., *Contemporary Portugal.* Austin: University of Texas Press.
Mandelbaum, Michael, ed. 1994. *Central Asia and the World.* New York: Council on Foreign Relations Press.
Mansergh, Nicholas. 1969. *The Commonwealth Experience.* New York: Praeger.
Marcus, Jonathan. 1992. "Israel's General Election: Realignment or Upheaval?" *Israel Affairs* 68, no. 4: 693–705.
Marseille, Jacques. 1976. "Commerce international et termes de l'échange." *RFHOM* 63, no. 232: 529–37.
———. 1984. *Empire coloniale et capitalisme français.* Paris: Albin Michel.
———. 1985. "The Phases of French Colonial Imperialism: Towards a New Periodization." *JICH* 13, no. 3: 127–41.
Marshall, Bruce. 1973. *The French Colonial Myth and Constitution-Making in the Fourth Republic.* New Haven: Yale University Press.
Martin, Lisa. 2000. *Democratic Commitments.* Princeton: Princeton University Press.
Martin, Lisa, and Beth Simmons. 1998. "Theories and Empirical Studies of International Institutions." *IO* 52, no. 4: 729–57.
Martins, Herminio. 1969. "Opposition in Portugal." *Government and Opposition* 4, no. 2: 250–63.
Matlock, Jack. 1995. *Autopsy of an Empire.* New York: Random House.
Mattli, Walter. 1999. *The Logic of Regional Integration.* New York: Cambridge University Press.
Maxwell, Kenneth. 1976. "The Thorns of the Portuguese Revolution." *Foreign Affairs* 54, no. 2: 250–70.
———. 1995. *The Making of Portuguese Democracy.* New York: Cambridge University Press.

Mayall, James. 1990. *Nationalism and International Society.* New York: Cambridge University Press.

McNeill, William. 1982. *The Pursuit of Power.* Chicago: University of Chicago Press.

McVey, Ruth. 1966. "Semaun: An Early Account of the Independence Movement." *Indonesia* 1: 46–75.

Meadwell, Hudson, and Pierre Martin. 1994. "Economic Integration and the Politics of Independence in the Developed West." Paper presented at American Political Science Association annual conference, New York.

Mearsheimer, John. 1983. *Conventional Deterrence.* Ithaca: Cornell University Press.

——. 1990. "Back to the Future." *International Security* 15, no. 1: 5–56

Medish, Mark. 1994. "Russia: Lost and Found." *Daedalus* 123, no. 3: 63–89.

Medvedev, Roy. 1975. *On Socialist Democracy.* New York: W. W. Norton.

Mendelson, Sarah. 1993. "Internal Battles and External Wars: Politics, Learning, and the Soviet Withdrawal from Afghanistan." *World Politics* 45, no. 3: 327–60.

Mendes, Hugo Fernandes. 1989. "Suriname: Military Threat and the Restoration of Democracy." *Internationale Spectator* 4, no. 11: 662–68.

Menon, Rajan. 1995. "In the Shadow of the Bear: Security in Post-Soviet Central Asia." *International Security* 20, no. 1: 149–81.

Menon, Rajan, and Hendrik Spruyt. 1997. "Possibilities for Conflict and Conflict Resolution in Post-Soviet Central Asia." In Barnett Rubin and Jack Snyder, eds., *Post-Soviet Political Order.* New York: Routledge.

——. 1999. "The Limits of Neorealism: Understanding Security in Central Asia." *Review of International Studies* 25: 87–105.

Merom, Gil. 1999. "A 'Grand Design'? Charles de Gaulle and the End of the Algerian War." *Armed Forces and Society* 25, no. 2: 267–88.

Meyer, Stephen. 1991–92. "How the Threat (and the Coup) Collapsed: The Politicization of the Soviet Military." *International Security* 16, no. 3: 5–38.

Michel, Marc. 1973. "Les Recrutements de tirailleurs en A.O.F. pendant première guerre mondiale: Essai de bilan statistique." *RFHOM* 60, no. 221: 640–60.

Mickelsen, Martin. 1976. "Another Fashoda: The Anglo–Free French Conflict over the Levant, May–September 1941." *RFHOM* 63, no. 230: 75–100.

Miles, Gary. 1990. "Roman and Modern Imperialism: A Reassessment." *Comparative Studies of Society and History* 32, no. 4: 629–59.

Miller, John. 1977. "Cadres Policy in Nationality Areas: Recruitment of First and Second Secretaries in Non-Russian Republics of the USSR." *Soviet Studies* 29, no. 1: 3–36.

Milner, Helen. 1987. "Resisting the Protectionist Temptation: Industry and the Making of Trade Policy in France and the United States during the 1970s." *IO* 41, no. 4: 639–66.

——. 1997. *Interests, Institutions, and Information.* Princeton: Princeton University Press.

——. 1998. "Rationalizing Politics: The Emerging Synthesis of International, American, and Comparative Politics." *IO* 52, no. 4: 759–86.

Minter, William. 1972. *Portuguese Africa and the West.* New York: Monthly Review.

Moe, Terry, and Michael Caldwell. 1994. "The Institutional Foundations of Democratic Government: A Comparison of Presidential and Parliamentary Systems." *Journal of Institutional and Theoretical Economics* 150, no. 1: 171–95.

Moodie, Graeme. 1971. *The Government of Great Britain.* London: Methuen.

Morris, Benny. 1996. "Israel's Elections and Their Implications." *Journal of Palestine Studies* 26, no. 1: 70–81.

——. 2002a. "Camp David and After: An Exchange. Interview with Ehud Barak." *New York Review of Books.* June 13.

——. 2002b. "Camp David and After: Continued." *New York Review of Books.* June 27.

Motyl, Alexander, ed. 1992a. *The Post-Soviet Nations.* New York: Columbia University Press.

——. 1992b. "From Imperial Decay to Imperial Collapse: The Fall of the Soviet Empire in Comparative Perspective." In Richard Rudolph and David Good, eds., *Nationalism and Empire.* New York: St. Martin's.

——. 1993. "Imperial Collapse and Revolutionary Change: Austria-Hungary, Tsarist Russia, and the Soviet Empire in Theoretical Perspective." In Jurgen Nautz and Richard Vahrenkamp, eds., *Die Wiener Jahrhundertwende.* Cologne: Böhlau Verlag.

——, ed. 1995. *Thinking Theoretically about Soviet Nationalities.* New York: Columbia University Press.

Mueller, Dennis. 1989. *Public Choice II.* New York: Cambridge University Press.

Mueller, John. 1988. "The Essential Irrelevance of Nuclear Weapons: Stability in the Postwar World." *International Security* 13, no. 2: 55–79.

Murphy, Philip. 1995. *Party Politics and Decolonization.* Oxford: Clarendon.

Nailor, Peter. 1996. "The Ministry of Defence, 1959–1979." In Smith, ed., *Government and the Armed Forces.*

Narizny, Kevin. 2003. "The Political Economy of Alignment: Great Britain's Commitments to Europe, 1905–39." *International Security* 27, no. 4: 184–219.

Navias, Martin. 1996. " 'Vested Interests and Vanished Dreams': Duncan Sandys, the Chiefs of Staff, and the 1957 White Paper." In Smith, ed., *Government and the Armed Forces.*

Nee, Victor, and Peng Lian. 1994. "Sleeping with the Enemy: A Dynamic Modeling of Declining Political Commitment in State Socialism." *Theory and Society* 23, no. 2: 253–96.

Nettl, J. P. 1968. "The State as a Conceptual Variable." *World Politics* 20, no. 4: 559–92.

Neumann, Robert. 1960. *European and Comparative Government.* New York: McGraw-Hill.

Newitt, Malyn. 1981. *Portugal in Africa.* London: Longman.

Nissman, David. 1993. "Turkmenistan: Ancient Heritage, New Politics." In Bremmer and Taras, eds., *Nations and Politics.*

Norden, Deborah. 1996. *Military Rebellion in Argentina.* Lincoln: University of Nebraska Press.

Noren, James, and Robin Watson. 1992. "Interrepublican Economic Relations after the Disintegration of the USSR." *Soviet Economy* 8, no. 2: 89–129.

North, Douglas, and Robert Thomas. 1973. *The Rise of the Western World.* Cambridge: Cambridge University Press.

Nove, Alex. 1977. *The Soviet Economic System.* London: Allen and Unwin.

Nye, Joseph. 1987. "Nuclear Learning and U.S.-Soviet Security Regimes." *International Organization* 41, no. 3: 371–402.

Odom, William. 1985. "Soviet Force Posture: Dilemmas and Directions." *Problems of Communism* 34: 1–14.

——. 1998. *The Collapse of the Soviet Military.* New Haven: Yale University Press.

Ofer, Gur. 1988. *Soviet Economic Growth, 1928–1985.* Los Angeles: Rand/UCLA.

Olcott, Martha. 1993. "Kazakhstan: A Republic of Minorities." In Bremmer and Taras, eds., *Nations and Politics.*

Olson, Mancur. 1965. *The Logic of Collective Action.* Cambridge: Harvard University Press.

Oren, Michael. 2002. *Six Days of War.* New York: Oxford University Press.

Ottolenghi, Emanuele. 2001. "Why Direct Election Failed in Israel." *Journal of Democracy* 12, no. 4: 109–22.

Oye, Kenneth, ed. 1986. *Cooperation under Anarchy.* Princeton: Princeton University Press.

——. 1992. *Economic Discrimination and Political Exchange.* Princeton: Princeton University Press.

Packenham, Thomas. 1991. *The Scramble for Africa.* New York: Random House.

Paxton, Robert, and Nicholas Wahl. 1994. *De Gaulle and the United States*. Oxford: Berg.

Penders, Christiaan. 1977. *Indonesia: Selected Documents on Colonialism and Nationalism, 1830–1942*. St. Lucia, Australia: University of Queensland Press.

Petersen, Phillip, and Notra Trulock. 1988. "A 'New' Soviet Military Doctrine: Origins and Implications." *Strategic Review* 16, no. 3: 9–24.

Peterson, Susan, and Christopher Wenk. 2001. "Domestic Institutional Change and Foreign Policy." *Security Studies* 11, no. 1: 53–76.

Petro, Nicolai. 1995. *The Rebirth of Russian Democracy*. Cambridge: Harvard University Press.

Pierre, Andrew. 1994. "Conflicting Visions: Defense, Nuclear Weapons, and Arms Control in the Franco-American Relationship during the de Gaulle Era." In Paxton and Wahl, eds., *De Gaulle and the United States*.

Pimlott, Ben. 1977. "Socialism in Portugal: Was It a Revolution?" *Government and Opposition* 12, no. 3: 332–50.

Pinto, Antonio. 1991. *The Salazar "New State" and European Fascism*. San Domenico, Italy: European University Institute.

Pinto, Antonio, and Pedro de Almeida. 1998. "On Liberalism and the Emergence of Civil Society in Portugal." Paper presented at Princeton University.

Pinto-Duschinsky, Michael. 1972. "Central Office and 'Power' in the Conservative Party." *Political Studies* 20, no. 1: 1–16.

Polèse, Mario. 1985. "Economic Integration, National Policies, and the Rationality of Regional Separatism." In Ronald Rogowski and Edward Tiryakian, eds., *New Nationalisms in the Developed West*. London: Allen and Unwin.

Posen, Barry. 1984. *The Sources of Military Doctrine: France, Britain, and Germany between the World Wars*. Ithaca: Cornell University Press.

———. 1993. "Nationalism, the Mass Army, and Military Power." *International Security* 18, no. 2: 80–124.

Przeworski, Adam. 1991. *Democracy and the Market*. New York: Cambridge University Press.

———. 1995. "The Role of Theory in Comparative Politics: A Symposium." *World Politics* 4, no. 1: 1–49.

Pundak, Ron. 2001. "From Oslo to Taba: What Went Wrong?" *Survival* 4, no. 3: 31–45.

Putnam, Robert. 1988. "Diplomacy and Domestic Politics: The Logic of Two-Level Games." *IO* 42, no. 3: 427–60.

Quandt, William. 2001. "Clinton and the Arab-Israeli Conflict: The Limits of Incrementalism." *Journal of Palestine Studies* 30, no. 2: 26–40.

Raby, D. L. 1988. *Fascism and Resistance in Portugal*. Manchester: Manchester University Press.

Raeff, Marc. 1984. *Understanding Imperial Russia*. New York: Columbia University Press.

Reid, Anthony. 1974. *The Indonesian National Revolution, 1945–1950*. Westport, Conn.: Greenwood.

Rice, Condoleezza. 1987. "The Party, the Military, and Decision Authority in the Soviet Union." *World Politics* 40, no. 1: 55–81.

———. 1991. "The Evolution of Soviet Grand Strategy." In Paul Kennedy, ed., *Grand Strategies in War and Peace*. New Haven: Yale University Press.

Riker, William, and Steven Brams. 1973. "The Paradox of Vote Trading." *APSR* 67: 1235–1247.

Rioux, Jean Pierre. 1987. *The Fourth Republic, 1944–1958*. New York: Cambridge University Press.

Roeder, Philip. 1991. "Soviet Federalism and Ethnic Mobilization." *World Politics* 43, no. 2: 196–232.

——. 1993. *Red Sunset.* Princeton: Princeton University Press.

Rogowski, Ronald. 1987. "Trade and the Variety of Democratic Institutions." *IO* 41, no. 2: 203–24.

Rooth, Tim. 1992. *British Protectionism and the International Economy: Overseas Commercial Policy in the 1930s.* Cambridge: Cambridge University Press.

Rose, Gideon. 1998. "Neoclassical Realism and Theories of Foreign Policy." *World Politics* 51, no. 1: 144–72.

Rose, Richard. 1961a. "Tensions in Conservative Philosophy." *Political Quarterly* 32, no. 2: 275–83.

——. 1961b. "The Bow Group's Role in British Politics." *Western Political Quarterly* 14: 865–78.

——. 1964. "Parties, Factions, and Tendencies in Britain." *Political Studies* 12, no. 1: 33–46.

Rosecrance, Richard. 1986. *The Rise of the Trading State: Commerce and Conquest in the Modern World.* New York: Basic Books.

Rubin, Barnett. 1993–94. "The Fragmentation of Tajikistan." *Survival* 35, no. 4: 71–91.

——. 1994. "Tajikistan: From Soviet Republic to Russian-Uzbek Protectorate." In Mandelbaum, ed., *Central Asia.*

Rutland, Peter. 1994. "The Economy: The Rocky Road from Plan to Market." In Stephen White, Alex Pravda, and Zvi Gitelman, eds., *Developments in Russian and Post-Soviet Politics.* Durham: Duke University Press.

Said, Edward. 2000. *The End of the Peace Process.* New York: Pantheon.

Sakwa, Richard. 1993. *Russian Politics and Society.* New York: Routledge.

Samonis, V. 1991. "Who Subsidized Whom? The Distorted World of Baltic-Soviet Economic Relations." *Current Politics and Economics of Russia* 2, no. 3: 241–43.

Sartori, Giovanni. 1994. *Comparative Constitutional Engineering.* New York: New York University Press.

——. 1999. "The Party Effects of Electoral Systems." *Israel Affairs* 6, no. 2: 13–28.

Scammel, G. V. 1981. *The World Encompassed: The First European Maritime Empires, c. 800–1650.* Berkeley: University of California Press.

Schaper, H. 1981. "Het Nederlandse Veiligheidsbeleid, 1945–1950." *BMGN* 96, no. 2: 277–99.

Schenk, Catherine. 1996. "Decolonization and European Economic Integration: The Free Trade Area Negotiations, 1956–58." *JICH* 24, no. 3: 444–63.

Schmitter, Philippe. 1975a. "Liberation by Golpe: Retrospective Thoughts on the Demise of Authoritarian Rule in Portugal." *Armed Forces and Society* 2, no. 1: 5–33.

——. 1975b. *Corporatism and Public Policy in Authoritarian Portugal.* London: Sage.

Schulten, J. W. M. 1987. "Soldaten, Legerleiding, en Thuisfront: Een Belangengemeenschap Onder een Ongelukkig Gesternte." In Teitler and Groen, eds., *De Politionele Acties.*

Schumpeter, Joseph. 1955. *Imperialism and Social Classes: Two Essays.* New York: Meridian Press.

Schwartz, Nancy. 1994. "Representation and Territory: The Israeli Experience." *Political Science Quarterly* 109, no. 4: 615–45.

Schwarz, John, and Geoffrey Lambert. 1971. "Career Objectives, Group Feeling, and Legislative Party Voting Cohesion: The British Conservatives, 1959–68." *Journal of Politics* 33, no. 2: 399–421.

Seyd, Patrick. 1972. "Factionalism within the Conservative Party: The Monday Club." *Government and Opposition* 7: 464–87.

Shalev, Aryeh. 1994. *Israel and Syria: Peace and Security on the Golan.* Boulder, Colo.: Westview.

Shamir, Michal, and Asher Arian. 1994. "Competing Values and Policy Choices: Israeli Public Opinion on Foreign and Security Affairs." *British Journal of Political Science* 24, no. 2: 249–71.

Sharkansky, Ira. 1999. "Israel's Political Economy." In Ehud Sprinzak and Larry Diamond, eds., *Israeli Democracy under Stress*. Boulder, Colo.: Lynne Rienner.

Shepsle, Kenneth, and Barry Weingast. 1984. "When Do Rules of Procedure Matter?" *Journal of Politics* 46, no. 1: 206–21.

Shevtsova, Lilia. 1992. "The August Coup and the Soviet Collapse." *Survival* 34, no. 1: 5–18.

Shirer, William. 1969. *The Collapse of the Third Republic*. New York: Simon and Schuster.

Shlaim, Avi. 1994. "The Oslo Accord." *Journal of Palestine Studies* 23, no. 3: 24–40.

———. 1998. *The Politics of Partition*. Oxford: Oxford University Press.

SIPRI (Stockholm International Peace Research Institute. 1974. *World Armaments and Disarmament: SIPRI Yearbook 1974*. Cambridge: MIT Press.

Skach, Cindy, and Alfred Stepan. 1993. "Constitutional Frameworks and Democratic Consolidation: Parliamentarianism versus Presidentialism." *World Politics* 46, no. 1: 1–22.

Skocpol, Theda, ed. 1984. *Vision and Method in Historical Sociology*. New York: Cambridge University Press.

Slater, Jerome. 2001. "What Went Wrong? The Collapse of the Israeli-Palestinian Peace Process." *Political Science Quarterly* 116, no. 2: 171–91.

———. 2002. "Lost Opportunities for Peace in the Arab-Israeli Conflict." *International Security* 27, no. 1: 79–106.

Smith, Alan. 1974. "Antonio Salazar and the Reversal of Portuguese Colonial Policy." *Journal of African History* 15, no. 4: 653–67.

Smith, Anthony. 1986. *The Ethnic Origins of Nations*. Cambridge, Mass.: Blackwell.

Smith, Paul, ed. 1996. *Government and the Armed Forces in Britain, 1956–1990*. London: Hambledon Press.

Smith, Tony. 1975, ed. *The End of the European Empire*. Lexington, Mass.: D. C. Heath.

———. 1981. *The Pattern of Imperialism*. New York: Cambridge University Press.

———. 1994. *America's Mission*. Princeton: Princeton University Press.

Snyder, Jack. 1984. *Ideology of the Offensive: Military Decision Making and the Disasters of 1914*. Ithaca: Cornell University Press.

———. 1991. *Myths of Empire*. Ithaca: Cornell University Press.

Soares, Mário. 1975. *Portugal's Struggle for Liberty*. London: Allen and Unwin.

Sofer, Sasson. 2001. "Israel in the World Order: Social and International Perspectives." In Sofer, ed., *Peacemaking in a Divided Society*.

———, ed. 2001. *Peacemaking in a Divided Society*. London: Frank Cass.

Solnick, Steven. 1996. "The Breakdown of Hierarchies in the Soviet Union and China: A Neoinstitutional Perspective." *World Politics* 48, no. 2: 209–38.

Solzhenitsyn, Alexander. 1981 [1974]. *From under the Rubble*. Chicago: Regnery Gateway.

Spechler, Dina. 1986. "The USSR and Third-World Conflicts." *World Politics* 38: 273–86.

Spruyt, Hendrik. 1994. *The Sovereign State and Its Competitors*. Princeton: Princeton University Press.

———. 1996. "Oversight and Control in Translocal Organizations." Paper presented at the International Studies Association conference, San Diego.

———. 1997a. "The End of Empires: Developing a Comparative Research Agenda for Imperial Dissolution in the Modern Era." *Acta Politica* 32, no. 1: 25–48.

———. 1997b. "The Prospects for Neo-Imperial and Nonimperial Outcomes in the Former Soviet Space." In Dawisha and Parrott, eds., *End of Empire?*

———. 2000. "The End of Empire and the Extension of the Westphalian System: The Normative Basis of the Modern State Order." *International Studies Review* 2, no. 2: 65–92.

———. 2001. "Empire and Imperialism." In Alexander Motyl, ed., *The Encyclopaedia of Nationalism.* San Diego: Academic Press.

Stargadt, A. W. 1989. "The Emergence of the Asian System of Powers." *Modern Asian Studies* 23, no. 3: 561–95.

Steinberg, Gerald. 1995. "A Nation That Dwells Alone? Foreign Policy in the 1992 Elections." In Elazar and Sandler, *Israel at the Polls 1992.*

Steinmo, Sven, Kathleen Thelen, and Frank Longstreth, eds. 1992. *Structuring Politics: Historical Institutionalism in Comparative Analysis.* New York: Cambridge University Press.

Stengers, Jean. 1982. "Precipitous Decolonization: The Case of the Belgian Congo." In Prosser Gifford and William Roger Louis, eds., *The Transfer of Power in Africa.* New Haven: Yale University Press.

Stinchcombe, Arthur. 1978. *Theoretical Methods in Social History.* New York: Academic Press.

Stone, Randall. 1996. *Satellites and Commissars.* Princeton: Princeton University Press.

Strang, David. 1991. "Global Patterns of Decolonization, 1500–1987." *International Studies Quarterly* 35: 429–54.

Strom, Kaare, Ian Budge, and Michael Laver. 1994. "Constraints on Cabinet Formation in Parliamentary Democracies." *American Journal of Political Science* 38, no. 2: 303–35.

Stuart, Robert. 1990. "Soviet Plan Targets and Achievements." *Communist Economies* 2, no. 3: 403–11.

Suny, Ronald. 1992. "State, Civil Society, and Ethnic Consolidation in the USSR—Roots of the National Question." In Lapidus, Zasklavsky, and Goldman, eds., *From Union to Commonwealth.*

———. 1993. *The Revenge of the Past.* Stanford: Stanford University Press.

———. 1998. *The Soviet Experiment.* Oxford: Oxford University Press.

Szporluk, Roman. 1994. "After Empire: What?" *Daedalus* 123, no. 3: 21–39.

Szulc, Tad. 1975. "Lisbon and Washington: Behind the Portuguese Revolution." *Foreign Policy* 21: 3–62.

Taagepera, Rein, and Mathew Shugart. 1989. *Seats and Votes.* New Haven: Yale University Press.

Taras, Ray, ed. 1997. *Postcommunist Presidents.* New York: Cambridge University Press.

Teitler, G. 1979. "Manpower Problems and Manpower Policy of the Dutch Colonial Army, 1860–1920." *Acta Politica* 14, no. 1: 71–94.

———. 1990. "1949 Afsluiting Zonder Afronding." In Teitler and Hoffenaar, eds., *De Politionele Acties.*

Teitler, G., and P. Groen, eds. 1987. *De Politionele Acties.* Amsterdam: De Bataafsche Leeuw.

Teitler, G. and J. Hoffenaar, eds. 1990. *De Politionele Acties: Afwikkeling en Verwerking.* Amsterdam: De Bataafsche Leeuw.

Thelen, Kathleen. 1999. "Historical Institutionalism in Comparative Politics." In *Annual Review of Political Science* 2: 369–404.

Thelen, Kathleen, and Sven Steinmo. 1992. "Historical Institutionalism in Comparative Politics." In Steinmo, Thelen, and Longstreth, eds., *Structuring Politics.*

Tignor, Robert. 1998. *Capitalism and Nationalism at the End of Empire.* Princeton: Princeton University Press.

Tilly, Charles. 1990. *Coercion, Capital, and European States, AD 990–1990.* Cambridge: Basil Blackwell.

Toumanoff, Peter. 1987. "Economic Reform and Industrial Performance in the Soviet Union, 1950–1984." *Comparative Economic Studies* 29, no. 4: 128–49.

Tsebelis, George. 1995. "Decision Making in Political Systems: Veto Players in Presidentialism, Parliamentarism, Multicameralism, and Multipartyism." *British Journal of Political Science* 25: 289–325.

———. 1999. "Veto Players and Law Production in Parliamentary Democracies: An Empirical Analysis." *APSR* 93, no. 3: 591–608.

———. 2002. *Veto Players*. Princeton: Princeton University Press.

van den Doel, H. W. 1996. *Het Rijk van Insulinde*. Amsterdam: Prometheus.

van Doorn, J. A. 1990. "De Verwerking van het Einde van Indië." In Teitler and Hoffenaar, eds., *De Politionele Acties*.

———. 1995a. *Indische Lessen*. Amsterdam: Uitgeverij Bert Bakker.

———. 1995b. "The Past Is a Strong Present: The Dutch-Indonesian Conflict and the Persistence of the Colonial Pattern." *Netherlands Journal of Social Sciences* 31, no. 2: 153–71.

van Doorn, J. A., and W. J. Hendrix. 1987. "De Planters Belegerd: De Positie van de Europese Planters Tussen Nederlandse Steun en Indonesisch Verzet." In Teitler and Groen, eds., *De Politionele Acties*.

Van Evera, Stephen. 1996. *Guide to Methodology for Students of Political Science*. Cambridge: MIT Monograph.

van Goor, J. 1987. "Nieuw-Guinea, 1950–1963." *BMGN* 102, no. 1: 53–56.

van Staden, Alfred. 1982. "American-Dutch Political Relations since 1945." *BMGN* 97, no. 3: 80–96.

Walder, Andrew. 1994. "The Decline of Communist Power: Elements of a Theory of Institutional Change." *Theory and Society* 23, no. 2: 297–323.

Wall, Patrick. 1960. "News Out of Africa." *African Affairs* 59, no. 236: 213–25.

Walt, Stephen. 1996. *Revolution and War*. Ithaca: Cornell University Press.

———. 2002. "The Enduring Relevance of the Realist Tradition." In Ira Katznelson and Helen Milner, eds., *Political Science: The State of the Discipline*. New York: W. W. Norton.

Waltz, Kenneth. 1979. *Theory of International Politics*. New York: Random House.

———. 1986. "Reflections on Theory of International Politics: A Response to My Critics." In Robert Keohane, ed., *Neorealism and Its Critics*. New York: Columbia University Press.

———. 1990. "Nuclear Myths and Political Realities." *APSR* 84: 731–45.

Wasserman, Gary. 1973. "The Independence Bargain: Kenya, Europeans, and the Land Issue, 1960–62." *Journal of Commonwealth Political Studies* 11, no. 2: 99–120.

Watson, Adam. 1992. *The Evolution of International Society*. New York: Routledge.

Weaver, R. Kent, and Bert Rockman, eds. 1993. *Do Institutions Matter?* Washington, D.C.: Brookings Institution.

Wheeler, Douglas. 1970. "Thaw in Portugal." *Foreign Affairs* 48, no. 4: 769–81.

———. 1979. "The Military and the Portuguese Dictatorship, 1926–1974: The Honor of the Army." In Lawrence Graham and Harry Makler, eds., *Contemporary Portugal*. Austin: University of Texas Press.

Whelan, Frederick. 1996. *Edmund Burke and India*. Pittsburgh: Pittsburgh University Press.

White, Nicholas. 1998. "Capitalism and Counter-Insurgency? Business and Government in the Malayan Emergency, 1948–57." *Modern Asian Studies* 32, no. 1: 149–77.

Wiarda, Howard. 1974. "Corporatism and Development in the Iberic-Latin World: Persistent Strains and New Variations." *Review of Politics* 36, no. 1: 3–33.

Wiebes, Cees, and Bert Zeeman. 1985. "Stikker, Indonesië en het Noordatlantisch Verdrag. Of: Hoe Nederland in de Pompe Ging." *BMGN* 100, no. 2: 225–51.

Williams, Philip. 1966. *Crisis and Compromise*. New York: Anchor.

Williamson, John, ed. 1993. *Economic Consequences of Soviet Disintegration.* Washington, D.C.: Institute for International Economics.

Williamson, Oliver. 1975. *Markets and Hierarchies.* New York: Free Press.

———. 1986. *Economic Organization.* New York: New York University Press.

Winks, Robin, ed. 1999. *Oxford History of the British Empire,* vol. 5: *Historiography.* Oxford: Oxford University Press.

Wohlforth, William. 1994–95. "Realism and the End of the Cold War." *International Security* 19, no. 3: 91–129.

World Bank. 1990. *The Economy of the USSR.* Washington, D.C.

Yarborough, Beth, and Robert Yarborough. 1987. "Cooperation in the Liberalization of International Trade: After Hegemony, What?" *IO* 41, no. 1: 1–26.

Yasunaka, Akio. 1970. "Basic Data on Indonesian Political Leaders." *Indonesia* 10: 107–42.

Yorke, Valerie. 1990. "Imagining a Palestinian State: An International Security Plan." *International Affairs* 66, no. 1: 115–36.

Zacher, Mark. 2001. "The Territorial Integrity Norm: International Boundaries and the Use of Force." *IO* 55, no. 2: 215–50.

Zakaria, Fareed. 1992. "Realism and Domestic Politics: A Review Essay." *International Security* 17, no. 1: 177–98.

———. 1998. *From Wealth to Power.* Princeton: Princeton University Press.

Zaslavsky, Victor. 1992. "The Evolution of Separatism in Soviet Society under Gorbachev." In Lapidus, Zaslavsky, and Goldman, eds., *From Union to Commonwealth.*

Zevelev, Igor. 1996. "Russia and the Russian Diasporas." *Post-Soviet Affairs* 12, no. 3: 265–84.

Zimbalist, Andrew, and Howard Sherman. 1984. *Comparing Economic Systems.* Orlando, Fla.: Academic Press.

Index

British Empire *(continued)*
  nuclear strategy and, 122–23
  public opinion and, 138
  and settlers, 127–29
  veto points absent in, 131–36, 144
  See also Aden; Kenya; Malaya; Suez
Bunce, Valerie, 81–82, 212
Bush, George. H.W., 234, 243, 254
business interests
  in British Empire, 119, 124, 127, 139,
    140, 144
  in Dutch Empire, 13
  flexibility of, 266
  French Empire and, 103–104
  in Israel, 237
  objectives of, 12, 27–8
  and Portuguese Empire, 80, 188,
    201–202
  and transaction specific assets, 8, 201, 265
  as veto players, 90

Caetano, Marcelo, 78–79, 177–78, 182, 193
  racial policies of, 187, 192n67
  reform tendencies of, 181n17, 191, 199,
    200–202
Camp David accord (1978), 63, 238–39
Camp David negotiations (2000), 235,
  258–59, 260n92
Cartier, Raymond, 71–72
case selection and research design, 10,
  31–36
Catholics (France, MRP), 96–100, 109, 116
  as favoring hard-line, 113
Catholics (Netherlands, KVP), 154–55, 163
  as favoring hard-line, 157, 160, 164–65,
    172–74
  and logrolling with Labor Party, 147,
    157–61
Chamberlain, Neville, 51, 72
China, 265
  and nationalist support, 56–58, 192
  and United States, 63
Churchill, Winston, 1, 53, 138
  and military, 121–22
  as reluctant to decolonize, 119, 131, 136,
    142
civilian control over the military
  in British Empire, 120–3, 144
  in Dutch Empire, 147, 151–3
  in French Empire, 89, 92–93, 109
  Israel and, 237, 240–41
  operationalized, 21–22
  in Portuguese Empire, 182
  USSR and, 207, 209nn11–12, 212

Clinton, William J., 234, 244n41
Colijn, Hendrik, 162, 167
Colton, Timothy, 21
Commonwealth (British) 42, 51, 72, 118,
  164
Communist Party (France, PCF), 72, 93–99,
  113
  as anti-system party, 97–100, 116
Communist Party (Netherlands, CPN),
  154–58, 161, 165
Communist Party (USSR)
  as center of an empire, 4, 205
  and defection of lower cadres, 223, 230
  Gorbachev's control of, 214–16, 231,
    270
  and nationalist movements, 228
  organization of, 225
  and reforms, 85, 222
Conservative Party (Britain), 119, 122, 125,
  139, 265
  and disengagement, 139–40, 144
  dominated by Whitehall, 131–35
  on India, 52, 142
  as pro-empire, 72, 124–126, 129, 138
consociationalism, 269–70
Coquery-Vidrovitch, Catherine, 69–70, 104
Council for Mutual Economic Assistance
  (CMEA), 81–82
counterfactual analysis, 34, 113, 265, 270
credible commitment
  initiation and implementation, 271–74
  See also Israel; USSR; *entries for individual
    empires*

d'Argenlieu, Thierry, 93
Dawisha, Karen, and Bruce Parrott, 3, 65,
  230n115
Dayan, Moshe, 243, 266
de Gaulle, Charles, 97, 109–111, 263
  allied relations with, 49, 112
  and Cartierisme, 72
  and constitutional reforms, 90, 96, 110
  Free French under, 48
  grand strategy of, 4, 110
  invoked by Barak, 236
  invoked by Spínola, 201
  invoked by Yeltsin, 217
  military and, 92, 95, 110, 116
  settlers and, 106
  veto points reduced by, 116, 274
Delgado, Humberto, 184
Desch, Michael, 22n43, 93, 183, 209n12
Deudney, Daniel, and John Ikenberry,
  231n117

Cornell Studies in Political Economy

A series edited by
PETER J. KATZENSTEIN